THE UNIVERSITY OF WISCONSIN COLLEGES 1919-1997

The Wisconsin Idea at Work

by Jerry L. Bower

THE UNIVERSITY OF WISCONSIN COLLEGES 1919-1997
The Wisconsin Idea at Work

by Jerry L. Bower

Library of Congress Cataloging-in-Publication Data

   ISBN 0-938627-55-4

Bower, Jerry L., 1938-
   The University of Wisconsin colleges, 1919-1997 : the Wisconsin idea at work / Jerry L. Bower.
      p. cm.
   Includes bibliographical references and index.
   1. University of Wisconsin System. I. Title.

LD6096. .B69 2002
378.775–dc21

                                                                                   2002025504

Publishing Services
New Past Press, Inc.
Friendship, WI 53934
newpastpress.com

Publishing Assistant: Carol Ann (Huber) Podoll
Designer: Jay Jocham, Big Flats/Hancock, WI
Index: Janet Josvai, Watertown, WI

Copyright © 2002, Jerry L. Bower and New Past Press, Inc.
All rights reserved: No part of this book may be reproduced in any form or by any electronic or mechanical means including information storage and retrieval systems without permission in writing from the publisher, except by a reviewer who may quote brief passages in a review.

Made in Canada

Contents

Preface		4
Chapter One	The Milwaukee Center Emerges	7
Chapter Two	The Depression Calls Forth Out-State Center: The Thirties	21
Chapter Three	Decline and Revival: The Forties	41
Chapter Four	The Centers Weather a Crisis: The Fifties	57
Chapter Five	The Center System is Created: The Sixties	71
Chapter Six	Merger within Merger: 1970-1974	97
Chapter Seven	The Center System and the Scope Reduction Report: 1975-1978	125
Chapter Eight	The Scope of the University is Reduced: 1979-1982	153
Chapter Nine	The UW Centers Achieve Stability: 1983-1991	173
Chapter Ten	The UW Centers Weather another Crisis: 1991-1997	199
The UW Colleges		219
Notes		265
Campus Directors, Deans and CEOs		288
Index		291
About the Author		300

Preface

If someone had told me when I began this project in 1989 that I would devote twelve years to writing the history of the University of Wisconsin's two-year campuses, I probably would have declined to undertake the task. Now that I am finished I am pleased that I persevered because I have learned a great deal. The history of the UW Centers (now the UW Colleges) is intricately entwined with state politics, University of Wisconsin versus Wisconsin State University politics and budgetary politics. I know that the academic community would like to think of itself as above politics but that expectation simply is not realistic. The Centers grew out of the economic woes of the depression of the 1930s and have had to struggle almost constantly to survive. Each time Wisconsin's higher education establishment has come under scrutiny the Centers became the first, and often the only, target for solving the problem.

But the two-year campuses, with the exception of the Medford Center which was closed in 1982, have survived for several very good reasons. The Centers starred as the epitome of the Wisconsin Idea—the promise that the boundaries of the University coincide with the borders of the state—by bringing the knowledge, research, and services of the University of Wisconsin to small communities such as Rice lake, Richland Center, and Marinette. The Centers always provided live-at-home, low-cost educational opportunities to students, many of whom were the first of their families to enroll in higher education. The Centers' faculty and staff, likewise, have always offered more personal attention to students than it is possible to provide at a larger institution. Finally, the fact that many of Wisconsin's legislators (72%) have a two-year campus in their districts gave the Centers the ability to mobilize political support to help itself and the entire UW System.

I owe a huge debt of gratitude to many persons who have assisted in this project. Chancellors Stephen Portch (who conceived this history), Lee Grugel, and now Bill Messner have supported me in numerous ways. The staff of the UW Archives, both in the Memorial and Steenbock Libraries, has been unfailingly courteous and tireless in assisting me to confirm facts and to follow leads in the thousands of University documents entrusted to its care. (Please permit me a digression here. Now that more and more business is being conducted in email and other paperless technologies, I wonder what resources future chroniclers of the UW will have at their disposal.)

I must thank the following who permitted me to interview them about their recollections: former Deans Henry Ahrnsbrak (Marathon County), Ted Savides (Baraboo/Sauk County), and Don Gray (Richland); former Vice Chancellor Daniel Van Eyck; and former media pioneer Jim Kirchstein who also piloted our chancellors across the state. They provided me with important insights and invaluable leads.

I have also greatly appreciated my faithful readers, truth-testers and occasional critics—Dean Dion Kempthorne (Richland); History Professors James Lorence (Marathon), Kerry Trask (Manitowoc), and the late Donald Dennis (Fond du Lac); former Centers Registrar Gladys Meier, former Assistant Vice Chancellor Antone Kucera, my English teacher neighbor Ruth Ghastin, and my ever-patient wife, Donna—who have critiqued the manuscript. Donna read the manuscript at least three times. Penny Sheafor, Richland's Faculty Secretary, also has earned eternal gratitude for deciphering my penmanship and muddy directions to produce clear pages of typescript.

There is a celebratory note to the appearance of the History of the University of Wisconsin Centers in the spring of 2002. The University of Wisconsin System will mark the 30th anniversary of the merger of the state's higher education system. Because the two-year campuses of the UW System were the first to truly experience a merger beyond changing logos and letterheads, I think the timing of this book is exquisite.

Jerry L. Bower
June 2001
UW-Richland

One

The Milwaukee Center Emerges

No one planned the University of Wisconsin Centers—they just happened. The story of the Centers gradual emergence is intricately tied up with the history of the University, of higher education in the state, and of Wisconsin politics. Until 1964 the two-year centers were called Extension Centers, and they were operated by the University's Extension Division. In 1964 the Board of Regents approved establishment of a separate Center System, headed by a chancellor who reported directly to the President of the University of Wisconsin. In the 1970's a merger of the State Universities and the UW doubled the size of the Center System to fourteen centers, by adding to the original membership four State University branch campuses and three two-year institutions previously attached to the UW-Green Bay. Born out of necessity, the University of Wisconsin Centers have played an important role in helping the University to carry out the Wisconsin Idea—providing educational opportunities to all of the citizens of the state.

Wisconsin's constitution, adopted in 1848, provided that the state legislature could establish a state university "at or near the seat of state government." Because of the crush of necessary business to launch the state government, no immediate attempt was made to implement this provision. In 1850, however, the legislature authorized the construction and operation of the

University of Wisconsin in Madison, the capital city. The task of establishing the institution progressed slowly. During the Civil War (1861-1865) the University received a significant boost when the state acquired thousands of acres of public land from the federal government under the terms of the Land Grant Act of 1862. Popularly known as the Morrill Act, after its sponsor U.S. Senator Justin Morrill of Vermont, the measure required any state which accepted federal land to provide four types of educational opportunities—agriculture courses, engineering courses, teachers institutes, and lecture series for general audiences. The state could fulfill these terms either by adding the programs to an existing state college or by establishing a new land grant institution.

Both state and University officials agreed that the most logical and least costly way to fulfill the Morrill Act's terms would be simply to add the courses to the University's existing curriculum. But their suggestion triggered considerable opposition from the faculty, who were firmly committed to the prevailing classical curriculum. Even if a student was solely interested in the practical knowledge of the agricultural and engineering courses, the faculty members insisted that he must first complete the classical program of study. Only then would he be permitted to enroll in the specialized courses. This serious rift between the administration and faculty prevented Wisconsin from even beginning to fulfill its obligations for over two decades.[1]

Finally, in the early 1880s, the State Agricultural Society and the Wisconsin Dairyman's Association forced the University to take action when they threatened to start a separate agricultural college because Madison had not responded to their needs. William Dempster Hoard of Fort Atkinson, and ardent advocate of dairying, had instigated this forceful nudge. Such a move, if carried out, would have diverted from the UW the federal dollars distributed under the Morrill Act. Thus inspired, the university administration asked the legislature to appropriate additional funds for both on-campus and off-campus courses in agriculture. The legislature enthusiastically responded with a $5,000 addition to the University's regular budget, an amount which greatly surpassed any other state's support for similar offerings.[2]

In November 1885 the University sponsored the first of many successful Farmers' Institutes in Hudson. The session was deliberately scheduled after the harvest season so that more farm families would be able to attend. Railroads cooperated by offering reduced rates to the attendees. The Institute speakers extolled the advantages of farm life and offered practical suggestions for improving the quality of rural life. Experts urged farmers to diversify their operations to cushion the adverse effects of competition and occasional crop failures. In addition, the college started a twelve week short course designed specifically for farm men and boys. Offered during the winter, it cost $60.00.

Although farm families enthusiastically responded to these initiatives, many University leaders in both the administration and the faculty remained skeptical; they believed that the institution had lost prestige by stooping to provide Farmers' Institutes and short courses.[3]

The successful launching of the Farmers' Institutes and agricultural short courses triggered demands that the University also provide courses for teachers and lectures for general audiences. Although a chair of the Science and Art of Teaching had been established in 1884, the program had attracted few students because a cheaper and shorter teacher training program could be obtained at the state normal schools. University President Thomas C. Chamberlain, who wished to strengthen the program, decided to try to use the Farmers' Institutes' approach in the teacher training field. Accordingly, Chamberlain convinced the 1887 legislature to authorize the offering of a teachers' institute in the summer, when teachers would not be holding school. In 1888 the first of many very successful summer institutes for teachers was launched in Madison.[4]

During the 1890-91 school year History Professor Frederick Jackson Turner offered a series of six off-campus, non-credit lectures in United States history. Turner first presented his lectures in Madison, then subsequently travelled to nearby communities to deliver the same addresses. Reacting to the success of Turner's series, the Regents, in June 1891 approved a limited "extension program aimed at a general audience." The Regents, however, provided no extra money for the program; it would have to be self-supporting. They also restricted the Madison faculty's participation to weekends, so that the extension work would not interfere with on-campus obligations.[5]

The following year (1892) the University enticed Professor Richard T. Ely of Johns Hopkins University to come to Madison to supervise the extension work. Chamberlain and Turner played large roles in convincing Ely to accept; they promised that they both would continue to support and work in the program. Ely and Turner worked especially hard but unsuccessfully to secure state support for the lecture series. They also failed to convince corporations and wealthy individuals to sponsor the lectures in their communities. Thus the financial burden, $60.00 for six lectures, fell entirely upon local community groups—teachers, churches, and civic and social clubs—which sponsored the series. These organizations eventually ran out of money and enthusiasm and by 1900 the general extension program was in deep trouble.

At the same time that demand for the lecture series declined, the faculty intensified its attacks upon the General Extension operation. Ely and Turner had decided to offer attendees the option of earning college credit by completing satisfactorily several assignments and taking an examination at the end of a lecture series. But very few enrollees completed the requirements, adding weight to the critics' assertion that the general audience attracted to the lectures sought entertainment, not education. And, they added, the University certainly had not been established to provide entertainment.[6]

The decline in interest in the general off-campus courses continued into the early 1900s. Some of the more popular lecturers, like Ely and Turner, withdrew from the lecture circuit because they could not continue to handle full time duties at Madison and travel on weekends to deliver their speeches. Audience interest also declined. Comments made about the courses reveal that many listeners found the material "above their heads." Then, too, the University's first avowed effort to cover the entire state stirred its competitors to action. The state normal schools stepped up their services to teachers. Private lecture series companies often offered better-known speakers, which enabled the local sponsors to sell more tickets. If the UW wished to serve the entire state effectively, it would have to do more than merely send out a few of its more popular, regular professors.[7]

The revival of the General Extension Division occurred during the presidency of Charles R. Van Hise, who served from 1903 until his untimely death in 1918. From the outset Van Hise expressed an interest in adult education but he, too, harbored doubts about whether the field was a proper one for a state university. Several men gradually persuaded Van Hise that the University should serve all of the state's citizens, not just those who could come to Madison to seek a degree. One of these men, Governor Robert M. LaFollette, Sr, leader of the progressive wing of the Republican Party, insisted that the University must at least attempt to fill all the citizens' higher education needs because they all contributed to its support through their taxes.

Frank Hutchins and Charles McCarthy also nudged President Van Hise to support a revived General Extension Division. Hutchins, the first executive secretary of the state's Free Library Association, understood well the citizens' deep desire for education and information, and he quietly lobbied Van Hise to enlarge the University's role in fulfilling this desire. McCarthy, who had earned a Ph.D. from Madison, worked with Hutchins in the Free Library Association and later became the first head of the Legislative Reference Bureau Library. The more vocal and politically astute McCarthy wanted the University to provide practical education to industrial workers and their employers, in the same fashion that the Farmers' Institutes gave farmers tips on how to improve their farms and homes. McCarthy backed up his arguments with data secured through legislative surveys—one significant survey revealed that Wisconsinites spent $800,000 annually out-of-state for correspondence study courses. Surely, McCarthy contended, the University could offer better courses and keep the revenue in the state.[8]

During 1905 the Regents and the University administration decided to reinvigorate the moribund General Extension program. President Van Hise led the way. In 1906 he announced what has since become known everywhere in the state as the "Wisconsin Idea," the campus of the University should extend to the very boundaries of the state and serve every home.[9] The University asked the legislature to appropriate $40,000 for the 1907-09 biennium for both agricultural and non-agricultural extension courses. Many legislators balked at this large sum, but powerful lobbying by the Milwaukee Merchants and Manufacturing Association and by other lakeshore cities which had a significant industrial base boosted the measure through intact.[10] At last, General Extension had found the type of political support that had sustained the appropriations of the Farmers' Institutes and short courses.

Van Hise began immediately to assemble an administration for the General Extension Division which, unlike the agricultural extension program, never would be absorbed into one of the University's colleges.[11] Louis E. Reber, dean of engineering at the Pennsylvania State College, arrived in 1907 to become the first Dean of Extension. Reber brought to the task solid academic credentials and a considerable amount of administrative and political experience. The latter was necessary because the Extension Division had to win continued legislative funding each biennium. William H. Lighty, meanwhile, had applied for and secured the position as director of the fledgling correspondence study program. Lighty, who had graduated from Cornell, was acquainted with Richard Ely and others connected with the earlier unsuccessful efforts to create a solid general extension program. Lighty used his contacts well; for instance, he worked carefully with Frederick Jackson Turner and other residence faculty to win their support for credit correspondence courses offered by Extension. This approach helped overcome some of the anti-Extension sentiment among the regular faculty.[12]

Dr. Charles McCarthy's interest in securing industrial training for workers spurred him to work along another line, even while he continued to support the development of general extension courses. From his post at the head of the Legislative Reference Bureau Library, McCarthy drafted a bill that authorized school districts to set up and operate vocational high schools. The bill included a provision that these vocational schools could contract with Extension for instruction and specified that Extension must provide a course in any part of the state if thirty people enrolled and a local agency agreed to underwrite the expense. This clause later became the key to the emergence of the freshman Extension Center program during the depression of the 1930s. The 1911 legislature passed McCarthy's measure, and a compulsory attendance law (to age 16) which assured that there would be a clientele for the vocational high schools.[13]

The revitalized Extension Division played an important role in carrying the Social Gospel of the Progressive Era to communities throughout Wisconsin. For instance, better health was promoted via a great variety of lectures and newspaper clippings which could be requested from Madison. Extension and the Federal Children's Bureau co-sponsored Better Baby Weeks, during which mothers received information about child development and had their infants' weight and height compared to standard growth charts. The Division also worked with the Wisconsin Anti-Tuberculosis Association in a campaign to reduce the incidence of this contagious disease. Practical correspondence courses were developed in subjects as diverse as credit management, home repair and dressmaking. In urban areas, Extension experts lectured about the dangers of smoke pollution from industrial plants and demonstrated the necessity for assuring a pure milk supply and sanitary bakeries.

In contrast to these successes, the Community Institutes—a project designed to "Americanize" quickly the various ethnic groups in the state's population—failed within two years. In this program, University professors made a half-day survey of a community; they returned later with advice on how to overcome ethnic or town/rural frictions. The scholars involved in the Community Institutes rapidly discovered that the true nature of a community cannot be perceived in one short visit, thus their advice often missed the mark by being far too general and too theoretical.[14]

Despite its considerable success, the Extension Division again became the target of criticism. Some employers blasted the courses for workers, saying the men emerged from them too union oriented, insisting upon better wages and working conditions. Contrarily, at first some unions had refused to endorse the workers' courses because they felt the material was too academic.

On the political front, the ongoing contest between the Progressive and Stalwart factions of the Republican party automatically embroiled Extension in political battles. Each bloc felt that its party line should be praised by people who received their pay from state appropriations. Some Regents even chimed in with criticism. For instance William Dempster Hoard feared that General Extension's success would eventually detract from the agricultural outreach programs and he proposed putting limits on Extension's role. Other Regents resented Extension's success in lobbying the legislature for its biennial appropriations. Even though the money was provided specifically for Extension programs, these Regents felt it should be placed in the total University budget and doled out by the Board. Needless to say, Dean Reber steadfastly resisted that suggestion. Fortunately, with the support of its newly won allies throughout the state, Extension overcame the criticism and won the major political battles.[15] But it, like the University, never was able to disassociate itself entirely from the political currents flowing in the state.

In late 1907, Extension Dean Reber opened a branch office in Milwaukee and put Kenneth Smith in charge. Smith's job was to coordinate Extension's programs in the populous southeastern corner of the state, where about one-third of Wisconsin's population lived. Smith kept extensive office hours (8:30-12:00, 1:30-5:00, 7:30-9:00 Monday through Friday and 8:30-12:00 Saturday) so that he could advertise the courses, enroll the students, and supervise the instructors. Very quickly an Extension "Center" emerged, much to the dismay of some University administrators and faculty who contended this branch college operation would sap the strength of the parent institution.[16]

It was here that the first freshman-sophomore center evolved. The evolution began in the engineering and business correspondence courses. These courses often were taken by a group of Milwaukee men in the evenings in their place of employment. Naturally, they studied together and used the shops of their employers as their laboratory. Soon, because these classes were large enough to warrant it, the Madison instructors decided to visit their students occasionally rather than limiting their interaction to the mail. Both instructors and students found these in-person sessions most rewarding, and their frequency increased. The instructors discovered that they could learn a great deal from men who applied the theoretical principles of engineering and business in their jobs. And the students no doubt enjoyed the question and answer sessions, the demonstrations, and especially the occasional opportunity to point out that a theory just did not work. Quite soon, groups of students began petitioning Extension to provide instructors for all their class sessions. Once it became evident that these courses would be self-supporting, more and more were offered, both on-site and at the Milwaukee Center. Indeed, by 1910, Extension had to find quarters that would provide a larger classroom, in addition to more office space. This willingness of Extension to adjust to the needs and desires of its clients earned it broad support in Milwaukee. Some civic leaders even suggested that Milwaukee had enough potential students to justify the establishment of a branch university.[17]

At the end of World War I, the flood of returning veterans who wished to utilize the benefits provided by both the federal and state governments accelerated the evolution toward permanent college credit classes at the Milwaukee Center. In 1919, the U. S. government contributed an unspent $37,000 from its War Emergency Fund to Extension to initiate a program for veterans. In addition the state granted each former soldier a $30.00 per month "bonus," if the man enrolled either in correspondence courses or in actual classes. In Milwaukee, the University through its Extension Division set up day classes to provide two-year vocational courses in Commerce, Engineering, and Building Design and Construction and a few regular freshman and sophomore college credit courses in the College of Engineering and the College of Letters and Science.[18] In mid-1921 a state Senate committee investigated the effectiveness of the programs for veterans. The committee report, issued in December 1922, emphasized that the work accomplished in Milwaukee was a bargain to the state. And reports from Madison indicated that students who transferred from the Milwaukee Center to the residence campus performed on a par with those students who had enrolled directly at Madison.[19]

Not long after the college credit daytime classes began in 1920, Extension officials in Milwaukee received inquiries from the parents of non-veteran college-age students about whether their sons and daughters could enroll in these courses. These parents noted that Madison lacked adequate housing for students during this post-war surge in enrollment and that they could save significant sums of money if their students could live at home while attending University classes.

When these requests were relayed to Madison, alarm bells went off. Many of the resident faculty had serious reservations about the entire Milwaukee operation. They considered the non-credit courses unworthy of the University's label and were concerned that opening up the college credit courses to all applicants might reduce the number of students on the main campus to a potentially dangerous level. (In 1921-22, the credit/day classes enrolled 258 students. Evidently the Madison faculty believed all of those students would be enrolled "on the Hill" if the Milwaukee classes did not exist.)[20] President Edward A. Birge eventually referred this important question to the Board of Regents.[21] In their August 1923 meeting the Regents failed to resolve the issue because the arguments on both sides were equally compelling, and they tabled the question. But three weeks later, in a special meeting, the Regents authorized the Extension Division to hold day classes for freshmen and sophomores for all applicants "at the Milwaukee Branch."[22] Obviously, a very important step had been taken to make college credit courses in Milwaukee a permanent part of Extension's services.

The surge in enrollment in the credit classes forced Extension to rent more space in downtown Milwaukee. Having to move between widely separated buildings quickly proved a burden to students, faculty, and administrators, alike. Fortunately, the state Senate committee which had reviewed the Milwaukee operation strongly recommended to the 1923 legislature that it appropriate money for the purchase of land and construction of an adequate building. Several Milwaukee groups lobbied vigorously for the measure. After much debate, the legislators added $150,000 to Extension's budget for the project. Much to their dismay, Dean Reber and his staff soon discovered that a suitable lot in downtown Milwaukee—the much preferred location—would be so expensive as to preclude construction of an adequate building. They did find a school building, not too far from the Civic Center, which the city was willing to sell. With some remodeling, this structure could be made to work. But the appropriation measure did not allow the purchase of an existing building, so the Extension Division leaders pleaded with the legislature either to amend the bill to permit the purchase of the school or to provide sufficient funds to acquire a downtown site and to construct an adequate building.[23] Before any decision was reached, a rather momentous change occurred in the University, and Marquette University publicly challenged the entire project.

In June 1925 President Birge retired. The Regents launched a nationwide search and thought they had secured Roscoe Pound, the eminent dean of the Harvard Law School, as a successor. Indeed, the press even announced the impending appointment and heartily approved. But just days later, Dr. Pound withdrew his name. Pound later explained that the major factor in his decision was what he had learned about Wisconsin politics, where the long-running battle between the LaFollette Progressives and the conservative Stalwarts had reached a new intensity. Pound feared he would be viewed as the appointee of "a party" and that when the other faction secured control of the capitol, both he and the University would be in serious difficulty. Glenn Frank, the Regents' remaining major candidate, however, expressed no fear of coming to Wisconsin. From the outset, he had been the favorite of Regent Zona Gale, of Portage. A renowned author, Gale had met Frank in New York City where he was the editor of *Century Magazine,* which had published several of her articles. Gradually, Gale and Frank overcame the reluctance of those Regents concerned about Frank's lack of a graduate degree or any academic administrative experience, and he received the appointment.[24]

While the appointment of a new president merely delayed the Milwaukee Center's building plans, the challenge issued by Dean Edward A. Fitzpatrick of Marquette University threatened the building project and all of Extension's credit classes. In mid-February 1925 Fitzpatrick wrote a long letter to state Senator Howard Teasdale of Sparta, the President Pro Tem of the Senate and a member of the Education and Public Welfare Committee, and carefully spelled out his concerns. He recalled that the credit classes begun in 1919 had been described by the University "purely as a tentative measure." Fitzpatrick asserted that the campaign to construct a state-owned building certainly suggested a permanent program because the credit class students would be the primary occupants during the daytime. Continuing, Fitzpatrick noted that the Extension operation and proposed building duplicated many of Marquette's programs and facilities, a wasteful expenditure of public funds. The Marquette Dean pointed out that his college was not exclusively for Catholics and that loan funds were readily available to students who could not afford the slightly higher fees ($87.50 per semester compared to $60.00 at the Extension Center). He also questioned whether the Milwaukee Normal School did not already offer "the substantial equivalent of two years of college work even for the prescribed pre-professional courses." Near the end of his letter, Fitzpatrick raised the most serious question—was it legal for the University of Wisconsin to establish a branch "at Milwaukee or any place other than at Madison?"[25]

While University officials rebutted most of Fitzpatrick's allegations themselves, they asked the state attorney general to render an opinion on the constitutional challenge. They pointed out that the Milwaukee Normal School, upon an order from the state Normal School Regents, had recently ceased giving "junior college" courses and that Extension had only responded to the pleas of teachers and prospective teachers when it provided education courses in Milwaukee.[26] Dean Reber noted that the credit program actually cost the state nothing, as the students supported it with their $5.00 per credit fees. He also denied that the University had any intention of establishing a full blown branch university in Milwaukee. The course offerings would continue to be limited to Engineering and Letters and Science, and to the freshman and sophomore levels. In time, the Attorney General, Herman Ekern, ruled that the proposed Milwaukee Center was proper and legal, for it was "an extension of the work of all the colleges and in no sense constitutes the establishment of any new department or college."[27]

Despite their success in winning the constitutional challenge and in refuting Dean Fitzpatrick's allegations, the University's leaders decided not to press further the building issue in the 1925 legislative session, for fear that it might jeopardize the biennial budget then under consideration. An administration change in Extension further delayed a resolution. Dean Reber, who had led the Division skillfully through many political battles, retired June 1, 1926. He recommended as his successor Chester D. Snell, who was involved in extension work in North Carolina. After an interview and reference checks were completed, the Board of Regents appointed Snell.[28]

Snell made the Milwaukee building project a top priority. He asked the 1927 legislature to appropriate sufficient funds to complete the plan. The legislators responded rather quickly, allocating another $175,000. The building, sited on a downtown lot, opened for classes in September 1928. The Capital Times described its virtues: "Twenty classrooms and lecture halls, six large modern laboratories, and a well-equipped library will provide the day school with facilities for giving high school graduates from Milwaukee and elsewhere studies equivalent to two full years of University residence at Madison."[29] The students' response justified all the struggle. The fall 1928 day class enrollment was 391, an increase of 52% over the previous year.[30]

The Extension Division had worked very carefully with the residence departments at Madison to assure that credits from the Milwaukee Center would be fully transferable. Consequently, Extension had only employed for the credit courses instructors drawn from the Madison faculty or persons approved by the residence departments. And it had attracted superior teachers by paying a premium salary for teaching in Milwaukee, in comparison with the compensation for teaching credit courses elsewhere in the state. The follow-up studies of the transferees from the Center consistently demonstrated that they competed academically on a par with students who had enrolled directly at Madison.[31]

When the credit class program started in earnest in 1920 and more Madison faculty had to teach in Milwaukee, the only reliable method of commuting was the train. Fortunately, several trains ran each day between the cities on both the Northwestern and the St. Paul and Milwaukee railroads. The trip normally took three hours, but a train from the north occasionally caused long delays at Watertown or Jefferson Junction, where the tracks intersected. A professor with a morning class at 8 o'clock had either to go over the night before or to ride the early morning milk train which, because of frequent stops, took four hours to complete the journey. They usually went the night before and stayed in a hotel. Extension paid these instructors $425.00 per class plus reasonable travel expenses, which could include a hotel room in Milwaukee. By comparison, those who taught an extension class in Madison, or a nearby community, received only $255.00 plus expenses.[32]

More and more instructors had to be employed to teach the every increasing number of credit classes in Milwaukee. By the late 1920s, a fairly sizeable residence faculty had been created, especially in the English and Business Departments. The development compelled changes in how the academic program was administered. For a few years, academic department chairmen in Extension had relayed communications between the Madison departments and their members in Milwaukee. But as the numbers grew this procedure became increasingly cumbersome and ineffective at both ends. Eventually the Madison departments appointed departmental representatives in Milwaukee and communicated directly with them. These representatives, after vigorous lobbying by their colleagues, won appointment to their respective departmental executive committees, with the right to discuss and vote on Milwaukee faculty members personnel decisions. Gradually, then, the academic chairmen in Extension relinquished their control over the university courses in Milwaukee.[33]

Despite the direct ties to the academic departments in Madison, those who taught for Extension struggled constantly to earn and keep the respect of their colleagues. Even the most outstanding professors could expect odd glances and snide remarks when they taught in Milwaukee or anywhere off the Madison campus. Part of the problems arose, no doubt, from an inability of the skeptics to distinguish between the credit and non-credit courses provided by the Extension Division. The lectures in entertainment and enlightenment arranged by the Instruction by Lectures Department were scathingly described as "the flea circus" and the term surely must have prejudiced some against anything offered by Extension. The instructors in the correspondence study program, especially, labored under a cloud. Correspondence courses, according to some resident faculty, could not equal a university course delivered in person in Bascom Hall. It did not matter, apparently, that the correspondence texts were almost always written by Madison faculty and that all had been thoroughly tested in residence classes before being published. Or that the texts and correspondence course procedures had been borrowed by dozens of other colleges and universities. The suspicion lingered, even after the UW, the University of Chicago, and the University of Michigan began to accept the correspondence credits at face value upon enrollment in a regular course of study on campus. [34]

The Extension Division and its Milwaukee Center had to remain flexible to serve a diverse and ever changing clientele. Most of the students in the early years were adults who enrolled in non-credit vocational courses—courses which they hoped would enable them to earn more money. The vocational high schools, however, gradually drew away most of these students after their establishment in 1911. [35] Indeed, Extension eventually negotiated a gentlemen's agreement not to compete directly with the vocational high schools; in return the vocational schools allowed Extension to use their facilities to conduct evening classes. In 1920 teachers comprised the greatest percent of Extension students—and by 1925 teachers filled almost 75% of the seats in the on-site evening classes being conducted across the state. The University, through its Education Department, encouraged these classes in the belief that better prepared public school teachers would graduate better prepared potential university students from the high schools. The students who enrolled in the daytime, college credit program at Milwaukee represented a cross-section of Wisconsin society. Many, as earlier mentioned, enrolled at the Center because they and their parents could save a sizable sum. The veterans, of course, often had families and jobs which tied them tightly to the metropolitan area. At the Extension Center they could test their abilities in college courses, while collecting the federal and state bonuses, and determine whether the required investment to move eventually to Madison would pay off. One important aspect of university life was lacking in Milwaukee—a lively social life and the comraderie that develops among students living in dormitories. Extension's leaders recognized this void, but the nature of their clientele made a solution difficult. Most of the students spent only a few hours each week at the Center to attend classes and do necessary work in the library, then they headed home or to jobs.[36]

As the twenties drew to a close, the University Extension Division could be proud of many accomplishments. It had infused new life into the Wisconsin Idea for the University; had secured allies for its programs among teachers, civic groups, unions, and legislators; and had, to a considerable extent, won support for its college credit courses from the resident faculty in Madison. The most notable achievement was the emergence of the Milwaukee Extension Center, housed in a state-owned seven-story building which bustled with activity. Here all sorts of activities were conducted: non-credit and credit classes, lectures for entertainment and enlightenment, and the rental of slides and motion pictures. In just a few years, the Milwaukee Center would be the model for a rapid expansion of daytime, college credit classes in communities throughout the state.

Two

The Depression Calls Forth Out-State Centers: The Thirties

The collapse of the stock market in late October 1929 marked the beginning of the severest economic depression the United States has experienced. Soon the disaster in Wall Street sent economic shock waves rippling across the country. Wisconsin's citizens shared fully this distress. For example, the state's manufacturing sector experienced a sharp decline in income, from $616 million in 1929 to just $173 million in 1932. Employment in manufacturing necessarily sagged, falling to 179,365 in 1932 compared to 309,397 in 1929. And workers lucky enough to keep a job suffered a twenty-five percent cut in their wages. These economic dislocations triggered a steep increase in the relief load throughout the state. Milwaukee County experienced the largest increase; in January 1930 the county's relief roll listed 1,000 families, by mid-1933 twenty percent of its families needed assistance.

Conditions were no better in the rural areas, although farmers may have been a little better able to secure food and shelter. Farmers' property taxes rose sharply (compared to ability to pay) as local governments struggled to meet rising relief costs. Farm prices plummeted fifty-seven percent between 1929 and 1932, while the prices farmers paid for commodities fell only twenty-nine percent. Total farm income declined almost by half in those three years.[1]

These adverse economic developments, of course, had a negative effect on the educational establishment in the state. During the 1920s many rural areas had constructed free union high schools under the terms of a 1921 enabling act. Still, the urban districts remained far ahead in providing these schools—in 1930 the number of potential secondary school students was roughly 50/50 between urban and rural areas, but just 31,836 were enrolled in the rural union high schools compared to 77,779 in city high schools. Working teenagers could seek further education in the vocational high schools, which could contract with University Extension to provide specialized continuing education courses. During the 1930s enrollments at all levels of education slumped because families lacked the resources to send their students to secondary school or to college.[2]

Enrollment in the Milwaukee Center's college credit classes defied the general trend and surged twenty-nine percent from January 1930 to January 1931.[3] Much of this increase no doubt occurred because students and their families could save a good deal of money by beginning at the Center, compared to living in Madison. A bill unsuccessfully introduced by Assemblyman John Ermene, a Milwaukee Socialist, in the 1931 session would have saved Milwaukee students even more money. Ermene's measure would have reduced the Center tuition from $75.00 to $24.50 per semester, the Madison rate. Ermene noted that the Extension students paid eighty percent of the cost of instruction while Madison students supported just six percent. Ermene argued that his measure was merely a matter of equity and he offered the opinion that its passage would enable many poorer families to secure at least two years of college for their students. President Glenn Frank thoroughly undercut support for Ermene's bill when he estimated that the state would have to add $200,000 to the University's budget to make up the lost revenue.[4]

The Center's sharp increase in enrollment provoked criticism from Marquette University and the Milwaukee Normal School. No doubt jealousy fueled some of the attacks, but more likely fear for their own institutions' survival triggered most of the accusations. Both asserted that Extension had plans to expand the Center's college operation into four full years. Extension Dean Chester Snell publicly denied this allegation and noted that the Attorney General's opinion, rendered during the building project dispute in 1925, clearly ruled out that option on constitutional grounds. Snell also pointed out that no student could earn more than half the required credits for graduation in non-residence courses, according to a rule adopted by the Madison faculty in 1906.[5]

By 1932 concern for Wisconsin's youth intensified. Principals of the public high schools knew that their graduates faced bleak prospects, while the directors of the vocational high schools labored to meet the divergent needs of their young day students. In March and April of 1932, at the suggestion of State Superintendent John Callahan, an ad hoc state committee met to discuss the problem and to propose solutions. In addition to Callahan, George Hambrecht, Director of the State Board of Vocational Education, Secretary F. G. Doudna of the Board of Regents of Normal Schools, Dean Snell of the Extension Division, and observers from the High Schools Principals Association attended these meetings.[6]

By late spring the group produced EDUCATIONAL PLANS for HIGH SCHOOL GRADUATES, a bulletin which reported the results of the committee's work. The authors noted that 23,000 youths had graduated from high school in 1932; normally forty percent would have continued their education and most of the rest would have found employment.[7] But these were not normal times. Local officials were becoming increasingly concerned about the rising number of idle young people and about the effect of idleness upon morale. Providing further educational opportunities, the authors wrote, would both reduce the youths' idleness and maintain their morale. But how could this be accomplished?

In the section of the bulletin Dean Snell authored, he pointed out the many services the Extension Division could offer to fill these needs. Thanks to the 1911 law, the vocational schools could contract with Extension to secure instructors for both credit and non-credit courses. Another statute permitted the city high schools to establish part-time college classes, for which Extension could also provide the teachers. And the Division's broad array of correspondence courses provided diverse options to the students. Snell suggested that a local school board might wish to provide a room where several correspondence course students could gather to do their lessons, although he cautioned that no assistance should be offered to them.[8]

Throughout the summer of 1932 meetings were held at each of the State Normal Schools. At these sessions, committee members explained the options to local school officials and introduced the Extension field representatives, who could help them make the necessary arrangements.

In the fall of 1932 the Extension Division experienced a significant increase in enrollment in its freshman level correspondence courses. The largest number enrolled in English, but history, foreign language and mathematics courses also recorded many more students. Consequently, in the spring of 1933 Extension employed seven English instructors who travelled from Madison to instruct classes in twenty cities.[9] When this experiment turned out favorably, the vocational school principals at Antigo and Sheboygan made inquiries whether a complete freshman program could be offered in their facilities.

Chester Allen, Extension's Director of Field Organization, relayed these inquiries to Dean Snell. From the outset, both men were enthusiastic about the potential of on-site freshman courses to help the Division weather its looming fiscal crisis. Snell immediately consulted with President Frank and Registrar Frank O. Holt about the idea. The two of them objected strongly to the proposal on the grounds that such out-state classes might further reduce Madison's enrollment. Snell, however, decided to ignore these objections because he felt the 1911 law required that Extension fill requests from the vocational high schools. So, Allen and his field representatives very quietly set up freshman courses in six cities for the fall of 1933.[10] These were the first Freshman Extension Centers to operate outside of Milwaukee. In the next two years, seven more cities opened Freshman Centers.[11]

Each Freshman Center was a lean operation which offered just two to four courses per semester, depending upon the number of students and their needs. English was almost always offered. The remaining courses were selected from among History, Geography, and Spanish. Geography became the laboratory science course by default because a "lab" could be set up in a standard classroom and did not require special equipment. A few students also enrolled in one or two correspondence courses to supplement these meager offerings. Sometimes an instructor requested some books from Extension's lending library and these volumes became the Center's very little library.[12]

The 1933 legislature unintentionally gave the Extension Centers a boost when it enacted Assembly Bill 922, a measure which appropriated $30,000 for each year of the 1933-1935 biennium to pay the tuition for unemployed persons for Extension courses. Dean Snell had given powerful testimony of the necessity for the scholarships when he noted that the "army" of young men roaming the state and nation swelled each month. And, he further observed, more and more adults were also joining these ranks when their resources and prospects gave out. Snell argued that the money would allow hundreds to be occupied "with constructive tasks and thus prevent individual and community morale from breaking down."[13]

The bill split the appropriation into thirds: $10,000 each was allocated to 1) correspondence courses outside of Milwaukee County, 2) fees for Extension classes outside Milwaukee County, and 3) students enrolled in Milwaukee County. To qualify a person had to be age 21 and employed less than fifteen hours per week. Any person receiving relief qualified. Young people between the ages of 18 and 21 could receive the scholarships if their parents were unemployed. On August 1, 1933, the Extension Division began accepting applications. In a little more than two months, on October 11, Extension announced that all the funds had been awarded. A follow-up study for 1933 showed that 2,452 Extension students had received an average of

$12.87 each. The largest number of recipients (1,029) attended out-state classes, including the college courses at the Centers. When not all of the Milwaukee County money was claimed, Extension received permission to transfer the surplus to the other groups.[14]

During the spring of 1934 the County Normal Schools in Mayville (Dodge County), Wausau (Marathon County) and Wisconsin Rapids (Wood County) contracted with Extension to provide a full freshman program in their facilities in the fall. When the *Wisconsin Rapids Tribune* praised this arrangement, someone brought the article to President Frank's attention and he censured Dean Snell and ordered a halt. Frank said his concern was for legalities—could Extension enter into a contract with any county normal without prior consent from State Superintendent Callahan? But even after Callahan gave his blessing, the President stalled. Chester Allen believed that the real basis of the delay was jealousy over Extension's ability to find new sources of revenue in the midst of the depression. Only after the three principals had written a pleading letter did Frank, on August 14, 1934, finally give his go-ahead.[15]

The cost to operate a typical Freshman Center program in a vocational high school was $1,500.00 per semester (25 students X 12 credits X $5.00 per credit). But the students often only paid $25.00 per semester out of their pockets, which generated $625.00 for the contracting school. State aid paid forty percent of the cost of instruction, or $600.00. That left just $275.00 for the community to raise. Most school boards paid this sum, justifying the expense by noting the economic advantages to the community of having its young people begin college at home. Each student, for instance, saved $400.00 in living expenses by attending a Center. In addition, surveys suggested that the instructors spent about $300.00 in each Extension Center community for meals, hotel rooms and other expenses during the course of a semester. These economic advantages created a good deal of enthusiasm for the program throughout the state.[16]

The Extension Division made a little money from each Center. Instructors received, on the average, $2,000 per year, plus $800.00 for travel expenses. This $2,800.00 represented the total instructional costs for a typical freshman program because the contracting school provided the facility, janitorial services, and utilities. Thus Extension cleared at least $200.00 per year from each of its Freshman Centers. This was a significant sum during the depression years and it enabled the Division to continue other services, such as correspondence courses, even though they operated at a slight deficit.[17]

The depression compelled the University to adopt some unorthodox fiscal procedures. The second semester had barely begun in Wausau when, in late January 1933, the town's banks announced they would close for a thirty day "bank holiday." Of course this meant that many students' fee payment checks could not be cashed until the banks reopened. Then, in March 1933, newly installed President Franklin D. Roosevelt imposed a national bank holiday to provide time for bank examiners to sort out the healthy from failing institutions. Extension, along with Madison, really had no choice but to continue the classes and hope that all of the checks could eventually be redeemed. Later that same year Dean Snell proposed to the regents a partial payment plan which would allow students to pay one-third of their fees when they enrolled, one-third in thirty days, and the last one-third in sixty days. Snell estimated the losses would be less than one percent and that the plan would mean $15,000 in income for Extension that would otherwise be lost. The regents approved. The field representatives who set up the freshman classes also regularly accepted post-dated checks from students. Chester Allen reported that not one cent was lost through this practice, and he was convinced that Extension earned inestimable good will by allowing this courtesy.[18]

But creative financial arrangements for students did not solve the University's basic problem—there just was not enough money to balance the budget. Each state budget through the mid-thirties decreased funds both to Madison and to Extension, which still received a separate allocation. Extension experienced an especially drastic change in its budget. At the beginning of the decade, the state provided about fifty-five percent of the operating budget and the remainder came from course fees. By the end of the thirties, the Division was compelled to earn almost sixty-five percent of its total revenue.[19]

The extra income earned via the freshman courses did not entirely offset the reduction in state funds and the decline in fee income in many of Extension's programs. Because the out-state Centers operated on a pay-as-you-go basis, they were not affected when the inevitable cuts occurred. But the Milwaukee Center definitely felt the crunch. By 1932 its program had grown to include a full array of sophomore courses, except for some pre-professional programs like engineering. Consequently, the number of permanent faculty in Milwaukee had also increased and some of them had earned tenure. These instructors shared fully in the so-called salary waiver program imposed in three consecutive years, beginning with the 1932-33 academic year. The theory behind the salary waivers was that the money voluntarily given up now would be restored when the state's finances improved. The restoration, of course, never occurred.

The salary waivers in Extension amounted to eighteen percent. All of the Milwaukee personnel and Extension's permanent employees throughout the state had their compensation reduced by this amount. In addition, the number of faculty at the Milwaukee Center was slashed by fifteen percent to bring its operating expenses in line with fee revenue. Despite the obvious pain these belt tightening measures produced, the Milwaukee Center retained and even attracted new, highly qualified faculty members because conditions in Wisconsin were far better than in many other states.[20]

During 1932 Dean Snell successfully warded off an attempt to combine Extension's and the University's budgets into one account. This move was proposed to the regents by President Frank, at the suggestion of the Business Office. Alarm bells immediately went off in Extension, where many believed that this was a bold scheme to get control of the Division's revenue so that it could be used to support Madison's programs. W.H. Lighty, the Director of the Department of Extension Teaching, drafted a long memorandum in which he recalled that Dr. Charles McCarthy had insisted upon a provision for a separate budget in the 1907 bill which had revived General Extension. Lighty also noted that, even though the legislature no longer made a separate appropriation for Extension, the regents had made and had kept a "gentlemen's agreement" to keep Extension's account isolated from the University's budget.[21]

Snell asked President Frank to put this issue on the agenda of the Deans Council. In the Council Snell campaigned vigorously against merging the accounts.[22] Apparently the anti-Extension prejudice on the Hill now proved an advantage. Several of the residence deans objected to the budget merger proposal because they feared their schools' funds might somehow get transferred to General Extension! Given Extension's brisk resistance and a lack of broad support among top administrators, President Frank and the regents allowed the resolution quietly to die.[23]

Tensions had been gradually building between Dean Snell and President Frank. Snell had quietly defied the President by starting the outstate Freshman Extension Centers and by later contracting with several county normals to offer the same program in their schools. The continual battles over the budget also strained their relationship. From time to time Madison deans complained about Snell's direct contact with legislators during state budget hearings, a privilege which they did not have.

During the budget building process in early 1934 Snell made what turned out to be a fatal error. He recommended, apparently without any consultation, that the four assistant professors at the Milwaukee Center be given one year contracts rather than the traditional three year agreements. The four affected faculty quickly complained to their union—Local 253, American Federation of Teachers—about Snell's arbitrary decision. The Union's executive committee set up a Fact Finding Committee to investigate the complaints against Snell.

After taking testimony from several Milwaukee faculty, the Union forwarded its report to President Frank during the summer of 1934. The report was highly critical of Snell. The Fact Finding Committee charged that Snell had made many arbitrary changes in the administration at the Milwaukee Center in order to gain more personal control and that he had granted salary increases only to faculty who supported his policies. L.E. Drake, the author of the report, described Snell as an "autocratic dictator," who terrorized his staff and who completely lacked the "human quality" essential in an administrator. Drake stressed the recommended one year contracts to the assistant professors as proof of these general allegations.[24]

President Frank apparently kept his own counsel about the union's report until October 1934 when, in executive session, the Regents voted to set up its own three man committee to investigate the Extension Division. Regent Vice President Harold Wilkie of Madison, who presided over this session, made himself chairman of the group. Later, accusations were made that this decision had been deliberately timed to occur during the absence of Regent President Fred Clausen, who presumably would have opposed undertaking the investigation. The Regent Committee operated entirely in closed sessions, taking testimony both in Milwaukee and Madison. When Snell finally learned that an inquiry into his Division was underway, he protested the secrecy and demanded to be told the objective of the investigation. Wilkie informed Snell that no charges had been lodged against him and that the probe was of a general nature.[25]

During its March 12-13, 1935, meeting the Board of Regents unanimously voted not to renew Snell's contract when it expired July first. However, the decision was not publicly announced so that President Frank could deliver the bad news and urge Snell quietly to resign. Snell asked for time to think about his response. According to Chester Allen, Snell's initial reaction was to go quietly, but gradually he became incensed over how badly he had been treated by President Frank and the regents.[26] Consequently, Snell refused to resign and resolved to fight his dismissal. Snell's combativeness compelled the regents to reaffirm their decision and to make public the reasons for terminating his contract. The regents asserted that Snell's ouster was not entirely a response to the complaints from Milwaukee and that ample reasons existed for their action wholly unconnected to that Center's operation.[27] Nevertheless, the press accounts of Snell's dismissal zeroed in on the allegations made by the Milwaukee teachers union as the real basis for the regents' action.[28]

This conflict in the University attracted the attention of the legislators and added fuel to the fires of political controversy. Philip LaFollette, younger son of Fighting Bob, had led his Progressive party to victory in the 1934 gubernatorial and Assembly races but the Democrats had retained control of the Senate. Early in 1935 the Senate Democrats seized upon alleged subversive activity on the Madison campus and set up a special investigating committee to look into the University's affairs. The Progressive majority in the Assembly decisively refused to make this a joint committee and labeled the Democrat's maneuver an attempt to embarrass the LaFollette administration, whose close ties to the University were well known. The Senate investigative committee immediately became known as the Brunette Committee, after its chairman, E. F. Brunette, a Democrat from Green Bay. Brunette and his four colleagues had just started the hearings when the Snell affair broke. They quickly decided to invite Snell to testify because, in addition to looking into communistic activities, they were empowered to probe "other irregularities" in the University of Wisconsin.[29]

Snell's account of the events that led to his dismissal totally contradicted the regents' and President Frank's explanations. Snell testified that he had gone confidentially to the President early in 1934 to tell him that he wished to dismiss four members of the Milwaukee Center faculty for improper conduct and immorality. Frank told him to proceed. Then, somehow, this information reached the affected persons and they mounted a campaign to discredit Snell. The alleged ringleader of the counter attack was Colin Welles, the son-in-law of former regent Meta Berger and the head of the Milwaukee County federation of labor unions. Welles enlisted Mrs. Berger in the fight and, according to Snell, she went directly to Frank and used her influence to turn him against the Dean of Extension. Snell told the Senators that he was confident he would still have his job if he had been willing to wink at the "irregularities" in the Berger family relationships. He also stated that Mrs. Berger had held a grudge against him ever since he had refused to put several members of her family on permanent contract in Milwaukee. For a while Snell had acceded to her requests for employment, but he had eventually tired of this "family job plan."[30]

President Frank, of course, related a very different story when he appeared before the Brunette Committee. Frank carefully outlined the defects he had found in Snell's administrative style and recounted his repeated attempts to convince the Extension Dean to correct these deficiencies. In regard to the Berger family allegations, he said that Snell had not produced any evidence of impropriety or immorality among the Milwaukee faculty, despite many invitations to do so. The President defended vigorously the Berger family's reputation and castigated Snell for his unsubstantiated allegations. Frank reiterated that Snell's dismissal had resulted from many administrative problems that the regents' investigating committee had turned up and not solely from the complaints made by the Milwaukee teachers' union.[31]

The Brunette Committee also called Regent Vice President Wilkie to the stand. In his first appearance Wilkie explained that Snell had been fired because he had lost the confidence of practically every leading educator in Wisconsin and of many co-workers in the Extension Division. The Dean had alienated all these people by being harsh, dictatorial, and petty in his relationships. For example, Snell had not allowed the Director of the Milwaukee Center, Professor Frank C. Purin, any real authority and required that Purin come to Madison for consultation before making any decision. Wilkie also scored Snell for his attempt to violate the University's tenure procedures by giving the Milwaukee assistant professors only a one year contract.

In a second appearance, however, sharp questioning by the Brunette Committee compelled Wilkie to concede that "there was nothing in the testimony taken by the [regents'] committee to substantiate any of the charges." Wilkie admitted that the regents, not Snell, had the final authority over faculty contracts and that, in any event, the Dean's recommendation for the one year contracts for the Milwaukee Center assistant professors had never been formally presented to the Board. Dr. Purin, moreover, had told the regents that he had been hired to teach, not to administer, and that he wanted no more authority than he had received. Wilkie admitted, too, that two personnel cases Snell had allegedly handled unfairly had, in fact, been decided by other persons in the Extension Division.[32]

"Snell Dismissal Was Unfair," read part of the *Capital Times* headline announcing the findings of the Brunette Committee.[33] The Committee's report asserted that President Frank deliberately brought the charges of Local 253 to the Board of Regents when he knew Regent President Clausen was out of town and that Frank had told some people in Milwaukee the Snell would be "got" in October 1934. The legislators listed three reasons for a finding of unfairness. First, the regent investigators had purposely deceived Snell as to the nature of the inquiry. Second, Snell had not been informed of the charges against him. Third, the regents kept the hearings closed, so Snell had no opportunity to respond to his critics. In addition, the Brunette Committee assailed the regents for not keeping a record of their secret meetings; the Board's secretary had admitted recreating some minutes from memory many months after one closed session and he grudgingly conceded that his recollections had been challenged by those who had attended the meeting. The report concluded that "to find a parallel we must go to the medieval inquisitions or to the present day Russia."[34] Needless to say, the regents rejected these findings and reaffirmed Snell's dismissal.[35]

University of Wisconsin Registrar Frank O. Holt was appointed Snell's replacement. He assumed the office on July 1, 1935, but also continued to serve as Registrar for almost a year. Several members of the Extension administration viewed Holt's appointment with suspicion because he had opposed the opening of the Freshman Centers and because he was generally viewed as being President Frank's closest advisor and confidant. These men feared that Frank would now secure greater control over the Division, something which Snell had diligently resisted.[36]

The Snell affair obviously caused a great deal of embarrassment for President Frank, the regents, and the University. Very soon Frank found himself under fire for mishandling it. Snell's dismissal and the messy business with the Brunette Committee evidently convinced several people that the President had to go. Regent Harold Wilkie, who was elected president of the board in June 1935, orchestrated the campaign. The anti-Frank forces received a boost in January 1936 when five new members joined the Board of Regents, bringing the total of Philip LaFollette appointees to eleven of the fifteen members. In mid-1936 three Regents visited with President Frank to inform him that the Board desired his resignation. Frank agreed. But, a few days later, he vowed that he would fight his dismissal on the grounds that it was politically motivated by the LaFollettes and their Progressive allies.

As with Snell's removal, this battle quickly turned nasty. The major allegation against the President was that he was a poor administrator, one who did not pay attention to necessary details. This defect, his detractors said, was compounded by his numerous and lengthy absences from the University during which he pursued his speaking and writing career. Zona Gale, who had played an instrumental role in bringing Frank to Wisconsin, defended him in the state and national press. The showdown occurred during the regents' January 1937 meeting. Wilkie presented the case against the President, then Frank spoke in his own defense. A few minutes after he finished his plea, the Board voted eight to seven to immediately dismiss him. Thus ended the Glenn Frank administration.[37]

The regents immediately initiated a search for a successor. The tremendous publicity surrounding both Snell's and Frank's dismissals certainly may have scared off some potential applicants. The search, however, moved rapidly along and in mid-1937 Clarence A. Dykstra was named President of the University of Wisconsin. Dykstra, a political scientist and historian, had taught for eleven years in various universities and then had worked in city government for seventeen years. At the time of his appointment, Dr. Dykstra was the city manager of Cincinnati, Ohio. Because of his expertise in politics and government, he served on over a dozen state and federal committees, commitments which he continued after he came to Madison. In contrast to his predecessor, Clarence Dykstra served a relatively uneventful seven year term as the chief executive of the University.[38]

The intense political battles of the 1930s naturally reflected the distress many of Wisconsin's citizens felt in the midst of the deep economic depression. It seemed to some that basic American values were being challenged as never before and they did not know what to do except strenuously to defend those values. Some also believed that anyone who would question even one of these "virtually sacred" values must be a communist bent on the overthrow of the entire American system. [39]

Consequently, an academic critique of America's institutions in the classroom sometimes placed the instructor in jeopardy. In one episode, Albert E. Crofts, a sociologist who taught in the Extension Centers in Green Bay, Manitowoc, and Fond du Lac, got himself into such serious controversy that he eventually resigned from the faculty. During a Green Bay class session Crofts blasted holding companies which controlled a large number of electrical power companies. Several employees of the Green Bay Power and Light Company happened to be enrolled in this class and they took serious exception to the instructor's remarks. A bit later, in Fond du Lac, Crofts delivered a lecture on the issue of social control by pressure groups, among whom he included the Roman Catholic church. A visitor to this class, a graduate of Notre Dame, registered a strong protest with a local priest, who relayed it to Extension administration in Madison. Dean Holt sent a representative to Fond du Lac to look into the allegations. Many students, including several who were Catholic, rallied to Crofts' defense. The priest, after visiting with Holt's emissary, announced publicly that he would have no objection to Crofts continuing to teach at the Center. Nevertheless, Crofts decided to seek employment elsewhere when his contract with Extension expired. [40]

In another case the Wausau American Legion Post demanded the dismissal of T. Harry Williams, an history instructor. On November 11, 1936, Williams delivered the annual Armistice Day address to the assembled Wausau High School students and, during the course of his speech, described Abraham Lincoln's Gettysburg Address as "the finest example of propaganda ever expressed in America."[41] When the Legionnaires met that evening all the talk focused on the report of Williams' speech in the *Wausau Record Herald*. The men decided to demand Williams dismissal, at the very least he should not be allowed to teach another class in Wausau. The next day E. A. Holm, the Director of the Wausau Vocational School where the Extension classes were held, announced that he would not allow Williams to hold his classes on November 13. Marshall Graff of Appleton, the District Extension Representative, also denounced Williams and said that Holm's decision had been approved by phone by Dean Holt. For the next several days, newspapers across the state carried accounts of affair drawn from the *Record Herald's* ongoing coverage. [42]

Williams stoutly defended his remarks, claiming that he had been quoted out of context and observing that every political leader uses propaganda in winning support for his policies. Williams asked the *Record Herald* to print the entire text of his speech and allow the readers to judge whether he had tarnished President Lincoln's reputation. Meanwhile, the University's History Department had initiated its own inquiry. It sent Bessie Edsall, who also taught Extension Center history courses, to meet with the Wausau school officials. She concluded that Williams had in fact been misquoted and that the local officials had acted with haste and undue emotion in deciding to terminate Williams' contract in Wausau. Even so, Dean Holt announced that Williams would not be returning to Wausau but would continue his other classes in Merrill, Rhinelander and Antigo. In a few days, however, Holt reversed himself when the History Department absolutely refused to appoint a successor to Williams at Wausau. The Department repeated that Williams had been both misquoted and quoted out of context and warned that he could seek redress in the courts for violations of his First Amendment rights if he was not reinstated. Williams also received strong support from his Wausau students, who stood to lose their credits if the impasse was not settled. The *Capital Times* blamed the whole affair on "Witch Hunters Over Rib Mountain" who were "old moss-backed reactionaries." At the end of November the *Record Herald* carried a joint announcement by the Extension Division and the Wausau Board of Vocational Education that Williams would return to his classes the next day. Thus the "Williams affair" quietly ended.[43]

During the 1936-37 academic year, S. I. Hayakawa, a Canadian of Japanese extraction who taught English in Rhinelander, Merrill, and Wausau, was a victim of prejudice. After he had been employed, the Extension Division field representative, Marshall Graff, encountered much resistance to a "foreigner" teaching English to white students. In addition, some complained that a foreigner ought not be hired when good American teachers remained unemployed. Invariably the local boards said that they had no objection to Hayakawa but they feared their communities would not be so open minded. Near the end of the second semester Graff conducted a survey of the three communities and found that, especially in Wausau, the resistance to retaining Hayakawa was strong. Graff recommended that Hayakawa not be reappointed. After consultation, Dean Holt appointed Hayakawa for one more year to a circuit where there was little or no outspoken opposition to him. Holt forthrightly admitted to Hayakawa that the anti-alien bias "out in the state" made his further employment a problem. In this instance, Extension clearly compromised in the face of overt racism.[44]

The instructors who taught in the Freshman Centers came primarily from the Madison Graduate School and the Milwaukee Center. Those from

Milwaukee faced a layoff if they did not accept an assignment to travel to the hinterlands. These professors were augmented as necessary with high school teachers, qualified housewives, and local professionals. In all instances the Madison departments maintained control over the appointmments and the evaluation of Extension's college credit class faculty.[45] The History Department regularly conducted inspection tours of the out-state classes to assess the quality of instruction and the morale of its instructors. The departmental visitors reported that faculty morale was pretty low because the Extension Center historians were isolated and had no opportunity to interact with colleagues. To remedy this, they recommended that each Extension history teacher receive one expense-paid research trip to Madison each month. The History Department also decided that it would limit the appointments of its graduate students in the Centers to three years. The other Madison departments were not nearly as active in keeping tabs on their Freshman Center classes and apparently did not adopt the three year maximum appointment rule.[46]

Because they travelled to three or four cities, Extension Center instructors were called circuit riders and itinerants. For example, in 1934 Howard Blackenburg, a historian who lived in Antigo, taught classes in the Antigo Vocational School on Monday and Friday mornings, travelled to Rhinelander on Tuesday for a three hour session which began at 9:30 A.M., and rounded out his week in the Marathon County Normal School in Wausau with classes on Wednesday afternoon and Thursday morning. Blackenburg received $250.00 per semester to defray his travel expenses. By contrast, R. J. Colbert, who taught economics and sociology, had a teaching schedule compressed into just two days—Monday and Tuesday. On Monday he taught Rural Sociology 25 in the morning at the Dodge County Normal in Mayville, then journeyed to Sheboygan where, between 4:15 and 9:30 P.M., he offered Economics 1B and Sociology 197. Each of these was a two hour class. The following evening Colbert taught Sociology 197 and Economic Trends (a non-credit course) in Fond du Lac.[47]

Because the majority of the instructors, like Colbert, lived in Madison, they travelled by train or automobile to their classes. Car pools were regularly formed to reduce the expenses, or for the simple reason that not every instructor owned a vehicle. Being on the road during a Wisconsin winter in the 1930s presented problems that our newer highways with wide shoulders have pretty much eliminated. The well equipped circuit rider's car carried chains, a shovel, and a lantern.[48] Mrs. Frank Rentz, who taught Spanish in the Centers for eight years during the Thirties, recalled that the winter of 1935-36 was very severe. She had to travel roads with only one plowed lane between snow banks that towered over the roof of her car. She remembered that twelve inches of snow remained on the ground in Sturgeon Bay at the end of May 1936 when she met her last class.[49]

John Bergstresser, the Assistant Dean of the University Extension Division, related that early in 1938 two fairly new Extension circuit riders were trapped by huge snow drifts in an overcrowded farm house for two-and-a-half days. The family and its many stranded guests subsisted on dried fish and slept on the floor in two hour relays.[50] L.H. Adolfson, who later became the Dean of the Extension Division, told a story of what happened to him when he was a political science instructor during that same rugged 1937-38 winter. He taught an afternoon class in Sheboygan and, as usual, rented a hotel room in that city before heading to Fond du Lac for an evening class. The weather was clear when he arrived in Fond du Lac but by the time he dismissed class a fast-moving Wisconsin blizzard had closed the road back to Sheboygan. So, Adolfson rented another room and spent the night. The next day he made an early start and struggled to reach Sheboygan for his 9:00 class. But the even greater struggle occurred when he had to explain to the business office why he should be reimbursed for hotel rooms in two different cities for the same night![51]

The Extension Center instructors taught in classrooms that varied considerably in quality from town to town. Commonly, the classes met in the city vocational school but high school and county normal facilities were also used. In Merrill the Center was located on the second floor of the City Hall.

Some of the residence departments periodically dispatched a faculty member or two to make an inspection tour of various Centers. These inspectors often found serious inadequacies. For example, Professor Mark Ingraham, Chairman of the Mathematics Department, complained about the inadequate blackboards in all four of the cities he visited—Green Bay, Manitowoc, Sheboygan, and Fond du Lac. He stressed that mathematical concepts and formulas had to be demonstrated on the blackboard and that students should have an opportunity to work problems on the board. At Green Bay, the students were wedged into youth-sized chairs and Ingraham demanded that the chairs immediately be replaced. In all four communities, he was gratified by his brief visits with the school officials, who were eager to try to make the corrections he suggested.[52] Historians William Best Hesseltine and R. L. Reynolds conducted class visitations in Manitowoc, Merrill, and Wausau. All of the classrooms lacked maps, which created a real problem for the instructors. At all three sites the halls resounded with noise because the students with free time had no where else to congregate and visit. They described the second floor of the Merrill City Hall as a "fire trap" and stressed that its busy atmosphere was not at all conducive to education. At Wausau Hesseltine and Reynolds found the library facilities so inadequate that they recommended the history class be dropped unless books could be provided for the students' research papers. The Wausau Public Library, they noted, could not fill the void because it owned only a dozen history books.[53]

Because this problem was not limited to Wausau, the Extension Division gradually created its own library in Madison. The books were selected from lists provided by the residence departments; often multiple copies were purchased so that several classes could be supplied with the same volumes. Each semester the books were shipped out at an instructor's request to the Centers. The instructors usually served as the librarian for their classes—checking the volumes out to the students, collecting them when due, and returning them to Madison at the semester's end.

The students who attended the Centers represented a good cross section of the youth of rural and small town Wisconsin. A study conducted in 1937-38 revealed that the freshman classes continued primarily to serve students who would not have started college if a Center had not been available. Extension's Assistant Dean, John Bergstresser, concluded that only ten percent of the students could have afforded to go directly to Madison. Most students worked part time to help pay their expenses; some were employed at the Centers by the N.Y.A. (National Youth Administration) for up to twenty hours per week at a rate of ten to fifteen cents per hour. The N.Y.A. was an important source of financial aid to depression era students. In April 1937, Dean Holt wrote to L. R. Evans, the Vocational School Director in Sheboygan, that, in Fond du Lac, out of a class of fourteen, twelve had jobs with the N.Y.A. Holt also noted that one young lady in that class, the valedictorian of her high school graduation, was so desperate economically that she was allowed to use one of her N.Y.A. checks as a down payment on eyeglasses rather than signing it over to Extension. Bergstresser noted that the Centers attracted good students—72% were from the upper half of their high school graduating class and just over 50% had ranked in the upper quarter. The students who continued at Madison did as well as those who began at the main campus. In 1936-37 the 67 former Extension students enrolled in the College of Letters and Science earned a 1.52 grade point compared to the College's 1.51 overall average.[54]

Shortly after Berstresser's appointment as assistant dean, he instituted, in July 1937, a guidance and counseling program to help the students make a smooth transition to Madison. Bergstresser was assisted by Dr. Louis E. Drake, a psychologist who had set up a counseling service at the Milwaukee Center. Dean Holt transferred Drake to Madison so that he could better administer the service. In Madison, a residence student committee made up of former Center students organized an orientation program for the transferees similar to the one offered to the incoming freshmen.[55]

The students who attended the Extension Centers, however, were short-changed in some respects. The student body lacked the diversity that existed in Madison. Because of space and staff limitations, the Centers offered almost no extracurricular activities during which the students could mingle and socialize. Thus loyalties remained with the local high schools instead of being transferred to the University. Some students also found that living at home interfered with their studies because parents expected them to shoulder numerous duties. For obvious reasons, the students from farms reported the greatest difficulty in this regard.[56]

The new Dean, Frank Holt, did not immediately take a firm grip upon the reins at Extension. For about a year Holt continued to serve as university Registrar; for almost another year Holt did not, in Chester Allen's opinion, offer strong leadership to the Division. Then, in mid-1937, Allen noticed a dramatic change—Holt firmly took charge and his attitude toward the Centers, whose establishment he had opposed, became much more positive. Allen attributed the change to a battle among the department chairs for more money. In order to make informed decisions, Holt had to visit several Centers and become knowledgeable about their operation. In the process the gregarious Holt met with local school officials, instructors, and students and when he encountered their enthusiasm, he was won over. In the fall of 1937 Holt began to use his great facility as a speaker to spread the word of the Extension Center program across the state.[57]

Holt, however, had not been entirely inactive in Extension's behalf. The 1935 Legislature had expanded the eligibility for legislative scholarships to the University to include Freshman/Sophomore Center students, provided they met the same academic standards as at Madison. But in the uproar over Dean Snell's contract, nothing had been done to implement the program. During the summer of 1936 Holt successfully lobbied President Frank and the Board of Regents for authority to award the money for the fall semester. The legislative scholarships provided fee remission to the recipients, a sum of $27.50 per semester.[58]

The state legislature paid more attention than usual to the Extension Division, and specifically to the Centers, after Dean Snell's removal. The publicity generated by the Brunette Committee's investigation may explain this phenomenon. In any event, the 1937 session considered two measures which proposed additional aid to the out-state college credit classes. Senator Earl Leverich (Progressive-Sparta) introduced legislation that would have added up to $30,000 annually to the vocational school aids to assist vocational school boards which contracted with Extension for freshman and sophomore courses. Leverich's measure would have reimbursed the boards for fifty percent of their aid to the college students, up to a maximum of $75.00 per student. In

1937 twelve districts would have benefitted from this program while five would have received nothing because they made no contribution toward their Extension Center student's expenses. Leverich promoted his bill as a measure for economic justice which would provide a college opportunity to the children of poor men who could not afford to send them to Madison. Dean Holt, State Director of Vocational Education George P. Hambrecht, and several directors of city vocational high schools testified in favor of the measure in the Senate hearings. Despite this testimony, the bill attracted little support and it quietly died when the legislature adjourned in early July.[59]

An amendment to the 1937-39 biennial budget proposed by Senator Roland E. Kannenberg (Progressive-Wausau) proved very controversial. Kannenberg wanted $165,000 added to the University allocation specifically for the purchase of a site and construction of an Extension building at Wausau. The Madison press vigorously denounced this scheme; the *Wisconsin State Journal* decried the threats of the "tombstone terror from Wausau" to tie up the entire University budget unless he got his way.[60] Attacks by the *Capital Times* finally moved Kannenberg to reply. He said that his motive simply was to provide good educational opportunities to the youth among the 100,000 residents of his senate district. The Senator denounced the *Capital Times* for desiring to continue Madison's monopoly over state funds.[61] Kannenberg's measure passed the Senate, 18 to 10, but was killed in the Assembly.[62]

In 1937 the state's Department of Justice gave the Extension Centers an apparent boost when the Attorney General ruled that a vocational school could admit students from outside its district to the college classes and that it could levy a non-resident fee. This decision pleased the smaller Centers because they could now augment their funds with the fees from non-resident students and collect state aid for them as well. But this simply meant that a limited number of dollars would have to be spread over more students, thus reducing the per-capita aid. Confronted with complaints from the vocational school districts that did not have Freshman Centers, the State Board of Adult and Vocational Education decided in mid-1938 that the subsidy to the college students would cease at the end of the biennium, despite strong testimony in favor of continuing the aid.[63] This decision placed several Centers in jeopardy. In an attempt to stave off a looming disaster, several vocational school directors met in Antigo in August 1938 to decide how to proceed. Dean Holt, State Superintendent John Callahan, State Director of Vocational Education George Hambrecht, and Regent Carl Drexler of Menasha accepted invitations to attend. The men decided to create a sub-committee which would draft a bill to be presented to the 1939 Legislature. They proposed that up to $100,000 per year in direct state aid be appropriated to the Centers to replace the funds being withdrawn by the State Vocational Board. Once the bill was outlined, they paid visits to several legislators to enlist their support. The legislators' favorable reactions made passage seem almost certain.[64]

But the election of 1938 shattered these well laid plans. In that canvass the Republicans swept the Progressives out of office, capturing the governor's mansion and control of both the Senate and Assembly. Joseph P. Heil, the new Governor, was a political neophyte who generally let the Republican old-timers in the legislature set the pace. The 1939 Legislature quickly approved a revision of the Board of Regents' statute to throw all fifteen incumbents out of office and replace them with inexperienced Heil appointees. In the midst of all this turmoil over university affairs, the bill to provide state aid to the Freshman Centers languished and eventually quietly died.[65]

In the late 1930s local school officials still wrestled with the fact that many graduates would be idle after they left high school. One possible solution they considered was to add a 13th and 14th year to the secondary schools and employ the high school teachers to teach both the college credit and non-credit vocational courses. University officials hastily pointed out that they would not accept the credits from such college courses unless they had certified in advance the course content and the instructors' credentials. Dean Holt, who certainly agreed with this assessment, urged the school districts interested in college courses for recent graduates to contract with Extension for the instruction. This arrangement would assure transferability of the credits because the circuit-riding instructors had been appointed by the Madison departments. After he had tried this idea out in a few meetings with secondary school principles without encountering any opposition, Holt wrote the text for a pamphlet which explained this option and underscored its advantages.[66]

Accordingly, early in 1939 the Appleton High School Principal contacted the Extension Division about setting up a freshman program in his building the following fall. In May he conducted a survey of the 1939 graduates which revealed that 36% of them would be "idle at home," 38% would be employed, and 25% would go to college. The survey also showed that a sufficient number of the 1939 graduates would enroll in a local Center to justify pursuing the arrangements with Extension. But before proceeding, the principal wrote to President Thomas Barrows of Lawrence College in Appleton to see if he had any misgivings about a freshman program operated under the auspices of the University of Wisconsin. Barrows objected strenuously. Barrows wrote Holt and told him that Lawrence had worked hard and successfully to assist Appleton students and that the proposed program was unnecessary. Holt sent Chester Allen and Marshall Graff, an Extension field representative, to visit with President Barrows. Allen reported that they got along fine, but that Barrows would not withdraw his opposition. In the end, Barrows won. The Appleton High School freshman center never opened.[67]

As the end of the decade approached, Holt eased his missionary work in behalf of the Centers and turned his attention to the Extension programs that were not doing nearly as well, such as the correspondence courses which had experienced a steady decline in registrations. By 1939 the Freshman Centers had become the mainstay of Extension's fee income, a fact demonstrated in 1938 when an unanticipated enrollment decline caused a $13,000 deficit. By careful management and aggressive recruiting the shortage had been made up and the fall 1939 enrollment was strong. Still, an uneasiness haunted the Extension administration. As the economy improved, it seemed inevitable that more high school graduates would opt to work than to attend a Center. Also, more students could afford to go directly to Madison or to a private college. The reduction in aid from the State Vocational Board had hurt some centers, most notably Antigo, where another $1,000 had to be raised from local sources to maintain the program. In September 1939 World War II erupted in Europe when Germany attacked Poland and the subsequent expansion of the United States military forces reduced the number of young men who might choose to attend college.[68] As the decade came to a close the Freshman Centers remained the fiscal backbone of the Extension Division, but that was to change very soon.

University of Wisconsin
Center System

Three
Decline and Revival: The Forties

The outbreak of hostilities in Europe in September of 1939 did not have an immediate impact upon the University of Wisconsin and the Extension Centers. During that month, however, President Franklin D. Roosevelt signed the Selective Service Act which required every male between the ages of twenty-one and thirty-six to register for the draft. By 1943 these ages would be expanded to eighteen through thirty-eight. Some men, especially the younger ones, decided to enlist immediately so that they might elect to serve in the branch of the military they preferred. By the time the six nationwide registrations were completed, some thirty-one million men had been enrolled. Almost ten million were eventually inducted into the service from this pool.[1]

Wisconsin contributed its fair share of personnel to the war effort. Over one million men registered for the Selective Service in the state and about one-third of them were called to duty. In addition, approximately 9,000 Wisconsin women served, primarily as nurses and office staff. The increased need for labor on the state's farms and in factories further reduced the pool of potential University enrollees. In 1941, as tensions between the United States and Japan heightened, many men left their studies in mid-semester either to volunteer or to respond to the draft.[2]

In September 1939 the General Extension Division responded to the need for military preparedness. George A. Parkinson, Assistant Director of the Evening School in Milwaukee and also the Lieutenant Commander of the local Naval Reserve unit, initiated a Civilian Pilot Training program. Its objective was to train rapidly as many pilots as possible for military duty. The Civil Aeronautics Authority worked with Extension to get this program underway and gave it a real boost in mid-1940 by convincing the War Emergency Board to build an Air Annex to house the burgeoning classes and to provide a lab for engine repair and other aircraft maintenance.[3]

The Engineering, Science and Management War Training (ESMWT) classes, which began in March 1941, aimed at increasing war material production for the United States military and for the Lend-Lease program, which shipped weapons to the Allies. By the end of the war, the ESMWT program had enrolled about 10,000 students from over 600 businesses and industries in 37 Wisconsin cities. The greatest number, of course, enrolled in the heavily industrialized Lakeshore District which included Milwaukee, Racine, and Kenosha.[4]

The largest and most successful Extension wartime program, by far, was the United States Armed Forces Institute (USAFI). USAFI, which operated under contract with the Department of Defense, provided both college credit and non-credit correspondence courses to military personnel throughout the world. The federal government paid all the fees, so the enrollments constantly climbed. The program quickly became the largest source of revenue for Extension and a surplus once again began to appear in the Division's accounts.[5] Through USAFI, many young men and women from families without a tradition of university education had an opportunity to try college. A significant number were successful and planned to complete a degree after the war.

In the midst of every-increasing uncertainty about enrollment, the University Extension Division went about its business as best it could. Chester Allen, still at his post as Director of Field Organization, and the field representatives opened sixteen Centers in the fall of 1940, which included a new one at Watertown. Two Centers (Manitowoc and Sheboygan) also offered sophomore courses for the first time. In addition to advanced courses in English, history and foreign languages, the sophomores could take economics and political science. Although the total enrollment sagged a little compared to the previous year, Dean Holt believed that his visits with prospective students and parents in several communities in the spring had prevented an even greater decline.[6]

In an attempt to bolster enrollment in the fall of 1941, Extension initiated college credit courses by correspondence in a few high schools. This high school program had been periodically discussed for several years but had always floundered when the final details could not be worked out. This time, Dean Holt successfully brought together the UW School of Education and the State Department of Public Instruction to make the arrangements. Extension advertised the program as a method by which small, rural high schools could offer introductory college courses to their graduates. The participating high schools provided a room where the correspondence students met regularly to complete lessons under the supervision of the principal. The cost was $5.00 per credit, the same rate charged at the Freshman Centers. Many of these students earned their tuition via National Youth Administration jobs, which paid $15.00 per month.[7]

In an attempt to increase its income, Extension worked out a cooperative arrangement with the state normal schools. In the past the normal schools had attempted without notable success to organize off-campus education courses for prospective teachers. Finally, during the summer of 1940 the Board of Regents of the Normal Schools accepted Extension's long-standing offer to use its personnel and experience to set up these classes. Because of the late start, just 190 students were enrolled in the fall of 1940; however, one year later, 575 teachers and prospective teachers flocked to the classes. Each course was sponsored by a particular normal school, whose instructors usually taught the classes. In January 1942, because these classes had proven so popular, the Normal School Board of Regents unanimously approved a resolution that allowed the students to apply up to sixteen credits from the off-campus courses toward graduation and to transfer the credits among the eight normal schools. These credits, however, could not be transferred into the University of Wisconsin, which resolutely maintained that the normal school classes were not truly college-level courses.

Despite the strong enrollment in these classes, Chester Allen remained unconvinced that they really helped the Extension Division. He noted that the net financial gain was very slight because, as usual, salaries and overhead ate up most of the income. In addition, Allen contended that the fifteen percent decline in the Centers' enrollment in the fall of 1941 could be directly attributed to these courses, rather than to the alarms of impending war. Allen conjectured that the Extension field representatives had devoted a great deal of time to filling the normal schools' classes and had significantly reduced recruitment of students for the Centers.[8]

During the 1941 legislative session a final attempt was made to convince the state to provide a direct subsidy for each Center student to replace the aid withdrawn by the vocational schools in 1939. Assemblyman Henry J. Berquist, a Progressive from Rhinelander, sponsored the measure. Despite Berquist's keen interest in the measure (both the Rhinelander and Antigo Centers were in his district), the bill died in committee. Partisan politics apparently doomed Berquist's measure. The Republicans and Progressives remained locked in a bitter struggle to control state government, with the Democrats a distant third. Because the Republicans controlled the Assembly and its Education Committee by a comfortable margin, they could easily defeat a Progressive's proposal.[9] The Republicans also noted that Berquist's measure would mean an increase in the state budget.

Somewhat ironically, however, this same session approved a bill which substantially increased Extension's USAFI income. Assembly Bill 194A authorized a "sum sufficient amount" from the state treasury for free correspondence courses for any Wisconsinite in the military. Furthermore, the state pledged to refund the fees paid by any soldier to Extension retroactive to October 14, 1940, the day the Selective Service Act had taken effect. This measure sailed unanimously through the Assembly and drew just three nays in the Senate.[10]

By 1940 the Milwaukee Extension Center's college credit program had become almost a separate operation, with the Extension Division office in Madison handling just the financial accounts and some administrative work. The academic departments in Madison handled all other matters, wielding especially strong control over the selection and supervision of the Milwaukee faculty and carefully monitoring course content. Milwaukee's freshman-sophomore enrollment slipped a good deal during the war, from 738 in 1939 to a low of just 274 in the fall of 1943. This was to be expected because the war was in full swing and men traditionally outnumbered women six to one in the college classes.[11]

Despite the close ties between the Madison campus and the Milwaukee Center, a squabble between the two units occasionally erupted. On Sunday, August 30, 1942, as A. W. Peterson, the University Comptroller, read his *Milwaukee Journal* he came across an advertisement promoting "The University of Wisconsin in Milwaukee." The next day an irate Peterson fired off a note to President Dykstra, along with the ad, calling Dykstra's attention to the fact that the Extension Division had again used the "offensive" name.[12] Dykstra subsequently asked Dean Holt for an explanation and requested that he take up the issue with the Milwaukee Center. In November the Milwaukee faculty formally petitioned that the Center be permitted to use "The University of Wisconsin in Milwaukee" in its literature and advertising. This was vital, the faculty contended, to make clear to the public that the college classes were bona-fide university courses, not non-credit correspondence courses and short courses generally associated with the Extension Division. They also pointed out that the Milwaukee press customarily referred to the institution as UWM (The University of Wisconsin in Milwaukee) and that a different title would have difficulty winning acceptance.[13] There is no evidence that this tiff was formally resolved by either the Regents or the President's office. But it clearly revealed that the Madison campus jealousies toward the off-campus college credit courses remained strong. In any event, the reference to the University of Wisconsin continued to be used in the Milwaukee Center's publicity and advertisements.

Extension's outstate college centers marked their nadir in the fall of 1943 when only five Centers operated with just 163 students.

ENROLLMENT 1943-44

	1st sem.	2nd sem.
Green Bay	45	52
Manitowoc	15	12
Racine	58	40
Sheboygan	16	11
Wausau	29	20

(Source: Allen, III:113)

In view of this dismal enrollment, one of the field representatives commented that the Extension Centers may as well be closed down because the students' fees barely covered the expenses of setting up and supervising them.[14]

That same October the Extension Division suffered a serious blow when, after months of discussion, its popular and effective Dean Holt was appointed Director of the University's Department of Public Service. This new public relations service, located in the President's office, had been created by the Board of Regents to assist President Dykstra, who was often in Washington, D.C., to fulfill his responsibilities as national director of the Selective Service System. In addition, Dykstra had not proven effective in public relations, a field in which Holt had several times demonstrated his mettle while the head of the Extension Division. Although Holt kept his title as Dean of the Extension Division, he obviously devoted most of his attention to his new assignment. His absence exacerbated the wartime personnel shortage in Extension's administration, where there already were five vacancies. And because Dykstra and the Regents seemed in no hurry to replace Holt, the staff members in Madison became concerned about the future of the entire Division.[15]

This uneasiness intensified the following month when several key people from the Madison administration, the Extension Division, the Milwaukee Center, and Agricultural Extension met to discuss a merger of the two extension services. One result of such a reorganization would have been to transfer total control of the college credit courses to the Madison academic departments. Chester Allen, who represented the Extension Division, believed that the academic departments would probably close down the outstate centers to secure for themselves at least the salary monies paid to the circuit-riding faculty. Allen and his colleagues in Extension quickly became convinced that President Dykstra, who did not attend this meeting, was the mastermind behind this transparent attempt to strip both General Extension and Agricultural Extension of some of their most important and income-producing responsibilities.[16]

Fears about Dykstra's motives intensified when Lorentz Adolfson was appointed Acting Associate Director of the Extension Division in February 1944. Adolfson, an associate professor of political science who had taught at several Centers and who was currently directing USAFI, was not the source of their concern. Rather, the veteran administrators were alarmed by the "acting" designation and by the apparent demotion of the Division's chief executive from the rank of dean to director. Dykstra told the Regents that for the present he personally would retain the decision-making authority of the director's office. Dykstra also explained that the "acting" label was necessary because further administrative changes might be made after the study of the Extension Division and Agricultural Extension was completed.[17] In the end, however, a merger did not occur, primarily because of a lack of enthusiasm for it among the principals. Even the academic departments, finally, did not support a merger, because they feared they might somehow lose rather than gain money and authority.[18]

President Dykstra's resignation in October 1944 to become provost of the University of California at Los Angeles also contributed to the demise of the merger discussions. Professor Edwin Broun Fred was appointed as Dykstra's successor in January 1945. President Fred had thirty years' experience at the University of Wisconsin as both a faculty member and an administrator. Most significantly for the Extension Division and the Centers, as Dean of the College of Agriculture at the time of his appointment, he brought a thorough knowledge of the University's outreach programs to his new office. Fred definitely did not favor a merger. He took quick action to end speculation about their futures when, in February 1945, he recommended that Adolfson be named Director of the Extension Division. The Regents unanimously concurred.[19]

Shortly thereafter, Adolfson delivered an address which focused entirely on the freshman-sophomore program. This speech clearly marked an end to the months of anxiety and indecision regarding the Centers' future. Adolfson predicted steady growth for the Extension Centers' college credit program because it provided many advantages. For instance, the Centers had ably carried out the Wisconsin Idea by extending college opportunities across the state at an almost ridiculously low cost. Adolfson also pointed out that both public and private colleges benefitted from the program when successful students continued their education, because without the Freshman-Sophomore Centers many of these young people would never have enrolled.[20] Adolfson's confident appraisal of the Centers appeared to be confirmed by the state legislature in September 1945 when it overrode Governor Walter Goodland's veto of a bill that lowered the Centers' fees to the level charged in Madison.

This important victory, however, came only after decades of struggle. In the 1930s, when the University had first offered off-campus credit courses, the legislature had concurred with a Regents' recommendation that these courses be completely self-supporting; the inevitable result had been a higher fee for any course not taught in Madison. In addition, as the legislature had increased the amount that the Extension Division had to contribute to its budget, the rates had steadily climbed. During debate in the 1943 session, testimony by Extension spokesmen revealed that while fees in Madison in both Letter and Science and Engineering were capped at $48.00 per semester, a student enrolled in the Milwaukee Center would pay from $150.00 to $203.00 for Letters and Science courses and from $193.00 to $274.00 for a full-time engineering program.[21]

During the hard economic circumstances of the 1930s, periodic attempts had been made to equalize the fees between Madison and the rest of the state. The sudden inability of many families to send their sons and daughters to Madison no doubt increased support for such a decision, as did general acceptance of the ideal of economic democracy which many New Deal programs promoted. Many now believed that access to public institutions of higher education should not be limited to the children of the well-to-do. Despite this increased support, the unequal fees had remained.

The 1943 session, which the Republicans dominated, rapidly passed a bill sponsored by the Assembly Committee on Education which stated that when Center courses were substantially the same as those offered at Madison, then ". . . the rates of tuition charged to the students at such extension center or other place of instruction shall be no higher than the rates of tuition charged for such courses at Madison."[22] The impetus for this measure came from within the legislature, rather than from the Board of Regents. Indeed, in February 1943, the Regents had declined to consider a communication from the University Board of Visitors which emphasized that an injustice was being done to the students at the Milwaukee Center by charging them substantially higher tuition.[23]

Despite strong support by his Republican colleagues in the legislature, Governor Goodland had vetoed the bill. In his veto message, he argued that the legislature should not interfere with the Regents' prerogative to set university fees. Goodland also expressed the fear that the sharp drop in income would compel Extension to curtail other programs to keep the Freshman Centers open, because the Education Committee had not proposed an increase in state aid to replace the lost revenue. The *Milwaukee Journal* printed the text of the veto message; then four days later it blasted both the Governor's and Regents' actions in a long editorial. The editor insisted that the Regents had had sufficient time to equalize the fees and that the legislature acted only when it was clear that the Regents did not intend to exercise their power. Therefore, Goodland's claim that his veto was necessary to preserve the Regents' prerogative was specious and the paper urged the legislators to override the Governor's decision. The real tragedy in all this, the editorial said, was that students who could not afford to attend Madison in the first place were being penalized by "severely" higher fees. The piece concluded with the pithy observation that the Regents were using their fee-setting authority to insure the continued supremacy of the Madison campus.[24] The legislators, however, made no attempt at an override, evidently because they agreed that the bill should have specified how the income shortfall would be covered.

In February 1945 another attempt at fee equalization began. The Board of Regents, bowing to heavy public and political pressure, now supported the proposal if the legislature agreed to increase the state aids. The Board estimated that it would need an additional $60,000 for the rest of 1945, $90,000 for 1946, and at least $150,000 annually thereafter. But the victory did not come easily. Goodland again vetoed the bill. He claimed that its cost to the taxpayers was excessive and that it was primarily a "Milwaukee bill." The *Milwaukee Journal* again ripped the Governor for refusing to sign. The editor reminded his readers that all communities with Centers would benefit from the measure and, furthermore, they deserved to benefit because they were providing the facilities used by the Extension Division. This time the legislators overrode the veto and a new, equal tuition rate was in effect when classes opened in September 1945.[25]

During that same summer (1945), the university administrators began to discuss how the anticipated post-war leap in enrollment could be accommodated. A large number of the new students would be veterans who would take advantage of the generous terms of the G.I. Bill of Rights. Some of these enrollees, no doubt, would have already earned college credits through USAFI. Another source of aspiring scholars was the ever increasing number of high school graduates. The percentage of secondary school graduates who attended college had been steadily rising in response to changes in the employment market, where the greatest number of new positions existed in occupations that required some type of post-secondary training. A third factor influencing the trend toward larger college enrollments was the massive federal and state aid for college education. Wisconsin had also consistently aided its students by keeping its tuition and fees as low as possible. [26]

The planning continued throughout the 1945-1946 academic year, when the total UW enrollment leaped from 7,779 in the fall to 12,429 in the spring semester. In March 1946 in a speech in Racine, President Fred explained that "[The influx of veterans] is a problem that can only be solved by establishing more university centers throughout the state." [27] A major component of the plan, then, was to keep as many freshmen as possible away from Madison by greatly expanding the number of Centers. In the early summer of 1946, Fred directed Adolfson to provide courses for at least 4,000 new freshmen, divided evenly between Milwaukee and the outstate communities. [28]

Consequently, the Extension Division staff worked furiously during that summer to set up additional centers. Because many more communities expressed an interest in hosting a freshman program than would be needed, a procedure was quickly developed to determine which invitations should be accepted. Whenever possible, an Extension representative visited a potential host community to meet with its leaders to assess whether a Center could enroll enough students and to evaluate the proposed facilities. Thirty-four centers had been established by the time classes began in the fall of 1946. Five of these were located in Milwaukee, where the downtown Extension Center operated satellites in South Milwaukee, Shorewood, Wauwatosa, and West Allis. The rest were scattered across the state, from Marinette in the northeast to Rice Lake in the northwest and from Janesville in the south to Rhinelander in the north. Naturally, the majority of the out-state Centers were clustered in the southeastern corner because almost half of the state's citizens lived there. The sparsely settled northwest quarter was served by a lightly enrolled circuit of Ladysmith, Rice Lake, and Spooner. [29]

The burgeoning enrollment created many problems. To staff all of the classrooms, the University recruited faculty from all over the United States and encouraged Wisconsin housewives who had college degrees to teach for a few semesters. Despite the urgency to find instructors, only teachers with solid academic credentials received President Fred's approval. Fred upheld his high standards by insisting that each departmental leader ". . . show me that the teacher at any one of these extension centers is fully qualified to teach and that if you had the funds, you'd be glad to have the individual on your staff." [30] Unless the chairman was willing to sign a statement to this effect, Fred refused to approve the appointment.

Because veterans swelled enrollments in all types of post-secondary schools, Extension found itself pushed out of some of the vocational school rooms it had traditionally used. When this happened, makeshift arrangements were hastily made. In Green Bay, for example, a temporary elementary school that had been used by munitions workers' children at the Badger Ordinance Works near Baraboo was moved and pressed into service. Because of its flimsily-constructed walls, it quickly became known as "Cardboard Tech." In Milwaukee, surplus barracks were moved near the main building and used as temporary classrooms. Center students in Merrill again ended up meeting in the City Hall, even in the council chamber. Textbooks were in short supply, too, even though the foresighted Extension Director of Teaching, Wilbur Hanley, had placed orders as early as the previous March. The nation's publishing houses just could not meet the tremendous demand, even by operating around the clock.[31]

One of the many problems caused by the tremendous leap in enrollments was a severe shortage of student housing and classrooms in Madison. This shortage, which obviously would not ease in just one year, inspired some Milwaukee Center sophomores to petition for a relaxation of the 60 credit rule, which required them to take their junior and senior years at Madison. The Regents had imposed the 60 credit rule in 1895 on correspondence courses taken for college credit and it had been extended in 1906 to any college course taken "in absentia." Like the tuition inequity issue, this was not a new concern and during the 1943-44 academic year a Madison Subcommittee on Transfer of Credits had made an extensive study which underscored how seriously the rule disadvantaged students transferring from the Milwaukee Center. For instance, Milwaukee students often needed just one more course to fill out their program; but if that course would put them over 60 credits, they were advised to take "any course" at Marquette because the limit was not stringently applied to Marquette's courses. In other instances, transfer students had been compelled to retake a course in Madison with the same instructor who had taught the class in Milwaukee![32]

Upon receiving the petition, President Fred sought Director Adolfson's advice. Adolfson agreed that the 60 credit rule should generally be retained because the Milwaukee facility lacked adequate laboratory space for advanced science courses. However, he recommended that the rule be waived in special cases and that transferring Extension students be given preference in the assignment of University housing. Subsequently, President Fred directed the executive committees of the various colleges to review carefully appeals of the credit limitation and to grant waivers to individuals who could not find housing in Madison and who also could enroll in appropriate junior level courses in Milwaukee.[33] Both the School of Commerce and the School of

Engineering implemented the President's suggestion for individual appeals during the 1946-47 year. In May of 1946 the School of Commerce proposed a general waiver for a few courses in Milwaukee of "sufficient degree of advancement"; the Regents concurred, with the stipulation that the waiver would expire once the housing crunch had eased. Engineering students, however, were not so fortunate. All they obtained, even after travelling en masse to Madison to confront President Fred and Engineering Dean Morton Withey, was permission to take up to 12 non-lab credits beyond their sophomore year.[34]

As a consequence of the debate over the 60 credit rule and in view of predictions that college enrollments would continue to rise, the question of merging the Milwaukee Center with the city's State Teacher's College to create a new four-year institution arose. In response a committee was established on the Madison campus to study the issue. In early 1948, it recommended that the two schools be merged and operated as a liberal arts college under the control of the University of Wisconsin. The committee also decided that the new institution should offer only undergraduate courses. The entire discussion came to an abrupt end when the Teachers College Regents unanimously opposed this suggestion because they wanted to control the merged institution. For the moment, then, the issue was dropped.[35]

The great bulge in enrollment created by the returning veterans passed quickly through the freshman centers. Thus even while the Extension Division operated thirty-four centers during the 1946-47 academic year, plans were made to reduce sharply the number for the following fall. Budget considerations also entered into the discussions because the enrollment in some Centers had fallen off drastically between semesters, largely due to drop-outs and academic dismissals. In April 1947 President Fred appointed a Committee on Extension Centers to provide advice on which centers should be continued. The members decided that a center should be kept open only when ". . . the enrollment would warrant a substantially full-time resident staff."[36] The Committee expressed the hope that the Centers left open would be large enough, also, to be provided with minimum laboratory and library facilities and with adequate counseling services and social activities. As a general rule, the members believed an enrollment of at least one hundred was necessary. After several meetings, the Committee recommended that just ten out-state Centers remain open, in addition to Milwaukee and its four suburban satellites.[37]

When he was informed of this decision, Adolfson wrote Fred that he anticipated some sharp criticism from several of the communities whose Centers would not be continued and he noted, in particular, that there would be no Center in the northwestern part of the state. Adolfson suggested that the Committee on Extension Centers reconsider its recommendations in the light of his observations and in view of the University's commitment to serving the entire state. Subsequently the Committee, by the narrow majority of one, added three centers (New Richmond, Spooner, Rice Lake) in the western part of the state. Just before the June 1947 Regents meeting, at which these recommendations would be ratified, Adolfson made a last minute plea to the president to add Antigo and Janesville. He pointed out that Antigo was the second oldest Center, preceded only by Milwaukee, and that it could be operated rather inexpensively in connection with Wausau and Rhinelander. Indeed adding Antigo to that circuit would allow the curriculum to be expanded a bit. Adolfson favored keeping Janesville open for political reasons. He had learned that some leading Janesville citizens were considering seriously the development of a junior college if their Center was closed. President Fred's recommendation, which the Board of Regents unanimously approved, included Antigo but not Janesville. [38]

Thus, in the fall of 1947 the Extension Division operated a total of nineteen Centers—five in Milwaukee and fourteen outside the metropolis. In a report to the President's office Wilbur Hanley, the Director of Extension Teaching, indicated that some important changes had been made at several Centers. Sophomore courses had been added at eight of the out-state sites—Fond du Lac, Green Bay, Kenosha, Manitowoc, Marinette, Menasha, Sheboygan, and Wausau—in response to petitions from students. Hanley noted that veterans made up half of the Centers' student body, compared to two-thirds the previous year. Full time Extension Center Directors had been appointed at Green Bay, Marinette, and Wausau because the field representatives could no longer adequately supervise their operations. These three administrators were the first appointed outside Milwaukee and marked the growing confidence that the out-state Centers would continue to be an integral part of the University's service to college students. [39]

These decisions had been made in the midst of a broad debate over the future shape of post-secondary education in Wisconsin. The focal point of the discussion was John Guy Fowlkes' and Henry Ahrnsbrak's report, "Junior College Needs in Wisconsin." This study had been authorized by the Regents in May 1945, when it was clear that the war would end fairly soon and that the University must be prepared to help shape the state's higher education system. Legislators were keenly interested in the study because of their concern about the ever-increasing share of the state budget claimed by the various post-secondary programs. Fowlkes and Ahrnsbrak carefully reviewed how each segment of the state-supported higher education establishment—vocational schools, State Teachers Colleges, and the University and its Extension services—had evolved. They then confronted the basic question: did

Wisconsin need a system of junior colleges, two-year schools which would offer both transferable college credit courses and non-transferable vocational programs? Their answer was a very qualified "yes." They suggested that junior colleges could be created in seven Extension Center cities by adding a vocational component to the existing college credit program, but they also noted that each campus would have to be constructed from scratch to assure the proper facilities. This recommendation was much discussed but no decisive action was taken to implement it by either the University Regents or the legislature. No doubt the great expense of the undertaking caused the report to be quietly shelved, but Fowlkes' and Ahrnsbrak's work would repeatedly surface as the state continued to wrestle with how best to provide for the post-high school educational needs of its citizens.[40]

In the spring of 1948 the Extension Division leaders again turned to the hard work of determining which Centers should remain open the following academic year. The task was made more difficult because the number of potential students continued to decline. The strong post-war economy, fueled by the need to rebuild Europe and Japan, provided high school graduates with many job opportunities. More entering freshman could now afford to go directly to Madison, too. Because of the Cold War and the looming threat of conflict with the Soviet Union, the draft still inducted many males and some men chose to volunteer, so that they could select a branch of the service. Consequently, the pool of veterans who would begin college studies in the fall of 1948 also continued to shrink.

In mid-April 1948 Adolfson recommended to the President that just ten Centers (Fond du Lac, Green Bay, Kenosha, Manitowoc, Marinette, Menasha, Milwaukee, Racine, Sheboygan, Wausau) should be continued. Subsequently the Regents set up a study committee which visited several of the cities to assess the sentiment toward the Centers. As a result of these surveys and in response to urgent appeals from several communities whose programs were slated to be dropped, the Regents added seven sites to Adolfson's list. Consequently, Antigo and Rhinelander retained their strictly freshman programs and Marshfield was also added to the Wausau circuit. The Janesville Center was reopened, despite strong objections from the nearby State Teachers College at Whitewater. The study committee, mindful of the promise of the Wisconsin Idea, rescued the small freshman course operations at Rice Lake and Spooner. Ladysmith was added in the hope that this northwest Wisconsin circuit would attract at least one hundred students and pay its own way.[41]

The ability of the Centers to pay their own way had become very important. When the state lowered the Center students' fees to the Madison level in 1945, the legislators had also placed all the UW state aid in Madison's budget. Consequently, the University would be compelled to make up any difference between income and expenses at the Extension Centers. This meant that the Centers' fiscal affairs received additional scrutiny from main campus officials who wanted to assure that Madison did not subsidize the Centers.

Actually, as Adolfson and Extension's other spokesmen often pointed out, the state received a bargain in supporting the Centers because the host communities paid for the facilities, utilities, and janitorial services. Normally, the Extension Center shared an existing building with a vocational school or a normal school. In mid-1945, however, the City of Racine had offered to provide a remodeled school for the sole use of the Extension Division and suggested that the University should pay for the utilities and upkeep. Although this seemed a fair proposition, Adolfson cautioned against accepting it because other Center towns would then demand similar treatment. The negotiations with Racine took on added urgency when the Marathon County Board offered the old normal school in Wausau to Extension for its exclusive use. By the time a policy was worked out in March 1948, Green Bay and Brown County had also joined the discussions. The 1948 Regent policy both confirmed the past practices and established important new provisions. When a Center shared a building with a vocational or normal school, the University would continue to provide the instructional and administrative services and the instructional supplies, while the community paid for the utilities and janitor's salary. But when a city or county provided separate quarters exclusively for Extension, the Regents agreed to supply all the furniture for the classrooms, laboratories, and offices and underwrite the expense of operating the facility. This policy committed the University more firmly to the continuation of the Extension Centers, especially those which now had their own building.[42]

This policy and an enrollment decline in September 1948 at the Oshkosh State Teachers College may have prompted its President, Forrest Polk, to exclaim loudly that the Centers at Fond du Lac and Menasha were drawing students away from Oshkosh. In fact, Polk asserted these Centers were unnecessary because the Teachers College provided the same courses. After several personal conferences, Director Adolfson and President Polk agreed to have a special committee conduct a survey of the students attending the Fond du Lac Center and of graduating seniors in that Center's drawing area to determine the validity of Polk's complaints.

The survey definitely did not support Polk's allegations. The forty-four Center students who responded to the survey indicted that, had the Fond du Lac option not been available, they would have chosen to attend Madison over Oshkosh. The high school seniors who intended to go to college echoed this finding: twenty-four chose the Center, nineteen preferred Madison, and only six selected Oshkosh.[43] Meanwhile, Polk expanded his allegation of unfair and unnecessary competition to include the freshman-sophomore programs in Manitowoc, Sheboygan, Marinette, and Wausau. This complaint caused Dr. Robert Doremus, Assistant Dean of the College of Letters and Science, to write to Adolfson. Doremus said, ". . ., it seems ridiculous to expect every existing institution such as Oshkosh must be surrounded by a sterile no man's land just that it can't possibly lose a student to some other place." Doremus observed that, following Polk's line of reasoning, the University of Wisconsin could argue that all the State Teachers Colleges were unnecessary competition because the UW existed first![44] Evidently because the survey results so decisively refuted his claims, President Polk refused to sign the committee report and he also forbade his Dean of Instruction, who had been a member of the committee, to sign it. By the fall of 1949 the controversy was practically forgotten, but it was indicative of increasing friction between the University and the State Teachers Colleges in the constant struggle to secure students and state aid.

The survey of the Fond du Lac students also provided the first extensive data about Centers' clientele and their families. The typical student was a male who had graduated in the second quartile of his class. He was undecided about his ultimate educational goal, but had narrowed the choices to the liberal arts or professional training. He received, on the average, direct financial support from his family of $100.00 to $400.00 per academic year. He worked about fifteen hours per week. Many of the students hoped to save enough by attending an Extension Center to finance most of the Junior year expenses in Madison. Of course, some males received G.I. benefits. The students' fathers generally held managerial positions or worked in skilled occupations. Mothers normally were not employed outside the home. A significant number indicated that they were the first members of their families to attend college.[45]

One of the students' persistent complaints had been that the Centers provided few of the extracurricular activities found at Madison. But this situation began to change in the late forties, thanks to a larger enrollment and the presence of veterans. The veterans proved to be self-starters who pitched in, organized activities, and sought out a faculty sponsor. The veterans who were elected to student government offices persuaded their classmates to assess themselves activity fees to provide modest support for social and athletic events. By the end of the decade, four inter-center activities had been founded: a Student Leadership Conference for present and prospective student government officers; a Music Festival that featured both instrumental and vocal performances; a Forensics Tournament with competition in discussion, original oratory, and interpretive reading; and a basketball league that included the team from the Milwaukee Center.[46]

At the close of the forties, the Extension Centers seemed well established in Milwaukee and nine out-state communities. Buildings (for Extension's exclusive use) had been provided in Racine, Wausau, and Green Bay. Indeed, in these cases, a formal agreement had been achieved between the communities and the University, which specified how the expenses would be shared. The achievement of fee parity had significantly boosted morale among the Centers' administrators and faculty and made attendance at a Center more affordable. Already, demographers were plotting the size of the postwar "baby boom" who would reach college age during the 1960s and whose numbers would surpass the capacity of all the public post-secondary educational institutions in the state. University and State College officials and the state's politicians took careful note of this prediction and began to plan how to accommodate the next generation of students.

Four

The Centers Weather a Crisis: The Fifties

The anticipation and hope with which the American people greeted the new decade was tempered by the ever increasing tension with the Soviet Union. The harmony among the Allies which had been instrumental in securing a victory over Japan and Germany had been quickly replaced with suspicion and recrimination. In 1947 the United States Congress had approved the Truman Doctrine, a pledge that the U.S. would assist any nation to resist a communist coup. In late June 1950, the North Koreans attacked South Korea, whose government quickly issued an urgent plea for aid. Within hours President Harry S. Truman had committed America soldiers to the fight to contain communism. The Korean War and the continuing confrontation with the U.S.S.R. inevitably influenced the entire decade.

The fifties were years of vigorous growth in Wisconsin. While the population grew fifteen percent during the decade, the number of school age children ballooned by forty-two percent. The baby boomers clearly were on their way through the state's educational system. The state budget, continuing its steady growth, increased ninety-eight percent during the ten years. At the close of the decade the state employed about 28,000—an increase of 10,500. Surprisingly, taxes and inflation remained stable. State revenues claimed roughly ten percent of total personal income, while the rate of inflation hovered between one and two points per year.[1]

Wisconsin's educational systems claimed a hefty portion of the increases in spending and employment. The amount expended for education (department of public instruction, university, and state colleges) increased two-and-one-half times and greatly exceeded the overall rise in the budget. A significant portion of the sizable increase in federal aid ($46 million in 1950, $109 million in 1959) was also earmarked for education. In addition, the University alone added nearly 5,000 members to its faculty and staff, which accounted for almost half of the new state employees.[2]

Wisconsin's 1950 gubernatorial contest concluded in the midst of the turmoil caused by the Korean War. Candidates Walter J. Kohler, Jr., Republican and Carl Thompson, former Progressive turned Democrat, campaigned vigorously about the need to limit state spending. Kohler, who easily won the first of three consecutive terms, immediately outlined his fiscally conservative ideas. In his inaugural message, in January 1951, he entreated all state agencies not to request an increase in their 1951-1953 budgets.

Upon hearing this unwelcome news, all departments of the University commenced a budget review. The major problem for Wilbur (Bill) Hanley, who was responsible for the out-state Centers' budget, was trying to predict enrollment. In a series of memoranda written in September and October of 1951, Hanley explained the problems and the options. In his original proposal, he had assumed an enrollment of 1,100 per year, but the Korean conflict now compelled him to evaluate that estimate. If eighteen year old males would not be drafted and if ROTC would be offered at the Centers, then enrollment would decline perhaps twenty-five percent, to 825 students. But if the draft included the freshmen and if there would be no ROTC programs, then the Centers' registrations could plummet by half.

Hanley pointed out that steps had already been taken to reduce the number of instructors to the absolute minimum. Further cuts in the teaching staff, Hanley warned, would require either excessive classroom hours for each teacher or a reduction in the course offerings. Hanley refused to recommend either of these options. An increased teaching load for the traveling faculty would, he believed, adversely affect the quality of instruction; and a reduction in the course offerings would push too many students into the remaining sections and might compel some to enroll in unneeded courses just to maintain their full time student status.[3]

Meanwhile the University enlisted legislators to defend the original proposal as necessary and reasonable. The nine Centers played an important role in this political effort. Scattered across the state and having direct contact with thousands of students and their parents, the Extension Centers helped line up votes. These efforts proved highly successful and the University ultimately received a slightly larger appropriation.

Fortunately, the actual enrollment during the biennium exceeded Hanley's estimates. The out-state Centers enrolled 906 scholars in the fall of 1951 and made a significant gain, to 976, in September 1952. None the less, the Fond du Lac campus was closed at the end of the 1951-52 academic year because its steadily declining enrollment had caused the cost per student to soar.[4] Extension officials believed that students from the Fond du Lac area could enroll at the nearby Menasha Center, where they would be able to select courses from a broader curriculum. Fond du Lac remained without a public collegiate institution until Oshkosh State University finally opened a branch campus there in 1968.

As events turned out, the 1951 budget struggle had been very mild, compared to what transpired in 1953. Governor Kohler had been keenly disappointed that the state agencies and the legislature had ignored his plea to support a no-increase budget. He was particularly upset that both the University and the State Colleges had succeeded in winning modest increases. The competition between these two systems for an ever larger share of the state's money, Kohler believed, made it very difficult for the state to hold down its spending. So, early in 1953, the recently reelected Governor proposed sharp reductions in the next biennium for several state agencies. For example, the University of Wisconsin would have to reduce its spending by two million dollars. When the Board of Regents examined the situation, it concluded that since the Centers (excluding Milwaukee) had a higher cost per student than the main campus, they should bear about twenty-five percent of the recommended reduction. Within days, Adolfson announced that such a sum could only be raised by closing five Centers (Kenosha, Manitowoc, Marinette, Menasha, Sheboygan), and scaling down the programs at the four remaining locations. These severe economies would save the state's taxpayers about $550,000.[5]

These dire figures quickly prompted the University to marshal its political forces. Actually, the Center communities did not need prompting and letters of protest soon appeared in the legislators' mailboxes. The Assembly members from each Center's district received a visit from Adolfson and top University administrators, as did state Senators who represented an Extension Center community. Late in March the Assembly passed Kohler's budget, but at the same time it unanimously enacted Resolution 41-A which stated the legislature's desire that all eight Centers continue to offer at least a freshman program. In short, the Regents would have to find the money somewhere other than in the Centers, unless they were willing to incur the wrath of the Assembly.

The Senate delayed a vote on 41-A until its Education Committee could hear testimony from President Fred, Director Adolfson, and other university administrators about the impact of the Governor's budget. President Fred reported that no definite plans had been made to close five, or even one, of the Centers. But he also stressed that the budget, as it now stood, meant that the University would need to make deep cuts. He told the Senators that if a minimum of $273,000 would be restored to the appropriation, then he would be able to comply with the intent of 41-A.

In his statement, Adolfson admitted that the Centers did cost more to operate in terms of direct costs. But he hastened to explain that other factors helped to offset the apparent red ink. He noted that the Centers' indirect costs were lower because the communities paid for the utilities, janitorial salaries, and maintenance. Adolfson also stressed anew the Centers' vital role in carrying out the Wisconsin idea—the promise that when a citizen could not come to the University, the University would come to him.[6] The University's budget experts explained that the Centers' operations were so intertwined that none could be shut down without adversely affecting the programs of the others.[7]

After hearing this testimony, the Senate concurred with Assembly Resolution 41-A. In the end, almost all of the Governor's suggested reductions in the University's appropriation were restored and the need to close any out-state Center disappeared. During the remainder of the 1950s, Wisconsin's budget picture gradually improved and there were no more intense struggles such as this one.

However, Governor Kohler did not give up his effort to end the costly competition between the University and the State Colleges. In January 1955, fresh from yet another reelection victory, Kohler proposed a merger of the University of Wisconsin and the State Teachers Colleges. In addition, he requested that a new four-year institution be created in Milwaukee by combining that city's Center and State Teachers College.

The Governor did not anticipate that the proposed mergers would save money immediately, rather he stressed that improved coordination and less competition between the two higher education systems would allow the state to better serve its students. For example, he noted that the State Colleges had empty classrooms and dormitory rooms, while Madison had been at near capacity for several years. Because all of the students in the merged system would receive a University of Wisconsin degree, Kohler expected that more of them would attend a State College and thus distribute the enrollment more evenly.[8]

The Governor sought approval for his proposal by personally lobbying the boards of regents and by a well-orchestrated publicity campaign designed to bring public pressure to bear on them. Kohler met in a closed two-hour session with the Regents of the State Colleges on February 10, 1955. They immediately supported his plan by an 8 to 2 vote.[9] On the contrary, the University Regents, without waiting for the Governor's visit, ratified a subcommittee's recommendation against a merger. The UW Board did leave the door open for reorganization someday, provided it would be achieved slowly and "not abruptly in a single all-inclusive step."[10]

The focus of attention over Kohler's bold suggestion quickly shifted to the legislature, where Senate bill 279S had been introduced. This measure would abolish both boards of regents and replace them with a single, fifteen member board. It also provided for the creation of a new, four-year university in Milwaukee.

Now the University leaders had a specific focus for their anti-merger arguments. Appearing before a joint hearing of the Assembly and Senate Education Committees, several UW Regents and President Fred vigorously voiced opposition to 279S. Even a Senate amendment that created two "sub-boards" of seven members to operate the two systems separately did not gain their approval.

When the Senate bill reached the Assembly, Speaker Mark Catlin (Republican, Appleton) deserted Kohler's team and proposed his own plan. Catlin's draft called for an eleven member "coordinating agency," whose membership would consist of five members from each of the two boards of regents and the State Superintendent of Public Instruction. This coordinating committee would be empowered to create policy in three major areas—educational programs (curriculum), facilities, and budget. The coordinating committee's authority would take precedence over any power previously granted to the boards of regents, but those boards would be retained to operate their respective systems. Later, the Assembly added four more members, so that there would be five individuals who could break deadlocks between the two sets of institutional representatives.

While the University considered Catlin's plan a great improvement, it still maintained its opposition. However, Charles Gelatt, President of the UW Board, realized the danger of maintaining a negative posture too long. So he and William McIntyre, his counterpart from the State College Regents, hammered out a compromise in a series of secret caucuses with key legislators. Most significantly, their proposal softened the coordinating committee's power to override the separate boards, except in the budget area. The major purposes of the new Coordinating Committee for Higher Education would be to prevent duplication of degree programs and, of course, to present one budget to the legislature for both systems. The Gelatt/McIntyre compromise even won Governor Kohler's support and it sailed through the legislature, attracting just one negative vote.

The only item in Kohler's original proposal that won approval was the merger in Milwaukee. The law specified that the University of Wisconsin would have control over the new institution and that it should begin operations in September 1956. The administrators and faculty of the Center and the State College spent a very hectic year working out the details of the merger, but they met the deadline.

Although the Extension Centers had not been prominently mentioned in the debate over merger, they were destined to have a prominent role in meeting the needs of the swelling tide of students. The establishment of additional centers seemed an attractive option because they would provide greater access to higher education and the host communities would underwrite a portion of the operating expenses. The competition among cities to be chosen to host a Center was keen. Cities realized that a Center offered an economic advantage by keeping students' money in the community and provided an important asset for attracting new industry. Of course, not every community that desired a two-year campus could support one. Politics also greatly influenced this competition. Both the University of Wisconsin and the State Colleges worked hard to win control over new Centers by lobbying the CCHE and state legislators.

The Coordinating Committee for Higher Education (CCHE) had the responsibility to determine how many two-year campuses the state needed and whether some should be established as junior colleges, which would offer both college-credit and vocational non-credit courses. The CCHE naturally inherited past discussions and resolutions concerning the existing two-year post-secondary institutions—the Extension Centers, the vocational schools, and the county teachers colleges. The junior college issue remained lively despite the definite tilt of the Fowlkes/Ahrnsbrak study against creating them in Wisconsin. In 1950, Governor Oscar Rennebohm's administration had engaged the American Council of Education to restudy the question. the Council's report urged Wisconsin to follow California's pattern, where the junior college movement was most prominent and successful. The Council believed the establishment of junior colleges would fill "one of the conspicuous gaps in the state's school program."[11] Governor Rennebohm's decision not to seek another term in 1950 no doubt explains why there was no follow-up to these recommendations.

In 1953, in the midst of the budget battle-royal over the state's higher education finances, Assemblymen Willis J. Hutnik (Rusk County) and Clarence Gilley (Oneida County) informally lobbied for the establishment of at least one junior college in northern Wisconsin. Specifically, they urged consideration be given to Ladysmith, Phillips, and Rhinelander as possible sites.

Hutnik and Gilley stressed that northern Wisconsin had always been slighted in the allocation of higher educational funds and institutions and that it was time to correct this inequity. Their recommendation had the support of State Superintendent George Watson, who noted that none of these communities had a vocational school. After testing the political waters, however, the two Assemblymen decided not to make a formal proposal.[12]

Nevertheless, Hutnik stubbornly stuck to his theme. Four years later, in May 1957, he introduced a resolution to set up a special legislative study committee to investigate the "possibilities of a state-directed junior college program in Wisconsin." the *Green Bay Press-Gazette,* which obviously supported Hutnik's objective, argued that the CCHE should conduct the study, since it had been created for just such a purpose. The editorial stressed that the state's "peculiarly formless system" of two-year post-secondary education cried out for more coordination.[13]

In response the CCHE set up an Extension Working Group in the summer of 1957 and gave it the task of determining whether Wisconsin should adopt the California model. When State Supervisor of Vocational Schools C. L. Greiber was asked his opinion, he emphatically rejected the idea. Too often, he said, when liberal arts courses and vocational programs were both offered, the liberal arts soon dominated the institution. In addition, Greiber contended that the presence of both an Extension Center and a vocational school in eight Wisconsin communities did "an excellent job of providing comprehensive community college services . . .," and negated the need for junior colleges.[14]

The Extension Working Group's report, "The Junior College," was issued in December 1957. It cited both the advantages and disadvantages of developing junior colleges in Wisconsin. The advantages included lower cost to the students, the provision of programs unique to a community's needs, and the easing of overcrowding in the freshman and sophomore years at Madison. The major disadvantage was that, frequently, junior colleges became little more than "advanced high schools." Consequently, they did not attract either the best students or the abler teachers. In addition, the report warned that many smaller communities might not have sufficient enrollment or adequate finances to support a junior college, even though the local citizenry might strongly favor the establishment of one.[15] In closing, the Working Group recommended strongly against the creation of a junior college system in Wisconsin.

The very next month, the CCHE accepted this recommendation. Although this action seemed to settle the junior college question with finality, the issue proved persistent and it periodically resurfaced. Consequently, the CCHE reiterated its position in January 1959 when it overwhelmingly adopted a resolution that said research into the state's higher education needs would proceed on the assumption that "[Wisconsin would] choose coordination and the development of existing institutions in solving its junior college problem rather than the establishment of new institutions."[16] The officials of the University (including the Extension Division), the State Colleges, and the vocational schools had worked together to maintain a strong position against junior colleges, which they saw as potentially damaging to their interests. Since the University and the State Colleges each had five regents on the fifteen member CCHE, they easily made their views the official position of the Coordinating Council.[17]

While the state's higher education systems underwent change, the Extension Division made important decisions about the local administration of the Centers. Just three—Green Bay, Marinette, and Wausau—had full time directors. At the other five, Extension field representatives handled the administrative details. But as enrollments escalated and interaction with the community increased, they found it increasingly difficult to cope with the workload. Consequently, in the mid-fifties, the Regents approved Adolfson's recommendation that the field representatives be relieved of these tasks and that at least a part-time director be appointed for each Center. These positions usually went to outstanding faculty members who continued to teach several sections each year. By the late fifties these local administrators had won the right to meet monthly with Adolfson and Hanley to discuss common concerns.[18]

Faculty appointments in the Centers remained almost unchanged during the fifties. Most still traveled a circuit of several campuses each week. They were supervised by subject area chairmen chosen by the Madison departments, but who were paid by General Extension. Thus the quality of the academic program was maintained by placing the selection and monitoring of the instructors squarely under the control of the Madison faculty.

Early in 1956 Adolfson, prodded by the faculty of the Kenosha and Racine Centers, began a campaign to improve faculty salaries. In a letter to the assistant to the President, he pointed out that the faculty at these two Centers could, with very few exceptions, earn more if they taught in the local high schools. The disparity with the high school teachers ranged from a low of about $300.00 per year to over $1,000.00.[19] Later that year Adolfson asked Hanley to provide him with some arguments and a plan to use in the salary negotiations with "big administration" in the President's office. Part of the strategy that eventually evolved stressed not only the adverse comparison with the high schools, but also the much greater demands placed upon instructors in the Centers, as compared to faculty in Madison. For instance, an Extension Center instructor often represented an entire academic depart-

FALL SEMESTER ENROLLMENT UW CENTERS

	1952	1953	1954	1955	1956	1957	1958	1959
Fox Valley (Menasha)	67	76	99	139	142	15	143	167
Green Bay	121	144	173	261	252	245	345	374
Kenosha	197	202	225	251	298	279	337	365
Manitowoc	63	51	82	118	97	90	91	131
Marathon (Wausau)	143	127	173	26	213	202	220	294
Marinette	47	43	37	49	38	40	38	37
Racine	280	309	348	348	377	380	397	431
Sheboygan	58	68	103	104	107	104	140	157
TOTALS	**976**	**1020**	**1240**	**1496**	**1524**	**1455**	**1711**	**1956**

Source: Fall Semester Enrollment Reports.

ment and thus had to assume work that could be shared or avoided in Madison. In addition, the community expected the faculty member to give public lectures, attend social gatherings, and participate in civic affairs. Despite the planning, the evidence, and the negotiations, Adolfson was unable to win any real improvement in faculty salaries. State officials contended they just could not afford more than token increases.[20]

The students of the fifties were not much different from those of the late forties. Many enrollees were the first persons in their families to attend college. A significant number chose to begin their college education at a Center to save money. Although the Centers lacked a broad extra-curricular program such as that provided in Madison, the students did not feel cheated. In fact, on a percentage basis, more Center students were involved in campus activities than those on the parent campus. Many students apparently made up for any lack of social functions by maintaining contact with high school friends and church groups.[21]

Most of the Centers had a strong intramural sports program and the students' fees also supported inter-Center competition in basketball, golf, and tennis. Athletes who met the participation requirements in these sports received an Extension Center "W." The non-athletic Centers-wide activities included an annual student leadership conference, speech tournament, and a music workshop. An art exhibition had been attempted in 1950, but was dropped due to low participation. It was revived, however, in the mid-fifties when the administration agreed to provide $250.00 to help defray the participants' expenses. [22]

Each Center was free to establish as many activities as it could support. For example, the Kenosha Center in 1955, with an enrollment of 250, held a homecoming celebration during and following a basketball game. The Kenosha student council also sponsored a formal dance at Christmas and in the spring. Both of these were scheduled during breaks in classes so that alumni would be home and could attend. Sixteen teams competed in the popular bowling league. And Kenosha, like most Centers, had a student newspaper. [23]

Some facets of student (and faculty) behavior have not changed with time—for instance, the urge to stretch a scheduled break by a couple of days. In December 1955 Adolfson returned from an Administrative Committee meeting where this practice had been discussed intensely. The high rate of absenteeism on the day before and the day after vacations on the Madison campus had come to public attention and some embarrassing questions had been raised. The conversation indicated that some professors allegedly allowed, if not encouraged, their students to cut class on these days so that they, too, could take the day off. Adolfson asked Bill Hanley about the situation in the Centers, so he could have a ready answer if the question arose. Hanley replied that the Centers did not share this problem with Madison, largely because their students were already at home. He observed that absences increased a bit before the Christmas holiday because more students were employed by local merchants to handle the shopping rush, but cutting a class here and there seemed more common than skipping an entire day. The local directors, faculty and counselors had indicated that they had the situation under control. Hanley added, however, that, "One phenomena peculiar to the Centers in the northern part of the state is the absentee rate during deer hunting season. No amount of reasoning, persuasion, or coercion has any effect upon the confirmed deer hunter. He just isn't there!" [24]

In April 1959 the Board of Regents, upon the recommendation of the University faculty, approved a resolution authorizing the Extension Centers to grant Associate in Arts and Associate in Science certificates. To qualify a student had to earn at least 60 credits and 120 grade points in courses which normally were required for a bachelors degree. [25] This authorization validated the quality of the Centers' academic program and recognized that more and more students were remaining in their communities for their sophomore year. The sophomore retention rate had gradually risen during the decade, from about 10% in 1950 to 22.9% in 1959-60. [26]

The steady rise in enrollment and the addition of more and more sophomore courses underscored the inadequacy of the facilities at many of the Centers. Especially critical was the shortage of suitable laboratory space for chemistry and physics classes. In the thirties and forties, when the Extension Centers had been strictly freshman operations, geography had been the sole science course because its lab requirements could easily be met; and the students could postpone taking other science courses until they transferred. In the fifties, however, many more students were choosing professional programs that required chemistry and/or physics during their first two years. Even when the building that Extension used contained a laboratory, it often did not meet the standards for a college-level set of experiments.

Because of the unique relationship between the University, the Centers, and the host communities, it took a great deal of coordination to address building and equipment needs. The city or the county (or both) had to provide the suitable space and the University had to agree to equip the facility. In the tight fiscal circumstances of the fifties, such an effort almost always involved a long struggle.

For example, the Marathon County board began early in 1955 to discuss a new building to replace the old County Normal building and the other "temporary" structures being used by the Center in Wausau. But the Board members wanted assurances that if they made the decision to proceed, the state and University would be firmly committed to equipping, staffing, and operating the facility for many years. The Marathon County supervisors were encouraged by the fact that the 1955 legislature had enacted two significant provisions that bolstered their plans. First, the statute which created the CCHE also contained the important stipulation that, "No educational program for which the legislature shall have made an appropriation existing at any institution of higher education shall be abandoned except with legislative approval."[27] Second, the legislators had amended an existing statute to allow counties to acquire land, appropriate money, and maintain Extension Centers "if their operation has been approved by the board of regents."[28] In November of 1955, the Board of Regents passed a resolution that pledged support for ". . . the continued operation of the Extension Center in Wausau under existing policies in an additional building to be provided by Marathon County, ..."[29] With these assurances in hand, the county supervisors worked tirelessly for two years to win approval for a bond issue to finance construction. Another three years passed before the building was completed. When it opened in January 1960, Marathon County had the first new Center building in the state and it had blazed the way for other counties and cities to follow.

Building needs remained urgent at many other Centers. In both Racine and Kenosha the current facilities were bulging, even the evening classes could barely be accommodated. The old Vocational School in Kenosha had absolutely no science labs or faculty office space. The Centers administration tried to convince the two cities to cooperate to construct a new building somewhere in the ten miles that separated them. Such a joint venture made great sense because the two Centers shared virtually their entire faculty and because students from one city often travelled to the other to take a particular course. These urgings, however, were not heeded. By early 1960 the city of Kenosha, in cooperation with Kenosha County, had broken ground for a new building, while the city of Racine was in the process of hiring an architect to design an addition to the McMynn School, which housed its Center.[30]

The situation in Menasha was the worst. The Center had shared space for many years with the high school, but the baby boomers had gradually swelled the secondary school enrollment to the point that Extension classes were pushed out. Finding new quarters proved almost impossible. Classes ended up being held in two rooms in a remodeled clinic and in one room in the Menasha Vocational School. At the clinic the front door opened directly into a classroom and the only access to the second room was through the first. Students quickly learned to be on time, unless they wanted to suffer the knowing glances of their classmates and the frown of the instructor. The clinic was not without its structural advantages, however. One of the back doors opened toward a pub only a few steps away, where many a quick one was quaffed by students between classes.[31]

The solution to Menasha's space needs required skilled diplomacy. The Winnebago County Board of Supervisors felt strongly that Outagamie County should provide one half the construction costs because so many of its citizens attended the Menasha Center. Outagamie's leaders, however, made a counter proposal. They suggested that they turn over their County Normal School in Kaukauna for use as a Center. Several Extension officials inspected this building and reported that very extensive, expensive remodeling would be necessary to make it suitable for college classes. As the two county boards wrestled with the knotty problem, the Appleton newspaper worried that the Fox Valley, with a population of over 100,000, would lose its two-year campus. The paper urged the supervisors to reach a compromise. In the end, they did exactly that. In the early 1960's the students and faculty moved into a new Fox Valley Center building in Menasha. The new name was deliberately chosen to emphasize the broad community support it had received.[32]

The library situation in the extension Centers had slowly improved since the 1930s when the History Department visitors had been appalled by its inadequacies. In 1949, Roger E. Schwenn was hired to coordinate all of the library activities of the Division, including the provision of library services to the Centers. Extension's central library in Madison still loaned out books semester by semester to those Centers that did not have their own collection. By 1956 four campuses—Green Bay, Kenosha, Racine, and Wausau—had established a small library and regularly augmented it with volumes borrowed from the central library. However, none of the Centers had a professional librarian. Consequently each Center depended upon faculty or administrators to supervise the library, but these volunteers could not give much technical assistance to the users. This was a problem the central administration pledged to address each time the budget hearings were held, but more urgent items seemed always to push funds for qualified librarians lower on the list of priorities.[33]

By the end of this decade the Centers seemed poised to move with assurance into the sixties. Although pared down in number to just eight out-state Centers, they seemed quite solidly entrenched in the state's educational establishment. The CCHE had clearly placed itself behind maintaining separate systems of two-year schools—Centers and vocational schools—rather than following a nationwide trend to combine liberal arts and vocational programs in a single institution. The state government had lent important support by empowering counties and/or cities to borrow money specifically for the construction and maintenance of Center facilities. And the Board of Regents gave a powerful endorsement in a June 1959 statement which said, in part, "The University is proud of its eight freshman-sophomore extension centers. Valuable now, these centers are certain to be even more important in the future. In the years of mounting enrollments immediately ahead, the centers will handle a larger percentage of the students in the University System."[34]

Five

The Center System is Created: The Sixties

The sixties were years of tremendous change and challenge for the United States. President John F. Kennedy, in his 1961 inaugural address, called the American people to accept the hard work of taming a New Frontier. The confrontation with the Soviet Union and the battle against communism continued; by the end of the decade thousands of our troops would be engaged in a war in Vietnam. A host of social problems at home intensified, problems made more urgent by the continuing increase in population. The baby boomers would begin to establish their own families, assuring that the pressure upon social agencies would not diminish. The trend toward urbanization also persisted. These phenomena would compel an ongoing reevaluation of the operative principles of American society, including those of the nation's colleges and universities.

The challenges facing Wisconsin, of course, mirrored the national issues. In state-supported higher education the challenge of steadily increasing enrollments was met through an expansion in the number of both two-year and four-year campuses and a major reorganization that phased out all of the County Teachers Colleges and many of the city vocational schools.

These changes required action by the state legislature; thus the history of the Freshman-Sophomore Centers during the sixties includes the political interaction between state government, the CCHE, the University of Wisconsin, the State Colleges, the County Teachers Colleges, and the State Board of Vocational and Adult Education (SBVAE).

In 1960, thirty-two percent of Wisconsin's eighteen to twenty-four year old citizens were enrolled in college. This was almost twice the national average and reflected the state's continued emphasis upon education. More and more of the enrollees chose to attend a public college or university. In addition, the number of students eighteen to twenty-one years old would continue to grow, as would the percentage of high school graduates who intended to pursue some form of higher education. In 1951, 63.5% of the state's college students had registered in a public institution; that number rose to 68.6% in 1960 and was projected to increase to at least 70% by the end of the decade. In the midst of all these numbers is the fact that, percentage-wise, the Centers' enrollment was growing more rapidly than either Madison's or Milwaukee's. From 1954 to 1964, the number of students attending a Center swelled by 177% while the number at Madison and Milwaukee grew, respectively, by 88% and 82% during the same interval. [1]

Director Adolfson, during his March 1961 Founders' Day speech in Green Bay, stressed that the Extension Division's operations would have to change dramatically to meet the challenge of an urbanized society. He noted that Extension ". . ., through its Centers, is in a good position to once again respond to the state's educational and research needs." He predicted that the Centers would eventually emerge as a special type of junior college. Adolfson believed that the Centers would increasingly attract instructors who had earned a doctorate and who intended to make teaching in the Center System their career. This would naturally give more permanence and continuity to the teaching staff. He applauded the efforts of the each host community to provide its Center with adequate facilities, but noted that there remained a critical need for more laboratories to offer a greater variety of science courses. Once again, he emphasized the Centers' close ties to the Madison campus as assurance that the students received a high quality education. Adolfson concluded with a reiteration of the key role the Centers would continue to play in fulfilling the Wisconsin Idea—providing citizens with access to the University across the state. [2]

Meanwhile, the CCHE, the fifteen-member coordinating council created in 1955 to head off a UW/WSU merger, continued its task of developing a master plan for Wisconsin higher education. In January 1961 the Council reported that a survey of the cooperation between the vocational schools, Extension Centers, and State Colleges had produced very positive results.

Indeed, these findings indicated that Wisconsin did not need to develop comprehensive junior colleges. Especially significant was the cooperation in guidance and counseling which assured that students were directed to the institution best designed to meet their particular educational goals.[3]

While the CCHE maintained its stance against developing community colleges in Wisconsin, its staff and various subcommittees worked toward important decisions which would affect all two-year post-secondary programs of study. In the fall of 1962 the CCHE approved a set of recommendations that called for the County Teachers Colleges to be closed by July 1, 1968. The cornerstone of the rationale was that two years of teacher education no longer sufficed, even for those serving one-room, rural elementary schools. A collateral recommendation urged that state teacher certification regulations be changed to require every public school teacher to have at least a bachelor's degree by the beginning of the 1972-73 school year. The same report recognized that closing the county colleges would compel more students to enroll in the University or in the State Colleges and would create significant geographic gaps in the provision of higher education opportunities in some parts of the state.

The CCHE proposed, consequently, that these gaps be filled by the creation of additional "extension centers," including some to be operated by the State Colleges. Naturally, criteria for the siting of these additional centers would have to be developed. Accordingly, a Committee Concerned with the Development of New Criteria for the Establishment and Operation of New Extension Centers was founded. It had ten members: four from the University, four representing the State Colleges, and two presidents of County Teachers Colleges. The committee was instructed to base its criteria upon the willingness of a community and/or a county to make a firm financial commitment to construct a new campus, on each site's distance from any public or private college and on the number of high school graduates within one hour's commuting distance.[4]

The University appointed its most influential spokesmen to this committee to promote its interests—President Elvehjem, Chancellor Edwin Young (Madison), Chancellor F.I. Olson (Milwaukee), and Extension Director L.H. Adolfson—and the State Colleges sent men of equal rank. Adolfson, because of his long experience with the Extension Centers, played a pivotal role in the deliberations. Indeed, the committee used his proposal for the minimum criteria as the basis of its deliberations. Adolfson recommended that if a proposed center site was 15 miles from another public institution, there must be a minimum of 900 high school graduates within a 20 mile radius; if the site was 16 to 30 miles from a state-supported college, there should be no less than 750 high school graduates within a 20 mile radius; and, finally, a center more than 30 miles from any public competitor should have at least 600 secondary school graduates within 20 miles. Adolfson explained that he had excluded private colleges from his calculations because students who could afford to attend a private institution would not consider seriously enrolling at a two-year campus. He also maintained that a proposed center should be able to enroll at least 150 to 200 students in order to provide an adequate freshman/sophomore curriculum.[5]

I.L. Baldwin, a member of the CCHE's staff, immediately challenged Adolfson's recommendations because he felt these criteria would permit centers to be too close to other public colleges and to one another. Baldwin also asserted that the minimum number of high school graduates in a center's primary drawing area ought to be increased, because CCHE's studies had demonstrated that a minimum enrollment of 300 to 400 students was required for a successful freshman-sophomore campus. The State College spokesmen vigorously supported Baldwin's views, noting that Adolfson's proposal would allow the siting of centers practically within "spitting distance" of their institutions. This latter point greatly intensified the debate over who should be authorized to establish and operate the new centers, the University or the State Colleges. The State College representatives vigorously rejected the University's argument that its experience made it the only logical sponsor of additional centers. They demanded the right to establish and operate two-year branch campuses in those areas where a state college would be the nearest state-sponsored institution.[6]

The public wrangling over the criteria for siting additional centers caused Democrat Governor Gaylord Nelson (1959-1963) and several members of the legislature to warn that if the CCHE could not reach a reasonable compromise, then the CCHE and both boards of regents might be abolished to merge the University and State Colleges into a single institution.[7] It is difficult to determine whether this threat spurred the committee members to settle their differences, however in late July 1962 they forwarded their report to the CCHE. The CCHE approved the recommendations in October 1962.[8]

The discussion of the minimum criteria for the establishment of additional centers had taken place in the midst of a raucous battle over the siting of an extension center in Wood County. For over two years that county's two major municipalities—Marshfield and Wisconsin Rapids—had been competing to be selected as the host community. In November 1961, the Wood County Supervisors had dodged making the choice when they pledged $350,000 toward construction costs in either city and forwarded their resolution to the CCHE. After completing its review, the CCHE passed the question to the UW Board of Regents. During the January and February, 1962, meetings the regents considered at length the competing claims of delegations from Marshfield and Wisconsin Rapids. The regents also closely questioned Extension Director Adolfson about his opinion. He observed that both communities could provide the present minimum of 150 students for a successful two-year program, and that both had prospects for growth to 200 to 250 students within five years. But, he added, the proximity of both Marshfield (36 miles) and Wisconsin Rapids (23 miles) to the State College at Stevens Point and to each other (33 miles) was a matter that deserved careful consideration. In June 1962 the regents finally chose Marshfield and established a timetable for securing the funds from the state for equipping the center.[9] Marshfield evidently won the competition because the city officials and the leaders of the medical community had planned and executed an intense lobbying campaign with the Board of Regents. Marshfield's greater distance from the Central State College at Stevens Point also helped. The State College Regents, of course, had followed this contest with intense interest. Once the decision to place an Extension Center in Marshfield had been made, they reacted. In a unanimous resolution, they asked the CCHE to delay construction of the Marshfield Center, or any center, until the future of the County Teachers Colleges had been determined and until the criteria for the placement of new centers had been completed. Consequently, the July 1962 meeting of the CCHE was a long and tense session. After a lengthy debate the CCHE members, by a tight seven to six vote, refused to reconsider the Marshfield/Wood County issue and gave the University the green light to proceed. This row opened up a permanent rift between the UW and the State Colleges that seriously damaged the CCHE's effectiveness as a coordinating body because the persistent issues of locating new centers and deciding who should operate them kept the CCHE membership sharply divided.[10]

On July 27, 1962, President Elvehjem died unexpectedly. A short time later Vice President Fred Harvey Harrington, a former Madison history professor, was elevated to the University presidency. In early August 1962, Gordon Haferbecker, an administrator at the Central State College at Stevens Point, wrote to Harrington, ostensibly to congratulate him on his appointment. However, Haferbecker devoted most of his letter to a proposal for an extensive network of higher educational opportunities in central Wisconsin. Haferbecker suggested that Central State College become a UW institution and that thereafter, it alone, or in partnership with the Extension Division, be given control over existing and projected centers at Wausau, Merrill, Rhinelander, Medford, Antigo, Marshfield, and Wisconsin Rapids.[11] Harrington's reply to Haferbecker was terse and non-committal; he agreed that both the University and the Stevens Point State College should continue their cooperation in the central part of the state. He made no comment on Haferbecker's bold proposal.

Much different was the President's memo of the same date to Vice President Robert Clodius and Dean [sic] Adolfson. In it he said the University must be ". . . out in front on this Center business—with us proposing and moving before a crisis develops." Harrington requested that Adolfson or one of his staff members prepare a response to Haferbecker's proposal to be used for planning purposes. Adolfson personally wrote the rebuttal. He noted that Haferbecker had made several good points, but the flaws in his scheme were fatal. First, Adolfson did not believe that the State College regents would give up Stevens Point or any of their institutions to the University. Second, he stated flatly that the State Colleges could not meet the diversified needs of the state's citizens as adequately as could the Extension Division through its Centers and other programs. Third, he adamantly rejected the suggestion that any Centers should be turned over to Stevens Point. However, Adolfson admitted that the legislature would probably authorize the State Colleges to operate branch campuses, so he urged that the University should be prepared to lay prompt claim to the projected centers in Rhinelander and in the Janesville-Beloit area.[12]

The need for Harrington's and Adolfson's advance planning became increasingly clear during the next two years, as the CCHE laid out detailed plans for at least six, and perhaps as many as twelve, additional two-year campuses in Wisconsin. When these plans and projections were formally announced, the State College leaders intensified the campaign to prevent the establishment of UW Centers in their proximity. The state government—the source of funds to equip and operate the Centers—was inexorably drawn into this momentous conflict.

The federal government added an important consideration to the ongoing debate in Wisconsin when it enacted Public Law 88-204, the Federal Educational Facilities Act of 1963. One of the cornerstones of President Kennedy's grand plan to strengthen American education, under its terms the federal government would finance 40% of construction costs and contribute significantly toward equipment purchases, especially for science laboratories. Each state would receive a percentage of the federal appropriation, allocated according to its financial commitment to the construction of new educational facilities. Wisconsin fared well in this competition for federal dollars, thanks to years of study and planning by the CCHE. PL 88-204 gave a great boost to potential two-year campus host communities and counties because they would now have to underwrite just sixty percent of the construction expenses. This feature made it easier, certainly, to convince local taxpayers to support bond issues. But PL 88-204 made the CCHE's task more difficult because it intensified the competition among prospective host communities and between the University and State Colleges to control the new institutions.

Following its usual pattern, the CCHE issued a preliminary report on new extension centers in March 1963 and in October approved a list of potential sites and a timetable for their development. Out of a total of twelve new locales, six were projected for development between 1965 and 1969. The University of Wisconsin was slated to operate new centers in Rock, Sauk, Washington, and Waukesha Counties, while the State Colleges would control the branch campuses in Barron and Waupaca/Shawano Counties. Then, depending upon how enrollment in these Centers developed, six additional communities would perhaps be given a two-year campus—Beaver Dam (Dodge County), Rhinelander (Oneida), Fond du Lac (Fond du Lac), Tomah (Monroe), Richland Center (Richland), and Lake Geneva (Walworth). Three cities—Medford, Monroe, and Wisconsin Rapids—were not on the priority list, but were kept under consideration. The CCHE promised to scrutinize their qualifications over the next decade to determine if they could meet eventually the minimum criteria for a center.[13]

To defuse the criticism it had received for recommending the closure of the County Teachers Colleges, the CCHE noted that a half dozen counties whose colleges would be closed already had a Center. If all of the projected new campuses were built, four more counties would be added to that number. The siting of the new institutions, the report noted, meant that the majority of Wisconsin youth would live within commuting distance of either a four-year or a two-year public college.

The State College Regents reacted negatively to the CCHE recommendations. Hewing to the line they had taken during the Wood County dispute between Marshfield and Wisconsin Rapids, they asserted that the State Colleges should be given control over any new campus closer to a State College than to Madison. The State College's Council of Presidents also joined the jurisdictional dispute, making especially heated remarks about the allocation of the Rock County Center to the University, when Janesville was a scant nineteen miles from the Whitewater State College. Both bodies observed that the UW had received the choicest sites, while the two projected State College branch campuses barely met the minimum criteria for their establishment. The University of Wisconsin evidently won the dispute over control of the Rock County Center because of strong lobbying of the CCHE by the Janesville Chamber of Commerce.[14]

In 1964 the situation became increasingly tense when the CCHE awarded both of the new four-year campuses at Green Bay and in the Kenosha-Racine area to the University. The CCHE based its decision primarily upon the fact that the new baccalaureate institutions would be created essentially by adding junior and senior year courses to existing Centers.

State College Regent John Thomson of Stevens Point, backed unanimously by his fellow regents, boldly attacked this decision. Thomson proposed that the State Colleges should specialize in undergraduate education while the UW concentrated upon its graduate programs. Consequently, he argued that the State Colleges should control the two new undergraduate institutions. Thomson urged that a new, separate board of regents be created to govern all two-year campuses—the existing and proposed UW Centers, the projected State College branch campuses, and the recently approved district-wide vocational-technical schools. Thomson asserted that his plan would finally end the jurisdictional disputes between the two systems and restore harmony to the CCHE.[15]

President Harrington reacted vigorously to prevent the "Thomson Plan" from obtaining support in the CCHE. Harrington wanted desperately to retain the Centers because they provided the University with important political support across the state. Once again, Harrington enlisted Adolfson. He asked Adolfson to write a "hard-hitting" one-page document that stressed why the University should both control the new four-year campuses and continue to supervise the Centers. He also suggested that Adolfson immediately send his staff members to visit key vocational school leaders to enlist their support in defeating Thomson's scheme. Harrington's carefully orchestrated campaign succeeded. In June 1964, one by one, the CCHE turned down Thomson's recommendations. The sole victory that Thomson and his fellow regents salvaged from this battle came when the state legislature approved changing the name of the State Colleges to State Universities to acknowledge that their curricula had been greatly expanded and that they would soon begin to offer masters degrees.[16]

Once Thomson's plan had been shelved, President Harrington confidently pressed forward with his ambitious plans to streamline the outreach activities of the University. Harrington wanted to merge the UW's three separate outreach arms—General Extension, Cooperative Extension (formerly Agricultural Extension), and WHA Radio & Television. He decided that the merger would be facilitated by first removing the Centers and their college-credit program from General Extension. He believed that most of the Centers' staff members would oppose any plan of unification with Cooperative Extension, because it offered almost exclusively non-credit courses and workshops. Thus, by separating the Centers from the Extension Division Harrington removed a large bloc of potential opposition to his merger scheme.[17]

Harrington unveiled his recommendation for creating the University Center System before the regents on September 3, 1963. He proposed that the Center System should start operations on July 1, 1964. A Provost, who reported directly to the President, would be its chief executive officer. The new System would consist of the eight existing Centers, the one under construction at Marshfield, and any new two-year campuses assigned by the CCHE. In addition, Harrington suggested that the Center System should have control over any new junior-senior programs authorized by the CCHE, because the upper division courses would be grafted onto existing Centers. In his rationale, Harrington noted that the Centers had experienced the fastest rate of enrollment increase in the University and that this rapid growth was expected to continue. Consequently, he was convinced this was the opportune time to relieve the Extension Division of the increasingly burdensome responsibility for administering the Centers. The Regents, after asking a few perfunctory questions, unanimously approved the President's plan.[18]

Within two weeks, President Harrington appointed a search committee which would provide him a list of qualified candidates for Provost of the Center System. In his comments to the Regents, Harrington had stressed the importance of finding the right person for this position, someone who could ably organize the new institution and who could command the respect of all those who worked for the Centers. Wilbur Hanley, the long-time Director of the Centers within Extension, avidly sought the post and apparently felt that his experience made him the obvious choice for the appointment. Hanley and his advocates arranged for letters of support to be sent to the search committee from Centers' faculty, county boards, and various municipal groups. The *Kenosha News* even editorialized in his behalf.[19]

Meanwhile, behind the scenes, Harrington and Vice President Robert Clodius worked carefully to avert Hanley's appointment and to persuade L.H. Adolfson that he was the only person who could get the Center System properly launched. Hanley's open eagerness for the post and the broad campaign in his behalf had peeved both Harrington and Clodius. A more substantial objection rested upon Hanley's renowned unilateral decision-making which, over the years, had antagonized the Centers' faculty, the Center directors, the Madison academic departments, and the top University administrators. Adolfson, on the other hand, was almost universally well liked. But he was not especially interested in the Provost's position , his eye was on the top administrative slot that would result from the merger of the Extension Division, Cooperative Extension, and WHA-Radio & Television. Patiently but persistently, Harrington and Clodius worked to get Adolfson to change his mind. They reminded him of all the successful battles he had fought on behalf of the Centers in his nearly twenty years as the leader of the Extension Division. Here was an opportunity, they said, to assure that the Center System was properly launched. Finally, in early March 1964, he agreed to accept the post. The next month the Board of Regents confirmed him as the Center System's first Provost.[20]

Adolfson faced a daunting task. In virtually all areas—administration, faculty governance, and relationships to the other arms of the University of Wisconsin—Center System personnel were required to be innovators. To be sure, the historical ties to the Extension Division and to the academic departments in Madison provided good starting points. But as the Centers matured, traditions sometimes had become an impediment to change. It is also perhaps fortunate that the Extension Division, itself, was involved in a merger at the same time the Center System was setting its course because those in Extension who would have been most inclined to try to maintain their ties to the Centers were kept very busy with the merger process and had little time to meddle with the Center System.

Adolfson and his colleagues had an important Working Paper on [The] Separation of Center System from University Extension Division to guide them. This document, issued in February 1964, represented the culmination of several months work by a committee whose members came from all University constituencies. The Working Paper's analysis of the administrative needs of the Center System was quite candid. The committee said the Provost would need to be strong yet flexible, a person who could boost morale and end uncertainty among the faculty, and an administrator who could set up from scratch a central office in Madison while overseeing eight widely-dispersed Centers. Adolfson managed to accomplish all this. The chancellor's office (Adolfson's title was changed from provost to chancellor in January 1965) that emerged contained five distinct functional areas. The vice chancellor was essentially an academic dean, who supervised the faculty and the curriculum. The business office, the registrar's office, and the assistant vice chancellor for student affairs handled most of the routine work. The secretary of the faculty was a new and important office. This person had the responsibility for all of the records associated with faculty governance.[21]

The Working Paper also analyzed the local directors' roles. It described the present directors as "weak," with no legal control over their Centers' faculty, budget or programs. It noted that in the new Center System the directors would become responsible for providing leadership in four areas: instruction, research, adult education, and public service. Consequently, the directors' authority needed to be augmented. However, in contrast to the precise recommendations made for the Provost's office, the Working Paper did not contain firm directions about how to strengthen the directors' roles. For example, the committee suggested that with regard to the faculty the directors could be empowered by one of three options: they could 1) be given complete control over faculty personnel actions (hiring, salary increases, promotions, granting of tenure), 2) hold a veto over the recommendations of the academic departments, or 3) share the decision-making with the departments. The third option of course presented the problem of where to draw the line of authority between the directors and the department heads. A similar dilemma existed with the budget: should each director receive a budget and have the sole responsibility to develop the courses/programs needed by his Center's clientele or should the director, Provost's office, and the departments collectively control the money? The committee observed that giving each director complete fiscal control would surely create powerful local administrators.[22] Because the local directors' roles intersected intimately with those of the department leaders and with faculty governance issues, the answers to these knotty questions only gradually evolved.

During the ensuing half-dozen years, the local directors' roles inevitably became larger. After the separation from General Extension, they assumed tasks that formerly had been shared with the central office and the Madison academic departments. The ambitious building programs of the sixties greatly increased the directors' visibility. In the fall of 1965 Adolphson recommended to the Regents that their title should be changed to "dean" in recognition of a greater workload and, especially, increased involvement with curricular issues. The Board readily approved.[23]

The Center System faculty took the greatest amount of time to settle upon an organizational structure. In 1964, the Center System employed 171 full-time teaching faculty and 122 part-time instructors. Ninety-seven percent of the full-time faculty were either instructors (65%) or assistant professors (32%), while just four persons held the rank of associate professor and only one had achieved a full professorship. Only thirty-seven of the full-time teachers had earned their doctorate; most of the others held a masters degree. Well over half of the graduate degrees had been awarded by Madison, vivid proof of the strength of the "Madison connection." By the mid-sixties, in response to rapidly rising enrollments, the vast majority of the full-time faculty had become resident faculty and had ceased to travel among the Centers. Indeed, in 1964 just 60 members of the faculty had split appointments and almost all of them were part-time instructors in special subject areas. This, then, was the teaching staff which had to shape its governance structure.[24]

The Center System faculty had virtually no experience in self-governance. Curriculum and personnel decisions, which normally would be made by faculty governance bodies, had been made by Madison's academic departments. Consequently, the Center System faculty faced the formidable task of creating its own governance structure and of writing the policies and procedures by which it would operate.

A faculty committee—the Interim Committee on the Organization of the Center System Faculty—consisting of one representative from each Center took on the task of setting up a faculty senate and of writing its constitution. The Interim Committee had been at work several months when the Center System was officially launched in July 1964, but did not make its report until February 1965. The proposed constitution enfranchised all half-time or more teaching faculty. Each Center would send at least one representative to the Senate; Centers with more than thirty voting members would elect two representatives. The department chairmen would select a senator from among themselves. The chancellor or vice chancellor would schedule the Senate meetings, prepare the agenda, and preside over the sessions. The report did not suggest how often the Senate should meet.

In addition to the Faculty Senate, the Interim Committee proposed the establishment of a five member Faculty Committee, whose duties would parallel those of Madison's influential University Committee. One member, elected at-large from all of the Centers' eligible faculty, would chair the committee. The other four members would be elected to represent a geographic region: area one consisted of Racine and Kenosha, two of Green Bay, Fox Valley, and Marinette, three of Manitowoc and Sheboygan, and four of Marshfield and Wausau. To be eligible for this committee, a faculty member had to have taught at least four years in the Center System. After consideration and debate at each Center, the faculty overwhelmingly approved the proposed constitution by a 165 to 18 margin. The next month, on May 7, 1965, the Board of Regents also gave its consent and faculty governance in the new Center System was officially underway.[25]

The chair of the Center System University Committee was automatically a member of the powerful UW Faculty Council which consisted of representatives from Madison, Milwaukee, and Extension, in addition to the Center System. The President of the University met regularly with the Faculty Council; the Council used these sessions to react to the administration's policies and to initiate policy proposals desired by the faculty. Within a short time, the Faculty Council created a Faculty Assembly which met at least once a semester to discuss and resolve issues of university-wide concern. Representation in the Faculty Assembly was proportional to each institution's size. In 1968 both the Council and Assembly were enlarged to include delegates from the new UW-Green Bay and UW-Parkside. Through these bodies the Center System faculty maintained strong ties to the Madison campus.[26]

One of the Senate's first tasks was to organize the academic departments. This task was complicated, as mentioned earlier, by the former ties to departments in the Extension Division and to the residence academic departments in Madison. The Senate considered several options. One possibility was to continue the association with the subject-matter departments in a reorganized UW Extension. This would be the least disruptive choice as, presumably, most of the same persons would continue as chairmen. But since the interaction of the Centers' faculty with the Extension Division departments had ranged from good to non-existent, this option was fairly quickly rejected. Second, the Senate investigated whether the faculty could be directly attached to their respective academic departments in Madison. This was an attractive possibility because it would perpetuate the "Madison connection." However, it would also mean that the Center System faculty would have their personnel decisions made according to Madison departmental rules—rules which did not take into account the far different nature of an appointment in the Center System. A third option called for the Centers to sever all former ties and to create their own independent academic departments. This alternative, too, was quickly dismissed, primarily because of the prohibitive cost of paying the entire salaries of the chairmen and of the potential problems in the transfer of Center System course credits.

In September 1966, the Faculty Senate developed a compromise which created independent departments in the Center System, but whose chairmen would hold a teaching appointment in a Madison department. Chancellor Adolphson would appoint the chairmen, upon the recommendation of the departments' executive committees and after consultation with the Madison Departments. This procedure was used until the appointment of chairs solely from among the Center System faculty became feasible. By 1972, only two departments (English and physical education) were still led by individuals who held joint appointments.

Each department's executive committee consisted of all its tenured members above the instructor rank, plus one member each from Madison and Milwaukee. The latter two representatives provided advice on policies and procedures and facilitated coordination of the Center System curriculum with Madison and Milwaukee. Each executive committee recommended promotions in rank, awards of tenure, and salary increases to the dean of the appropriate Center. The dean then added his comments and forwarded both reports, as appropriate, to either the Biological and Physical Sciences Division or the Humanities and Social Science Division executive committee for review. The divisional executive committee's advice went directly to the Chancellor, who ultimately forwarded a request for approval to the Board of Regents. With this procedure the Center System faculty had steered a careful course which allowed them to maintain important ties to the Madison departments, but which also permitted them to write their own personnel policies and procedures.[27]

In the fall of 1964 the Center System petitioned the Board of Regents to revise the "60 Credit Rule," which stipulated that all UW students must earn one-half of their graduation credits in residence. The Board of Regents had originally adopted this rule in the 1890s to limit the number of credits that a student could earn by correspondence and extension courses. In the 1930s the 60 Credit Rule had been applied to the Freshman Centers. Now, however, that limitation conflicted with a new Regents' policy which encouraged the development of a summer session in the Center System. If, for example, a student averaged 15 credits a semester for four semesters, the 60 credit limit was reached and that student could not enroll in even one summer course. The Faculty Senate, in November 1965, submitted to the regents its rationale for allowing the Centers' students to transfer a maximum of 72 credits to Madison. In its Memorandum the Senate argued that this revision would accommodate the better students, who wanted to carry more than 15 credits per semester and/or to enroll in a summer session, would reduce the overcrowding in Madison, and would help the Center System establish a viable summer session.[28]

Transfer problems had intensified, generally, after the Center System was established because many of the special ties to the Madison campus had disappeared. Consequently, students from the Centers began to encounter increasing difficulty when they moved on for their junior and senior years. In the worst instances, some of the Madison colleges insisted that Center students apply for admission, as though they were new students. Naturally, Chancellor Adolfson took up this crucial issue in the Administrative Council where he argued that transfer students from the Centers ought not to be treated differently than a UW-Madison student who changed majors and had to be admitted to a different college. President Harrington agreed and directed the Deans of the colleges from both Madison and Milwaukee to meet with Center System representatives to work out a smooth transfer policy. The policy, produced in September 1966, pledged the senior campuses to a liberal policy in accepting transfer credits and directed the Center System to assume the initiative in conferring with the individual colleges to assure that its courses would meet degree requirements. The policy also required each college to name a person who would handle questions and appeals. Shortly afterward, the Centers initiated the practice of having UW college representatives visit their campuses to talk directly with prospective transferees. These face-to-face conversations enabled students to learn first-hand about requirements they had to meet and which Center System courses would satisfy those requirements. These visits gave important reinforcement to the on-campus counseling in the Centers. Subsequently, most Center students were able to transfer smoothly to either Madison or Milwaukee.[29]

The Centers' libraries grew very rapidly in the sixties, especially after the separation from the Extension Division. Now the focus could be upon building a network of purely academic holdings, rather than having to share the resources with many non-academic departments. Roger Schwenn, the

Director of the Libraries, noted many of these improvements in his June 1968 Center System Progress Report. In all cases, Schwenn contrasted the situation in June 1964 with June 1968. The number of volumes in each Center library had at least doubled and at Manitowoc and Sheboygan it had quadrupled. In order to catalog all these books, periodicals, films, records, and other materials, the processing center in Madison had been compelled to lease space at two additional locations to augment its original area in the Extension Building. Schwenn noted that the state had been generous in appropriating money for the University libraries. The Center System basic book fund, for example, leaped from $30,000 in 1964-65 to almost $123,000 in 1966-67. The state added nearly $436,000 in "enrichment funds" during the 1965-67 biennium and the federal government granted $10,000 per library during the same interval. The Centers, in 1967, finally reached a long sought goal of having a professional librarian operate each library. The local librarians, Schwenn, and the professionals on his staff met in Madison four times each year to plan and coordinate their work. In addition, a Centers-wide faculty library committee met periodically with Schwenn to provide him with advice on acquisitions needed to accommodate new courses and to strengthen weak areas. Schwenn also noted that several campuses, in addition to the ones recently built at Marshfield, Janesville, and Waukesha, had new libraries which provided pleasant, efficient surroundings for the patrons. Schwenn believed that the Center libraries would be near a goal of at least 20,000 volumes, each, by the end of the decade. This was certainly a sharp contrast to a Center library of the 1940s that had housed 200 well-worn books shelved in the corner of a classroom or an office. Like the Center System, itself, the libraries had matured and were on a solid footing.[30]

During 1965 and 1966 the community college/junior college question returned to center stage. Warren Knowles, a Republican who had been narrowly elected governor in 1964, triggered this episode with a letter he sent to the CCHE in December 1964, a month before he took office. Knowles asked a dozen questions about the CCHE's long-range plans; four of the queries focused directly upon community colleges and made it clear that the governor-elect believed Wisconsin should build several of them. He asked that the CCHE reply by mid-February. Governor-elect Knowles' decision to push community colleges arose from his desire to provide adequate post-secondary educational opportunities at an affordable cost. Knowles believed that the CCHE would never be able to overcome the UW-WSU competition to gain control over any new two-year campuses. Knowles had decided the best solution would be to construct a few dual-track community colleges in areas of the state not presently served by a public institution of higher education. He also believed that control over these community colleges should be given to the

State Board of Vocational and Adult Education (SBVAE) to avoid antagonizing either the University of Wisconsin or the Wisconsin State Universities. Giving control to the SBVAE would, Knowles hoped, prevent the academic track from dominating these institutions.[31]

In a move that surprised many, the CCHE, in early February 1965, abandoned its hard-line against community colleges and proposed that dual-track institutions be authorized for construction in Rhinelander, Rice Lake, and Wisconsin Rapids. The resolution recommended these three as "pilot projects" and justified them on the basis that neither a vocational-technical school nor a two-year college, alone, could enroll sufficient students in these communities to be educationally or fiscally sound. By providing both a vocational training program and liberal arts transfer courses, a community college hopefully could succeed. This sudden abandonment by the CCHE of long-held and often-reiterated opposition to community colleges drew much criticism. For example David Obey, a rising Democrat Assemblyman from Marathon County, wrote the CCHE to warn that he would oppose funding for these pilot projects from his position as Vice Chairman of the powerful Joint Committee on Finance. Obey had three major objections: first, where vocational and academic programs were combined, one became dominant and the other languished; second, Wisconsin could not afford to establish institutions of higher learning "all over the state"; and, third, Obey believed that the CCHE had caved in to political pressure in approving the three sites.[32] However, instead of backing down, in its March 1965 meeting the CCHE decided to reevaluate the preliminary plans for the new two-year campuses authorized for Waukesha, Janesville, and Richland Center to determine whether a vocational-technical component should be added to their curriculums.[33]

Governor Knowles was deeply disappointed by the CCHE's response to his questions about whether the state should create new community colleges. In particular Knowles was angry because the CCHE recommendations contained no estimate of the costs to carry them out and because the recommendations dealt primarily with liberal arts education and gave little attention to technical training. Consequently, Governor Knowles kept up the pressure with a special message to the legislature, "Crisis in Education", in late March. In a series of bold proposals, he repeated his call for the establishment of community colleges, suggested revamping the CCHE's membership to reduce the influence of the University of Wisconsin and of the Wisconsin State Universities, and recommended the creation of new four-year colleges in the Fox River Valley and in the Racine-Kenosha area. In the latter instance, Knowles proposed to add junior and senior year courses to one of the UW Centers in each area.[34]

Because of Governor Knowles' campaign, the 1965 legislative session grappled with several educational issues, including the vocational school/community college question. The traditional city-sponsored vocational high schools which Wisconsin had pioneered clearly were in decline. CCHE studies revealed that a major factor in the shrinking enrollments was that more and more high school students were electing a college prep program of study. After hearing hours of testimony on various proposals, the legislators passed a bill that would close the remaining vocational high schools by 1970 and replace them with multi-county vocational-technical school districts. Each district would build a new campus which would be supported by a district-wide property tax levy.

The original proposal would have granted the SBVAE (State Board of Vocational and Adult Education) the option to authorize any or all of the new institutions to offer liberal arts college transfer courses in addition to their traditional programs. However, Assemblyman Frank Nikolay (Democrat—Abbotsford), prompted by University of Wisconsin and State University lobbying, successfully amended the enabling legislation to prohibit the transfer of liberal arts credits to either the UW or the State Universities. Nikolay's amendment, though, exempted both Madison's and Milwaukee's Vocational-Technical Schools from the prohibition because they had already demonstrated sufficient support for both a high quality liberal arts curriculum and a top-notch vocational training program. Nikolay's proviso effectively halted the community college movement in Wisconsin, with the exception of the Nicolet Community College in Rhinelander.

Armed with the CCHE's February 1965 recommendation, the persistent lobby group from Rhinelander pressed the legislature to authorize a dual-track, two-year college for the northern Wisconsin region. The Rhinelander interest group also had the governor's support for a "pilot project" to establish a community college in north central Wisconsin, an area whose residents often complained that they were not adequately served by state-supported higher education. During the 1966 session the legislators acquiesced. The Nicolet Community College was the only dual-track institution of the three recommended by the CCHE to be constructed. In a special message Governor Knowles had spelled out his reasons for advocating the reorganization of the CCHE. Knowles based his case upon the allegation that the UW and State University representatives so thoroughly dominated the council that it had failed to coordinate anything. Therefore, considerable duplication in academic majors in the two systems had occurred, accompanied by steadily increasing budgets. The Wisconsin taxpayer could no longer afford the CCHE's failures, Knowles said. The legislature took up the Governor's suggestion and in the fall of 1965 it sent Knowles a bill which revamped the

Coordinating Council. The measure only slightly reduced the body's size from nineteen to seventeen members. But the institutional representation from the University of Wisconsin, the State Universities, and the SBVAE was dramatically reduced by half, while the number of citizen members (appointed by the Governor) was increased from four to nine. From now on the council would have a citizen majority. As he signed the bill, Knowles expressed the hope that the new CCHE would do a better job in providing adequate higher education opportunities at a reasonable cost to taxpayers.[35]

The busy 1965 Wisconsin Legislature enacted yet another measure which affected the Center System. This statute authorized the University of Wisconsin, working with the CCHE, to construct two new four-year campuses. Green Bay was quite quickly chosen as the site for the Fox River Valley institution, but a spirited competition between Racine and Kenosha held up the siting of the Parkside Campus for several months.

President Harrington's original intention, expressed at the time the Center System was created, was for these new institutions to offer just junior and senior year courses and for them to be operated by the Center System. Neither of these concepts proved practical. A study by the CCHE provided convincing evidence that juniors and seniors often needed also to take lower division courses, especially if they had changed their major, and that it would be terribly inconvenient for them to commute to a Center to take those courses. It made more sense for UW-Green Bay and UW-Parkside to absorb nearby Centers and to offer all four years of undergraduate work. This decision led naturally to a subsequent one to establish a separate administration for each of the new campuses, on a par with that at UW-Milwaukee.[36]

The decision that these new four-year campuses should absorb nearby Centers was easy to implement in Racine and Kenosha, but not in the Green Bay area. Reasonably close to the Green Bay Center were three other Centers: Manitowoc (37 miles), Marinette (55 miles), and Fox Valley/Menasha (39 miles). Students from these Centers might logically finish their undergraduate studies at Green Bay, rather than at Madison, which strengthened the argument that these 3-M Centers, as they were popularly known, should be attached to Green Bay to better key the curriculum to that campus. President Harrington and Chancellor Adolfson supported this transfer of control. Harrington, however, clearly indicated that the three Centers should ". . . not be satellites, run from Green Bay in the colonial manner." Instead, Harrington envisioned that they would be fully integrated into Green Bay's structure and faculty.[37]

The faculty of the three Centers were not happy with the pending transfer to Green Bay. Because the UW-Green Bay was undertaking a bold experiment with its curriculum, these Centers' faculty feared that as the courses became oriented to Green Bay's program, students would find it increasingly difficult to transfer to other colleges.

For example, the Manitowoc Center's faculty was especially apprehensive about a transfer to Green Bay and the potential effect upon their careers. They feared that the greatest rewards would go to researchers and that mere teachers would be relegated to a secondary role. They also expressed concern that tying Manitowoc's courses to Green Bay's innovative, inter-disciplinary curriculum would make the Center less attractive to students who did not intend to earn a baccalaureate degree from Green Bay. At the end of the 1967 spring semester the Secretary of the Manitowoc Faculty urgently requested that President Harrington meet with a faculty delegation to hear first-hand their misgivings. In a terse reply Harrington declined to receive a delegation. Instead he said that the top administrators—himself, Adolfson, and newly appointed Green Bay Chancellor Edward Weidner—would again discuss the issue. If that conversation took place (there is no record of it in Harrington's file), the same conclusion was reached: Manitowoc would be placed under Green Bay's control.

Later that year, in early November, the faculty of four Centers—Fox Valley, Green Bay, Manitowoc, and Marinette—received notice from Chancellors Adolfson and Weidner that they had until mid-month to decide whether to apply to UW-Green Bay for a teaching position or to remain in the Center System. Those who chose the latter option would, of course, have to accept a transfer to one of the seven remaining Center System campuses. Faculty who applied to Green Bay would not automatically receive an appointment; they would be interviewed by an appointment committee, which would make the final recommendations to Chancellor Weidner. The entire process was extremely distasteful to the Centers' faculty and morale remained low at the 3M Centers during the years they were attached to Green Bay.[38]

On July 1, 1968, the Center System became a much smaller institution. Three Centers—Green Bay, Kenosha, Racine—were directly absorbed into the new four-year institutions and Green Bay now operated the 3-M Centers. Thus just seven Centers remained in the Center System: Wausau, Sheboygan, Waukesha, Janesville, Marshfield, West Bend, and Baraboo. The latter two were still under construction and scheduled to open in the fall. Of these seven, only Wausau and Sheboygan had unbroken roots that stretched back to the 1930s.

Naturally, the Center System faculty now had to modify its constitution and procedures to reflect the dramatic changes that had taken place. The faculty approached this task with a confidence and determination that had been lacking in the drafting of the original documents. The Committee on the Future Role and Organization of the University of Wisconsin Center System took clear note of this when it reported that "Center System faculty are ready to effect independent exercise of full departmental prerogatives within their own System. . . ." In order to facilitate the exercise of this authority, the committee recommended that all faculty should be members of an academic department and that the departments should meet periodically to discharge their responsibilities. The committee also urged the administration to reduce the teaching load of the department chairmen to provide adequate time to do their work. The committee also stressed the important role of the departments and the two Divisional Executive Committees in approving new courses and other curriculum modifications because the Center System now prepared students to transfer to four other UW units, not just to Madison. By the end of the 1968-1969 academic year, the Faculty Senate had approved all of these recommendations and had accomplished the necessary amendments to the faculty documents.[39]

Both the Center System administration and the CCHE staff continued to study intently the Centers' student body, hoping to gain insights crucial to wise decision-making. One clear trend concerned the county of residence of the students. In the fall of 1962, 98% of the students enrolled in the Center System lived in the county which hosted their Center. By September 1969 that percentage had dropped almost twenty-seven points. This pronounced broadening of each Center's drawing area resulted from the students' increased mobility, who were now able to commute longer distances to classes and still live at home. The number of women students rose dramatically during the decade. Just three of ten students were female in the 1960 fall enrollment; however, they constituted 44% of the student body in 1969. The quality of the entering freshman class, measured by class rank, had improved just slightly. In 1963, for example, 44% of the new enrollees had graduated in the upper quarter, while 77% had been in the upper half of their senior class. The figures for fall 1969 were 46.2% and 82.3%, respectively. Entering women students ranked significantly higher than the males and the increase in the number of females no doubt primarily accounts for the improvement in academic quality of the freshman classes.[40]

In 1963 Madison Professor L.J. Lins, who was the Coordinator of the Office of Institutional Studies, and Allan P. Abell made an extensive study of Center System transfer students. The major finding echoed the theme of earlier studies—that former Center students, after a one semester adjustment period, earned a GPA equal or superior to those who had enrolled as freshmen at Madison. What is unique about this study is its analysis of the so-called "transfer shock" experienced by the students from the Centers. Lins and Abell noted that while all transferees' grades slipped during the initial semester in Madison, those who had spent two years at a Center, rather than just one, recovered more quickly and sustained a higher GPA for the remainder of their undergraduate careers. Here was positive proof that students were well advised to remain at a Center for a sophomore year. Lins and Abell concluded that the Centers succeeded in helping students to realize their potential for college work and prepared them well for transfer to Madison.[41] Nine students, one from each Center, appeared before the Board of Regents in May 1966 in response to an invitation to present an evaluation of their experiences in the Center System. All nine indicated that they had gathered comments from classmates and from former Center students in preparing their remarks. They reported that, because most of the students came from the hometown high school, the same cliques reappeared at the Centers. They felt that this situation could be improved by providing more diverse social and cultural activities and programs. The students said a survey of former Center students revealed that the curriculum and the rigor of the courses was adequate to prepare them for junior and senior year courses. They remarked that they especially appreciated the personal approach to teaching by the Centers' faculty in comparison to the large lecture sections in Madison. However, they related that a few faculty members seemed to be just marking time while they sought a teaching position at a four-year school. One student concluded her testimony by underscoring that accessibility was the Centers' greatest advantage for students. She estimated that fifty to seventy percent of the current student body would not be in college, if a Center had not been nearby.[42]

The next year, Dr. Martha Peterson, UW-Madison Dean for Student Affairs, echoed what the nine students had said. Peterson, who had gathered her "Impressions of Center Students" from many interviews, both in Madison and on the two-year campuses, described her findings during a workshop for the Center System Student Affairs staff in July 1967. She had drawn three major conclusions. First, living at home created a problem, both for the student and the parents, particularly during the first semester. The tension apparently arose from the fact that society placed a great value on "going away" to college and, consequently, ones acquaintances looked askance at any family whose student enrolled at a Center. However, she added that no one had demonstrated that there was any educational value in going away to college and that this expectation rested solely upon appearances and subtle concerns about status. Second, Center students did not see themselves as the "cream of the crop." Peterson believed that this self-deprecation dampened their desire to learn and to perform up to potential. Third, Peterson reported that Center students realized that they had a limited geographic, social, and cultural background. Unfortunately, the faculty and staff sometimes dramatized the situation by referring to a Center as "Siberia," in comparison to Madison. The Center System would have to work hard to broaden its students' horizons, Peterson warned, to reduce the eventual transfer shock.

Dean Peterson also listed the Centers advantages. First, because the students lived at home, the Centers' staff did not have to perform "in loco parentis" duties, allowing them to focus upon more beneficial activities. Second, she had found that Center students generally underestimated their abilities and knowledge. Consequently, the faculty had a great opportunity to awaken these students to their potential. Third, because the student body was fairly homogeneous in background and in preparation for college, the instructors could accurately target the courses to the clientele's needs. Finally, Peterson explained that, deep down, the Center students she had talked to believed that the Centers provided a good education and that they had not chosen a second-rate institution in which to begin college. Peterson concluded by underscoring the important role that Centers were playing in the University of Wisconsin. [43]

Center System administrators were, of course, aware of the need to broaden the students' cultural horizons. The lack of sufficient funds remained the major impediment to solving the problem. Back in 1965, the legislature had dictated that the Center System's tuition could not exceed the amount charged by the State Universities. At the time Adolfson had been privately unhappy because the law effectively placed the WSU Regents in charge of the Centers' tuition. The State Universities charged a separate student activity fee of $80.00 per year, but the UW Regents had imposed a "no fee" policy upon the Centers. In November 1966, Adolfson asked President Harrington to review that prohibition in light of the Center System's need to expand its cultural arts and lecture series. Harrington replied that he wanted to retain the no fee policy because it made attending the Centers slightly less expensive than enrolling in the State Universities. However, Harrington promised that he would provide additional dollars to the Center System for the Fine Arts. With this encouragement, the Center System Lectures and Fine Arts Committee developed a budget of $18,500 for 1967-68, to be allocated equally among the eleven Centers. At each Center the fine arts committee chose its programs from among Public Affairs, Drama, Science, Art, and Music. By using a central booking procedure, popular performances were scheduled at several Centers on successive evenings to stretch the funds. By these means the Centers provided a greatly expanded Fine Arts and Lecture series. [44]

Intercollegiate athletics was another concern of the Center System in its quest to provide its students with a complete college experience. Since the late 1940s the Centers' basketball teams had played one another but no other sports had been offered on a regular basis. In the summer of 1968, months of discussion and negotiation concluded successfully with the formation of the

Wisconsin Collegiate Conference. The WCC, for its initial season, had fifteen members: the seven Center System campuses, the four WSU Branch Campuses, the 3-M Centers, the Green Bay Center, and the new UW-Parkside, whose team would be drawn from the Kenosha and Racine Centers. The new athletic conference sponsored competition in cross-country, basketball, wrestling, fencing, golf, and tennis. For the basketball season, the WCC divided into a northern division of eight teams and a southern division of seven teams. A play-off at the season's end between the divisional champions determined the Conference championship. The member institutions decided that the basketball games with Parkside should not count in the Conference standings, because its team would be drawn from two Centers. Once these two Centers and the Green Bay Center were absorbed by the new four-year campuses they, of course, ceased to be members of the WCC.[45]

In the mid sixties, as the United States increased its involvement in Vietnam, college students across the nation visibly demonstrated their opposition to or support for the federal government's policy. The Madison campus was frequently the scene of violent anti-war protests that drew national attention. Center System students also demonstrated on both sides of the issue, but they avoided the use of violence. In Racine, for instance, co-eds baked and sent over 2,000 dozen cookies to service personnel in Vietnam, while students at the Kenosha Center donated 84 pints of blood during a "bleed-in." At Fox Valley a group of anti-war students circulated a petition that said, "we believe the present U. S. policy is neither ethical nor according to national interest." At several Centers, student government leaders worked with the local administration to arrange "teach-ins." In a typical teach-in, classes were suspended and students were invited to attend special lectures and to discuss the issues. For example, the Green Bay Center and nearby St. Norbert's College jointly sponsored a State Department panel that presented the government's position. All of the student newspapers, of course, contributed to the discussion with editorials, columns, and letters to the editor.[46]

One outgrowth of the anti-Vietnam war demonstrations was a nationwide movement among students to achieve greater participation in the governance of colleges and universities. In December 1966 forty-four student leaders—four from each Center—met with student affairs staff members from Madison and the Centers to discuss student government problems and issues. The conferees drafted several resolutions: one demanded more significant student participation in the Faculty Senate and in each Center's faculty meetings; another called for the establishment of an inter-Center student government council. Responding quickly, Chancellor Adolfson arranged to have the eleven student senate presidents meet in Madison the following spring, at which time they organized themselves and agreed to meet at least once each semester and to maintain communication with one another between meetings. In the spring of 1968, the Faculty Senate approved a Student Government Association resolution that called for "voting student representation" in the Center System Faculty Senate and all of its committees, and in each Center Faculty Senate and its committees. Gradually, the faculty constituencies amended their constitutions to provide for student representation and voting rights in all governance bodies (except the committees that dealt with personnel issues). This significant development opened up new and better lines of communication between students, faculty, and administrators.[47]

While the Center System was organizing itself and drafting policies, the development of the Wisconsin State University Branch Campuses had been moving forward. The Barron County branch of WSU-Stout opened in the fall of 1966 in the former County Teachers College building in Rice Lake. During the first year it offered only freshman courses and the initial enrollment was far below estimates, but the addition of basic sophomore courses the following year caused Barron's enrollment to increase dramatically. Its new campus was completed in 1968. The Richland Campus, operated by WSU-Platteville, started instruction in new, but not entirely completed, buildings in September 1967. Thus Richland became the first new WSU campus to open since 1916, when Eau Claire had joined the system. Richland, of course, had not been scheduled by the CCHE for construction until the 1967-1969 biennium, but President Marjorie Wallace of the Richland County Teachers College, State Senator Jess Miller, the Richland County Board of Supervisors, and numerous other community leaders had lobbied successfully for permission to begin construction early in 1967. WSU-Oshkosh's two-year campus in Fond du Lac enrolled its first class in September 1968. After an interval of sixteen years, a state-supported collegiate institution again operated in this city at the southern tip of Lake Winnebago.[48]

The fourth WSU two-year campus, the Medford/Taylor County Branch Campus, did not begin operations until September 1968. The decision even to open it had been difficult to reach. The CCHE's initial intent (in 1963) had been to study the enrollment potential over ten to twelve years before making a recommendation whether to proceed. The Center System's Wilbur Hanley was brutal in his analysis of the CCHE's preliminary findings on Medford. Hanley estimated that a two-year campus there would not attract more than fifty students. Hanley naturally felt that potential students in Medford's orbit would be better advised to attend the Centers at either Marshfield (39 miles) or Wausau (48 miles), because both had a broader curriculum than Medford could ever hope to develop. Hanley asserted that much of the pressure to develop the Medford Campus arose from the fact that the Taylor County Teachers College had an almost new building. However, he had visited the facility and concluded that its "ordinary classrooms" were unsuitable for a Center-type program. Although its estimate of potential enrollment was considerably higher than Hanley's, the CCHE staff was well aware that a two-year campus in Medford would always be a marginal operation. But the politics of siting the new institutions and, especially, the heated rivalry between the Wisconsin State Universities and the University of Wisconsin had ruled out a wait-and-see approach.[49]

Even after the Taylor County Board agreed, in September 1965, to construct an entirely new campus, the State University Regents proceeded very cautiously. Over the next two years, they received periodic verification from the CCHE of the enrollment estimates and they learned that the costs per student at Barron County and Richland were significantly higher than anticipated. They were also concerned because the competition for federal dollars, under PL 88-204, was intensifying in the state, now that the newly authorized Vocational-Technical School districts were also scrambling to secure these funds. Even WSU-Stevens Point President Lee S. Dreyfus, whose school would oversee the Medford campus, expressed misgivings about going ahead too rapidly. Dreyfus preferred that a freshman program be tried for a couple of years in the County College building before Taylor County began construction of new facilities. On the other hand, WSU Executive Director Eugene McPhee argued that the Regents had accepted jurisdiction over Medford and had "made commitments that could not be rescinded." Finally, on April 26, 1968, the WSU Board voted 9 to 3 to initiate a one-year program in the Teachers College building in September 1969. If Medford maintained an enrollment of 125 full-time equivalent (FTE) students until October 15, 1969, the Board committed itself to authorize an addition to the County College and a two-year curriculum for the following academic year. The target enrollment was achieved and the Medford Branch Campus was finally launched.[50]

The Branch Campus faculty members, unlike their Center System counterparts, did not have an inter-campus faculty organization. Indeed, there was virtually no interaction among them. However, each Branch Campus did send a representative to the Faculty Senate of its parent campus and thus had a voice in that chief policy-making body. The relationship between the two-year campus faculty and their parent departments was not specified by policy. For example, during the five years Richland was attached to Platteville, a member of the history department recalls that he was invited to just one department meeting and had no input into its curricular decisions. Conversely, the content of the Richland history courses and the selection of textbooks was not dictated by the department.[51]

The Sixties ended on a disappointing note for the Center System. In

February 1969 Governor Knowles, who had become increasingly concerned about the rapidly escalating cost of operating the state's higher education institutions, established a special Governor's Commission on Education. Knowles selected William Kellett, a successful, retired businessman to lead the group, which soon was labeled the Kellett Commission. The Governor asked the commissioners "to examine the huge public educational machine from top to bottom, from the inside out, and to make recommendations about how it can function better on the one hand, and more economically on the other." The Kellett Commission was expected to make its report in early 1971.

The progress of the Kellett Commission, which held public hearings across the state, was followed intensely by the governor, state legislators, and officials from both the Wisconsin State Universities and the University of Wisconsin. By late 1969 it had formulated four options for the Center System. First, the Center System could continue its cost reduction program until it reached an acceptable cost-per-student and be maintained as a high quality collegiate transfer institution. Second, the seven Centers could be nucleated (i.e. attached) to a nearby four-year UW or WSU campus. For example, the Marathon County Center would most logically be attached to the WSU-Stevens Point. Third, an enlarged Center System could be created by bringing in the WSU Branch Campuses. And, finally, the Centers (and Branch Campuses) could be merged with the Vocational-Technical Schools.[52]

But, of course the Center System was only a small part in the Kellett commission's assignment. In looking at the larger picture of public higher education in Wisconsin, the Kellett Commission studied intently a potential merger of the University of Wisconsin and the Wisconsin State Universities. The projected savings from a merger would be substantial. Elimination of the CCHE and one board of regents and central administrative staff, an end to costly duplication of academic programs and perhaps the elimination of repetitive programs that were already in place would all reduce costs. The leaders of both the UW and the WSU lobbied hard against this option. President Harrington feared a merger would damage seriously the UW's reputation as one of the nation's leading research institutions while the WSU leadership issued the alarm that Madison would capture an even larger share of the budget in a merged system, causing the withering of their campuses and a weakening of the Wisconsin Idea. As the decade drew to a close, it was obvious that the Kellett Commission would play a pivotal role in shaping the future of not just the Center System but of all of Wisconsin's higher education institutions.

Six

Merger Within Merger: 1970-1974

President Richard Nixon, in his 1970 State of the Union Address, placed special emphasis upon two major issues—the continuing conflict in Vietnam and the increasingly alarming economic news. Shortly after he had taken office, Nixon had announced that United States combat troops would gradually be withdrawn from South Vietnam. For a few months this hopeful new policy defused antiwar protests on the nation's college campuses. But as time passed and the war continued, the protests flared anew. In January 1970, after the old Red Gym on the Madison campus was firebombed, the *Daily Cardinal* ran an editorial which approved of the use of firebombs "to rid this campus once and for all of repressive ideas and institutions." Then, in August of the same year, in the early morning, a tremendous blast heavily damaged Sterling Hall, which housed the Army Mathematics Research Center; it killed a young physics' researcher who happened to be in the building. These incidents elicited calls from state legislators for UW President Harrington to resign, while anxious parents sought assurances that their sons and daughters could safely attend the Madison campus.[1]

The economic news was puzzling, even to the experts. The United States was experiencing "stagflation," a word coined to describe an economy that had stalled while at the same time the inflation rate continued to rise.

Stagflation meant that all government budgets—local, state, and federal—were being squeezed hard. This budget pressure had convinced Wisconsin Governor Warren Knowles to create the Kellett Commission in 1969 to study the state's entire public education establishment and to recommend how it could be streamlined to achieve greater efficiencies.

Both of these issues played a prominent role in Wisconsin's 1970 elections. As usual, most of the attention focused upon the governor's race, which had been thrown wide open by three-term Republican Governor Knowles' unexpected announcement that he would not seek another term. In addition, the 1970 gubernatorial election would for the first time choose someone for a four-year, rather than two-year, term of office. Both parties' candidates were selected in primaries: Republican Lieutenant Governor Jack Olson handily won his party's contest, while Madison real estate magnate Patrick J. Lucey rather easily became the Democrat nominee.[2]

During the campaign neither Olson nor Lucey devoted much attention to higher education issues. Both said they would assist UW officials to get tough with the small number of students who were continually disrupting the Madison campus.[3] In the sole speech that he devoted to higher education, the Democrat nominee focused almost exclusively upon economic issues. Lucey pledged to keep tuition low and affordable and promised to support salary increases, at least equal to the rate of inflation for the faculties of both the Wisconsin State Universities and the University of Wisconsin. Lucey, however, made no comment on the Kellett Commission's highly publicized suggestion that the two university systems should be consolidated under a "super board of education," which would operate all public education in Wisconsin, preschool through graduate school.[4]

When the ballots were counted, the Democrats were elated. Pat Lucey had bested Jack Olson by a 135,000 vote margin out of over 1.35 million votes (55% to 45%). In addition Lucey's broad coattails had carried many Democrats to victory in Assembly races, where they would enjoy a 67 to 33 margin. The Republicans, however, had retained a strong seven vote majority in the 33 member Senate.[5]

Since the Kellett Commission report on public education in Wisconsin was scheduled for completion by the end of November 1970, speculation immediately began about how Lucey would react to recommendations made by a task force appointed by his Republican predecessor.[6] Governor Knowles had appointed the Commission in February 1969 and had requested that it complete its work by the following January. However, the commissioners quickly discovered that the issues they needed to examine were too complex to meet that deadline. Instead, they issued a preliminary report in February 1970 and promised to complete their task shortly after the fall election.[7] After the preliminary recommendations were made public, the commission's various committees held public hearings to gauge reactions to their proposals. Commission Chairman William Kellett often chaired these hearings, especially when a controversial issue was examined.[8]

The Commission's Study Committee on Education for Employment had unveiled in December 1969 a proposal which directly involved the state's two-year campuses. It recommended creation of "a state-wide system of comprehensive area colleges" which would be empowered to offer programs in four areas: adult education, vocational education, technical education, and the liberal arts. The plan suggested forming as many as ten of these comprehensive colleges outside of Madison and Milwaukee, via a merger of existing and projected vocational and technical schools with either a nearby UW Center or a WSU branch campus. Because fears had surfaced that the liberal arts college credit component could overshadow the other programs, the Study Committee recommended that the liberal arts enrollment be limited to twenty-five percent of each institution's total enrollment. The proposal cited the significant savings that could be achieved by this merger—a reduction by at least half of the administrative staffs, less duplication in the physical plant, and much better utilization of the faculty. It also asserted that students would be better served by being able to transfer easily from a liberal arts curriculum to a vocational-technical program without the stigma that was often attached to such a move.[9]

Strong opposition to this scheme was quickly voiced by the Center System, the University of Wisconsin, the State Board of Vocational, Technical and Adult Education (SBVTAE), and labor representatives. The Wisconsin State University Board of Regents did not comment on the comprehensive area college proposal, perhaps because the WSU had just four branch campuses at risk, while the UW could potentially lose all ten of its two-year campuses. The State Universities also supported the Kellett Commission suggestion which recommended that the relatively new UW four-year campuses at Green Bay and Parkside (Racine) be transferred to the WSU System, thus leaving UW-Madison and UW-Milwaukee to concentrate primarily upon graduate education.[10]

In early February 1970 Chancellor Adolfson sent to President Harrington two position papers which detailed the Center System's opposition to the proposed merger. President Harrington and other UW officials often used Adolfson's arguments in the campaign against the merger.[11] Adolfson noted that the missions of the Centers and the Vocational-Technical institutions were significantly and deliberately different and that serious damage would occur to both if they were compelled to merge programs. He pointed out that the Centers were unlike either junior colleges or community colleges because of the intimate connection to UW-Madison. Any attempt to turn them into community colleges via a forced merger would "abolish their present function," Adolfson believed, and would fail to create viable new institutions. Contrary to the expectations of the Study Committee on Education for Employment, the Chancellor offered his opinion that most of the Centers' administrators and faculty members would seek new employment rather than continue to serve in a radically different institution. Hiring a substantially new group of teachers would raise anew issues of the quality and transferability of the liberal arts credits, which so far had been ensured by the Centers' long association with the University of Wisconsin. Adolfson agreed that Vocational-Technical education deserved to receive more emphasis but he argued that the proposed merger would not achieve that goal; indeed, the merger would no doubt result in the liberal arts program, even with limits on enrollment, overshadowing technical education. Adolfson also faulted the Study Committee's data, which included national, not state, figures; outdated and too high cost calculations for the Centers and too low enrollment projections for the Centers. Finally, he observed that the Kellett Commission had not calculated how much money its plan would save. Actually, Adolfson believed that a merger would cost the state more money.[12]

Officials of the SBVTAE and the state AFL-CIO Apprenticeship Conference also attacked the comprehensive area college plan. For example Joseph Noll, chairman of the SBVTAE, spoke out against the idea at a public hearing in November 1969. Noll feared that a merger would mean the eventual dominance of the liberal arts program, because that had been the experience in every state where community colleges had been created.[13] Clarence Greiber, the long-time director of the SBVTAE, supported Noll's remarks and added the observation that both California and Florida, which had comprehensive community colleges, had found it necessary to construct separate technical schools in order to assure an adequate supply of well-trained employees for technical occupations.[14] The delegates to the Wisconsin State AFL-CIO Apprenticeship Congress, who met in February 1970, added their voices to the chorus of protest. They, too, agreed that all the evidence indicated that when both liberal arts and technical programs were offered in a single institution, the former by far overshadowed the latter. The delegates also expressed fears that organized labor would lose its direct input into the vocational training programs if the state implemented the Kellett Commission recommendation.[15]

The Kellett Commission submitted its formal recommendations to Governor Knowles in late November 1970. Evidently the combined opposition of the UW, the SBVTAE, and the state AFL-CIO to the creation of community colleges had been effective. The Commission's final report, entitled

"A Forward Look," did not propose a merger but left the door ajar by urging that the SBVTAE "be authorized to phase into the Technical College System two-year university branch campuses and two-year centers where appropriate."[16] Also of keen interest to both the UW and the WSU was the final word on a much larger merger—one which would combine these two systems under a single board of regents. On this issue, also, the commissioners had bowed to criticism and recommended retaining the status quo. However, the report discussed at length the rationale for an eventual union and the Commission urged that further study of this issue be undertaken immediately by the state government.[17]

Governor Knowles received the long-awaited report amid much fanfare, thanked the commissioners for their hard work, and bestowed his approval upon their recommendations. But, of course, the lame duck Republican Governor's reactions to "A Forward Look" were relatively unimportant. Consequently, attention quickly shifted to Governor-elect Lucey's reaction.

As noted previously, during the campaign Lucey had not devoted much attention to higher education issues. And even now, with all of the work that had to be accomplished prior to assuming office, he had little to say about the Kellett Commission's recommendations. So, until Lucey revealed his views, the press had to make do with speculations and with trying to ferret out hints about how the Lucey administration might handle the state's higher education systems. For example, the *Milwaukee Sentinel,* shortly after the election, conjectured that Lucey would try to merge the two boards of regents in an attempt to reduce administrative expenses and, more importantly, to end the costly duplication of academic programs. The same article noted that the Coordinating Committee for Higher Education (CCHE) was in a very precarious position due to its failures to halt this duplication. In fact, the *Sentinel* suggested that even Republican senators probably would not complain if Lucey found a way to eliminate the CCHE.[18]

In December 1970, during the governor-elect's preliminary budget hearings, speculation about a merger of the two state financed university systems received new fuel from the testimony of Lee S. Dreyfus, the President of the WSU-Stevens Point. Dreyfus, a close personal friend of Lucey, made a lengthy, careful comparison between the mission, enrollment, and budget of his institution and that of UW-Green Bay. Although the first two, he stressed, were nearly identical, Green Bay's budget was far larger than Stevens Point's. Dreyfus argued that this fiscal inequity could not be justified and it was evidence that the CCHE had failed to coordinate the two systems' programs and budgets. He concluded his testimony with the observation that "The best way to eliminate the need to coordinate the systems is to . . . merge them."[19]

Governor Lucey officially ended his silence on February 4, 1971, when he outlined the major features of his biennial budget proposal. He strongly hinted that he would request a merger of the UW and WSU Systems by the simple expedient of eliminating funds for the CCHE and for the two separate system administrations from the budget. Lucey asserted that his primary motivation was to save the taxpayers' money—he believed that up to $4 million could be saved in the first biennium and that future savings would be even greater as cooperation replaced competition. The Governor slammed the CCHE's failure to prevent duplication of academic programs with the observation that after a bruising battle, both WSU-Stevens Point and UW-Madison had received permission to set up a School of Forestry. Lucey said bluntly, "the creation of satellite two-year campuses as a political trade-off [between the two systems] must end."[20] He also justified his recommendation by pointing out that undergraduate education in the WSU was almost identical to that provided by UW-Green Bay and UW-Parkside, yet the latter two were much more generously financed. Since undergraduate education was equal in quality throughout the state's universities, Lucey believed it was time to issue a University of Wisconsin degree to all graduates and, thus, end the myth that a UW diploma was more valuable than one from a State University.[21]

Naturally the merger proposal became one focal point of debate over the 1971-1973 budget. The CCHE staff and the University of Wisconsin Board of Regents quickly and loudly voiced their opposition. Within a short time, the faculties of Madison, Green Bay, and Parkside also joined this chorus. The CCHE staff believed the Governor's projected savings would not materialize and that he had greatly overestimated them, in any case. The UW opposition stemmed almost exclusively from a fear that the University's reputation for high quality education would be irreparably damaged by the merger.[22] By contrast, the WSU regents gave unanimous support to the proposal after their Executive Director, Eugene McPhee, announced he favored the plan. The WSU faculty remained ambivalent for several weeks; however their organization, the Association of Wisconsin State University Faculties (AWSUF), eventually endorsed the measure. The WSU support represented a reversal of the negative position previously taken toward merger. In the past the State University leaders had feared that Madison would so thoroughly dominate a merged system that their situation would become worse, not better. Now, apparently, they believed Governor Lucey when he promised that the WSU would have parity with the University in the single board of regents. Support was also received from the faculty of the UW-Milwaukee, the Wisconsin United Auto Workers political action committee, and the Executive Board of the Wisconsin National Farmers Organization.[23]

In the state legislature the attention focused primarily upon the Senate because the Governor needed at least four Republican votes, even if all thirteen Democrat Senators voted the party line. The large Democrat majority in the Assembly seemed certain to enact the merger/budget bill. Early on, the Senate Republicans offered their own merger plan, to which the Governor had serious objections. But gradually the two sides drew together through compromise—either as a result of direct negotiations between Lucey and the Republicans or as a result of trade-offs in the Joint Committee on Finance. Finally, on September 22, 1971, the Senate approved the 1971-1973 budget, which included merger approval, by the narrowest of margins, 17 to 16. About two weeks later the Assembly ratified the Senate's decision by a comfortable 57 to 43 vote. The merger bill immediately combined the two boards of regents and their central administrations and authorized creation of a Merger Implementation Committee, which would draft a statute to govern the new University of Wisconsin System.[24]

The measure contained several items of particular interest to the Centers and branch campuses. Prominent among these were the provisions that the new board of regents would operate all fourteen two-year campuses as a single institution and that no campus could be closed without the legislature's approval. In addition, a potentially damaging clause that would have given the SBVTAE the authority to establish college transfer programs in its schools had been deleted.[25]

This was not the first time that the SBVTAE had attempted to compete directly with the Center System and the branch campuses. While the legislators were debating the merger budget, the SBVTAE executive committee, in mid-February 1971, had endorsed a sweeping resolution: three Centers (Baraboo, Marshfield, Wausau) and one branch campus (Rice Lake) should be closed and their facilities turned over to the local vocational-technical district. In addition, careful study should be made of the Manitowoc, Marinette, and Sheboygan Centers to determine if they, too, should be taken over by a vocational school. Joseph Noll, President of the SBVTAE, supported these recommendations with the argument that the state could not afford both a college transfer campus and a vocational-technical school in communities with a limited potential student population. Noll asserted that a VTAE district could offer necessary college transfer courses without harm to its technical programs, thereby reversing the position he had taken just a few months earlier in testimony to the Kellett Commission. The following day, February 17, Noll elaborated on the recommendations when he presented them to the entire board of directors. He explained that the Mid-State Vocational, Technical and Adult Education School (Wisconsin Rapids) would centralize all of its health occupations courses at the Marshfield/Wood County Center, where it could collaborate with the Marshfield Clinic and Hospital. Noll described the Baraboo campus as "unsuccessful" in attracting sufficient students. Its facilities, he said, could be used as the nucleus of a vocational-technical operation which would serve the northern portion of the five counties in the Madison VTAE district. Likewise, either the Manitowoc or Sheboygan Center buildings could be employed in a similar manner by the Lakeshore VTAE district. In his remarks to the SBVTAE members Noll explained that these recommendations were trial balloons sent up to gauge the reaction from the public and the University of Wisconsin. Noll added that he expected the UW opposition to be strong—a prediction that proved very accurate. The full SBVTAE did not adopt the resolution, but it kept the issue alive by returning it to the executive committee for further study.[26]

In a joint statement, Chancellor Adolfson and Vice Chancellor Durward Long mounted a strong counter offensive to keep the Center System intact. They argued that Noll's proposal rested upon inflated enrollment estimates for the new schools because they included all of the currently enrolled Center students; Adolfson and Long believed that many, perhaps a majority, Center students would go directly to a four-year UW campus rather than enroll in VTAE-sponsored college transfer programs. The two men stressed the deliberate choice the host communities had made when they built their Centers and the commitment the state had made to equip and staff those facilities for a UW college transfer curriculum. To turn some Centers over to the SBVTAE would not only negate those agreements, but would override the strong public support of the Center System expressed at the Kellett Commission hearings. Long said it would make just as much sense for the Center System to take over some of the vocational-technical schools. Long also observed that the Centers enrollment problems would quickly disappear if their students' tuition and fees were reduced to the VTAE level.[27]

Noll floated these suggestions once more—in the last CCHE meeting he attended as President of the SBVTAE, in July 1971. During this session he said action should be taken "pretty damn quick" to demonstrate to legislators, who were then debating the merger budget, that the CCHE could make tough decisions. In his remarks Noll especially attacked the wheeling and dealing that had allowed the WSU-Stevens Point branch campus at Medford to be built. With a flourish Noll pronounced the Medford Campus "dead. It just has to lay down now."[28] Despite Noll's impassioned remarks, his bold proposal eventually died a quiet death, along with the CCHE, when the merger budget was approved.[29]

The merger of Wisconsin's fourteen two-year campuses—the seven members of the Center System at Baraboo, Janesville, Marshfield, Sheboygan, Waukesha, Wausau, and West Bend; the four branch campuses at Fond du

Lac, Medford, Rice Lake and Richland Center; and UW-Green Bay's 3-M campuses at Manitowoc, Marinette, and Menasha—presented some knotty problems to the authors of the merger bill. Governor Lucey had taken note of these issues in his proposals when he suggested that there were at least three options from which the legislators could choose: 1) create an enlarged, separate system of two-year campuses that reported directly to a merged UW System administration, 2) attach the campuses to a nearby four-year institution, or 3) require the campuses to operate cooperatively with a nearby vocational school.[30]

In June 1971, the CCHE staff released its analysis of these options. First, it noted that a "Super Center System" of fourteen campuses could readily be created without a large increase in central office costs, or the Center System central office functions could be returned to UW-Extension, which had operated the extension centers until 1964. Second, the central office could also be eliminated by attaching (nucleating) the two-year campuses to a nearby four-year public college, which would probably produce only a modest increase in the administrative costs of the parent institution. In its analysis of the third option, greater Center/VTAE cooperation, the CCHE staff conjectured that some savings could be achieved by eliminating duplicate programs and by expanding the VTAE college transfer programs, whose cost to the state was significantly less than that of the Centers.[31]

The merger budget, which passed in October 1971, did not include any details about how the merger should be consummated. Consequently, in November 1971, the new UW System Board of Regents asked Attorney General Robert W. Warren to provide advice on three questions: 1) should the merger of the two-year campuses take place at once, 2) should the regents postpone the appointment of a new Center System chancellor to replace Adolfson, who had announced his intention to retire at the end of June, 1972, and 3) should the branch campuses now be designated as Centers? In less than a month the Attorney General responded. Warren advised that the merger of all fourteen campuses should occur immediately, but that they should continue to operate under their respective Chapters of the Wisconsin Statutes (UW—Chapter 36, WSU—Chapter 37) until the Merger Implementation Study Committee had written a new statute. He said, further, that the search for a successor to Adolfson could begin immediately and that the branch campuses would, indeed, become Centers when they were detached from their parent campuses and brought into the Center System. Accordingly, UW System President John Weaver asked the Regents during their December 1971 meeting for permission to appoint a committee which would specifically help the fourteen two-year institutions achieve merger and a search and screen committee to advise him on the selection of Adolfson's successor. The Regents gave their unanimous permission.[32]

President Weaver moved quickly to appoint both committees. The search and screen committee had the important task of finding someone who could engineer the Center System's "merger within merger." As his retirement approached the accolades for Adolfson's long career mounted. He had begun his career with the Extension Centers in 1938 as a circuit riding political science instructor at the Sheboygan and Fond du Lac Centers, while he worked on his doctorate at Madison. Six years later, in 1944, Adolfson had been appointed to head the Extension Division, a position he held for twenty years. During that tenure he maintained Wisconsin's leading role in all aspects of Extension education; for example, he was among the first educators in the nation to urge the use of television to deliver educational programming. Then, in 1964, Adolfson had been chosen chancellor of the newly formed Center System. President Weaver noted in congratulatory remarks during Adolfson's final regents meeting, in June 1972, that he had given eight years of exemplary leadership as Chancellor and that "the greatest monument that is left in his wake . . . is the University of Wisconsin Center System."[33]

Just moments later Weaver announced that Dr. Durward Long had been selected as Adolfson's successor. But Long would be able to devote only a few days each month to the chancellor's office until October 1, when he would finish his consultancy on the California Master Plan for Higher Education. Long's academic training was in history, which he had taught at several southern universities, while gradually moving into administrative positions. Long had co-authored a book (*PROTEST: Student Activism in America*, 1970), and had written over two dozen history and higher education journal articles.[34] Clearly, President Weaver had selected Long from among the search and screen committee's candidates because of his previous experience as the Center System's vice chancellor. Weaver believed Long's familiarity with Wisconsin's higher education system made him the best choice to preside over the immediate merger of the state's fourteen two-year campuses. This would not be an easy task. The challenge not only involved implementing the merger, but also included overcoming the suspicions of the faculty of the seven Center System campuses to Long, personally, and wrapping up unresolved problems inherited from Adolfson.

The faculty of the seven Center System campuses had come to view Long as an opponent of strong faculty governance. Faculty were convinced that Long had been trying to dilute, perhaps even eliminate, the central role of their academic departments in governance and in recommending personnel actions. When Long, shortly after taking up his duties full time, rejected the recommendations of the Consolidation Task Force (CTF) for faculty governance and substituted his own charter, he confirmed the suspicions of many Center System faculty. Long's difficulties were compounded by the complicated task of trying to bring together fourteen two-year campuses which had three quite different backgrounds and experiences.

Among the issues left unresolved when Adolfson retired was a bitter struggle between Dean George Condon and his faculty at the Rock County Center in Janesville. On February 21, 1972, the faculty had turned down by just one vote a resolution asking Condon to resign. Before the vote, those faculty who wanted to force Condon out made several allegations of misconduct against him: that he had ordered department chairmen not to hire Madison graduates or anyone under 40 to teach at Rock County because they would likely be too radical, that he had attempted to have two professors transferred or fired because of personality conflicts, and that he had refused to support a department's recommended merit salary increase for a professor whose wife wrote for an underground newspaper. They also blamed the Dean for Rock's slumping enrollment which was due, in part they alleged, to his failure to support strongly a student recruitment program among African-Americans, Mexican-Americans, and poor whites. In March the number of anti-Condon faculty increased to 22 and they passed a resolution that labeled the Dean's performance as "unacceptable." Afterward, a faculty delegation visited Chancellor Adolfson and laid their case before him. After listening to them Adolfson indicated that Condon would not be replaced unless he resigned.[35] Shortly after Long was appointed Chancellor, a *Wisconsin State Journal* reporter sought him out and asked what he intended to do about the situation. Long said he would thoroughly review the case and that he would assure that all parties received due process. Long added that it appeared the anti-Condon faculty had not followed university due process procedures because they had not informed Condon of the allegations against him prior to the initial no-confidence vote. He also noted that Condon apparently intended to stay because the Dean had appealed to the citizens of Rock County for support.[36] This battle continued into the 1972 fall semester, when Condon resigned to take another position.[37]

The Center System Consolidation Task Force held its initial meeting in February 1972. The CTF had 17 members—15 chosen from among the administrators, faculty, staff, and students of the two-year campuses, a UW System representative, and a representative of the four-year campuses. The latter, Dr. Harold Hutchison, Vice Chancellor of the UW-Platteville, was chosen by President Weaver to head the CTF. During this inaugural meeting, the CTF organized itself into four subcommittees, one for each of the major areas in its charge: Faculty Governance, Instructional Organization, Mission Statement, and Clientele. Further, the CTF decided to hold its subsequent sessions on various Center campuses, to distribute widely its minutes, and to allow ample time for reaction to its decisions. Weaver asked the CTF to submit its recommendations to him by the end of May.[38]

Faculty governance immediately surfaced as the most prickly issue for the CTF to resolve. Faculty governance involved numerous problems which had to be solved wisely in order for the merged Center System to succeed. These problems concerned not just the faculty senate but also the division of decision-making authority among the faculty, the deans, and the Chancellor's office, the amount of local autonomy for each Center in personnel and curricular decisions, and the role that the existing Center System academic departments ought to play in governance and decision-making.[39]

The faculties of the seven Center System campuses naturally favored the existing governance structure, which was legislated in the UW statutes, and advocated expanding it to accommodate an additional seven campuses. The chairmen of the Center System academic departments lobbied the CTF hard to maintain the broad decision-making power of the departments in personnel and curricular matters. The department leaders stressed that this was necessary to maintain the transferability of Center System course credits and to maintain the high quality of the faculty. They feared that granting autonomy to each Center to make curricular and personnel decisions would result in a lowering of standards. In addition they noted that the Center System, between 1964 and 1969, had successfully operated a thirteen member institution via this structure.

The four Branch Campus faculties expressed strong opposition to simply expanding the existing Center System governance structure. They did not want most of the decision-making authority in the hands of system-wide academic departments. Their communications to the CTF argued that the departments would be very costly to operate and that it would be unwise to forge such a costly structure at a time when the pressure was on the University of Wisconsin to hold down spending. They also cited communication difficulties as mitigating against an efficient system-wide organization—a chairman could not possibly know each faculty member well enough to make an informed decision in personnel matters. Nor, could a chairman know the local factors which needed to be incorporated into curricular decisions at each Center. Consequently, they recommended that local campus committees be empowered to have the final say in personnel issues and in shaping the curriculum. In this structure, the academic departments would have primarily an advisory role.

The faculty of the three UW-Green Bay Centers—Manitowoc, Marinette, and Menasha/Fox Valley—told the CTF that they wanted more local authority than they had under Green Bay's highly centralized administrative system. Under Green Bay's tutelage the 3-M faculty had endured low salary increases, a lack of promotions, and curricular decisions which did not take into account local student needs. These faculties also thought their campus deans should participate in decision-making. But they did not oppose the academic departments also having a voice in both personnel and curricular issues. Thus the 3-M faculty, without spelling out a particular plan, took a position somewhere between giving exclusive authority to the academic departments or to local campus committees.[40]

Cost was a major consideration for the CTF as it studied the alternatives for faculty governance. UW central administration had become alarmed when a cursory budget review revealed that the cost per student was higher at a majority of the two-year campuses, compared to freshman/sophomore instruction at the degree-granting institutions. President Weaver had urged the CTF to make a start toward whittling down the Center System figure by making a cost effective decision.

Accordingly, Steve Bennion of Vice President Dallas Peterson's staff prepared a study which compared the costs of expanding the current Center System department structure with the cost of a system-wide divisional structure, which would be headed by four full-time divisional chairmen. Bennion estimated that the existing departments would spend about $153,000 in 1971-72, plus he predicted another $84,000 would have to be expended to serve seven additional Centers. Thus, Bennion's best guess was that an enlarged academic department structure would require approximately $237,000 in the first year of merger. He compared that figure with the projected $130,000 cost of a systemwide divisional structure and concluded that at least $100,000 could be saved if the CTF opted for the divisions rather than for the departments.[41]

Edward McClain, chairman of the Philosophy Department, who attended the CTF meeting at Rice Lake as the spokesman of the Center System department chairmen, sharply contested these figures. To start with, McClain noted, the 1971-72 estimates were far too high. For example, Bennion had pegged the Philosophy Department's cost at $11,800 while McClain testified that he would actually spend $2,900. Then, Bennion had not included an amount to operate fourteen local campus executive committees under the divisional system. McClain and his colleagues believed that it would cost about $10,000 per campus to operate those committees, for a total of $140,000. When this amount was added to Bennion's estimate of $130,000 to operate a systemwide divisional structure, retaining and expanding the present academic departments became the better bargain.[42] After McClain addressed the CTF, the members spent an hour in heated discussion over whose figures were more accurate. Finally, CTF Chairman Hutchison ruled that the Task

Force had to move on to other issues and should leave the shaping of a recommendation to the subcommittee on Faculty Governance. On May 22, 1972, right on schedule, Dr. Hutchison forwarded the final report of the Consolidation Task Force to President Weaver. In the transmittal letter, he reiterated that the most controversial issue had been whether the system-wide academic department structure of the Center System should be extended to fourteen campuses. Hutchison also noted that the CTF would not provide copies of the final report to anyone until Weaver had decided how and when he wished the report distributed.[43]

The Task Forces's final recommendation for faculty governance and instructional organization can only be described as complex. At each Center, the voting faculty were designated as those who had at least a half-time academic appointment and any staff persons granted "faculty status for purposes of governance." The faculty would be assigned, according to academic discipline, to one of five academic divisions—Biological Sciences, Humanities, Performing and Visual Arts, Physical Sciences, or Social Sciences. One divisional representative would be elected from each to a Center Executive Committee, whose membership would be brought to a total of seven by the selection of a chairman and chairman-elect by the entire Center faculty. The Center Executive Committee had a great deal of power. In addition to handling routine matters such as preparing the agenda for faculty meetings and making policy recommendations to the local faculty, it would make recommendations to the Center dean on all faculty personnel matters including appointments, merit increases, promotions in rank, and the awarding of tenure. The local Executive Committee, likewise, held the primary decision-making authority on curricular issues. The Executive Committee was directed to seek the "advice" of the appropriate Discipline Resource Committee in both personnel and curricular matters, but there was no stipulation requiring further consultation should the Executive Committee decide to ignore that advice.[44]

Each Center would elect at least one senator to the Center System Faculty Senate. A Center with more than 45 voting faculty would elect two senators and any Center which had more than 90 voting faculty would be entitled to a third senator. These senators would be joined by the five members of the Faculty Council, who would be chosen by the members of each of the academic divisions. The chairman of the Faculty Council would also chair the Faculty Senate, but neither the Chairman nor the Council members had voting rights in the Faculty Senate. The Faculty Senate's duties of course encompassed the responsibilities normally associated with faculty governance—the development and approval of policies "pertaining to areas of faculty concern, the establishment and staffing of committees, and supplying advice to the chancellor upon request."[45]

Even before the Consolidation Task Force sent its final report to President Weaver, the faculty and staff of the Centers were registering their approval or disapproval of its contents. Predictably, the reactions generally followed the lines laid down during the debate over governance. The faculty and staff of the former branch campuses strongly supported the CTF's proposal because it placed a good deal of power in the hands of the individual Center Executive Committees, while the faculty of the original seven UW Centers strongly condemned the recommendations for precisely the same reason. After this brief flurry of initial comments, silence reigned because most of the faculty were on summer break. During the summer President Weaver's staff studied carefully the CTF's proposals, paying particular attention to the budget implications.[46]

When Durward Long had been appointed Chancellor, in June, he was provided with the System administration's analysis. President Weaver urged Long to have a plan of action mapped out so that it could be rapidly implemented after he assumed his Center System duties full time on October first. Accordingly, on October 4, 1972, Long distributed his personal proposal for moving the fourteen Centers toward final merger by the end of the year.[47] Long noted that the Task Force deliberations had revealed "deep divisions which could not be resolved by any Solomon." Reacting to the broadly expressed displeasure with the CTF's elaborate and expensive structures for faculty governance and instructional organization, Long made bold to present his own plan and asked that it be accepted for a two-year trial period. Near the end of the trial period, a Charter Review Committee would be created to assess how well Long's governance system had worked. He also sent along the CTF proposal so that faculty, staff, and student governments could choose between that plan and his. In a separate letter to the Deans, marked "confidential," the Chancellor gave instructions for the two documents to be duplicated and distributed on October 11 and for the Deans to hold a special faculty meeting no later than October 13 to obtain the faculty's preference. Long closed his memo with the pointed observation that, "It is imperative that we do everything possible <u>to get acceptance of the alternative I am proposing</u> and as little conflict as possible (underline added)."[48]

Long's proposed Charter greatly streamlined the CTF's governance structure. His system-wide Collegium contained 22 voting representatives: 14 faculty members, 5 students, a dean, a librarian, and a student services representative. In place of the CTF's robust instructional organization, Long proposed just 13 academic departments (reduced from 19) whose chairmen and advisory committees would advise Center-based committees on faculty personnel and curricular issues. Long's plan, like that of the CTF, placed the primary responsibility for deciding these important faculty issues in the hands of faculty committees on each campus, rather than leaving it in the hands of the departments. At the local level the Charter provided for a campus collegium, which would also include students and professional staff members, a steering committee, and other committees necessary to carry out the collegium's responsibilities to oversee the curriculum and to provide advice to the chancellor on personnel actions.[49]

Late in the afternoon of October 13, Vice Chancellor Allan Hershfield telephoned each Dean to obtain the results of the special faculty meetings. When those were tallied, Long's Charter had easily defeated the Consolidation Task Force plan. Long quickly relayed this news to President Weaver and asked him to place his Charter on the Board of Regent's December agenda for approval.[50] When he appeared before the Regent Education Committee to discuss the Charter and the process used to secure approval of it, Long chose his words carefully and explained that his plan "...had support from a majority of faculty from a majority of the Centers." While these words accurately described the result, they did not convey the strong reservations voiced by many faculty, including some who had supported the Charter, that their options had been limited to two seriously flawed documents and that they had been pressured to vote without adequate time to analyze the alternatives. However, the major objection to Long's Charter was that the faculty had no input into drafting it, contrary to the statutory mandate that each UW faculty determine the form of its governance structure. Many faculty regarded Long's assertion that there had not been sufficient time for consultation as yet another of his flagrant attacks upon faculty self-governance. The Regent resolution, itself, noted that the Center System personnel had been under pressure to act quickly on a governance structure so that the merger of the two-year campuses could be expeditiously completed. But the Regent resolution left the door open for future change in the Charter by referring to it as an interim structure which might require amendment once the state legislature had enacted the merger implementation law. The Board of Regents, after hearing the report of the Education Committee, unanimously approved the resolution, thus completing the Center System's "merger within merger."[51]

While the Center System was concentrating on its own merger, the entire newly merged University of Wisconsin System was carefully watched to see if Governor Lucey's plan for public higher education would actually save money. In this context of close scrutiny of all aspects of the University's operation, the Center System repeatedly found itself under a budgetary microscope operated both by state and university officials. Actually, many of the Centers had operated for some time under a mandate to reduce their composite support index (CSI), which measured the average cost per student. For example, as noted earlier, one of then Vice Chancellor Long's major tasks in the late 60s and early 70s had been to reduce the Center System's CSI because it greatly exceeded that of the other UW campuses. And the four branch campuses had been under similar pressure from the WSU Board of Regents to reduce expenses; indeed, budget issues had delayed the construction of the Medford branch campus. Only the 3M Centers had escaped budgetary constraints, but that was primarily because Green Bay had kept those campuses' expenses to the bare minimum.

Governor Lucey and the state legislature kept the pressure on the University to trim its budget by keeping the 1972-73 UW budget at the premerger level. On May 19, 1972, a joint meeting of the Board of Regents and the members of the State Board of Vocational, Technical and Adult Education (SBVTAE) investigated whether the UW System and the Technical Schools could reduce their respective costs through greater cooperation. Because the Center System campuses were most like the Technical Schools, they naturally became a focal point of this discussion. In fact, the SBVTAE pressed the regents hard on the question of whether facilities could be shared by the Technical Schools and the Center campuses in Fond du Lac and Rice Lake. In Fond du Lac the Moraine Park Technical School lacked adequate space for its burgeoning enrollment while the adjacent Center was using just sixty percent of its capacity. The situation in Rice Lake was somewhat different—the Indianhead Technical School did not yet have its own campus and held classes at eight sites scattered around the city. The Barron County Center, too, had excess space and its enrollment projections suggested a steady or slightly declining enrollment. Thus, one solution to Indianhead's problem could be renting space from the Center, which would enable it to consolidate its classes at just three sites.[52]

During this same meeting the two boards also explored the feasibility of a complete merger of the Center System and the Vocational-Technical Schools. The consensus was that liberal arts Centers were not a good match for the Technical Schools and the state's citizens would be ill-served by combining the two systems. Those who spoke against a merger used arguments that had been voiced many times in the past when the legislature or CCHE had considered the same issue. For example Gene Lehrmann, Executive Director of the SBVTAE, said that the philosophy and objectives of the two types of campuses were substantially different and that, consequently, they each attracted students with different educational and vocational objectives. Regent Bertram McNamara reiterated that when mergers had occurred, the academic track by far had overshadowed technical education. Other regents pointed out that the Center host communities had made a heavy financial commitment to provide a liberal arts education to area citizens, a commitment which could not be ignored in any merger discussion. While the participants concluded that a union was not desirable, they did agree that the Technical Schools and the University had to intensify their cooperation to avoid duplication in programs and over-building their facilities, especially in communities where sharing would be practical. They also agreed to set up a small liaison committee of two members from each board who would meet periodically to discuss issues of common concern.[53]

Despite the agreements reached in May, in the fall the SBVTAE mounted a public campaign to obtain control over the Centers in Fond du Lac and Rice Lake. If successful, those Centers' liberal arts courses would just be dropped. Burt Zien, the SBVTAE member who leaked this scheme to the press before officially presenting it to the UW, justified this proposition by explaining that UW-Oshkosh was just 20 miles from Fond du Lac and could easily accommodate students who might have gone to the Center. At Rice Lake the distance would be greater, but the Barron County Center students could go either to UW-Stout (50 miles) or UW-Eau Claire (60 miles).[54]

Zien's proposal elicited a prompt response from the University. Among the options discussed in internal communications between System administrators and Regents McNamara and Bernard Ziegler, who were the regent members of the Liaison Committee, were 1) push for a complete merger, which the legislature would have to approve, in the expectation that this preemptive counterattack would confound the SBVTAE, 2) curb duplication and competition between the Center System and the Technical Schools by requesting the legislature to clearly differentiate the two systems' mission in a statute, and 3) counterattack by recommending that control over the three existing college-credit programs in the Technical Schools at Madison, Milwaukee, and Rhinelander (Nicolet) be transferred to the Center System.[55] By the time the liaison committee met in late October, both the VTAE and UW positions had been well aired in the state press. During that meeting Zien pressed hard the proposal that the two Centers be turned over to their respective VTAE districts. Regent McNamara repeatedly parried Zien's thrusts with the assertion that this was not a simple take-it-or-leave-it proposition, for its consequences would affect all of higher education in Wisconsin. The Board of Regents, McNamara said, needed more time to consider the ramifications of such a transfer. By the end of the session, the two SBVTAE representatives' ardor for the takeover had subsided considerably.[56]

In the midst of this furor, President Weaver and Executive Director Lehrmann quietly established three joint administrative committees: the Joint Administrative Committee on Academic Programs (JACAP), the Joint

Administrative Committee on Continuing Education (JACCE), and the Joint Administrative Committee on Physical Facilities (JACPF). All three, of course, were designed to increase cooperation between the UW and the Technical School systems. The first fruits of these endeavors appeared in December 1972 when the Board of Regents approved a proposal to permit the renting of Center facilities to the technical school districts in Fond du Lac and Rice Lake. The proposal also included a plan to review the curriculums of the rival campuses to eliminate overlapping courses and a plan for a low fee experiment at the two Centers, which would reduce the UW tuition to the fee level of the Technical Schools, $80.00 rather than $500.00 per year. The SBVTAE accepted the entire proposal during its January 1973 meeting.[57]

The low fee experiment ran for three years, from the Fall 1973 semester through the 1976 summer session. It provided an opportunity to test some theories about higher education in Wisconsin, especially whether the comparatively high UW tuition was forcing some students, who really desired a liberal arts education and a baccalaureate degree, to enroll in a technical school. A survey of the fall 1973 students at the Barron County and Fond du Lac Centers produced startling results which apparently confirmed the belief that high tuition was denying many students access to the University. Three hundred additional students had been attracted by the low fees and they pushed up the enrollment at these Centers dramatically (23% at Barron, 47% at Fond du Lac), while the entire Center System saw just a seven percent increase. However, a later study by Professor W. Lee Hansen of UW-Madison's Department of Economics concluded that the sharp increase in enrollment at the two Centers could not be ascribed solely to the low fees. Hansen discovered that convenient location was just as significant as the low fees in influencing students' decisions to enroll. He noted that both the Indianhead and Moraine Park Technical Schools had also experienced a surge in enrollment coincident with that of the Centers. Hansen's observation that the experiment cost the University about $600,000 in lost tuition revenue, which other Centers and other UW campuses had to cover from their revenues, no doubt carried a great deal of weight when the decision was made in 1976 not to continue the project.[58]

In the early months of 1973, as Governor Lucey and his staff worked on the 1973-1975 biennial budget, they issued a governor's policy paper which focused upon the Center System. Following tradition, they had sent the paper to the Legislative Audit Bureau to conduct a fiscal analysis. The LAB's report began by noting that the merged Center System's average cost of instruction for each full time student (this figure is the "composite support index" or CSI), had ballooned from a pre-merger $1,720 to $1,880, an increase of $160 per student. This increase had arisen primarily from three factors—the much higher CSI of the four former WSU branch campuses ($2,280), a decline in enrollment at some Centers, and the high inflation rate. The LAB also noted that the Center System's CSI was several hundred dollars per student higher than Madison's and Milwaukee's ($1,470), or that of the former WSU campuses ($1,320), for freshman and sophomore instruction.

Having laid out the numbers, the LAB report proceeded to analyze five alternatives for helping the Center System to reduce its operating budget. Two of the possible options concerned the Centers and the VTAE schools: should the two systems be merged or, a much less drastic remedy, required to coordinate better their respective course offerings and facilities usage, where a Center and a VTAE school were in close proximity? With regard to a merger, the LAB candidly observed that such a proposal would surely increase, not decrease, tensions between the SBVTAE and the Board of Regents because both would fight hard to gain control over the merged institution. Requiring more Centers/VTAE cooperation appeared to be both a reasonable and an achievable objective. However, the LAB reminded its readers of the very recent struggle between the Board of Regents and the SBVTAE over how best to solve the VTAE's shortage of space in Fond du Lac and Rice Lake. The joint discussions of the two governing boards, at least at the outset, had produced more controversy than cooperation. An obvious third option would be to close the five lowest-enrollment, highest-cost Centers. But the LAB study observed that in the past individual UW Centers with similar enrollments had been able to operate at a lower cost, so there was certainly a possibility that these five Centers (Medford, Richland, Barron County, Baraboo, and Fond du Lac) could reduce their CSI. Indeed, the fourth alternative suggested that costs could be reduced through a combination of increasing enrollments, increasing the faculty's teaching load, and decreasing support staff, perhaps by pairing Centers to share a dean, a business manager, and/or a student affairs director. The fifth LAB alternative—acknowledging the public service mission of the Centers and removing its cost from the instructional budget—was the only new proposal. But the removal of the almost insignificant $76,000 the Center System spent each year on its public service activities would have had a negligible impact upon the average CSI.

The LAB also discussed some policy changes the state government or the Board of Regents could make to assist the Center System. For example, the state could authorize the University to charge a significantly lower tuition at all Centers, which would presumably increase their enrollments. However, the reduced tuition income would have to be made up through tuition increases at the other UW institutions or by increased state funding specifically for the Center System. Either of these options would pit the Centers against the rest of the University in what no doubt would become a bruising battle. A perhaps less controversial policy change would be to include the Centers as active participants in a "regents statewide university," which was then under discussion. If that was done, the Center System would have to work more closely with UW Extension and would need to have its mission amended to include the authority to offer more adult and continuing education programs and even more public service activities. The proposed regents statewide university was yet another revival of the Wisconsin Idea—the obligation of the University to provide a variety of educational opportunities and information to citizens throughout the state. The LAB, in commenting positively on the Centers' potential role in providing credits toward a regents degree, said it made sense to utilize existing facilities rather than building new ones. But the LAB also issued a caution, if the Center System had to develop new programs to fulfill a new mission, those programs might also turn out to be high cost and compound the problem rather than solving it.

Finally, to conclude its analysis, the LAB presented some numbers and commented upon the impact various budget reductions would have upon the Centers. For the Center System to lower its average CSI in the 1973-75 biennium to its pre-merger level, over $1.3 million would have to be excised from its budget, a reduction of 8.52% over two years. The LAB observed that such drastic medicine, administered in a short time, could devastate the institution. So, instead, it recommended that the Center System be required to give up a lesser amount each year of the biennium, either $50.00 per student or $30.00 per student, for a cumulative budget reduction, respectively, of $839,700 or $503,820. In its concluding comments, the LAB backed a suggestion in the governor's policy paper that each individual Center be required to bring its CSI reasonably close to the Center System composite average CSI, but it did not recommend an acceptable deviation from that figure. From all of these options and analysis, the policymakers in the state government and in the University would shape their decisions.[59]

In mid May 1973 Chancellor Long made the startling announcement that he would leave his post at the end of September, after just a year on the job, to move to California to become a vice president at Berkeley. Long explained that he made this early announcement so that a successor might be selected by the time he departed.[60] Many faculty cheered Long's announcement. They felt that he had trampled on their traditional rights with his Charter; with his unilateral decision to telescope 19 academic departments into 13; and with continuing budget cuts, most of which came from reducing the number of faculty positions and increasing the faculty's teaching load—all decisions made without any consultation with a faculty committee. The record also reveals that Long had some problems with System administrators. For example, in June, President Weaver expressed his amazement when Long complained that he had not received a salary increase for the few months that he would serve in fiscal 1974. Weaver wrote that it never occurred to him that Long ". . . would expect an increase in salary for a year subsequent to your announcement of your resignation. There is no way, I would have thought you would have understood, that I could have persuaded the Board to approve such an action." On another occasion, when Weaver was writing a recommendation for Long, he cautioned the search committee to consider whether Long had "the sensitivity to handle the great range of personal relationships . . ." a college presidency requires, because he has an aggressive and hard-hitting administrative style which causes him sometimes "to run a little roughshod over people." On the positive side, Weaver described Long as "extremely bright in his analysis of problems," particularly in budgeting, and as an administrator who would make decisions and keep things moving.[61]

Because there were so many unanswered budget questions about the Center System, President Weaver did not follow Chancellor Long's suggestion to immediately initiate the search for his successor. Instead, the Board of Regents accepted Weaver's recommendation that an acting chancellor be appointed to serve until the various pieces of the budget puzzle had been sorted out.

Rather quickly, the System administrators also put aside Long's proposal that the Centers just be given more time to bring their budget under control because this proposal would require additional staff in the central office, especially in the business and payroll areas. Naturally, Weaver did not want any expansion to occur, even if in the long run it might prove a reasonable investment. Instead, some believed that the Center System administration ought to be remerged with Extension's administration.

UW-Stevens Point Chancellor Lee Dreyfus explored this option at length in his keynote speech to the 1973 annual Wisconsin Chamber of Commerce convention. As Dreyfus saw it, such a move would restore statewide visibility to Extension's outreach efforts and would provide important administrative savings to the Center System.[62] But Dreyfus's option would raise anew the old issue of a blurred identity for both the Center System and Extension—would the merged institution's major mission be college credit courses or non-credit adult education?

During the summer another plan emerged, one that seemed to provide help for both the Center System and Extension and allowed each to continue its special mission. This plan would create a new office of Provost for University Outreach and place both Extension and the Center System under its administrative umbrella. This plan would foster Weaver's desire to reinvigorate the Wisconsin Idea and would permit Extension to provide sorely needed business operations and payroll services to the Center System without an actual merger. Indeed, this option seemed brilliant—Extension would be spared the necessity of paring its administrative staff and the Centers would receive vital services at a far lower cost than by expanding its central office.

Also under discussion during the summer of 1973 were two very drastic propositions. One was "nucleation." Nucleation would dissolve the Center System and attach a Center, or perhaps two, to a nearby four-year UW institution. Thus, the Centers' high administrative expenses and CSI would disappear into the averages of the parent campuses. The other drastic solution would leave the Center System intact, but with fewer than fourteen members. This option would have the Board of Regents request that the state legislature, as required by the merger law, approve the closing of the highest-cost, lowest-enrollment Centers. Naturally this would reduce the Center System's budget, but it would also raise the specter that future budget difficulties could trigger more closures.[63]

During June and July President Weaver, his advisers, and Chancellor Long and his staff studied the various options for reducing the Center System's expenses. Their deliberations took place amid strong and frequently voiced expectations that the University's 1973-1975 biennial budget had to at least hold the line on spending, to support Governor Lucey's prediction that merger would save money. In the materials he sent to the members of the Board of Regents a few days before their August 1973 meeting, Weaver recommended creation of an office of Provost for University Outreach, which would oversee both the Center System and Extension. In an accompanying paper, Senior Vice President Donald Smith explained that this plan would immediately merge the budgeting, purchasing, and payroll operations of the two institutions to eliminate any need to expand the Center System's central office and, at the same time, utilize more fully the Extension staff. Indeed, Smith believed, the projected savings would be sufficient to finance the Provost's office for two to four years, during which time plans could be made and carried out to better coordinate the University's outreach programs. Smith also explained that an outright merger of the two units had been rejected because it "could in the end prove more costly," especially in terms of lower morale.[64]

In presenting the Provost proposal to the Regents, President Weaver explained that nucleation had not been pursued because it would totally destroy the progress the Center System had made within the past year toward "merger within merger" and because the WSU branch campus structure had proven only "erratically successful in holding down costs." The Center System, Weaver argued, deserved an opportunity to demonstrate that it could bring its costs under control. The Provost for Outreach option provided that opportunity with the least alteration to the existing Extension and Center System structures. In addition, this plan held the prospect for considerable long range administrative savings.⁶⁵

Chancellor Long, however, spoke against the President's proposal. He argued that the Provost's office was unnecessary because the Center System had already made great strides by reducing its biennial budget request by half a million dollars and by operating fourteen campuses with about the same number of central office staff who had previously managed just seven Centers. Long felt that the proposed plan sent a signal that the Center System could not properly manage itself and he insisted that implication was not true. Despite Long's plea for delay, the Regents only briefly discussed Weaver's recommendation and then unanimously approved it.⁶⁶

Agreement on a new administrative arrangement did not automatically remove the Center System from intense budget scrutiny. The legislature and governor had included in the biennial budget a requirement that the Regents and System Administration study all UW institutions to determine whether any of them should be closed because of high operating costs and/or low enrollments. Five Centers—Barron County, Fond du Lac, Manitowoc, Medford, and Richland—qualified for special scrutiny because of their unreasonably high CSIs, as did four baccalaureate institutions—Platteville, River Falls, Stout, and Superior. The Baraboo/Sauk County Center was added to this list when its fall 1973 enrollment plummeted from 301 to 267 students.⁶⁷

The Regents scrutinized the six high cost/low enrollment Centers via a mission hearing held on each campus. The public was invited to testify at these hearings. These sessions elicited a great deal of support for the six Centers. The citizens' testimonies reiterated that students saved a significant sum by beginning their college education while living at home, that smaller classes provided more individual instruction, and that the quality of instruction was excellent. In addition, adult (or non-traditional) students testified that they could handle a few classes each semester and still maintain their work and family obligations. Without a Center, they said, they would not have been able to attend college.⁶⁸

These hearings also brought forth suggestions of alternate solutions to the Center System's low enrollment problems. At Baraboo, for example, Leo Rodems, a former CCHE member, pushed the idea that capping the enrollment at Madison and Milwaukee would necessarily increase enrollments in the Centers and at the four-year campuses. Some witnesses pleaded for the low tuition program, which was just beginning in Rice Lake and Fond du Lac, to be extended to all Center campuses. Lowering the Center tuition to the VTAE level would enable many more students to afford to attend a Center. Richland's Acting Dean Marjorie Wallace urged that the Regents lift the 72 credit rule, which required Center students to transfer when they reached 72 credits, because some students could legitimately earn more than 72 credits toward their baccalaureate degrees at a Center.[69]

While public attention was focused on the mission hearings, System administrators worked with Center System leaders to prepare a greatly pared down biennial budget and to demonstrate that closing a Center would save very little money. For example, the state potentially could save $415,000 annually by closing down the Fond du Lac Center. But, the analysts pointed out this amount had to be adjusted by the additional expenses incurred when tenured faculty were employed by another Center ($189,917) and when students paid more to attend another UW institution ($156,000). And Fond du Lac County would be saddled with repaying a $3.3 million debt. Indeed, the investigators speculated that the state might be liable to repay $1.84 million of that debt, itself, if the Fond du Lac Center buildings were no longer used for educational purposes because the state had endorsed the county's Title I grant proposal for that sum. If this came to pass, the state would have to wait several years before realizing any fiscal benefit from shutting down the Fond du Lac Center. Finally, the economic impact report noted that the host community would suffer an annual economic loss very close to $3.0 million. The numbers for the other five Centers included in the analysis—Baraboo/Sauk County, Barron County, Manitowoc, Medford, and Richland—revealed similar results. The state could save a few hundred thousand dollars in each instance, but many costs would be laid upon someone else and the impact upon the host community would be devastating.[70]

Ultimately, System Administration proposed that the Center System's budget be gradually reduced by about $1.5 million. Large segments of this sum would be drawn from three major areas. First, the Center System would repay UW System $458,000 through adjustments in the enrollment funding formula. Second, increasing the faculty teaching load at the ten former UW Centers from nine to twelve credit hours per semester would save $409,000. In addition, some instructional dollars would be saved by offering low enrollment courses less frequently and by eliminating a few such courses from the curriculum. Third, savings of $207,000 would be realized from cutbacks in support programs, such as student services and maintenance. Lesser amounts would be saved from a variety of other efforts, such as the reduction of summer session programs by twenty percent and a reduction in the number of promotions to associate and full professor by ninety percent. If all of these plans came to fruition, the impact upon the cost per student at the most expensive Centers would be dramatic: Manitowoc's cost per student would decline $100.00, Medford's $422.00, and Richland's $831.00. In addition, the Center System's composite CSI would be significantly reduced.[71]

In late August 1973, the final details were worked out to appoint Barron County Dean John Meggers the acting chancellor of the Center System when Chancellor Long departed for California. Meggers, a native of Sheboygan, had earned his undergraduate degree from Oshkosh and had later completed both his master's and doctorate at Madison. Because Meggers would be spending much time away from his family in Rice Lake, President Weaver decided that he should receive the full salary and exercise the full authority of a chancellor. System administration also agreed to provide extra staff support for the special projects the central office would have to undertake to accommodate the budget reductions. Dr. Meggers' appointment was officially announced at the September 1973 Board of Regents meeting.[72]

In December 1973, the Board of Regents adopted a resolution, requested by Acting Chancellor Meggers, that promised no Center would be closed during the 1973-1975 biennium. However, Regent support beyond the end of the biennium was contingent upon two conditions or "tripwires," as they were quickly labelled. First, if the average cost per student for the entire Center System exceeded the average costs for a comparable group of two-year university centers, the Regents would reassess their continued support. Second, any individual Center whose average cost per student exceeded the Center System average by 20% or more for two consecutive years would be subjected to special scrutiny.[73]

Naturally, Acting Chancellor Meggers immediately focused most of his attention upon plans to assure that no individual Center snagged the 120% tripwire set by the Board of Regents. But the prospect that Medford could avoid setting off that alarm was especially bleak—its cost per student was the highest in the Center System and its fall 1973 enrollment numbered just 131 students. Meggers' own former Center, Barron County, despite its healthy 1973-74 enrollment of 506 students, was perilously close to the 120% CSI tripwire, as was Richland, whose fall 1973 enrollment totalled 300.[74]

During the summer months of 1974 the Chancellor's Search and Screen Committee worked hard to fulfill its responsibility to recommend to President Weaver several candidates for the Center System's vacant position. Acting Chancellor Meggers aggressively sought the appointment, but ultimately Dr. Edward B. Fort, the Superintendent of Schools in Sacramento, California, was selected. From the list of candidates forwarded by the screening committee, Weaver had interviewed only Meggers and Fort. Weaver tried to assuage Meggers' disappointment by writing him that the decision was "a narrow judgement call" and that it in no respect reflected a lack of confidence in Meggers' leadership ability.[75] Indeed, behind the scenes Weaver was poised to appoint Meggers in the event that Fort could not secure a release from his contract in Sacramento.[76]

Weaver announced Fort's appointment on August 13, 1974, and the Board of Regents confirmed the decision during its September session. The new chancellor assumed his duties at the beginning of October and Acting Chancellor Meggers returned to his duties as dean of the Barron County Center. Edward Fort, a native of Detroit, had earned his baccalaureate and master's degrees from a hometown institution, Wayne State University. He earned his doctorate, in English, from the University of California at Berkeley. Fort had gained broad experience as a teacher and administrator in the Detroit public schools, prior to becoming the head of the Sacramento public school system. In his remarks describing Dr. Fort's qualifications to the Regents, President Weaver stressed that Fort had acquired "substantial administrative experience and budget management capabilities" that would be put to good use in the Center system. Most noteworthy, of course, was the fact that Ed Fort was an African-American, the first black to be appointed to head an institution within the University of Wisconsin System.[77]

In early November 1974, while Chancellor Fort worked hard to grasp the complexities of the Center System, Governor Patrick Lucey overwhelmed his Republican challenger, William Dyke, to capture a second four-year term. During the campaign, which featured a series of debates between Lucey and Dyke, the candidates focused primarily upon economic issues. A brief Arab-Israeli war in the waning months of 1973 had convinced the Organization of Petroleum Exporting Countries (OPEC) to place an embargo upon sales of crude oil to the United States to punish the Americans for their lop-sided support of Israel during repeated Middle East crises. The effect of this embargo, even though it lasted just five months, was dramatic. Prices for petroleum products leaped 350% almost overnight. The ripple effect of this tremendous upsurge in oil prices looked ominous for the nation's economy—a leap in the inflation rate (1973-6%, 1974-11%), a rise in unemployment, and eventually a slowdown in the entire economy. Indeed, a long recession began in 1975.[78]

Consequently, economic issues were very much on the minds of Wisconsin voters, who expected to hear from the candidates how they would meet the constitutional requirement that the state budget be balanced. Once again the University of Wisconsin did not figure as an important issue in the campaign. Indeed, the only comment Governor Lucey made about the University came during one of the debates in response to a question about the 1975-1977 biennial budget. On that occasion, he said that he would not include in his budget proposal, if reelected, money to offset a tuition decrease suggested by the Board of Regents. The Regents' formula was designed to hold the level of tuition at twenty-five percent of instructional costs, but Lucey said that UW students would have to bear their share of the economic pain that loomed on the horizon. When his turn to respond came, candidate Dyke tersely agreed with the Governor's assessment of the Regents' request.[79] In view of the general economic climate, it seemed clear that the University System would experience other blows to its 1975-1977 budget proposal by the time Governor Lucey and the legislature finished their work.

Seven

The Center System and the Scope Reduction Report: 1979-1982

Escalating oil prices compelled the Governor to immediately adjust the state budget. Just three weeks after his reelection, in November 1974, Lucey sent a letter to all state departments instructing them to save one percent of their 1974 fiscal year budget in the next seven months. The Governor also issued specific directives to freeze hiring, to curtail state employees' travel, to ban new consultancy contracts, to reduce printing expenses, and to sharply cut back overtime expenditures. The University's central administration quickly decided to prorate the burden among all the System's institutions. The Center System's share was $98,379. When Chancellor Fort relayed this discouraging news to the deans, he noted with alarm that this sum would be added to the Regents-required productivity savings of $140,000 for fiscal year 1974.[1]

A short time later, Regent President Frank Pelisek received more bad news from the Governor. Lucey began his letter by reminding the Regents of the great commitment Wisconsin taxpayers had made and sustained over many decades to assure both broad access to the University and the high quality of its programs. He underscored this point by observing that Wisconsin's per capita support of the UW ranked third in the nation, despite her 27th rank in per capita income. Then, he flatly stated that this level of support could not continue in these severe economic times. Specifically, Lucey informed Pelisek that, in the 1975-1977 budget, there would be no increase for supplies and expenses (S&E); a reduction in the amount of state dollars for support services, computing services, and instructional supplies; and no additional state dollars to accommodate any increased enrollment. He suggested the faculty's workload be increased to absorb additional students. The Governor closed his letter by admonishing the University of Wisconsin to maintain the high quality of its educational programs as it planned how to meet these budget constraints. Accordingly, to meet this challenge, he directed the Board of Regents to provide to him, by April 15, 1975, a plan for "phasing out, phasing down, or consolidating existing centers, campuses, colleges, and programs of the System." Thus began what quickly became known as the "scope reduction study."[2]

Shortly thereafter, on January 19, 1975, the *Milwaukee Journal* Sunday edition carried a long article that summarized the findings of budget analysts in the Department of Administration (DOA). Among DOA's recommendations were several directly affecting the Center System: 1) closure of the Medford and Richland campuses; 2) transfer of seven Centers (Baraboo, Barron County, Fond du Lac, Manitowoc, Marinette, Marshfield, Washington County) to the VTAE System and reduction of their state support to the VTAE average of $750.00 per student, and 3) transfer of control over four Centers to nearby four-year University of Wisconsin institutions (Fox Valley and Sheboygan to UW-Oshkosh, Marathon to UW-Stevens Point, and Rock County to UW-Whitewater). Consequently, only the Waukesha Center would remain an independent two-year campus, and even it would be constrained to operate within a budget pegged at the average per student cost for Level 1 instruction (freshman-sophomore courses) of the University Cluster. This restriction promised to slash Waukesha's budget by approximately $300.00 per FTE student, a 15% reduction.[3]

The DOA claimed that the state would save about $3.3 million during the 1975-77 biennium if the governor and legislature implemented all of its recommendations. However, it acknowledged that the savings could be reduced by $150,000, if the state had to assume the debt service for the Taylor and Richland County construction bonds; and, in the worst case scenario, if the state was required to repay entirely the grants obtained from the federal government for these facilities, the savings would drop to a meager $210,000.

The DOA study also admitted that the transfer of seven Centers to the VTAE System could occur only if some very knotty issues could be resolved. One of those questions involved the VTAE System's lack of enthusiasm for more college parallel programs; the issue was certain to arise because merger was likely to touch off a struggle for control in each new dual-track institution between the academic and the vocational-technical personnel. Another large obstacle was the cost of accommodating those tenured Center System faculty who refused voluntarily to transfer to the VTAE schools. Moreover, the DOA estimate failed to assess the negative economic impact of closing Medford and Richland upon their host communities or upon families who would now have to send their students to another UW institution.

The authors of this study contended that, "It [economic impact] is a consideration that should really not play a part in determining what the educational value of a campus is." They argued that the University had overbuilt during the sixties and that the location of some of the Centers appeared to be the result of political trade-offs between the WSU and UW Systems, without regard for economic and educational necessity. The evidence of the political struggles between the WSU and UW Systems in the 1960s, as described in Chapter Five, to gain control over as much of Wisconsin higher education as possible supports the DOA Study's conclusion. However, its hard-hearted dismissal of the adverse economic impact upon a community whose UW Center campus would be closed appears in sharp contrast to state government's willingness to assist private businesses to continue operations so that the state could avoid the much higher costs of assisting a community which lost an important employer.

The DOA study also made recommendations about three smaller baccalaureate institutions—Platteville, River Falls, and Superior. These four-year campuses had been singled out because their current and projected enrollments for the early 1980s would remain under the 5,000 FTE students required to be cost effective. However, these institutions were to be closed only as a last resort; first, the UW could phase out any under-enrolled majors and eliminate departments and colleges to bring costs under control. The study also suggested that System Administrators discuss with University of Minnesota officials a possible merger of Superior and River Falls with the Minnesota campuses at Duluth and Minneapolis, respectively.

Once the press corps learned of the DOA report, they rushed to the governor's office to ask about his view of its recommendations. They were aware that the governor had received the report about five weeks before he sent his letter to Regent President Pelisek and they wanted to know whether he had used it in drafting his November directive to the University, and whether he would preempt the Regents' deliberations by including any of the DOA's proposals in his 1975-1977 budget. Robert Dunn, the Governor's executive secretary, explained that Lucey had not yet read the report and that the Governor would await the University's report before drawing any conclusions about closing campuses. Lucey's press secretary, Jeff Smoller, reiterated this point by saying, "Lucey will not recommend any campus closings in his budget bill."[4]

Reporters also sought reactions from various University officials. Regent Vice President Bertram McNamara labelled the suggestion that Medford and Richland be shut down as a "trial balloon." McNamara disputed the DOA's estimate of the savings from closing these campuses, noting that it omitted costs that would inevitably continue, such as state support for Medford and Richland students who enrolled elsewhere and the salaries of faculty who transferred to other System campuses. Senior Vice President Donald Smith sharply criticized DOA's decision to ignore economic impact in its calculations. Smith also predicted it would be six to eight years before any savings would be realized, concluding that, "[The] projected savings in this biennium are pure fiction." Chancellor Fort echoed these observations. He added that even if the entire $3.3 million could be captured in fiscal 1976, the net savings would be a minuscule .006% of the annual $495 million UW System budget. Fort especially disagreed with DOA's suggestion that seven Centers could be easily transferred to the VTAE System. He cited his knowledge of California's junior colleges, which were the scene of expensive, ongoing power struggles between the academic and vocational-technical faculties. Indeed, Fort predicted that such a merger would actually result in higher costs.[5]

Roger Gribble, education reporter for the *Wisconsin State Journal*, sought out reactions to the possible closing of the Richland Campus. Richland's Dean, Marjorie Wallace, related that about seventy citizens had gathered on the campus the day after the story broke to develop a strategy to "shoot down the DOA trial balloon." Asked to comment on the subject, Wallace insisted that a merger of Centers with VTAE schools would not save the taxpayers' money because the VTAE System per student cost of $2,040 was higher than the Center System average of $1,964 per FTE student. A merger would merely shift expenses from the state budget to the property taxpayers of the vocational-technical school districts. Richland's State Representative Joanne Duren (D-Cazenovia) and State Senator Kathryn Morrison (D-Platteville) pledged strong support to keep Richland open. Duren emphasized that this Center provided access to public higher education for people who otherwise would not have an opportunity to take college courses. Richland County Board Chairman Foster Patch bluntly promised, "there'll be a battle if the legislature actually receives a proposal to shut down the Center."[6]

While the public reactions of UW System administrators to the DOA study were politely critical, such was not the case within the confines of the

System offices in Madison's Van Hise Hall. There, UW System staff members Elwin Cammack, Gene Arnn, and Jim Kolka drafted "Alternatives for Dealing With the Problem of Underutilized Center System and University Campuses." This hard-hitting critique blasted the unwarranted assumptions, the overblown estimates of savings, and the anti-UW tenor of the DOA paper—a paper these men labelled a "polemic." They contended that DOA's budget people displayed a bias toward a "quick fix" budget cut that required very drastic measures to achieve a very modest reduction in the state's general public revenue (GPR) support of the University System. Indeed, Cammack, Arnn, and Kolka stressed that the estimated savings from campus closings were inflated primarily because closing and transition expenses had not been taken into account. For example, no attempt was made to calculate the increased cost to UW-Madison's engineering department should Platteville be eliminated, thus forcing its engineering students onto the Madison campus. The DOA estimates also conveniently overlooked the fact that tenured faculty contracts required a one year notice of a layoff, so even if a Center or a Campus could be quickly closed down, the obligation to continue faculty and other salaries would almost wipe out the short term savings. This document challenged each of the DOA's calculations and conclusions and raised important policy questions.[7]

During its January 1975 meeting, the Board of Regents unanimously directed President Weaver to appoint and convene a System Advisory Planning Task Force to "define those actions which, by reducing the size of the System, would help to generate over the next four to six years the resources needed to maintain the quality and health of the System as it would then be organized."[8] The Task Force would need to work quickly to meet Governor Lucey's mid-April deadline. Within two weeks Weaver announced that he had chosen 29 administrators, faculty, and students to be members of the Task Force and that he had selected Senior Vice President Donald Smith to chair the group. From the Center System, Chancellor Fort and Assistant Professor Veldor Kopitzke (Business Administration/Economics, Fox Valley) were appointed. Wilson Thiede, Provost for University Outreach, whose domain included UW Extension and the Center System was also named to the group. During its initial meeting the Task Force divided itself into four study groups, each of which was assigned the task of examining a particular perspective: Committee 1—Phase out of universities and centers; Committee 2—Phase down of institutions through phase out of schools and colleges; Committee 3—Phase out, phase down or consolidation of academic or support programs; and Committee 4—Alternative approaches to planning for the 1980s.

Each study committee was directed to consider several factors in its deliberations, such as the correlation between a campus's current enrollment and its projected 1984 enrollment, the number of UW institutions in a service area, the ratio of current and projected enrollment to campus capacity, and, of course, the average cost per student.[9] Even before the Task Force was appointed, President Weaver had attempted to reassure the chancellors that the Task Force would not, itself, decide what ought to be closed or scaled down, but rather would develop criteria to use in reaching such decisions and would run simulations in an attempt to predict the consequences of applying those criteria.[10]

Committee 4, responsible for suggesting "Alternate approaches to planning for the 1980s," ran a simulation to determine the potential savings if the Marathon County, Marshfield/Wood County, and Medford Centers were consolidated with the UW-Stevens Point. The logic behind this particular simulation was that these three Centers were within 35 miles of one another and two of them (Marathon and Marshfield) were not much farther from Stevens Point. Using Fall 1973 enrollment data for the three Centers and Stevens Point's formula for allocating a full time faculty position, the model suggested that 54 FTE faculty would be sufficient to staff the classes at the Centers, a reduction of 18 faculty. This would generate a savings of $216,000 ($12,000 average x 18). The simulation also calculated savings from transferring most of the administrative functions from Marathon, Marshfield, and Medford to Stevens Point at $89,000 (reduction of 7 FTE administrators), to produce a total potential saving of $305,000.[11]

In addition to stressing the relative proximity of the four campuses, the study group noted that projections for the 1980s indicated that the enrollment at all four would decline. Thus, this simulation suggested a solution that would help the three Center System campuses and UW-Stevens Point. At the same time, the Committee admitted the Centers' students would experience some disadvantages. Obviously, these students would have little direct access to student services, especially counseling, business office operations or the commuting faculty. In fact, the Committee speculated that the Medford resident faculty could eventually be entirely phased out, so those students would have no full time university personnel on campus to assist them. Finally, it was noted that there would be a short term workload increase for Stevens Point personnel, but that would be resolved in the early eighties, when the projected enrollment decline began.[12]

Responding to an invitation for comments, Medford Dean Darwin Slocum, whose campus had been a branch of UW-Stevens Point until the merger, indicated that he and his faculty and staff did not desire to renew that relationship. Since merger, Medford's course offerings had been broadened to enable her students to transfer readily anywhere in the UW System, rather than being funneled primarily to the Stevens Point Campus. Slocum also told the Committee that the Center System's greatest strength arose from the varied backgrounds of the personnel of the 14 Centers, whose talents could be pooled to solve problems. Chancellor Fort echoed Slocum's comments and predicted that the proposed elimination of virtually all student services personnel from the three Centers would mean rapidly declining enrollment because students, particularly freshmen, needed readily accessible advising and counseling services. Fort also asserted that the expenses necessary to maintain a commuting faculty (one-fourth release time and travel reimbursement), would consume a significant amount of the estimated savings. The Chancellor passed along the Marathon Center's concern that its enrollment would drop precipitously when its curriculum became geared to Stevens Point's course offerings, because Marathon had traditionally stressed transferring students to UW-Madison. In conclusion, Fort stated that this plan would do serious harm to the Center System, while producing very little monetary savings for the University System and the state. [13]

Committee 1 of the Task Force had the assignment to study "phase out of universities and centers" that elicited the most widespread fear throughout the University of Wisconsin System. Four University Cluster campuses—Green Bay, Platteville, River Falls, Superior—and five Centers—Baraboo/Sauk County, Barron County, Marinette, Medford, Richland—were chosen for this simulation because of their low enrollment, high cost per student, projected enrollment decline, and geographical proximity to another UW institution. This lengthy "hit list" caused so much alarm and rumor-spreading that System Vice President Donald Smith felt compelled to write all the chancellors to remind them that this was just a study of options and that "no prior judgements have been made about when any closings may actually occur." Smith urged the chancellors to stress this point in the midst of "all the inevitable rumors." [14]

A lengthy list of questions was considered in simulating the elimination of each Center. These questions were arranged in four broad categories: Educational Consequences, Human Consequences, Fiscal Consequences, and Economic Consequences. The educational consequences of closing the five Centers would be minimal because students could enroll in similar freshman and sophomore courses elsewhere in the UW; however, the communities would be deprived of the cultural and social activities these Centers provided. The assessment of the human consequences produced sharply contrasting results. While most students, it was believed, could pursue their educational goals elsewhere, the employment outlook for the faculty and staff was bleak. There was a surplus of university teachers nationwide, and the local economies provided few job opportunities that would match the salaries staff persons presently received. The examination of the fiscal consequences naturally focused upon potential savings of state revenue. But this, too, was a complicated calculation, for the simulation model had to reduce savings by the cost of educating each student who enrolled in another UW institution, the expense of terminating tenured faculty, the salary of any faculty who found a position elsewhere in the UW, and any federal grant funds the state might have to repay. The economic consequences, ultimately, were not calculated because it took longer than anticipated for the state Department of Administration and the UW System staff to produce the data.[15]

Using Fall 1974 student data, Committee 1 discovered that each Center served primarily a very local clientele, for almost 80% of these five campuses' students lived within a 25 mile radius of the Center. This data also revealed that almost two-thirds of the students were recent high school graduates, while the remainder were over age 21. Medford deviated from this pattern because it drew about half of its scholars from the non-traditional pool. Medford used this figure as evidence that it provided vital access to the UW for many Taylor County citizens. These statistics failed to address the key question: how much money could Wisconsin save by closing these five Centers? The model estimated the savings at various points in time—the Centers being closed immediately (1975), in 1980, in 1986, and in 1992. The latter three calculations were founded upon enrollment projections. The largest sum, almost $610,000, would be gained if all five were closed immediately and if, as the statisticians assumed, 80% of the non-traditional students did not enroll in another UW institution. As is evident in the accompanying chart (see page 133), the projected savings declined after 1975 Moreover, if all the Centers' students continued their education in the University of Wisconsin, the state would have to pay an additional $437,000 to accommodate them.[16]

In mid March 1975, the System Advisory Planning Task Force transmitted its findings to President Weaver, who circulated drafts of the report to his staff in Van Hise Hall, asking for their comments and advice. Most noteworthy were Steve Bennion's observations to Vice President Donald Percy. Bennion contended the Centers were not "Launched with the idea that their instructional costs would approximate" those of the smaller four-year campuses. As proof, Bennion cited the Board of Regents' pre-merger decision in the 1960s to keep the Centers' tuition below that charged of either UW-Green Bay or UW-Parkside. This policy, which had been continued since the merger, suggested that access was the "major intent in building the Centers to expand educational opportunity throughout the state." Bennion remarked that the Center System already was making its salary dollars go farther by keeping a much greater percentage of its faculty at the instructor and assistant professor ranks, compared to the University Cluster. He also observed

DATA FROM SIMULATION OF CLOSING FIVE CENTERS

Center	% Traditional	%Non-Traditional	% of Students 25 mi. radius	Savings to State (Assume 80% of non-trads do not continue)				(COST) to State 1975 All Students Continue
				1975	1980	1986	1992	
Baraboo Sauk Co.	60.4	39.5	89.0	$117,504	$107,912	$91,126	$93,524	($61,897)
Barron Co.	78.6	27.6	77.0	$164,776	$150,322	$106,960	$138,277	($176,182)
Marinette	57.7	40.0	59.0	$133,092	$127,097	$87,529	$88,728	($57,503)
Medford	55.0	50.0	94.0	$75,884	$64,386	$49,439	$51,739	($56,929)
Richland	66.1	36.8	79.0	$118,260	$76,212	$76,212	$76,212	($84,320)
TOTAL	63.6	38.8	79.6	$609,516	$525,929	$411,266	$448,480	($436,831)

*Based on Fall 1974 student data, % do not total 100% exactly.
Source: Book I. Report of the System Advisory Task Force, March 1975.
Chapter IV: Summaries of Simulation Studies, pp. 58-114.

that the Centers could not squeeze more dollars from its instructional program without calling into question the quality of the curriculum. He concluded by noting that the Centers were worn out from all the scrutiny that had been focused upon them since the late 1960s; it was time to leave them alone or make a straight-forward recommendation to close the two or three smallest Centers.[17] John Weaver presented his "Scope Reduction Report" to a special meeting of the Board of Regents on April 18, 1975. Seating space in the Board Room, on the 17th floor of Van Hise Hall, was at a premium because members of the press and keenly interested administrators and faculty representatives had flocked to the meeting. The President began by dramatically describing the UW's dilemma—how to balance the tension between budget, quality, and access, so that the Wisconsin Idea could continue to thrive. He observed that Governor Lucey had admonished the UW not to expect any increase in state GPR support during the 1975-1977 biennium. Indeed, the UW was being asked to reduce its budget request by almost $10 million and to absorb a predicted $19 million in inflationary price increases during the upcoming biennium. Given those fiscal facts, he questioned how the University could absorb the predicted additional 6,000 students and reduce its expenses without harming the quality of the academic program. Weaver believed that access to the UW would have to be scaled down by raising admission standards, capping enrollments, or closing some campuses or Centers. For the University to accept more students without an increase in state resources, Weaver thought, was "an inescapable prescription for irreversible mediocrity."[18]

Weaver then turned to the closure simulations that had been conducted. The trial runs clearly indicated that substantial savings would be realized only if a closure was accompanied by a limit on enrollment. If a substantial number of students from a closed campus enrolled elsewhere, almost no savings would be realized. In addition to less access to the UW, a closing also meant a loss to the host community in intellectual, cultural, recreational, and economic benefits. Weaver reiterated his plea that state government find a way to stabilize the System budget, so that citizens' access to higher education and the high quality of the UW's academic programs could be maintained.[19]

Weaver then presented his "decision agenda for Wisconsin state government"—an agenda that contained just two options. State government, Weaver said, had to choose between A) ordering the University of Wisconsin System immediately to begin to reduce its scope and to limit access or B) allowing the Board of Regents to continue its "current planning approach to accommodating an uncertain future." If Option A were selected, Weaver suggested the state could direct the Board to phase out up to three Centers (Baraboo, Medford, Richland) by 1977, or to mandate an alternate use for those Centers, such as having UW-Extension establish a "life-long learning center" at each campus. Secondly, by 1979, selected four-year campuses would be closed and, finally, by 1981, the University's budget would be reduced to reflect the savings. The President added the ominous observation that, if any four-year campuses were to be shut down, all of the nearby Centers ought to be closed first in an effort to shunt sufficient enrollment to that institution to permit it to survive. If the governor and legislature selected Option B, then Weaver pledged the continuation of the systemwide "program audit and review" process to eliminate unwarranted duplication of academic majors.[20]

Having placed the current three smallest Centers on the table as possible candidates for closure or mission redefinition, President Weaver spelled out the criteria to be used to decide whether a particular Center needed "special scrutiny." Weaver suggested that no course of action be chosen until meetings had been held with the Center's faculty, staff, and community members, and an open hearing had taken place. Then, the Board would make its decision and spell out the legal and policy steps required to implement its decision. If the recommendation was to shut down a Center, all this information would be passed on to the governor and legislature, who would make the final decision.[21]

Because the Center System had loomed so large in the Task Force's work and in the President's Report, Chancellor Fort was invited to address the Regents. He questioned the Department of Administration's predictions that the current economic doldrums would continue for several years and that the

UW's enrollment would decline sharply in the 1980s. Fort observed that the enrollment of significant numbers of older students was already making earlier projections inaccurate. From a historical point of view, Fort asserted that the Centers had been founded with the idea that they would not be as cost effective as a larger institution, but rather their purposes were to provide, at relatively low cost, greater access to the University, a smaller class size, and a personalized education. Fort reminded his listeners that closing small Centers would generate only negligible, or, probably, no savings. He called upon state government to renew its support of the Wisconsin Idea and to provide the University System with adequate resources.[22]

After considerable discussion, the Board of Regents unanimously adopted Weaver's Report as its plan of action.[23] Thus, the smaller Centers would have to at least avoid the "tripwire" which stipulated that if any Center's cost-per-student exceeded the Center System average by 20% or more for two consecutive years, it would be given special scrutiny to determine whether closure was warranted. And it appeared that the entire Center System might be heading into dark days, depending upon the directives included in the 1975-77 Biennial Budget bill.

Now the focus of attention shifted to the State Capitol at the other end of State Street. In his letter of transmittal, Regent President Frank J. Pelisek emphasized the most prominent conclusion drawn from the Task Force's data, ". . . a decision to close down a particular campus will not produce major dollar savings," unless the state, at the same time, releases the System from any obligations to accommodate the displaced faculty and students.[24] When reporters queried Democrat Senator William Bablitch (Stevens Point), a co-chairman of the powerful Joint Finance Committee, about his reaction to the Regents' recommendations, he said that campus closings should not be included in the budget bill, so that this important issue could receive the intense study it deserved.[25] However, a few days later Department of Administration Secretary Anthony Earl told the press that he was trying to find a Democrat legislator who would move to insert just that provision into the budget bill. Earl believed the Regents should be granted the authority to close Centers without legislative approval. He added the observation that the ". . . Centers at Medford, Baraboo, and Richland Center are thought to be expendable."[26]

Most of the attention, quite naturally, concentrated upon the deliberations of the Joint Finance Committee, to which the majority Democrats looked for guidance on the biennial budget. On the second of May, the JFC reached consensus on a three-point resolution addressed to the Board of Regents, which included a directive to the Regents to "Proceed during 1975-77 with the development of plans to phase out or otherwise change the use of

Centers failing to meet performance criteria set by the Regents." The Board was further instructed to send a progress report on its development of these plans to the Legislature by October 15, 1975.[27] The next three weeks were filled with maneuvers by various factions concerned with the Centers' future. In the end, the Assembly passed a resolution, sponsored by state Representatives Joanne Duren (D-Cazenovia), Michael Farrell (D-Racine), and Norman Anderson (D-Madison), which deleted campus closings or phase downs from the budget bill.[28] Nonetheless, the Center System, and especially the Baraboo, Medford, and Richland campuses, remained under heavy scrutiny, as the System administrators and Board of Regents tried to figure out how best to manage the University's resources.

Ironically, the Center System, as an institution, had made good progress toward reducing its cost-per-student or CSI. The composite support index (CSI) was a formula developed by UW System to compare the cost-per-student among UW institutions. The CSI included the cost of instruction; the supplies and expenses (S&E); the cost of support services such as admissions, advising, and other student services; and administrative overhead; all calculated on a per student basis. The cost cutting measures introduced by Chancellor Adolfson and Vice Chancellor Long in the early 1970s had been continued after the merger. Consequently, in just one year, 1973-74, the Centers had lowered its CSI by $100.00 per student.[29] This was very impressive, since it had been accomplished in the midst of an inflationary economy.

But what was an appropriate CSI for the Center System? This question had puzzled System Administration ever since merger. One large problem was that there was no exactly comparable institution in the entire United States, against which the Centers could be measured. After a good deal of investigation, System Administration decided, in summer 1975, to compare Center System costs to those of six sets of two-year institutions that seemed "most comparable."[30] In November 1975, a progress report to the Legislative Fiscal Bureau on the Center System noted that its cost-per-student was within $15.00 of the average for these six institutions. Furthermore, it appeared that by 1976-1977, the Centers' collective CSI would be below this average, because the comparable budgets were rising, while the Center System continued to trim its operating costs. Consequently, the progress report urged the LFB not to conduct further studies of the Centers, because the negative publicity that accompanied such scrutiny hurt morale and, more importantly, dissuaded students from enrolling at a Center undergoing scrutiny.[31]

However, it was too late to ask state government to take the spotlight off the Center System because the smallest Centers had already been caught in its glare. And the Board of Regents kept them there, as it followed up on the Scope Reduction Report. Even if the Center System's fiscal health was improving, serious questions still remained about Medford, Richland, and Baraboo. In July 1975, Chancellor Fort reported to Senior Vice President Donald Smith that his and Outreach Provost Wilson Thiede's assessment was that Baraboo and Richland would be able to meet both of the Regents' criteria—at least 250 FTE and costs no more than 20% above the Center System CSI—but that Medford would never achieve the mandated minimum enrollment. Thus, Fort suggested that he and the System administrators meet to explore the options which might be exercised in Medford's case.[32]

That meeting produced five options. For example, the Medford campus could be turned over to UW-Extension to be operated as a "Northwest Wisconsin Continuing Education Center." As an alternative, Medford could be eliminated. Another possibility was to transfer the facilities to the North Central Technical Institute, located in Wausau.[33] The fourth option would reduce Medford to a "freshman Center," similar to the earliest Extension Centers of the 1930s and 1940s. The final alternative would have reattached Medford to UW-Stevens Point, which could hopefully provide needed administrative and student services to Medford's students without adding significantly to its own costs.[34]

The preliminary Fall 1975 enrollment figures revealed the welcome news that the Center System had about 800 more students, a ten percent increase, compared to the previous fall. But, this increase was unevenly distributed among the fourteen campuses. Tiny Medford had 187 students (118 FTE), its second highest enrollment ever. Despite this, Medford still needed to reduce its budget by $26,000 to bring the cost-per-student within the +20% criteria. Baraboo's enrollment had shot up by 120, a 38% increase which removed that campus from the special review list. But Richland's student body plummeted by 15% (48 fewer students), causing its budget reduction to more than triple, from $23,000 to $76,000.[35] Richland reported that it had contacted 52 students who had preregistered but who did not actually enroll. This survey demonstrated that most of them had been "scared away" from Richland by the negative publicity about the campus possibly being closed.[36]

Throughout the Fall 1975 semester, Chancellor Fort and Provost Thiede worked with President Weaver's staff to find the dollars that Medford and Richland needed to refund. They tried hard to leave the instructional budget intact but in the end had to take $10,000 from Medford's and $29,000 from Richland's. The results of these deliberations were forwarded to the Regents for their action in January 1976. Provost Thiede, in his address to the Board members, noted that a slight decrease in enrollment at a small Center resulted in a huge increase in its CSI. For example, Richland's 15% enrollment decline had caused its per-student-cost to jump more than 30%. On the other hand, Baraboo's handsome enrollment increase had diminished its CSI to very near the Center System average. Thiede urged the Regents to relieve the Center System from making annual budget adjustments, because annual changes to dollars and personnel were difficult to quickly accomplish.

Chancellor Fort echoed the Provost's remarks, then presented a broader perspective on the Center System's dilemma. Fort contended that, because an "averaging down" was underway, even a Center whose enrollment rose modestly might find itself in fiscal difficulty. Closing a high cost, small Center would not solve this problem, Fort noted, because there inevitably would be another Center to take its place on the "chopping block." The Chancellor then questioned the validity of the 250 FTE figure, which the Regents had decreed was the minimum number of students needed for a Center to sustain a curriculum broad enough to guarantee completion of an associate degree in four semesters. Fort announced that he had appointed a Basic Curricular Program Task Force, which would investigate the issue and report in May 1976 the minimum array of liberal arts courses a Center needed to offer over two academic years to enable students to earn an associate degree. Fort suggested that this "minimum module" or core curriculum might be an acceptable alternative to the 250 FTE tripwire. If so, perhaps even Medford could be maintained as a UW Center.[37]

After hearing the speakers' comments, the Regents debated the requirement that Medford and Richland fully repay their debts by July 1, 1976. Several Regents expressed sympathy for these Centers' plight. Ody Fish argued that the Regents' criteria were too rigid and that they must remember the UW's partnership with the communities in which Centers were located. That partnership ought not be dissolved, he argued, except for the most critical reasons and the current circumstances did not constitute a crisis. John Levine observed that, since the Scope Reduction Task Force data indicated it would cost the state more to accommodate a closed Center's students elsewhere in the System, it made no sense to him to "spend money to close campuses." Gradually a consensus emerged around a resolution suggested by Regent Joyce Erdman that suspended the budgetary axe hanging over Richland and Medford. The Regents agreed to await the report of the Basic Curricular Program Task Force before taking further action. In the meantime both campuses were admonished to continue their efforts to bring their CSI within 20% of the Center System's average.[38]

The Basic Curricular Program Task Force produced a Liberal Arts Core Curriculum (see p. 139), consisting of forty-six courses drawn from all academic disciplines. Each Center was permitted to add courses to this bare minimum as its budget allowed. In addition, each Center was directed to develop and publish a four semester sequence of courses to be used in advising students.[39] The recommendations of the Task Force were forwarded to the

LIBERAL ARTS CORE CURRICULUM

Each campus must be able to offer, within a two-year period, the following distribution of courses as a minimum.

In Mathematics and Natural Sciences
Twelve courses, representing each of the following subject areas:
- Biology
- Chemistry
- Physics
- Math, Pre-Calculus and Calculus
- Physical Geography or Geology

In Humanities
Twelve courses, representing each of the following subject areas:
- English (Literature)
- Art (not applied)
- Music (not applied or performing)
- Philosophy
- Communication Arts
- Foreign Language

In Social Sciences
Twelve courses, representing each of the following subject areas:
- Economics
- History
- Psychology
- Sociology
- Anthropology
- Political Science
- Cultural Geography

Among Non-Distributive Courses
Ten courses, representing each of the following offerings:
- English (Writing Courses)
- Applied Music Courses
- Performing Music Courses
- Studio Art Courses
- Performing Drama Courses
- Applied Journalism Courses
- Activity Courses in Physical Education
- Professional Courses in Physical Education

Courses for the Underprepared Student as Appropriate

Source: Chancellor Edward B. Fort, Report on the Liberal Arts Core Curriculum, February 1977.

Center System Senate in Fall 1976, discussed thoroughly by the local collegia, and ultimately ratified by the Senate in January 1977.[40] With the Senate's approval in hand, Chancellor Fort forwarded the Liberal Arts Core Curriculum to the Board of Regents in February 1977. In his report he recounted how the core curriculum had been developed, noting that all fourteen Centers would be able to comply with it and also remain within the Regents' cost guidelines. He described it as a "living document," one which would be reviewed annually and adjusted to meet students' needs. Fort told the Regents that the core curriculum should now be substituted for the 250 FTE enrollment criterion for the minimal size of a Center campus.[41]

In March 1977, Chancellor Fort presented his 1976 Annual Report to the Board of Regents. There was much good news to report, especially concerning finances. Fort underscored that the Center System CSI now stood at just 10% above the University Cluster average. The Centers had enrolled 6.2% of the University's total enrollment but expended only 3.5% of its GPR budget. Further, more of the individual campus CSIs had been compressed toward the average through reallocation. The range had been reduced from more than 20% above the average at the time of merger to about 9% during the 1976-1977 fiscal year.

In addition, the Chancellor reported that the Center System had a new constitution, which replaced former Chancellor Long's much maligned Charter, and that the North Central Association of Colleges and Schools visitation committee had unanimously awarded the institution ten years accreditation as a "separate unit of the University of Wisconsin System."[42]

The drafting of a new constitution had actually begun in October 1974 when Acting Chancellor Meggers appointed a ten-member Charter Review Committee. The revised constitution had to win three separate votes to be adopted. First, the Collegium needed to initiate the approval process by a two-thirds vote, then ten of the fourteen local collegia needed to give their assent and, finally, the Collegium needed to ratify it by another two-thirds margin.[43]

While the Charter Review committee was organizing its work, an important debate and vote took place in the Collegium concerning a vital constitutional issue. Both the recently enacted merger law (Chapter 36: University of Wisconsin System) and the Board of Regents' Faculty Personnel Rules, which were solidly based on Chapter 36, mandated that the faculty be given the primary responsibility for making personnel decisions and determining the curriculum. This responsibility was to be exercised through the appropriate "academic department or its functional equivalent." The "functional equivalent" phrase recognized that both the Center System and UW-Extension were not single-site institutions where the faculty could conveniently gather to deliberate and make personnel and curriculum decisions.[44]

CENTER SYSTEM ENROLLMENT
(Headcount and Percent Change)

	1971-72	1972-73	1973-74	1974-75	1975-76
Baraboo	268	301	267	313	433
		12.3%	-11.3%	17.2%	38.3%
Barron	392	411	506	518	548
		4.8	23.1	2.4	5.8
Fond du Lac	545	496	729	799	952
		-9.0	47.0	9.6	19.1
Fox Valley	438	432	518	684	942
		-1.4	19.9	32.0	37.7
Manitowoc	262	230	270	307	301
		-12.2	17.4	13.7	-2.0
Marathon	725	796	861	844	812
		9.8	8.2	-2.0	-3.8
Marinette	348	340	358	350	406
		-2.3	5.3	-2.2	16.0
Marshfield	355	402	425	394	473
		13.2	5.7	-7.3	20.1
Medford	177	142	131	165	187
		-19.8	-7.7	26.0	13.3
Richland	316	298	300	307	259
		-5.7	0.7	2.3	-15.6
Rock	593	520	531	583	660
		-12.3	2.1	9.8	13.2
Sheboygan	518	560	603	583	646
		8.1	7.7	-3.3	10.8
Washington	532	539	539	539	543
		1.3	0.0	0.0	0.7
Waukesha	1,421	1,418	1,592	1,671	1,701
		-0.2	12.3	5.0	1.8
TOTAL		6,890	6,885	7,630	8,057	8,863
			-0.1	10.8	5.6	10.0

Source: The University of Wisconsin System Student Statistics—Term 1, 1981-82 Undergraduate Enrollment with 10-Year Profile (March 9, 1982)

On November 14, 1974, the Collegium convened in a special session to determine the Centers' functional equivalent. University of Wisconsin System Legal Counsel John Tallman addressed the delegates, laying out the legal requirements of the merger law and faculty personnel rules. Then each senator had an opportunity to describe the stance of his or her constituency. After considerable debate of a resolution which would have designated the academic departments as the functional equivalent, the Collegium convincingly voted it down, 4-yes to 18-no. Next, a proposal specifying, "the local Center Collegium, through its committees," as the functional equivalent was debated. The senators ultimately passed this motion, 15 to 6.[45]

The simple report of the votes, of course, understates the strong emotions expressed in the debate. The lines drawn in this meeting held throughout the entire constitution-writing process. On one side stood the faculties of the four former WSU branch campuses—Barron, Fond du Lac, Medford, and Richland. They resolutely resisted having the ultimate control over personnel decisions taken from the local appointments and evaluation committees, where Long's Charter had placed it. Their opposition also arose from these campuses' pre-merger history; they had traditionally made these decisions themselves. In addition, anxiety stemmed from worry about how they might be treated by the academic departments. A few key faculty members from the original UW Centers had expressed misgivings about the professional qualifications of the former Wisconsin State University faculty members, because they believed the WSU appointees had not been subjected to rigorous academic department scrutiny, such as they had received from the UW-Madison departments.

The faculty senators from these four Centers had been joined in crucial votes by the academic staff and student senators. The academic staff representatives' opposition arose from the fear that they would lose their voting rights in the new constitution, although the librarians and student services directors would continue to elect delegates. The five student senators apparently had been won over by the comments made by the faculty senators from Barron, Fond du Lac, Medford, and Richland and by the concerns expressed by the two academic staff senators.[46]

On the other side stood those faculty members who wished to return control to the academic departments. Led, especially, by senators from Fox Valley, Marathon, Washington, and Waukesha, they lobbied the Charter Review Committee to ignore the Collegium vote and to restore the primary power over personnel decisions to the departments. This faction was also upset at the fact that Long's Charter permitted non-faculty senators to vote upon issues which exclusively concerned the faculty.[47]

Meanwhile, the Charter Review Committee, led by Professor Fred Moss

(English, Waukesha), started its work by inviting the faculty, staff, and students to communicate their ideas for the new constitution to the group by mid-December 1974. While awaiting this deadline, the Committee members met with Legal Counsel Tallman and System Administrators, who explained the legal requirements of the Faculty Personnel Rules. The Committee also gathered constitutions from other UW institutions to use as guides. The Committee met several times between semesters to draft a new constitution.

Moss gave the Collegium a progress report in March 1975. On the central issue, he said that the academic departments would be given primary authority over personnel decisions, but that they would be required to consult with local committees to appoint, promote, and tenure faculty. Moss explained that this resolution of the functional equivalent issue appeared best suited to win approval from the System lawyers, who would review the Constitution before it was forwarded to the Board of Regents. Moss also told the senators that most of Chapters 4 and 5, dealing with Academic Departments and Appointments and Promotions, respectively, had been taken word-for-word from the Faculty Personnel Rules.[48] Having completed its work, the Charter Review Committee sent a proposed Constitution to the Center System Collegium in mid-April 1975.

During its April session, the Collegium voted to initiate the Constitution as an amendment to the Charter, and sent it to the 14 local collegia for discussion and a vote by October 1, 1975. The Collegium also decided to conduct a faculty-only advisory referendum before the academic year ended. In this referendum, seventy-one percent of the faculty approved the Constitution.

When the Collegium met in October, the Steering Committee Chair reported that ten Centers had approved the Constitution, which cleared the way for its final test—a two-thirds vote of the Collegium. After several hours of heated debate, the Collegium fell two votes short of the required two-thirds, supporting the Constitution by only a 13 to 8 margin. This result caused consternation practically everywhere, except at the former WSU branch campuses (Barron, Fond du Lac, Medford, Richland), which had led the campaign against it. The Waukesha Center urged Chancellor Fort to simply bypass the Collegium and to take the document directly to the Board of Regents, noting that the faculty had overwhelmingly approved the Constitution and that the votes of the student and academic staff senators had defeated it. System Vice President Donald Smith, too, was upset at this development because only the Center System lacked a constitution that implemented the Faculty Personnel Rules. Smith directed Fort to communicate the urgency of breaking the impasse to all Center System personnel. In special meetings with the Steering Committee, Fort explored the possibility of sending forward just crucial Chapters 4 and 5, on the premise that these had been approved by more than two-thirds of the faculty. This would bring the Centers into compliance with the Faculty Personnel Rules. However, the Steering Committee, after broad consultation via telephone, decided against a piecemeal approach and called a special session of the Collegium, on November 22, to take another vote.

This meeting, held at UWC-Waukesha, was tense from beginning to end. Each faction reiterated its position. The faculty senators from the ten campuses which had approved the Constitution warned of dire consequences, should the Center System again fail to come into compliance with the Faculty Personnel rules. The faculty senators from the opposing four Centers repeated an appeal to leave the locus of power on the campuses. The two academic staff senators again expressed their dismay over the loss of voting rights under the Constitution. The five student senators explained that it was this point, primarily, that had caused them to vote en masse against the Constitution. Although they would retain voting rights, they were sympathetic to the plight of the academic staff. After almost six hours of emotional debate, the crucial roll call vote began. Of course, everyone kept a tally as the names were called. When the 20th name—that of Professor Victor Wrigley of Waukesha—was called and he loudly voted "aye," cheering erupted because his was the decisive vote in favor of ratification. After several minutes of celebration, the remaining two names were called and the final count, 16 in favor and 6 opposed, was announced. Richland Senator Jerry Bower and two student senators had changed their votes, compared to the October Collegium meeting, to put the Constitution over the top. The Board of Regents approved the Constitution in February 1976 and ruled it would take effect July 1, 1976. [49]

While a few of the constitutional changes were primarily cosmetic—such as naming the systemwide deliberative body the "Senate," while the local governance body continued to be the Collegium—most were quite dramatic. Representation in the Senate would now be proportional to the number of ranked faculty at each Center, with the result that Marathon had two senators and Waukesha three. [50] Many observed that if this democratic feature had been present in Long's Charter, the arduous struggle over ratification of the Constitution would not have occurred. The student senators, to be selected by the council of student government presidents, were reduced in number from five to three. The two academic staff senators lost their voting rights, although they could participate in Senate debate and serve on Senate committees. [51] Two new Senate committees were created. The Budget Committee, which almost everyone felt was needed, would consult with and advise the Chancellor on the annual budget and serve as an academic planning council.

The other new committee, the Faculty Consultative Committee, would not be staffed by senators; instead each Center collegium would choose one ranked faculty member to serve. The Faculty Consultative Committee had just two duties: first, to determine the form of seniority to be used if tenured faculty layoffs became necessary and, second, to consult with the Chancellor, should a declaration of fiscal emergency be under consideration.[52]

The most significant changes in faculty governance were spelled out in Chapter 4—Academic Departments and Chapter 5—Appointments and Promotions of Ranked Faculty. Totally erasing former Chancellor Long's antipathy toward the academic departments, the Constitution gave them the primary responsibility for all personnel decisions. In short, no appointment, promotion in rank, or grant of tenure could be made without the appropriate department's approval. Although each Center continued to have a local appointments and evaluation committee, it could make no decisions independent of the departments.[53] In conjunction with this enhancement of the academic departments' authority, Chancellor Fort agreed to the separation of several large departments thrown together by Long. Thus, English was separated from Philosophy, Psychology from Anthropology and Sociology, and Art from Music.[54] Finally, the Constitution referred to department "chairpersons" in recognition of an ongoing effort to eradicate sexist language from the UW institutions.

Aside from the dramatic changes in the local appointments and evaluation committees' functions, the Constitution specified only a few modest alterations in the local collegium procedures. Long's Charter had bestowed the right to participate in governance upon all faculty and academic staff who held at least a half-time appointment; the Constitution now restricted that right to the ranked faculty. Academic staff persons who wished to have a vote in local affairs would have to petition the Senate to be granted "faculty status for purposes of governance."[55] The faculty senators routinely bestowed faculty status upon members of the instructional academic staff because they were employed with the departments' approval, but they grappled for years to establish the criteria for granting faculty status to members of the non-instructional academic staff. Later, in 1985, a Board of Regents policy—The Role of Academic Staff in Governance—spelled out the eligibility of academic staff persons to participate in governance, thus removing the issue from the hands of the faculty.[56] The local collegium continued to have student representatives and the local committee that budgeted the student activity fees would have a Regent-mandated student majority.[57]

Because attracting more students clearly was the surest way for the Center System to solve its financial problems, the Center System Office of Research conducted two major surveys to determine how the Centers could better market themselves. Herman Kroll's "A Survey of Student Opinion, 1975-1976" produced a profile of that year's student body: almost half of the enrollees were women (49%), the median age was 20, one-fourth were non-traditional students (over age 24), 26% were married, 60% lived with their parents, and 64% were employed. Kroll observed that the vast majority of married students were women and that they often were part-time students, so that they could handle both academic and family responsibilities.[58] When Kroll asked about the reasons for attending a Center, the students reiterated the responses of previous generations: lower cost, smaller classes, good teachers, and the opportunity to try out college in a supportive atmosphere. The respondents listed the major drawbacks as a "high schoolish" atmosphere and a lack of diversity, because most of the students lived in the immediate area.[59] When Kroll inquired about the students' "Feelings About the Institution," the vast majority gave the Center a very high rating. In particular, they felt they had been treated as adults and that the professors were interested in them as individuals. Students at the smaller Centers rated their experience more positively than did colleagues at the larger ones, no doubt because it was easier to become acquainted.[60]

In October 1976, Teresa Shen, Richard Schwartz, and Beverly Drier released "The UW-Center System Transfer Study," which surveyed a stratified random sample of just over one thousand students who had been enrolled in a Center in the fall of 1973 to learn their circumstances three years later. The study revealed that 60% of the respondents had continued their education, with 78% of them transferring to a UW four-year campus. The most popular transfer institutions were Madison (29%), Milwaukee (18%) and Oshkosh (13%). Center System transferees earned just slightly better grades at their new college, which confirmed the assertion that the Center System prepared its students well for junior and senior level courses.[61] While neither of the studies contained any startling new information, both underscored the Centers' claim that they provided access to the University of Wisconsin for many persons who, otherwise, would not have had an opportunity to enroll. This was especially true for older and married students, who were more place-bound than recent high school graduates.

Ironically, while the smaller Centers struggled to attract more students to fill up under-utilized classrooms and laboratories, several of the larger Centers needed more space to handle their burgeoning enrollments. Many of the campuses constructed in the 1960s had been minimally outfitted and now facilities were overtaxed. A 1975-1976 survey revealed that five campuses lacked a gymnasium, six had no theater or performing arts area, numerous libraries were cramped, most Centers were without a student union or commons area where students could gather, and three Centers needed more classrooms and laboratories.⁶² Three Centers—Fox Valley, Washington County, Waukesha—had experienced enrollment growth far beyond the original estimates. For example, Waukesha juggled the schedules of 1,200 students on a campus designed for 750.⁶³

The unique arrangement between a Center's host community, which built and maintained the facilities, and the Board of Regents, which supplied the moveable equipment and paid the faculty and staff, meant building projects in the Center System took a long time to negotiate. At Fox Valley and Washington County such negotiations were even more complicated. Fox Valley was sponsored by Outagamie and Winnebago Counties, who had split the initial bond issue 50/50. However, Winnebago County resisted continuing this pact because two-thirds of the Fox Valley students now resided in Outagamie County. The presence of UW-Oshkosh in Winnebago County, which competed for students with the Center, further complicated the negotiations. During the protracted dispute between the two counties, the *Appleton Post-Crescent* accused UW-Oshkosh faculty of orchestrating opposition to a settlement.⁶⁴

In Washington County there were different antagonists. Here, the City of West Bend had shared the cost of erecting a new campus in the late 1960s with Washington County, on a 40%/60% basis. Now with the buildings crammed with 150 students above their capacity, the city sought to reduce its share to twenty percent. Naturally, the County Board resisted. After two years of argument, Reuben Schmahl, the County Board Chairman, wrote to Governor Martin Schreiber to urge the state to assume responsibility for all of the Center System facilities. Coached by Center System administrators, the Governor's reply reminded Schmahl that his county had won a spirited competition to host a Center; a competition it had eagerly entered because of the educational, cultural, and economic advantages that would accrue to the community. Schreiber warned that if the state secured ownership of the Washington County campus, it could be closed without any input from the County Board or Board of Regents. The governor therefore urged Schmahl and his fellow supervisors to continue to seek a solution to the impasse.⁶⁵

Among the many items included in the merger implementation statute was a directive that the Board of Regents assure that all UW System faculty and academic staff with comparable training, experience, and responsibility receive equitable compensation. The 1975 state budget bill repeated this mandate and set up a Legislative Study Committee to investigate salary equity, "…paying particular attention to salaries provided in the Center System."⁶⁶ Subsequently, the Legislative Committee asked the Board of Regents to supply it with data on UW System salaries and an explanation of any apparent inequities. This request, as usual, was passed on to each institution. Thus, in

November 1976, the Center System Senate created a four member Faculty Salary Equity Committee to conduct an investigation. UW System Administration directed the Committee to first determine whether there were any internal salary inequalities among the fourteen Centers before comparing the Centers' salaries to those of the University Cluster campuses.[67]

The Faculty Salary Equity Committee uncovered great salary inequities among the campuses. The Committee concluded that external factors had created these differences. First, it noted that the Center System had three "parents"—UW-Madison (7 Centers), the former Wisconsin State Universities (4 branch campuses), and UW-Green Bay (the 3-M Centers)—which had treated their two-year campus faculties quite differently. Second, just prior to merger, the legislature had handsomely boosted the salaries of the State University system's personnel, with the result that faculty at Barron County, Fond du Lac, Medford, and Richland received raises that put them ahead of their Chapter 36 colleagues. Third, the rapid inflation of recent years had so eroded purchasing power that the Center System had been compelled to increase starting salaries to attract new faculty.

This policy had produced a new problem—a few of the new hirees' salaries topped those of some veteran faculty members. This salary compression naturally struck hard at morale. The Committee made two recommendations, to be implemented over two academic years, to correct the internal inequities it had uncovered. First, it recommended that the injustices created by the different starting salaries for the past four years, 1973 through 1977, be corrected, at a cost of $20,000. Second, the Salary Equity Committee urged that all other faculty salaries be adjusted to remove the inequalities between campuses. Under this proposal, which would require $245,000 to implement, the Barron County faculty would receive no equity increase, while the other Centers' faculty would receive boosts ranging from 2.5% at Fond du Lac to 7.6% at Baraboo.[68]

With these recommendations, the Faculty Salary Equity Committee had completed the first portion of its task. It then began comparing the Centers' faculty salaries with those in the University Cluster and urged Chancellor Fort to request that System Administration conduct a similar study. The committee members noted that they lacked the time to do a detailed study of academic staff compensation and they asked the Senate to set up a separate committee to investigate those salaries. The Senate quickly acceded to this request.[69]

On July 1, 1977, the reins of leadership were passed to different hands at both ends of State Street. University of Wisconsin System President John Weaver, who had announced his intention to retire the previous July, left his post to become a Visiting Distinguished Professor at the University of

Southern California. The Board of Regents' search for Weaver's successor resulted in the selection of UW-Madison's Chancellor H. Edwin Young as the University's sixteenth president. Young, who had first arrived in Madison in 1947 as an economics instructor, had led the Madison campus for nine years. He had enjoyed strong support from the Regents because he had dealt effectively with student demonstrators. The only negative comment on Young's appointment came from TAUWF (The Association of University of Wisconsin Faculties), which claimed its membership primarily among the former Wisconsin State Universities' faculty. TAUWF believed the selection of Madison's chief executive to head the System meant that the interests of the out-state campuses would be ignored.[70]

The transition at the state capitol was equally smooth. When Governor Lucey resigned to become President Jimmy Carter's ambassador to Mexico, his lieutenant governor, Martin J. Schreiber, succeeded him. Schreiber had been second-in-command since 1971 and before that he had served two terms in the state Senate.[71]

The 1978 governor's election proved to be extremely interesting from the University's standpoint. On the Republican side, UW-Stevens Point Chancellor Lee S. Dreyfus surprised the political pundits when he announced, in April 1978, that he was resigning his post to seek the Republican gubernatorial nomination. A political neophyte, who had not previously even announced his political affiliation, Dreyfus brought to his campaign great skill as a public speaker and trademark red vests. Despite Dreyfus's impassioned plea to remain neutral in the primary, the Republican state convention endorsed U.S. Representative Robert Kasten. Undaunted, Dreyfus fought on and scored a smashing upset in the September primary. The Democrats, meanwhile, had a much less controversial convention and primary. Although challenged by Madison businessman David Carley for the top spot on the ticket, Governor Schreiber easily defeated Carley in the primary.[72]

The Dreyfus/Schreiber campaign brought forth two issues directly related to Wisconsin higher education. The candidates devoted a good deal of time describing how they would dispose of a totally unexpected $300 to $500 million budget surplus. Dreyfus, naturally, blamed Democrats' overtaxation for the surplus and promised to return it to the taxpayers, perhaps through a two or three month income tax withholding moratorium. Schreiber, who insisted that the surplus resulted from inflation-related "tax bracket creep," proposed to dispose of it through program spending, targeted to critical needs. The governor suggested some spending to increase salaries for UW and other state employees, whose purchasing power had been severely diminished by inflation The second issue concerned the financing of the state's vocation-technical education system, which Dreyfus proposed to shift from local property taxes to state government. The vocational-technical schools' supporters strongly backed Schreiber's attack on Dreyfus's scheme. They feared that such a tax shift would lead directly to more state control over the Voc-Tech System and, perhaps, even to demands that some districts reduce their cost per student to a statewide average, just as the Center System was being pressured to do.

Dreyfus, the political newcomer, rapidly overcame Schreiber's early lead with populist-style campaign techniques drawn from his earlier career as a UW-Madison professor of speech. By contrast, Schreiber appeared ill at ease and displayed occasional flashes of temper in dealing with the press corps. Dreyfus's lead continued to build throughout the early fall and the question soon became whether his coat tails would be long enough to give the Republicans control of at least one chamber of the legislature. On election day, Dreyfus handily defeated Schreiber, 816,000 to 674,000, but the Democrats maintained their comfortable margins in both the Senate and Assembly.[73]

Many in the University speculated about how a governor, who had been a faculty member and a top administrator, might treat the UW. Of course, because Dreyfus inherited higher education policies from his predecessor, there probably would not be any immediate, dramatic change of direction proposed for the 1979-1981 biennial budget. When queried about what he might do about the underutilized Center System campuses, Governor-elect Dreyfus said, perhaps they could be used for Department of Natural Resources regional offices. He argued that this use of the facilities would cushion the negative economic impacts of closing a Center, because the state would pay rent and the DNR would employ secretaries and other support staff. Dreyfus also noted that such an arrangement would make the DNR personnel more accessible to the public.

Although Dreyfus did not name a specific campus in his comments, reporters speculated that Medford and Richland were the most likely candidates for conversion to DNR use. When contacted for his reaction, Chancellor Fort bluntly labelled the suggestion "nonsensical" and "ridiculous" and noted that the governor would need the Democrat legislature's approval before any Center could be shut down. President Young was more measured in his response. Young thought that Dreyfus had just been thinking out loud and that the only valid reason for closing a Center would be if it consistently failed to achieve its enrollment and cost-per-student targets. He went on to explain that the Centers were important points of access to the UW for many citizens. He also reminded reporters of his September testimony before the Assembly Education Committee, in which he had observed that the

Center System's CSI now was comparable to that of the baccalaureate institutions. DNR top officials, who were definitely against the governor-elect's idea, were convinced that dispersing even a portion of their personnel to the hinterlands would reduce, not increase, the agency's efficiency.[74]

Eight
The Scope of the University is Reduced: 1979-1982

While Chancellor Fort could fend off rather easily the suggestion that the smaller Centers be turned over to the DNR, he had considerably less success coping with two other events during the Fall 1978 semester. These events foreshadowed the most turbulent, stressful four years in the history of the Center System. The first development was an unanticipated enrollment decline of 2.4% to 8,389 headcount. While this drop, by itself, might appear insignificant, it gave credence to a Legislative Fiscal Bureau report that predicted the UW System enrollment would plunge by at least 25% by 1993. Such a drastic decline, the LFB said, would surely result in tenured faculty layoffs. While the 21.4% enrollment decline projected for the Center System was considerably less than the 30% to 40% rate expected for several four-year campuses, it renewed the concerns about the ability of the smaller Centers to attract enough students to maintain a high quality academic program at a reasonable cost.[1]

The LFB predictions touched off a great deal of activity in the state capitol and in Van Hise Hall, the headquarters for System Administration. As enrollment declined, the University's leaders would have to carefully trim the

System's scope in response to diminished demand and a simultaneously reduced state budget. Consequently, the 1979-1981 budget bill directed the Board of Regents' Education Committee to report by November 30, 1979, how the University planned to cope with an enrollment decline and less money. The Education Committee's preliminary report, "Preparing for a Decade of Enrollment Decline," indicated that existing academic program audit and review procedures would suffice to gradually scale down the scope of the University's offerings in all except two institutions, the Center System and UW-Superior. Accordingly, the Board of Regents ordered President Young to appoint special task forces to conduct in-depth reviews of enrollment and budget prospects for those two units. The Center System Task Force was to pay particular attention to the outlook for Barron County, Medford, and Richland. [2]

Behind the scenes while the "November 30th Report," as it was popularly labelled, was still in the draft stage, Chancellor Fort argued strenuously with the President's staff. He contended that the entire Center System was not a legitimate candidate for a far-reaching review. Fort lodged his contention on the language of the budget resolution, which required a review for any UW institution whose cost of instruction exceeded the University Cluster average CSI by 130%. He reminded the System administrators that the Center System's CSI was just 123.3% of that average, compared to Superior's 146.8%. While Superior's options obviously needed to be investigated, he argued, the Centers deserved to be excused from this round of special scrutiny. [3] In a pithy letter, an angry Vice President Donald Smith demolished Fort's arguments. Smith pointed out that Fort had focused upon just one portion of a broadly worded resolution; the Board of Regents needed to respond to all of the issues it raised. Even though the Center System CSI was below the legislature's threshold, the three named Centers had stumbled over the Regents' 1975 tripwire that required individual Centers to keep their cost of instruction below 120% of the Center System's average. In addition, Medford was far below the 250 FTE minimum and the enrollment projections for Barron County and Richland were not promising. At some point, a campus's academic program might become so constricted that it could no longer meet the quality standards of the University of Wisconsin. Smith closed with the reminder that the Center System's budget contained $700,000 more than her enrollment warranted. The Board of Regents and System Administration needed to demonstrate that steps were being taken to bring the Centers' fiscal affairs into balance. [4]

Shortly after New Year's Day, 1980, President Young appointed an eleven member "Special Task Force to Review the Programs of the UW-Barron County, UW-Medford, and UW-Richland, Within the Mission of the

UW Center System," and named UW-Madison Professor Richard Rossmiller as its chairperson. None of the eleven were from the Center System; however, Thornton Liechty, assistant to the chancellor, and Peter Okray, chair of the Senate Steering Committee, were designated as resource persons to the Task Force. Young told the members that the Board of Regents had given them a broad mandate, including the freedom "to rethink the wisdom of the current alignment of the Center System, or individual Centers." Young requested that the Task Force work hard and quickly, forwarding its recommendations to the President by June 1, 1980.[5]

The Task Force's report, however, would actually go to new UW System President Robert M. O'Neil because Young retired at the end of January. O'Neil, the first President in decades who did not have previous ties to the UW, came from Indiana University at Bloomington, where he had been vice president and chief academic administrator. A Harvard Law School graduate, O'Neil was nationally known as an expert on the First Amendment's freedom of speech clause. O'Neil's personal style was unorthodox—he typed many of his own letters and either walked or rode a bicycle to Van Hise and to appointments in Madison, spurning the use of the car and driver traditionally provided to the President.[6]

The Task Force held a public hearing in each of the three communities to gather the opinions of students, faculty, and the general public. The group also conducted interviews with campus administrators, faculty, and community leaders to learn of the plans they had for guiding their Center through this crisis. And, of course, the Task Force used previous reports on the Center System in its deliberations.[7]

The Special Task Force's "Report to the President" began by sketching the fiscal problems of the Center System. It noted that the Centers and System Administration had already negotiated budget reductions of $150,000 for 1980-81 and another $400,000 for the following year, which would repay most of the debt. However, the Task Force estimated that the Center System would accumulate an additional $600,000 in red ink by the mid-1980s due to the projected enrollment decline. Consequently, closing all three Centers would not fully address this looming fiscal disaster. It seemed apparent that only a fundamental restructuring of the Center System could solve its lingering and future financial problems.[8]

The Task Force quickly decided that maintaining the status quo would not solve the Center System's huge budget problem. Proportional budget cuts spread across all fourteen Centers would not solve it either because even the strongest campuses' academic program would be devastated. Likewise, transferring some Centers to four-year campuses was not a practical solution. The remaining Centers would still confront a bleak fiscal future and the negative publicity generated by this policy seemed likely to scare away potential students. The two remaining alternatives sought a solution outside the Center System. A remerger of the Centers with Extension received only brief consideration because the latter had its own serious financial problems. Finally, the creation of community colleges via a union between the Centers and the VTAE schools was also set aside, in light of Wisconsin's repeated decisions to keep the two systems separate.[9]

The Task Force firmly recommended the closing of Medford, but left the timing to the Board of Regents and state legislature. The public hearing in Medford had naturally elicited an outpouring of support. County officials and campus personnel bitterly charged the UW with perfidy for never giving the Center the support that it needed to become solidly established. While the Task Force acknowledged that the campus's troubled history had kept Medford in a negative light, it concluded that the demographic data did not predict a viable future.[10]

After it established that a fundamental change should occur in the Center System's structure, the Task Force proposed the reorganization of the Centers into regional groups as the best way to achieve that goal. The Report described four possible configurations; only one is discussed here, as an example. Configuration I envisioned three groups: Region I would include the northern tier of Centers—Barron, Marshfield, Marathon and Marinette; Region II would lie along the shores of Lakes Michigan and Winnebago and consist of Fond du Lac, Fox Valley, Manitowoc, Sheboygan and Washington; Region III would sweep across the southern part of the state, from Richland to Baraboo to Rock and, finally, to Waukesha. This arrangement allegedly produced savings of $1.4 million, including $282,000 garnered from a reduction in the number of central administration staff in Madison and all of Medford's $215,000 budget. The remainder would come from cutbacks in each Center's administration and from a reduction in the number of faculty in each region. Ten campus deans' positions would be trimmed to half-time, and proportional reductions would be made in every Centers' library, business office, student services, and classified staff. The number of faculty in each region would be slashed by assigning some faculty to travel throughout the region and by offering traditionally low enrollment courses less frequently. Overseeing each region would be a modest administrative staff (8.5 FTE), which would provide services no longer available on the campuses or from central administration. The Task Force recommended the creation of a new Office of Academic Affairs to be headed by a vice chancellor to coordinate and supervise the regional curricula.[11]

The Task Force decided the Center System should be dismantled only as an extreme last resort. Nevertheless, it studied what might be gained by closing several Centers and assigning the rest to nearby four-year institutions. For example, $3.5 to $4.0 million could be gained by closing six smaller Centers (Baraboo, Barron, Manitowoc, Marinette, Medford, Richland), phasing out entirely the central administration, and assigning the eight survivors to various UWs to be operated as branch campuses. The model the Task Force used envisioned these pairings: Fond du Lac and Fox Valley with UW-Oshkosh, Marathon and Marshfield with UW-Stevens Point, Sheboygan and Washington with UW-Milwaukee, Rock with UW-Whitewater, and Waukesha with UW-Parkside. This drastic option would reduce access for people living in the vicinity of the closed Centers and could result in the cannibalization of the remaining campuses by the parent campuses as enrollments and budgets declined. In addition, these projected savings would be diminished by the costs of closing six campuses and of educating those Centers' students elsewhere in the UW.[12]

The Task Force Report also recommended several policies for consideration by the Board of Regents and state government. It suggested that the Regents should use a three-year rolling CSI average, instead of annual figures, to identify Centers for special review because small Centers' cost of instruction could fluctuate tremendously from year to year. Once the Center System's future had been decided, the Board of Regents and state government should promise not to conduct a special review of any Center for six years to allow adequate time for the corrective measures to take effect. Finally, the Task Force called upon the governor and legislature to support the entire University of Wisconsin System with adequate resources to maintain both access and the quality of the academic program. The Report closed with a question, does the state "have the will to preserve one of its most valuable resources?".[13]

In May 1980, while the Special Task Force was winding up its work, the Center System faculty was astounded to learn that Chancellor Fort had overturned tenure recommendations for five probationary faculty. Fort based his decision on the need to avoid excessive "tenure density" in any academic department. If the tenure density in a department exceeded 75%, Fort believed he would not have the flexibility needed to make staffing adjustments when the Center System's enrollment declined or if a campus was closed. The tenure density issue was not new to the Centers or other UW institutions, as it had been discussed periodically for several years. The key concern of the Board of Regents and the System Administration was that each institution maintain sufficient staffing flexibility so that tenured faculty would not have to be laid off in the event of a severe enrollment decline, because that would require a declaration of a fiscal emergency.[14]

The five affected persons soon filed a grievance with the Senate

Appeals and Grievances Committee, requesting a reversal of the Chancellor's decision. Their central argument was that Fort's rationale for denying them tenure was not among the criteria for awarding tenure in the Faculty Personnel Rules (UWS 3.06(b)), which required an evaluation of a probationary faculty member's ". . . teaching, research, and professional and public service and contribution to the institution." In each case, the department executive committee and campus evaluation committee had decided that the person had met these criteria and had earned a tenure appointment. Because Fort's decision was not made public until late May, the academic departments, campus collegia, and the Senate did not have an opportunity to voice an opinion in this dispute until the Fall semester began. When they did speak, they solidly backed the appellants. In January 1981, the Senate passed unanimously a resolution that called upon the Chancellor to reverse his decision because his ". . . actions ignore and supersede faculty responsibility for shared governance." In the 1981 Spring semester the Appeals and Grievances Committee granted all of the appeals and formally requested Fort to send forward the five tenure recommendations to the Board of Regents. He reluctantly did so.[15]

The issues raised by these tenure density cases reverberated throughout the University of Wisconsin. Ever since merger various faculty groups had expressed alarm at the increasing number of instructional academic staff (lecturers), who were teaching courses. Since these lecturers were not "faculty," they were not protected by the Faculty Personnel Rules and were usually employed on a semester to semester basis with the position dependent upon sufficient enrollment. Concerns about this practice, along with an increasing emphasis upon avoiding high tenure density, were not limited to the UW. In 1973, the American Association of University Professors (AAUP) had issued a statement on tenure density that read, in part, "To make appointments which are destined to lead to non-retention because of a fixed numerical quota of tenured positions, . . ., is to depart from a basic feature of the system of tenure and thus to weaken the protections of academic freedom."[16] The highly publicized furor in the Center System caused System Executive Vice President Joseph Kauffman to request a legal opinion from UW Legal Counsel John Tallman. He asked whether a chancellor could make tenure decisions on criteria other than those specified in the Faculty Personnel Rules. Tallman replied affirmatively, arguing that a chancellor, according to the Personnel Rules, had the authority to also take into account ". . . the mission and needs of the particular institution and its component parts." Tallman added that several Regents' policies specified the need to maintain staffing flexibility. Indeed, some UW institutions had responded by establishing a specific tenure ratio.[17]

Eventually, the Center System Senate adopted a tenure policy, but avoided setting a specific maximum for the number of tenured faculty. The Policy included "Institutional Need as a Criterion in Defining Tenure Positions" and "Program Flexibility" as factors the academic departments and campuses were to consider in making tenure recommendations. The policy required each department to conduct an annual review of its core curriculum and the enrollment history and projections for its courses to ascertain the number of tenured positions the department could justify. Each year every probationary faculty member was to receive a letter that assessed "the anticipated institutional need for positions" in his/her academic discipline.[18] The provisions of this document laid the foundation for many other policies still in force—the annual four semester sequence review, the need for a department to justify the existence of a tenurable position before it receives permission to advertise a faculty position, and policies which mandate the primary role of the departments in the employment and evaluation of the instructional academic staff.

In May 1980, as the System Task Force was polishing its report, Chancellor Fort began preparation of an institutional response to its recommendations. He appointed a seven member Coordinating Committee to write a critique of each of the Task Force's proposals. Fort requested that the Coordinating Committee's conclusions be sent to him no later than September 1.[19]

The Coordinating Committee's report, "Meeting the Challenges of the 1980s," concurred with many of the Task Force recommendations. For example, it reluctantly agreed that Medford should be closed, but expressed the hope that some of the dollars saved could be shunted to Barron and Richland to enable them to recruit more students and improve their chances of survival. The members also agreed that the amount realized from closing the smaller Centers would be negligible. In addition, they observed that transferring the survivors elsewhere could touch off a competition to gain control of these stronger Centers that would be potentially damaging to the entire University of Wisconsin System. The Coordinating Committee approved the suggestion that the Center System should reduce the size of its administration since the faculty already had been severely trimmed. If fewer students meant fewer teachers, it also meant less demand for the services administrators provided. The Committee believed that the Central Administration in Madison was especially overstaffed.[20]

The Coordinating Committee disagreed with the Task Force's conclusion that the Center System allegedly could not overcome its fiscal difficulties as it was currently organized and that the Centers should be rearranged into regional groups. It asserted that, just as an enrollment decrease in 1978 had created much of the problem, the enrollment increase in Fall 1979 (316 students, 3.8%) and the one projected for September 1980 would enable the Centers to repay almost all of its debt. The members also proposed that at least twelve positions could be pared from the central administration, saving $250,000. Having established its confidence in the Center System's ability to reduce its budget, the Coordinating Committee moved to a critique of regionalization.

The major advantages claimed for regionalization were a reduction in administrative overhead costs and enhancement of the Centers' ability to attract and serve students. The Coordinating Committee attacked both of those claims. Using figures supplied by Assistant Chancellor for Administrative Services Antone Kucera, it argued that the Task Force had vastly overestimated the savings from regionalization and had dangerously understaffed the regional offices. For example, the Task Force had neglected to include money for S & E (supplies and expenses) in its budget, an oversight that Kucera estimated would reduce the savings by $340,000. Kucera also worried that the proposed cuts in the business operations staff would ensure that a regionalized Center System would fail one of Wisconsin's rigorous audits. Kucera's concerns were backed up by comments from Manitowoc Business Manager Steven Bendrick, who related that for eight months he had also operated Fox Valley's business office. He reported that services at both campuses had suffered and that, while they were able to "get by," sharing a business manager would not work over the long haul. Bendrick predicted that the regionalized business staff would be unable to cope with the heavy workload on the campuses, especially during final registration when tuition and fees were collected.[21]

Using data supplied by Assistant Professor Stephen Portch (English, Richland), the Coordinating Committee declared that, with regionalization, services to students on the campuses would be seriously deficient. For instance, the students would be unable to obtain adequate academic advising and counselling from the half-time student services officers. Students would find it difficult to arrange a time to meet with circuit-riding faculty. The campus libraries would be open fewer hours. Non-traditional students would suffer the most from the effects of reduced student services and they were the very group that the Centers were being urged to work hard to attract. National studies had repeatedly demonstrated that non-traditional students made greater use of these services. The net result, then, would be a declining enrollment as word spread that the Centers could not meet students' basic needs.[22]

Chancellor Fort's speech, "The Issue Before The House: The UW Center System and Access For the 1980s," to the Board of Regents in October

1980 disappointed anyone who anticipated hearing new ideas for leading and managing the Centers. The Chancellor agreed with the Coordinating Committee's conclusion that the Center System did not need to be restructured and assured the Regents that the necessary reductions would be made at Barron and Richland to bring their budgets to an acceptable level. However, he did not propose cutbacks in the Central Administration staff; instead, he said the matter would be studied. Fort made a plea for the President and Regents to consider seriously the creation of a "basic financial module" for the Center System, which would take into account the diseconomies of scale that arose from the geographical dispersion of the Centers.[23]

Especially disappointed with Fort's remarks were the two UW-Madison professors, William Lenehan and Richard Rossmiller, who had been members of the Task Force. Lenehan wrote Rossmiller that he was pleased that everyone agreed that Medford should be closed but he blasted Fort's request for further study of issues that both the Task Force and Coordinating Committee had thoroughly investigated. Lenehan complained that Fort had asked for more money, so that he would not have to face "the necessity of finding ways to live within the Center System's current and projected budget." Rossmiller forwarded Lenehan's letter to Vice President Kauffman, who had also served on the Task Force, adding his own observation that Fort "still does not seem willing to face reality."[24]

In December 1980, President O'Neil brought to a close a year's intense study of the Center System, when he made his recommendations about its future to the Board of Regents. He began by reviewing the Centers' major strengths—they provided relatively low cost access to the UW, the faculty and staff were extremely dedicated, and the Center System was fulfilling its mission to deliver a high quality academic program to freshmen and sophomores. But because the Centers faced a potential $1.5 million debt by 1986, some changes had to be made. O'Neil confirmed that Medford would be closed. He followed the Task Force's lead in recommending that Barron and Richland remain open, but admonished them to increase their enrollments and to keep their costs under control. The President reported that he had been persuaded by the Coordinating Committee's strong arguments against regionalization and had decided to give the Center System some additional time to decrease its institutional CSI. On that topic, O'Neil said he would not propose a basic financial module for the Center System, but that its instructional costs would continue to be compared to those of the freshman-sophomore CSI in the University Cluster. He added that, in this era of fiscal stringencies, he could not justify cutting the Center System free from standard measures of cost effectiveness. In an effort to facilitate the search for more efficient ways to operate, O'Neil said his office was willing to arrange talks between a Center and a baccalaureate UW institution that might eventually result in formal affiliation between the two. The President concluded by saying that he would give the Board periodic progress reports and in one year's time he would decide if further action was necessary to assure that the Center System would reach its objectives.[25]

Even before President O'Neil made his encouraging remarks about formal affiliation between a Center and a four-year UW, both the Fox Valley and Marathon County Centers had begun exploring the possibility of attaching themselves to UW-Madison. This development understandably alarmed Chancellor Fort. If Fox Valley and Marathon, the second and third largest Centers, respectively, left the Center System, the remaining campuses would find it much more difficult to meet the Regents' enrollment and financial goals. In time, President O'Neil also became concerned. His major concern was political. UW-Stevens Point and UW-Oshkosh had already objected to the possibility that nearby Centers might leapfrog over them to establish ties with Madison. O'Neil realized that both institutions had a valid complaint. In addition, if these two Centers were permitted to attach themselves to Madison, the infighting among the UW System campuses would surely intensify. So O'Neil sought a strategy that would permit him to gently defuse the situation.[26]

In late April 1981, President O'Neil met with the Senate Steering Committee to discuss the affiliation issue. During this session, he used points provided by Chancellor Fort to list four major conditions that any affiliation negotiations would have to meet. First, a two-year planning period must precede any formal proposal for affiliation. Second, that planning must include a study of the impact of the affiliation upon the Center System and upon all other UW campuses. Third, O'Neil stressed that several governing bodies—the Center's host community, the Board of Regents, and perhaps even the legislature—would have to give their consent to the proposed affiliation. Finally, the President observed that it was unlikely that he would view favorably an affiliation between a Center and a "remote" UW, because of the negative impact on the nearby UW campuses. The Senate Steering Committee Chair widely circulated these requirements which dampened considerably the enthusiasm for affiliation by Fox Valley and Marathon.[27]

Meanwhile, Chancellor Fort appointed a Long Range Planning Committee, whose major responsibility was to write a six-year plan for the Center System, describing how the institution would manage diminishing resources during an era of declining enrollments. In his initial letter to the committee members, the Chancellor outlined the parameters of the task. They were to assume that the current Center System structure, minus Medford, would be maintained. They were asked to outline the staffing and program changes necessary to enable the Centers to accommodate current and future givebacks to the UW System and the state. In addition, the long range planners were to recommend any necessary changes in the administrative and governance structures. Because the task was so broad, Fort gave them almost a year to do the work, asking that their plan be forwarded to him by December 1, 1981.[28]

While the Long Range Planning Committee pored over the numerous studies of the Center System, interviewed department chairs and deans, and consulted with the Senate Budget Committee, once again state and federal economic problems intervened and made its task more difficult. In mid-May 1981, as state legislators worked on the 1981-1983 biennial budget, Governor Dreyfus suddenly announced that the proposed biennial budget needed to be reduced by six percent to balance the state's books. Dreyfus explained that the still lethargic economy had compelled the Legislative Fiscal Bureau to reduce its estimate of revenue over the biennium. In addition, because of similar difficulties in Washington, newly installed President Ronald Reagan had announced cutbacks in Supplemental Security Income (SSI), Medicaid, and several block grant programs which would diminish federal aids to Wisconsin by $220 million over the same interval. The Governor and his Republican colleagues believed the best way to avoid red ink was to cut expenses. The Democrats, who controlled the legislature, responded that the state should cover the deficit through selective tax increases in order to maintain the integrity of these important social welfare programs and to underwrite a 1981-1983 state budget at least at its current level.[29]

Speaking on behalf of the University of Wisconsin System, President O'Neil reacted very negatively to Dreyfus's proposal. He noted that, so far, the UW had accommodated successive cutbacks in state funding, including an $18.5 million giveback imposed in Fall 1980. But he insisted that this most recent paring down of $51 million for the biennium, coming in the midst of a 5,000 student increase in enrollment, would produce "unspeakable results."[30]

The Center System's share of the looming reduction was $750,000 or 35 positions. The Senate Budget Committee, in close consultation with the Long Range Planning group, took the lead in drafting a proposal for meeting this crisis. The Budget Committee reported that a cutback of this magnitude could not be squeezed entirely from faculty positions, which had borne the brunt of previous decreases. Consequently, it recommended that 15 positions be slashed from the Central Office staff, reducing it from 35 to 20 full-time slots. The Budget Committee supported its dramatic proposal with the observation that every group which had studied the Center System since merger had concluded that the central administration was overstaffed. What is more, the Chancellor's failure to make any significant cuts in his office had created a serious morale problem on the campuses, where the budget axe had repeatedly fallen. Another twelve positions would be gained by selective trimming of the Centers' administrative staffs. This might be done, for example, by reducing annual contracts by a month or two, especially at Centers where the summer session was very small or where one was not offered. The remaining eight positions would have to be trimmed from the instructional staff.[31]

In the midst of this latest budget turmoil, Chancellor Fort, on June 13, 1981, announced his resignation to become the Chancellor of the North Carolina Agricultural and Technical College in Greensboro.[32] Naturally, Fort's announcement triggered speculation about his reasons for leaving. Some believed that after seven years of incessant strife, he was burned out from defending the Centers. While that was the most visible explanation, a few insiders also knew that Fort's relationship with President O'Neil and key members of the President's staff had grown increasingly tense. Throughout the Task Force process, the Chancellor had repeatedly insisted that the entire Center System should not be under scrutiny, because it had not met the legislature's criteria for a special review.[33] By the time of his resignation even the Deans had stepped up their criticism of Fort's steadfast refusal to consider deep cuts in the Central Office Staff.[34]

When queried about the anticipated search for Fort's successor, President O'Neil replied that he intended to take his time and study the wisdom of a thorough reorganization of the Center System.[35] The President's remarks sent a shock wave through the Centers. The alarm intensified two weeks later when Vice President Joseph Kauffman told the press that the coincidental resignation of Extension Chancellor Jean Evans had provided an opportunity for the UW System to weigh options for slashing the administrative costs of both institutions. Kauffman observed that one possibility for streamlining the Center System was to entirely eliminate the Central Office, give each Center administrative autonomy under a "super" dean, and have the System Administration oversee the operation.[36]

Kauffman's remarks appeared to unveil a plan already adopted in the President's office. As an interim measure O'Neil then announced the appointment of Robert R. Polk, his Associate Vice Chancellor for Academic Affairs, as the half-time Acting Chancellor of the Center System. Polk, who had earned his Bachelor's Degree from the Naval Academy in 1944 and who had been a naval officer and pilot from 1944 to 1949, had long been connected to the University of Wisconsin. He had served as a faculty member and chair of the UW-Oshkosh Geography Department from 1957-1967. Then he had moved into full time administration at Oshkosh. After the merger, Polk had been appointed to his current post in the President's office.[37]

O'Neil, sensitive to the fears that would surely arise from Polk's selection, arranged a meeting to introduce the acting chancellor to representatives of the faculty, the academic staff, and the deans. These representatives reported, "The President said there was no hidden agenda for Center System reorganization," but that he was also convinced that significant economies could be achieved in the Centers' administration. O'Neil told the delegates that he felt Polk, who had a thorough understanding of the Center System's difficulties and of the UW System, would be able to assist the Centers in defining and implementing these economies. Polk impressed the representatives with his candor and his pledge to help the Centers get their affairs in order.[38]

Acting Chancellor Polk repeated O'Neil's theme when he met for the first time with various constituencies—the Central Office staff, the Deans, the Board of Visitors, the Academic Staff Advisory Committee, and the Senate. In his initial Senate session he said, "I want to assure you that I have no charge to dissolve or unbundle the Center System but we will have to undertake some restructuring actions cooperatively and with dispatch. In the past the Center System has given outsiders the impression that it is unable to make a tough decision. This has to change."[39] To help him accomplish the restructuring, Polk appointed a Special Planning Committee (SPC), and charged it with two major tasks: recommending specific reductions in the Central Office staff and developing a procedure to be followed if a Center decided it wished to affiliate with a four-year institution. Polk directed the SPC to use the System Task Force and the Center System's Long Range Planning Committee Reports as it discussed the possible elimination of Central Office positions. Polk requested the SPC's final report by February 1, 1982.[40]

In November 1981, the Long Range Planning Committee published its report, "Adjusting the UW Center System to the Demands of the 1980s. A Six Year Plan." The Six Year Plan became the blueprint for the Centers' payment of its debt to UW System, of state-mandated budget reductions, and trimming of program and staff as the enrollment declined in the 1980s. While the Six Year Plan set goals and suggested processes or formulas for achieving them, it left the details of implementation to be worked out by the chancellor and the Senate.[41]

Of course, given the circumstances, much of the Long Range Planning Committee's report dealt with financial issues. The Committee proposed that the Center System gradually reduce its CSI to approach the average cost-per-student of the University Cluster campuses' freshman-sophomore programs by 1987. It also recommended that processes be established so that budget reductions could be sensibly made as enrollment declined, rather than waiting, as in the past, until a huge debt had accumulated. A key to achieving these goals lay in changing the method for allocating resources within the Center System. Since merger, tradition had prevailed in the setting of each Center's annual budget, thus funding inequities had been compounded over the years. Although some Centers, such as Barron and Richland, had experienced deep emergency budget cuts to bring their campus CSIs within acceptable limits, the greatest fiscal burden had been borne by the larger Centers. Consequently, these campuses' academic and support services programs were seriously underfunded and their faculty and staff felt overworked. To rectify this situation, the Six Year Plan proposed a formula, based on the student credit hours generated at each Center, that would be used to allocate all positions (administrative, support staff, faculty) to each campus. Over a few years, this formula would correct the most glaring funding inequities among the campuses and bring them all within a narrower range of the institution's average CSI. To complement these important proposals, the Committee recommended that a Reinvestment Fund be created to underwrite innovative programs and to provide matching funds for grant proposals. This was something that had been proposed every year since merger, but never implemented due to repeated budget restraints. [42]

In order to facilitate the reallocation of positions and money among the Centers, the Long Range Planning Committee urged the Senate to create an annual academic program planning process to be conducted by the academic departments and relevant campus committees. The departments would play a pivotal role in this process because they had a systemwide perspective of the curriculum and could allot fairly the faculty and lecturer positions needed to staff the academic program at each Center. To make clear the departments' control over the academic program, the Six Year Plan recommended that the Constitution be amended to stipulate that no course could be offered and no instructor could be employed without the express approval of the relevant department chair. [43]

The path-breaking Six Year Plan proved to be an invaluable tool as the Center System worked toward bringing staffing into balance with enrollment. Now data had been gathered to support or debunk long-held notions about who was underfunded and who was overfunded. Formulas and procedures had been created to enable the Centers to meet budget crises in a more rational manner. And mechanisms had been created to assure that long-range planning would be an ongoing process, so that the Centers could anticipate and adjust to the changing tastes of their student clientele.

Acting Chancellor Polk's Special Planning Committee made extensive use of the Six Year Plan and its supporting data to prepare its recommendations for paring down the Central Office staff. In addition, the SPC interviewed each staff member to better understand the position and how it fit into the services provided by the central administration. Consequently, the SPC believed it was on solid ground when it proposed to Polk a reduction of the Central Office staff from 35 to 20 positions.

The SPC recommended that two positions (media services and institutional research) be eliminated. The remainder of the reductions would be accomplished by transferring several data processing and business office positions to UW System Administration and by terminating the employment of those classified staff whose services were no longer required. The members of the SPC had also discussed at length the chancellor's office itself. In view of these staff adjustments, it seemed that the Center System no longer needed a full-time chief administrative officer. Then, too, Polk's excellent performance as a half-time Acting Chancellor was a powerful argument in favor of a somewhat streamlined position. Ultimately, the SPC decided that the Center System could be adequately served by a two-thirds time chancellor and suggested that the balance of the new position continue to be lodged in System Administration. The SPC had taken into account the potential impact of these recommendations upon the administrative staff at each Center, where the dean, the student services director, and the business manager would experience an increased workload. Following precisely the Six Year Plan, the SPC proposed that, if a Center's non-instructional/administrative costs exceeded the Center System average by 20% or more, its administrative staff should be trimmed to bring its personnel into balance with the workload.[44]

The SPC's final recommendation concerning the Central Office moved in a different direction. The SPC proposed that one new position, an assistant chancellor for student services, be created. Again, this need had periodically been discussed but Chancellor Fort had steadfastly refused to make the necessary adjustments to create the post. This assistant chancellor would supervise the operation of the Registrar's and Financial Aids' Offices and work with the Centers' directors of student services to resolve transfer issues. It was also anticipated that the assistant chancellor would help coordinate the student recruitment and retention endeavors by bringing the directors together periodically to plot effective strategies.[45]

The SPC also drafted an Affiliation Protocol to be followed if a Center decided to try to attach itself to another UW institution. The SPC followed the guidelines already laid down by President O'Neil and Chancellor Fort in shaping the Protocol. The process could only begin upon a two-thirds vote of the entire collegium membership. Once that vote was secured, the Center was to investigate the effect of its departure upon the Center System, on each one of the other UWs, and, perhaps most importantly, upon the employment status of each person in the new relationship. The Center would also have to secure the consent of its host community to transfer its allegiance from the

Center System. Finally, the Center was required to convince the Chancellor to recommend secession to the President and the Board of Regents, who had the ultimate authority to approve or veto the proposal. The Affiliation Protocol, a daunting, three-page long list of requirements, thoroughly squelched interest in pursuing new affiliations. Of course, the prospect that the implementation of the Six Year Plan would finally put the Centers on a solid footing no doubt also contributed to the quieting of this issue.[46]

Acting Chancellor Polk was very pleased with the Special Planning Committee's Report. In transmitting a copy to President O'Neil, he observed that it was ". . . succinct and on target, in my view." He told O'Neil that he would soon give notice to four staff members that their positions would be terminated as of the first of July. In addition, he immediately began working to facilitate the transfer of three data processing personnel to UW System Administration offices. Polk moved quickly on these tasks so that the morale of remaining Central Office staff members would rise—the uncertainty of the past six months had taken a heavy toll on everyone's spirits. When all of these transitions were completed, the central administration would be at the level proposed by the SPC.[47]

Now Polk turned his attention to lining up support, both inside and outside the Center System, for the Special Planning Committee recommendations. With a sense of relief, the various Center System constituencies endorsed the Report. For example, the Faculty Senate did so unanimously in April, including even the votes of senators from campuses which had expressed an interest in affiliation with UW-Madison.[48] A few days later, Polk appeared to have won support from President O'Neil, who announced that he was removing the "Acting" from Polk's title. This meant that Polk would be the Center System's Chancellor until May 1983, when he would return full time to System Administration. In making this announcement, however, O'Neil, ominously noted that this interim appointment would provide time ". . . for the UW System Administration to review various alternative structures and options . . ." for the Center System. These were most disquieting words because they suggested that O'Neil had lingering doubts that the thirteen Centers should continue to operate as a single institution.[49]

Polk, who had become convinced that the Center System was a valuable asset to the University, wrote a long letter to O'Neil concerning these remarks. He reiterated his conclusion that the Center System was now on the right track. Polk insisted that the major elements in the Six Year Plan and the Special Planning Committee proposals preserved "the best of the Center System whose liberal arts transfer mission and function as an access point for thousands of Wisconsin students are in my view indispensable contributions to the University of Wisconsin System. That the Center System is still there to be salvaged is remarkable in itself after all the buffeting it has received." Polk reviewed the key items that remained to be accomplished and closed with, "Before we can, as a Center System, move toward implementing some necessary internal management improvements, we need badly a corroboration of the plan so that we can do away with the arguments of those who say we should not proceed with further activity until we know that we will be permitted to continue as a System of Centers."[50] Polk urged O'Neil to provide this reinforcement when he came to the May Senate meeting.

It is clear that Polk had carefully calculated his strategy. A week before he sent his letter to O'Neil, he had written confidentially to Therese Rozga, Chair of the Senate Steering Committee, asking her to prime the senators to express to O'Neil, "The depth of their concern about any imposed change of planning direction which would disregard progress in the past months and throw the Center System into turmoil once again." Polk mentioned that he also had arranged for two members of the Board of Visitors to be present at the Senate meeting, to make strong statements of support for keeping the Center System intact.[51] The transcript of the senators' comments and O'Neil's responses clearly reveal that he was surprised by the extensive support for maintaining the Center System. When he remarked that he had heard from a few faculty who continued to talk favorably about affiliation with Madison, several senators responded that this was the minority opinion even on those campuses and that O'Neil should not listen to these lingering malcontents. Instead he should weigh heavily the position of the official governance body, the Senate, in shaping his recommendations to the Board of Regents about the future of the Center System.[52] A couple of weeks later, O'Neil reassured Polk that he approved of the steps already taken to reduce the central office staff and asserted that his "careful consideration" of the SPC Report did not mean that he disagreed with it. O'Neil asked Polk to relay this message to the Centers and to arrange for O'Neil to meet with the Board of Visitors and the Deans to discuss the Report.[53]

In the fall of 1982, as the President worked to shape his recommendations to the Board of Regents, Polk tried hard to steer him toward keeping the Center System intact. But O'Neil had also received pressure from people outside the UW System and from some Regents to make ". . . significant changes in the present organization of the Center System."[54] After he finished drafting his recommendations in mid October, O'Neil asked Polk to distribute the text for comment to the Board of Visitors, the Deans, and the Faculty Senate leaders. While there was much in the draft that pleased Polk and these groups, they were greatly concerned about three points. Polk wrote that they were worried about O'Neil's observation that alternate structures, such as those in the Special Planning Committee Report, ". . . remain attractive and potentially viable for the future." Faculty leaders were especially concerned that this remark signaled that the Center System would remain under intense scrutiny and that an alternate structure might yet be "imposed" upon them. Polk asked O'Neil to recast the sentence, "Additional economies [in Central Administration] should be considered and implemented as soon as possible.," because it had totally deflated the morale of Polk's staff. Polk suggested that O'Neil might simply enumerate the central office reductions already made and stress that progress had been made toward establishing a Central Administration that could provide necessary services at "the lowest cost practical." [55]

The third point, however, was the most alarming. In discussing the need to appoint a search and screen committee to select Polk's successor, O'Neil had written, "I believe there may be much value in changing the title from Chancellor (as it now is) to something a bit more modest, . . . [because] it would signal that the academic and administrative leadership of our Centers resides in their Deans and campus-based colleagues—even though major personnel and policy decisions would remain centrally." Polk reported that this proposal alarmed everyone because it would signal a lesser role for the Centers in the UW System decision-making process. In addition, the reference to the Deans as the Centers' academic leaders thoroughly upset the faculty leaders because the academic departments, under the Constitution, had the primary role in making faculty appointments, awarding tenure, and monitoring the curriculum. The department chairs, Polk observed, guarded their prerogatives "jealously" against any encroachment by the Deans. To cushion the impact of changing the title of the chief executive, Polk counseled O'Neil to enumerate the powers of the office to clarify that its holder would meet with the other chancellors. Further, he recommended that the reference to the Deans as "academic leaders" be dropped, and that O'Neil explain that they have assumed a somewhat larger "administrative" role, due to the cutbacks in the central office. [56] Ultimately, O'Neil accepted each of these three suggestions.

Polk continued a personal struggle to prevent a change in the chancellor's title until the eve of the November Board of Regents meeting. He also helped arrange a meeting with O'Neil for the Senate Steering Committee, which hoped a last-minute appeal might change the President's mind. It did not. O'Neil told the Steering Committee that he would recommend to the Board, in two days, both a new name for the institution and a new title for its chief executive. He cautioned the Steering Committee not to make its displeasure public, because there were many individuals, including some Regents, who anticipated that much more drastic medicine would be prescribed for the Center System. [57] The next day, November 4, Polk wrote

O'Neil that he, too, had advised the Steering Committee not to go public with its concerns. Polk then informed O'Neil that he did not want to be called upon for comment in the Regents' meeting because he would have to politely disagree with the President's recommendations.[58]

Except for Polk and the Steering Committee, President O'Neil's announcement that he was recommending a new institutional name for the Center System and a new title for its chief executive caught everyone at the Board meeting by surprise. O'Neil proposed "UW Centers" as the new institutional label to remove confusion that arose from having two "Systems" in the University. The new title, "Executive Dean," he explained, signaled that the Centers had made significant progress in the last year and a half toward coming together in an effective thirteen campus federation. He emphasized that the executive dean would have the statutory powers of a chancellor and would meet with the Council of Chancellors. O'Neil concluded his report on the Centers by requesting the Board to authorize the recruitment of "an Executive Dean of the University of Wisconsin Centers." When asked whether the Centers' staff had been made aware of the President's recommendations or expressed opposition, O'Neil chose his words carefully. He replied that he had met with the Steering Committee and that he had sensed "some concern" among its members, as well as among the Deans and other groups, that the changes would signal a lesser stature for the Centers. But "As we talked and as I explained some of the thinking that went into the recommendation and shared with them my desire to strengthen and to recognize the role of the Centers, rather than of a central administration, it seemed to me that there was understanding, if not in all quarters complete happiness with the change." The Regents then unanimously endorsed the new name and authorized the search for an Executive Dean.[59]

When Chancellor Polk retired from his Center System duties, in May 1983, faculty, staff, and administrators regretted his departure. In his twenty-two months with the Centers, he had compiled an impressive list of accomplishments. He had taken charge of a dispirited team in August 1981, had dispelled fears that he had been assigned to break up the Center System, and had initiated a planning process to implement the recommendations of the System Special Task Force and of the Centers' Long Range Planning Committee. After he had assessed the situation, he moved quickly to pare down the central office staff, a step that Chancellor Fort had avoided for years. Through his System vice presidency, Polk had communicated to O'Neil and his staff his growing admiration for the hard-working people he met. Moreover, he had brought two mutually suspicious groups—the deans and department chairs—very near to an agreement on a curriculum planning protocol that recognized the academic departments' primary role in approving the courses and the instructors who would teach them. Perhaps most importantly, Robert Polk had restored the morale of those who worked in the Centers. When he left, they looked forward to a second straight fall semester with an enrollment over 10,000 students. And there was no budget crisis on the horizon!

Nine

The UW Centers Achieve Stability: 1983-1991

On July 1, 1983, the renamed University of Wisconsin Centers came into existence, signifying a new beginning for the two-year campuses. The institution also had a new leader, Lorman "Larry" Ratner, who began his duties as the Centers' first Executive Dean in September. Ratner, a historian and experienced administrator, had spent the last six years at UW-Parkside as its vice chancellor and dean of the faculty. Because Parkside, too, had been under intense scrutiny for its excessively high costs and sagging enrollment, Ratner understood well the pressures he would experience in his new position. But he also knew that the Centers were in better shape than at any time since merger, thanks to the efforts of Acting Chancellor Robert Polk, the faculty, and the staff, who had developed long-range plans for the institution.

Ratner assumed his office knowing that a large share of his time would be devoted to consolidating the Centers' recent gains and pushing toward fulfillment of its long-range goals. In budgetary terms, the institution needed to become even more efficient to further reduce the cost-per-student (CSI). The Long Range Planning Committee had recommended that these efficiencies be achieved by careful annual and long-range planning of the academic program to enable the Centers to make wise rather than expedient reductions during any future fiscal crises. The Centers also needed to work hard to maintain and even increase enrollment. In Fall 1983, it enrolled 10,454 students and was the sixth-largest institution in the UW System.

Ratner was also determined to improve the image and clarify the role of the Centers. The Scope Reduction episode had again demonstrated that very few persons outside the Centers really understood how the two-year campuses fit into Wisconsin higher education. For example, many still referred to their local two-year campus as the Extension Center, even though the connection with UW Extension had been severed in 1964. In addition, numerous citizens perceived the Centers as community or junior colleges, rather than as a fully accredited unit of the University of Wisconsin. Even some UW System administrators saw the Centers only as a troublesome entity which had repeatedly drawn unfavorable attention. Indeed, former Chancellor Polk had begun his duties skeptical of the ability of the Center System to surmount its problems. However, he had been won over as he came to understand the unique contributions the Centers made in providing access to higher education for thousands of students and in assisting the UW to fulfill the Wisconsin Idea. Polk had also recognized the political potential of the Centers, whose service areas included all or part of the districts of fifty Assembly representatives and of twenty-one state senators (72% of the state legislators) but he had not found the time to stage an event that would bring them together. Now, with the Centers' circumstances much improved, Ratner intended to do so.

Ratner's featured event was a legislators' luncheon, officially initiated in February of 1984 by the Centers' Board of Visitors (BOV). The BOV, consisting of one leading citizen from each Center community, had been established by Chancellor Fort in 1979. The Visitors had proven quite effective in contacting local legislators, regents, and even President O'Neil to plead the Centers' case, so it made great sense to employ them in this endeavor.[1] Amazingly, 47 legislators attended the inaugural luncheon, held at the Edgewater Hotel in Madison. Although primarily a social gathering, Executive Dean Ratner and President O'Neil presented a few key facts about the Centers and the UW System. Ratner capitalized on this introduction with follow-up visits to twenty legislators in the state capitol. Additionally, he directed the deans to invite their area representatives and senators to come to the campuses and become better acquainted with the Centers and its vital role in the communities. The legislators' luncheon became an annual event, one that has been very useful over the years, not just to the Centers, but to the entire UW System.[2]

The campaign to better acquaint the Regents and the top UW System administrators with the Centers pushed ahead when the Centers hosted the October 1984 Board of Regents meeting at the Marathon County Campus.

The persistent efforts of Marathon County Dean Stephen Portch finally brought the regents to a Centers' campus so that all the board members could learn first-hand about the Centers. The Centers seized this opportunity to showcase its best features. Four students, two former and two current, including one who had dropped out of high school and had returned to school at age 25, captivated the Regents with their accounts of how the Centers had helped them toward their goals. Collectively, the students recited the advantages that had convinced them to enroll at the local Center—they saved a great deal of money by living at home and keeping their part-time jobs, they could readily participate in student government and cultural events, and they found the staff and faculty readily accessible and attentive to their needs. The two who had already completed baccalaureate degrees testified that the Centers had prepared them well for upper division courses.

Roy Valitchka, a member of the Centers' Board of Visitors, stressed the community services provided by the campuses. Among many examples, he described faculty consultants working to solve local problems, the College for Kids program at seven Centers, the sharing of facilities between Barron County and the Indianhead Technical School, and the campus-community bands and drama groups at several Centers. Kerry Trask, Chair of the Senate Steering Committee, completed the "show and tell" session with a profile of the Centers' 345 faculty members. He illustrated that they held as many doctorates and had published as many books and scholarly articles as the University Cluster faculty.[3] Following this successful occasion, the Centers have periodically hosted a Board of Regents meeting.

By 1983 it was clear that the days when the University could rely on an ever-expanding state budget, as it had during the 1960s and early 1970s, were gone forever. Governor Lee Dreyfus, who had entered office in 1979 amidst a debate over how most responsibly to spend a budget surplus, left to his successor, Democrat Tony Earl, the problem of overcoming a deficit to balance the state's accounts.[4] Indeed, economic issues had dominated the 1982 governor's campaign, when Earl and Republican Terry Kohler each asserted that he was better qualified to revive Wisconsin's economy and bring down her 11.3% unemployment rate. The poor economy, naturally, meant declining tax revenues, at a time when demands on the state's coffers were increasing. During the 1982 campaign, the UW System released a study which revealed that, although its budget for 1981-82 had been increased by 4%, the University had actually received $54.6 million less in constant dollars compared to 1973-74.[5]

The Centers' budget situation in the early 1980s, of course, mirrored the increasingly tight fiscal circumstances of the entire University. Inflation, fueled primarily by the OPEC oil crises of 1973 and 1979, had greatly eroded the purchasing power of the dollar. In addition, the Centers' and the UW's enrollment had defied predictions and had continued to climb, putting even more pressure on budgets. Because the enrollment increase was not evenly distributed among the thirteen two-year campuses, some Centers, particularly the larger ones, were quite seriously underfunded and, in a few instances, understaffed. On the positive side, attracting more students enabled the Centers, in 1984, to reduce its CSI to sixth among the fourteen UW institutions, the best ratio ever.[6]

The Centers' unique configuration—thirteen campuses scattered across the state—compounded its fiscal straits. Executive Dean Ratner repeatedly made this point in his communications to the President's office, seeking a fairer and larger share of the UW budget, to compensate somewhat for the institution's inability to achieve the economies of scale available to a single-site campus.[7] One concern he noted was that the Centers needed a healthy infusion of money to begin replacing old-fashioned and worn-out instructional equipment, much of which dated to the 1960s or even earlier. The problem was particularly acute in the laboratories. Ratner pithily noted that the Centers received $150,000 per year to maintain and upgrade thirteen sets of labs (97 labs, total), the same amount that his former institution, UW-Parkside, received for one set of laboratories. President O'Neil responded with a $200,000 no-interest loan so that the most pressing new instructional equipment needs could be addressed; but, because a loan mortgaged future equipment budgets, it did not solve the Centers' perennial difficulty in providing the latest equipment for all of its classes.[8]

Another concern was that the Centers' libraries also desperately needed more money. The dollar amount of the libraries' allocations had remained practically constant since merger, consequently the ability to maintain up-to-date collections had been eaten away by inflation. Hence the library directors increasingly had to prioritize book purchases and to prune the periodicals' subscription list to balance budgets. In addition to these routine expenses, the Centers' libraries were becoming connected with the Ohio Colleges Library Consortium (OCLC). When completed, OCLC would enable a student or faculty member to access a shared database for all the cooperating libraries in North America to search for a particular book or periodical article. Naturally a considerable expense was attached to converting the thirteen libraries' catalogs to a machine-readable format and to provide the hardware, software, and network wiring necessary to become effective users of OCLC. Executive Dean Ratner repeatedly pled with UW System for additional funds to help underwrite these modernizing expenses.[9]

Yet another concern was that faculty salaries had not been maintained at a competitive level. In the successful effort to trim operating costs, the

Centers had held down starting salaries for new faculty. Since annual salary increases were awarded as a percentage of all salaries, this stratagem also held down the size of the pie available for distribution. The state's fiscal constraints, too, contributed to the problem. A succession of raises far below the annual rate of inflation had caused a salary crisis throughout the entire UW System because the real dollar value of faculty salaries had declined by twenty percent since 1966.[10] The UW found it increasingly difficult to attract and retain top-notch teachers and scholars. When advertisements of vacant positions failed to attract suitable candidates, Centers' starting salaries were increased. This, however, created a salary compression problem by providing a few new hires with an initial salary very close to, or perhaps even exceeding, those of veteran teachers. Salary compression and inadequate raises were very demoralizing and caused some experienced faculty to leave the Centers for better paying positions.

The crisis peaked in the summer of 1983 when Governor Earl announced that, in order to balance the state's accounts, all state employees' salaries would be frozen at their current level for one year. Naturally, this decree drew strong protests from the state employees' union and the Board of Regents. These groups asserted that persons who worked for the state were being arbitrarily compelled to shoulder an unfair share of Wisconsin's economic burden. Subsequently, in September 1983, Governor Earl, in close cooperation with the Board, established a sixteen-member Faculty Compensation Study Committee. To increase the legitimacy of the group, the Committee had a non-UW majority and included just three faculty members. Professor Ted Kinnaman (Rock County—Music) secured one of the faculty slots.[11] The Governor directed the study to be completed by the end of March 1984.

The Faculty Compensation Study Committee selected three out-of-state university peer groups (one for Madison, one for Milwaukee, one for the University Cluster and Centers) to which UW faculty salaries would be compared. Initially, the Committee planned to compare Centers' salaries to those of other states' two-year institutions, but the search for a comparable group proved futile, and the Centers' compensation instead was measured against the University Cluster's peer group of fifty institutions. A few University Cluster faculty leaders loudly complained about the inclusion of the Centers in their peer group. They believed that, because the Centers' faculty taught just freshmen and sophomores, the Centers' teachers were less qualified than the Cluster's faculty. However, Ratner produced data that showed that two-thirds of his faculty held a Ph.D. or other terminal degree in their academic fields, a statistic that stacked up well against the Cluster faculty achievements, and that the scholarly output of several departments outpaced that of the Cluster departments.[12]

The peer group comparisons produced startling results. The Madison faculty was paid on average 15% less; Milwaukee's faculty was 11% behind; the Cluster faculty, who came closest to matching their peers' compensation, still was paid 6% less; and the Centers' faculty salaries had ranked a miserable 48th among the 50 peer institutions. This meant that a 17% raise would be required to raise the Centers' compensation to the median of the group.[13] Indeed, the survey also indicated that Centers' salaries were well below those paid in the VTAE System and even beneath those paid to most Wisconsin public school teachers.[14]

Armed with these figures in the fall of 1984 the Board of Regents developed its catch-up salary proposal for the upcoming biennium. The Centers' proposed increase, 15%, was the same as Madison's but, of course, the dollar value of the average increase was vastly different. The Madison average came to $5,351, while the Centers' figure was $3,588. These amounts would lift Madison's compensation to the middle of its peer group, but leave the Centers 3% below the median of its colleagues. UW-Milwaukee's 11% ($3,416) would put her in the middle, too. The University Cluster fared the best because its 9% ($2,588) would elevate the average faculty salary 3% above the median. These catch-up increases, if approved by the legislators, would be paid in addition to the normal pay package and would be phased-in in three steps—40% paid in January 1986, 30% in July 1986, and 30% in January 1987.[15]

Even though the data clearly showed that the Centers' faculty deserved to receive the same percentage of catch-up as Madison's, a few vocal University Cluster faculty leaders continued to complain publicly about this so-called preferential treatment. This opposition, potentially, could have jeopardized the entire catch-up salary process by giving naysayers in the legislature the opportunity to assert that no plan should be approved until the entire UW System had come to an agreement. In the midst of this bickering, Executive Dean Ratner used his political contacts to line up support for the Regents' proposal. The annual legislators' luncheon, February 6, 1985, attracted 45 legislators, giving both Ratner and President O'Neil a forum in which to promote the catch-up package. Ratner also urged the deans and their steering committees to invite area legislators to local campuses and lobby for the proposal.[16]

Because Governor Earl and his party's leaders in the legislature had pledged to support the recommendations of the Faculty Compensation Study Committee, the various UW faculties began planning how to divide the catch-up money. Naturally, the prospect of having $1,265,000 to distribute elicited differences of opinion among the Centers' faculty over how the money ought to be disbursed. The senior faculty, for example, favored a straight 15%

increase for everyone, since, as the data showed, they were the furthest behind in compensation and had suffered the longest. The junior faculty, on the other hand, preferred an across-the-board award of $3,600 to each person, because everyone had equally suffered from the effects of inflation and years of inadequate raises.[17] As it turned out, however, the Board of Regents' guidelines for dividing the funds specified that the distribution plan could not be across-the-board but that it must weigh heavily the merit ratings each faculty member had received since 1981 and must include a market adjustment factor for those departments whose members were at greatest risk of being lured away by higher salaries.

The Senate Budget and Steering Committees jointly developed the Centers' plan. Adhering to the System guidelines, they determined that the greatest portion (62%) of the catch-up dollars would be distributed by multiplying ones total merit points earned during the previous five years by the value of a single merit point ($127.77). This formula would award the largest sums to the most outstanding faculty members. Then, thirty percent would be divided through the use of a rank factor (Instructor - 1.50, Assistant Professor - 1.75, Associate Professor - 2.25, Professor - 3.0), multiplied by one's average merit. This calculation distributed the largest amounts to those in the upper two ranks, thus addressing somewhat the salary compression issue. Finally, the remaining eight percent would be used to counteract the market pressures on the salaries of the most meritorious members of five departments—computer science, mathematics, business, economics, and psychology.[18] This carefully crafted formula has since been used, with necessary minor modifications, each time the state has provided special "catch-up" or "keep-up" raises for UW employees.

The legislature's eventual approval of the Board's catch-up plan greatly bolstered the morale of the Centers' faculty and academic staff. Their elation, however, was dampened a good deal by the state's latest budget crisis. It was the same old story: the revenue department had reduced its income projections for the next 18 months, January 1986 through June 1987, which forced Governor Earl to order state agencies to reduce spending by $33 million for that period.[19] The UW System had to bear almost half of the total reduction, $15.6 million, with the Centers' share pegged at $600,000. This figure included $100,000 that the Centers would contribute toward funding the catch-up compensation package.[20]

Once again, the suddenness of the mandated budget reduction compelled the Centers to extract most of the money from the instructional program, even though that meant reducing the number of sections of basic courses, such as entry level English and mathematics. Thus, $325,000 was trimmed from the instructional budget by cutting out eleven lecturers' positions and by not filling some existing vacancies. The instructional equipment budget was slashed by $110,000, wiping out much of the progress that had been made with the loan to update laboratory equipment. The remainder of the giveback was skimmed from faculty salaries, primarily from the difference in compensation for a retiree and a new hire.[21] Given the Centers' record enrollment, these decreases meant that some freshmen would have to delay their enrollment in basic English and math courses and the faculty would shoulder a heavier workload.

Meanwhile, the Centers continued to work on two issues of Systemwide importance. First, the Board of Regents had directed, in April 1982, that UW-Extension faculty be integrated with the faculties of the thirteen degree-granting institutions.[22] Secondly, the increased employment of non-tenure track instructors—or lecturers as they were popularly labeled—was a problem considerably less clear-cut in both its extent and its solution.

Historically, in the early days of the Extension Centers, the field agents in a Center's district had also arranged non-credit, continuing education courses. In a Center community, these courses were usually offered at the Center campus. Elsewhere in the district, the Extension agent contracted with a vocational high school or with a business, which had the necessary equipment, for space to offer adult continuing education programs. This arrangement ceased, of course, in mid 1964, when the Center System was created. At that time, only three Centers—Baraboo, Fox Valley, Marinette—had retained a continuing education coordinator.[23] The other Centers were either served by an Extension agent whose office was off-campus or they did not have a continuing education program.

The UWC-Continuing Education Long Range Plan, sent to Extension Chancellor Patrick Boyle by Executive Dean Ratner in April 1984, listed six continuing education needs which had been identified via surveys of the Centers' service areas. These needs included, first, education, with a special emphasis upon providing courses for public school teachers to enable them to fulfill recertification requirements; second, technology, especially workshops that provided instruction in using microcomputers for data management and literacy in specific software programs; and third, health, with workshops focused primarily upon stress management, maintaining good health, and aging. The third need recognized an important demographic trend and aimed at assisting senior citizens to make the most of their retirement years. The fourth need—personal development and enrichment, which would be met via a wide range of non-credit courses that fostered cultural enrichment and the productive use of leisure time—also responded to this trend. Business, with a particular focus upon employee and management training and development was the fifth need identified in the surveys. Sixth, the surveys identified a need for inservice training for human services and law enforcement employees.[24]

To implement this plan, Extension Chancellor Boyle authorized the transfer from Extension to the Centers of ten half-time continuing education coordinators' positions and start-up funds for each.[25] On behalf of the Centers, Ratner pledged that the Center dean, business manager, public information officer, and a secretary at each campus would devote approximately ten percent of their time to assist the coordinator in developing and expanding continuing education programs.[26] It was anticipated that the continuing education courses and workshops, in addition to helping the University fulfill the time-honored Wisconsin Idea, would acquaint hundreds of adults with the local two-year campus. It was hoped that these adults would prompt their children and grandchildren to enroll at the Center.[27]

In September 1983 System Vice President for Academic Affairs Katharine Lyall presented the Board of Regents with four reasons for the increased use of lecturers. All four concerned maintaining sufficient fiscal flexibility so that UW System could balance its budget. First, Lyall cited the regents' own mandate that UW institutions maintain enough staffing flexibility to avoid tenured faculty layoffs in a time of fiscal crisis. Second, she explained that the state sometimes provided limited-term positions and funds so that the University could accomplish a special project; these positions could not be filled with tenure track faculty. Third, Lyall noted the state's repeated last minute budget givebacks as a reason for using lecturers, because they could be laid off mid-year to free up funds. Finally, Lyall described the continuing economic uncertainty as the fourth reason to hold down the number of tenure track appointments.[28] As the years passed the number of lecturers employed in the UW System has steadily increased. Indeed, the situation became so serious at some Centers that questions were raised whether some academic staff would need to be removed from local collegium membership in order to maintain the constitution-mandated faculty majority in the collegium and on its committees.

Lyall's explanation (particularly her remarks about maintaining staffing flexibility to meet fiscal constraints) corresponded well with the Centers' experience in employing lecturers. Indeed, Chancellor Fort's consideration of these factors had prompted him, in May 1980, to attempt to deny tenure to several probationary faculty members to regulate tenure density. At the time Chancellor Fort made his announcement, the Senate had under consideration a "Policy on the Use of Teaching Academic Staff" which was designed to prevent vacant full time positions from being filled by lecturers. The Policy stipulated that any vacant full-time position should be staffed by a faculty appointee, unless one of these conditions existed: it became vacant too late to follow the prescribed appointment procedure; the candidates were unqualified; the opening was temporary because a faculty member was on leave; or enrollment projections raised serious concerns about the long-term stability of the position. The Policy provided, further, that after a position had been filled by a full-time lecturer for two years, it should be reviewed by the chancellor, the dean, a faculty representative from the Center, and the relevant department chair to determine whether a faculty appointment could be sustained in future years. If the decision was affirmative, the vacancy would be advertised and filled by a tenure track faculty member.[29]

Interestingly, nineteen eighty-six was a year of many transitions in the University and in state government. A new president took office at UW System; the Centers welcomed a new chief executive with the restored title of chancellor; and voters ousted incumbent Democrat Governor Earl in favor of Republican Tommy Thompson. In January 1985 President O'Neil confirmed rumors that he had accepted the presidency of the University of Virginia, as of the Fall 1985 semester. O'Neil explained that he could not pass up an opportunity to lead a university founded by Thomas Jefferson. Vice President Katharine Lyall served as Acting President for five months, until the new president assumed office.[30]

The new System President was Kenneth "Buzz" Shaw. Shaw, who had headed the multi-campus Southern Illinois University System since 1979, was appointed in September 1985 but assumed office February 1, 1986. Shaw, whose academic credentials included a Ph.D. in sociology from Purdue University, drew a good deal of Wisconsin media attention because he had been a star basketball guard in high school and at Illinois State University during his undergraduate years. Only 46, Shaw impressed the search committee with his success in convincing the Illinois governor and state legislature to significantly increase funding for the SIU System.[31]

Meanwhile, Executive Dean Ratner tendered his resignation, effective July 1, 1986, to Acting President Lyall. He explained that he would become the Dean of Liberal Arts at the University of Tennessee-Knoxville, thus fulfilling a desire to return to a single-campus institution. Just shortly after O'Neil's departure, Ratner had requested Acting President Lyall to support the restoration of the title of chancellor for the Centers' chief executive. After due consideration, Lyall forwarded the proposal to the Board of Regents, which unanimously gave its approval. President Shaw, in his first meeting with the Regents, also strongly supported the restoration, noting that, with more than 10,000 students, the Centers ranked among the largest institutions in the UW System and that ". . . it was not fair for the institution to be headed by a chancellor in fact, but not in title." Long-time Regent Ody Fish observed that he had very reluctantly supported the change to executive dean and that he now embraced the opportunity to vote to restore the chancellor title.[32]

In August 1986, President Shaw announced that the Centers new chancellor, who would assume office on November first, would be Stephen Portch. Portch, a native of England, had earned an undergraduate degree from the University of Reading and had subsequently studied at Pennsylvania State University, where he earned a masters degree (1976) in English and a doctorate (1980) in higher education administration. Portch had served on the UWC-Richland faculty as a professor of English from 1976 to 1981, at which time he became dean of the UWC-Marathon County. Chancellor Portch, in his inaugural visits to each Center, stressed three major goals he wished to achieve—a significant increase in sophomore retention, a Systemwide transfer of credit policy, and the creation of a new curriculum with a beefed-up associate degree.[33]

The 1986 governor's election pitted incumbent Democrat Tony Earl against Republican Tommy Thompson, who had served ten terms in the Assembly, including several as his party's minority leader. As usual, economic issues played an important role in the campaign. Much of the debate was shaped by a fifteen-minute video, titled "Choices," that blamed many of the state's business community's woes upon excessive state taxation and spending. In particular, the video's three sponsors—the Council of Small Business Executives, the Independent Business Association of Wisconsin, and the Milwaukee Metropolitan Association of Commerce—asked whether Wisconsin could continue to afford all thirteen four-year campuses of the UW System, its generous welfare benefits, and the high level of aid to local governments and public schools.[34] "Choices" did not endorse a gubernatorial candidate; however, the Democrats quickly charged that the sponsors were pushing to elect Thompson, a known fiscal conservative. That allegation gained credence when Thompson, in early October, indicated that if he became governor, he would require all state agencies, including the University, to demonstrate how they would operate with a 5% budget reduction in the 1987-1989 biennium. Regent Ody Fish, a key figure in the Republican party, responded that the Board would be very hard pressed to operate the System with 50 million fewer dollars. Indeed, the regents' Study Group on the Future of the UW System, which Fish chaired, had recently proposed a $50 million increase in the upcoming biennium to enable the University to maintain the quality of its academic program in the midst of ever-increasing enrollments. Thus, if Thompson would become governor and he implemented his 5% reduction, the University of Wisconsin's 1987-89 budget would be $100 million less than the amount estimated to maintain quality and the current record enrollment. Fish summed up his observations with the comment, "There must be a limit somewhere to just how many of these [reductions] we can take and not hurt educational offerings." [35]

Although the Democrats pasted an "anti-education" label on Thompson for his campaign promises to reduce state expenditures for both the UW System and aids to local school districts, he easily defeated Earl, 773,458 (53%) to 683,172 (47%), in the November balloting. However, the Democrats retained majorities in both chambers of the legislature, assuring a spirited battle over the biennial budget. [36] Two days after the election, news surfaced that Thompson, several days prior to the voting, had reassured Regent President Laurence Weinstein that the UW would not be required to plan for a 5% budget reduction, as would other state agencies. While this was welcome news, the fact that Thompson also warned the regents not to anticipate any increase in state support meant that the UW's proposed 1987-1989 budget would be underfunded by at least $50 million. [37]

Throughout 1986, the Board of Regents' Study Group on the Future of the UW System, chaired by Regent Fish, had labored over budget issues. The Group worked with the understanding that a significant increase in state support for the University would not be forthcoming. Thus, the Study Group's major task was to determine how to bring the UW's enrollment and resources back into balance, while maintaining both access for students and a high quality academic program. The budget already was millions of dollars out of balance primarily because, contrary to predictions, a larger percentage of Wisconsin high school graduates had chosen to enroll, increasing the UW enrollment rate from 24.5% in 1979 to 31.5% in Fall 1985. This unexpected trend had pushed the UW enrollment almost 16,000 students above budget. Some of this increase was being accommodated by faculty and staff shouldering a heavier workload. But, at the most popular campuses, such as Madison, Milwaukee, Eau Claire, and La Crosse, this workload expansion had reached its limit, resulting in long lines of frustrated students during registration, who were forced to rework their schedules because key courses were closed. [38]

The Board ultimately settled upon a four-year plan, known as Enrollment Management I, to reduce gradually the System's enrollment by 7,000 FTE students. The regents believed this reduction, which would parallel a projected decline in the number of high school graduates, could be made without denying qualified students access to the University. The key to Enrollment Management I was beefed-up admission standards for high school graduates. Another objective of the plan was to encourage more students to enroll at UW institutions that were currently underutilized, such as the Centers, Superior, and Parkside. [39]

The regents allocated the Centers an additional 2,250 students, the largest increase under Enrollment Management I. Tuition in the Centers was deliberately made the lowest in the System, as an economic enticement. In addition, the Centers remained the only open enrollment institution, thus it served as an access point for students who had graduated in the lower half of their class and who probably could not meet the stiffened UW admission requirements. The Centers, thus, would continue to provide the academic late-bloomers with an opportunity to try out college.[40]

During the development of Enrollment Management I, the Study Group had been informed that important policy changes would be necessary to enable the Centers to attract more students. President Shaw, in his first meeting with the Board, had urged the Regents to strengthen the systemwide credit transfer policy to require acceptance of the Centers' Associate Degree as fulfilling all four-year UWs' general education requirements. Such a policy, Shaw said, would assure each Centers' student that all the credits would transfer, making a Center an attractive place to begin a UW education.[41]

Executive Dean Ratner, during his last six months in Wisconsin, worked hard to persuade the regents to support President Shaw's proposal. Addressing the Board in February 1986, Ratner said that, "The issue of transfer needs to be acknowledged as a System concern and the best solution to it as one which emanates from the System. . . . An unambiguous transfer policy would encourage more students to attend a Center and [convince] more students to remain at a Center for more than one year."[42] A few days later, Ratner delivered the same message to nearly 60 state representatives and senators, who attended the annual Centers' Legislative Luncheon.[43]

The Centers' Senate and its Steering Committee, chaired by Professor Jim Lorence (history—Marathon County), represented the faculty and academic staff and reinforced Ratner's efforts. On February 26, the Steering Committee sent Working Together: The Centers in the University of Wisconsin System to the Regents' Study Group. Four of the five issues addressed in Working Together concerned transfer. First, the Steering Committee described an "increasing tendency at baccalaureate institutions to mandate early transfer by requiring students to complete preprofessional program requirements and foundation courses in the sophomore year and, in some cases, even in the freshman year."[44] It called upon the UW System to monitor the baccalaureate academic programs to prevent the placement of preprofessional courses in the freshman or sophomore years, unless it was absolutely necessary.[45] Another issue concerned the variation in the general education requirements at the thirteen baccalaureate campuses, which caused difficulty in properly preparing students for transfer. The best solution, the Steering Committee suggested, would be for the regents to "direct the full systemwide acceptance of the Associate Degree as meeting the general education requirements."[46] It noted that six degree-granting UWs already accepted the Centers' Associate Degree for this purpose.

Third, the Steering Committee pointed out that a transferee could encounter difficulty when degree and/or major requirements were changed by one campus and this information was not promptly disseminated to all other UW institutions. When this occurred, the student was naturally angry and felt that credits had been "lost," even though all the Center's credits counted toward graduation. To solve this problem, the Steering Committee proposed creation of a systemwide computerized information system which would list the requirements for all majors and the course equivalencies for all UW institutions.[47] The final section in Working Together concerned non-academic problems. The most common difficulty arose when a degree-granting campus treated a Centers' transferee as a "new," rather than as a "continuing," student. This meant that the transferee, even if qualified for junior status, was compelled to register last. Often this meant that upper division courses the transferee needed were filled by the time he registered. Steering recommended that the Board mandate that a Centers' transferee be treated as a continuing student. The Steering Committee supported its proposal with the observation that a Centers' student, who had earned an Associate Degree, or who was bumping against the 72 credit rule, absolutely had to transfer. It just did not seem fair that a student was penalized when he transferred.[48] Throughout its paper, the Steering Committee sprinkled reminders that the Centers would not be able to fill completely the role envisioned for the institution during Enrollment Management I unless each prospective student was assured that all Centers' credits would transfer smoothly throughout the UW System.[49]

The Report of the Regents Study Group on the Future of the University of Wisconsin System, issued in November 1986, contained solid evidence that the Centers' lobbying efforts had borne fruit. For example, Policy Decision Summary #5, concerning Undergraduate Credit Transfer, said:

> A student transferring a UW Associate Degree to a UW university will be considered as having fulfilled the general education requirements of that university. The President, with advice from a systemwide ad hoc committee, will recommend minimum standards for general education requirements for the associate degree.
>
> To facilitate the transfer process, the UWs will establish a systemwide faculty appeals committee, a computerized course equivalency and degree requirement matrix, and will require recording on the transcript of the receiving institution all undergraduate credit courses previously completed at another UW institution.[50]

Policy Decision Summary #9 reaffirmed the UW Centers' mission and status:

> The Board reaffirms the distinct education and transfer mission of the Centers and the locally owned status of the Centers' physical plant. . . . Centers are directed to streamline their course offerings by reviewing all courses to ensure that they are appropriate to the freshman and sophomore level; they are also directed to seek additional joint activities with the VTAE. Regents' planning thresholds [250 FTE students and a cost index of 120% of the Centers' average cost] will be used by the Centers' chancellor in biennial reports to the System President to assure that each Center is appropriately utilized.[51]

This statement, after its adoption by the Board, required that the Centers eliminate all courses from its curriculum numbered above 200. The former UW Centers were still offering a few courses numbered 300, 400, and even, occasionally, 500, because their curriculums had been primarily crafted for transfer to Madison. While these statements by the Study Group were most encouraging, much hard work remained to assure that the recommendations became System policy.

During the first month of his tenure, new Chancellor Stephen Portch led and coordinated a campaign to implement the transfer recommendations. Portch's three major priorities—increase sophomore retention, a Systemwide transfer of credit policy, and creation of a new Centers' curriculum and associate degree—meshed smoothly with the Enrollment Management I goal to increase the Centers' enrollment by over 2,000 (1,200 FTE) students. Early in 1987, Portch communicated to President Shaw his concern that the two-year campuses could not achieve this goal unless an associate degree transfer policy was adopted. Without it, he predicted, many students would continue to transfer after their freshman year.

Portch also described two additional policies that he considered vital to assist the Centers to achieve its goals. One was an "articulation agreement" between the Centers and each of the four-year institutions, which would precisely specify the transfer and academic major requirements for a student who transferred before earning an associate degree. The Chancellor envisioned that each articulation agreement would also contain a course equivalency table, to enable students and advisors to plan a program of study that would fulfill these requirements. The other policy was the pending tuition differential, which would set Centers' tuition at $400 per year less than Madison's and Milwaukee's and about $100 less than the University Cluster's.[52] Its adoption would make enrollment in a Center even more economically attractive, especially if a student remained two years.

The Board of Regents took a big step toward helping transferees, in July 1987, when it approved the Minimum General Education Breadth Requirements and Associate Degree Transfer Policy. The minimum general education breadth requirements stipulated that a UW Associate Degree must require a minimum of 60 credits with a "C" average, including at least 40 credits in the following breadth areas—humanities and the fine arts, 9 to 15 credits; natural sciences and mathematics, 12 to 16 credits; and social sciences, 9 to 15 credits. Once a UW institution's associate degree contained these minimum requirements, all other UWs had to accept it as fulfilling their own "university-wide, college and school general education breadth requirements." [53]

Chancellor Portch, building on this success, in October 1987, wrote to President Shaw to solicit his support for a new Regents' policy that would guarantee a Centers' transferee would be treated exactly as a continuing student for registration and admission to university housing and to academic major courses. He asserted that a Centers' student deserved this so-called "preferential treatment" because he had to transfer whereas a student enrolled at a four-year UW campus had the option to transfer or remain at the current school. [54] A couple of weeks later, Portch sent Shaw a letter which outlined a "suggested policy on transfer treatment of UW Center students." He provided data that showed how the thirteen bachelors degree granting UWs presently treated a Center transferee. Six of these campuses—Eau Claire, Green Bay, La Crosse, Madison, Milwaukee, Oshkosh—already treated a Center transferee the same as their continuing students. Consequently, Portch argued that requiring the other seven baccalaureate UWs to do likewise would not be a major policy change. [55]

In November 1987, no doubt with President Shaw's permission, Portch broached this subject, via letter, to his chancellor colleagues. With his rationale he included transfer data for the previous five years that demonstrated the number of Center transfers to each institution had remained stable. Thus, this new policy would not create a "management nightmare" for anyone. [56] Portch went on to explain that because his fellow chancellors had been so receptive to his preliminary survey on this issue, he now believed a Regents' policy was unnecessary to achieve the Centers' goal. Instead, Portch proposed that a statement describing that a Centers' transferee would be treated as a continuing student be included in the Articulation Agreements. This statement would spell out exactly how many credits (and in which courses) a student could earn at a Center in various majors prior to transferring to a particular four-year campus. The accord would also indicate how many semesters the transferee could expect to spend completing a bachelor's degree. In this letter, Portch announced that he was reorganizing his staff to appoint a "transfer liaison," who would negotiate the Articulation Agreements and troubleshoot transfer problems. Once all these formal understandings were in place, Portch believed that the UW System could honestly say that any remaining transfer difficulties were "of the student's own making."[57]

Despite the good progress toward ironing out the long-standing transfer problems, Enrollment Management I meant that the enrollment situation was fluid, as each baccalaureate campus adopted enrollment management policies most advantageous to itself. Consequently, new alarms about the treatment of transfer students arose. For example, in early January 1988, Chancellor Portch informed his deans and department chairs that a trend seemed to be developing toward a policy which required a higher GPA for a transfer student to be admitted in "good standing" than was demanded of a continuing student.[58] President Shaw quickly reacted to this development, warning the chancellors that he did not want the four-year UWs to undo, with their transfer standards, what the System was trying to accomplish with its "tuition and Associate Degree policies." Shaw illustrated his concern by noting that a few four-year units had decided that a transfer student needed a 2.5 GPA for good standing, while a continuing student needed just a 2.0 to maintain that status. Shaw feared that this policy would cause students to bypass the Centers and destroy the work of the enrollment management program. Shaw said that he intended to discuss this issue with the chancellors, during their next council meeting.[59] Shaw's intervention proved decisive, for Chancellor Portch reported, in mid February, that 11 of the four-year campuses had agreed to treat a Center transferee exactly as they treated a continuing student. The remaining two—Oshkosh and Stout—were reviewing their policies and Portch expected that they, too, would eventually sign the agreement.[60]

In January 1989, Chancellor Portch reported to the Board of Regents and UW Center legislators the tremendous progress made toward ironing out transfer difficulties. He used the analogy of a three-legged stool to illustrate the three key developments: the Centers' recently revised associate degree and its acceptance by all UW transfer campuses as equivalent to their general education requirements; joint admissions agreements which permitted a high school senior to apply both to a Center and his intended baccalaureate campus to insure his acceptance as a junior in two years; and articulation agreements that listed the course requirements and Centers' equivalents for majors throughout the UW System. The latter policy served well the two-thirds of Centers' students who, for a variety of reasons, chose not to earn an associate degree.[61] Snags in the transfer process, of course, continued to arise but, with these policies and agreements in place, a process to rapidly resolve them had been created.

As a result of a lingering recession and years of inflationary price increases, late in 1986 alarm bells went off about the deteriorating fiscal condition of Wisconsin's Vocational, Technical, and Adult Education System. The crisis had been triggered by the same adverse economic factors that plagued the University of Wisconsin—increased energy costs and, especially, the erosion of the dollar's purchasing power. But, because of the VTAE System's unique financing arrangements (12% from tuition, 28% from state aid, 60% from local property tax levies), the early 1980s recession in agriculture had devastated the VTAE's largest source of funds by causing property values to plummet. As a result, four VTAE districts—Southwest in Fennimore, Blackhawk in Janesville, North Central in Wausau, and Mid-State in Wisconsin Rapids—were experiencing serious financial problems because they had reached the maximum property tax levy. Several more districts were rapidly approaching that limit.[62]

Initially, many thought the solution lay in changing the fiscal rules that governed the VTAE district's budgets. For example, the state could increase both the local property tax mill rate and the 12% limit on the tuition a vo-tech school could charge. Another possibility would be for the state to sharply increase its aid, thus reducing reliance on the property tax levy. However, none of these were politically palatable, in view of the state's own budget crunch and the public schools' pleas for more state aid. Some of the VTAE System's own leaders expressed concern that increased state aid would naturally entail more state mandates and a corresponding loss in local autonomy.[63]

A Governor's Study Commission on the VTAE was appointed by Thompson in March 1987 to investigate and recommend solutions. One time-worn proposal that soon surfaced was a merger of the Centers and VTAEs to create community colleges.[64] At first glance, this had always sounded like a sensible proposal—one which would save money through staff reductions and elimination of duplicate courses. Chancellor Portch quickly mobilized the deans, faculty, and staff for an offensive against a merger. He pointed out that, historically, Wisconsin had deliberately separated the two systems, so that each could concentrate on its distinct mission: job training for the VTAE and college transfer for the Centers. Portch also cited the Report of the Study Commission for Increased Cooperation between UW-Fox Valley and Fox Valley Technical Institute (1985), which had concluded, "The UW Centers do not offer a single course that is related to the primary mission of the VTAE" and "there are no [general education] courses similar enough to be comparable" to demolish the notion that a merger would eliminate a large number of duplicate courses. He asserted further that a merger would not save tax dollars because the VTAE average faculty salaries ($29,386) were much higher than in the Centers ($26,037).[65]

After also hearing considerable opposition from staunch friends of the vocational schools, the Governor's VTAE Study Commission eventually decided not to conduct an in-depth study of a merger. For example, Jim Haney of the Wisconsin Manufacturers and Commerce testified against the community college idea because he believed a merger would decrease the emphasis upon vocational skills education. Likewise, the AFL-CIO repeated its long-standing antipathy to a merger.[66] Even Governor Thompson eventually weighed in against the community college idea.[67]

Once they saw that a merger would not occur, a few aggressive VTAE directors began a campaign to secure state authorization to establish college-credit parallel programs, like those already in operation in Madison, Milwaukee and Rhinelander (Nicolet Vocational-Technical School). Dr. Mel H. Schneeberg, Director of the Midstate Technical Institute in Wisconsin Rapids, took the lead in this endeavor. For example, during his negotiations with the Marshfield/Wood County Center to determine which general education courses the Center should offer in Wisconsin Rapids, Schneeberg claimed that the University of Wisconsin really needed to provide junior and senior courses, because Midstate already supplied the general education courses![68] However, Schneeberg's assertion was seriously undercut when a Legislative Audit Bureau Study discovered agreement by the thirteen VTAE institutions without college-credit programs that their general education courses were "considerably different from those of university general education courses." This same study revealed that the UW seldom accepted general education course credits in transfer from these thirteen VTAEs, unless a student transferred into a specific vocation-oriented program.[69] The LAB report also contained data about the cost of Nicolet's college parallel program ($5,282 per FTE) that proved the Centers' costs ($3,506) were much lower. Again, neither the state nor the VTAEs would save money by creating additional college-credit parallel programs.[70]

Eventually, as the nation's economy improved, the VTAE fiscal problem diminished. However, two specific changes occurred as a result of the scrutiny given the VTAE System. First, the VTAE State Board voted, in July 1987, to change the schools' names from "technical institutes" to "technical colleges," as of January 1, 1988.[71] The second change, no doubt because it required extensive negotiations between the UW System and the VTAE System, took over two years to achieve. In June 1989, the UW Board of Regents finally approved a two-page Statement of Principles on the Transfer of Credit From the Vocational, Technical and Adult Education System to the University of Wisconsin System. The key provision, from the VTAE viewpoint, authorized

UW institutions "to accept up to fifteen (15) general education credits from a successfully completed non-college parallel Associate Degree program at a VTAE System institution." [72] The Centers regarded the "successfully completed . . . Associate Degree program. . . ." qualification as crucial to protecting its interests. This meant that the VTAE Colleges could not entice students to enroll just for their general education courses, with the expectation that those credits would readily transfer into the University of Wisconsin. In addition, the two systems exchanged "assurances" that (1) neither would seek to expand their missions into the other's statutory responsibilities, (2) the VTAEs would offer only those general education courses required for their Associate Degree programs, and (3) that ". . . college parallel programs will not be initiated in other VTAE System districts." [73] The third assurance was particularly vital to the Centers because it ruled out increased competition for college-bound freshmen.

When Chancellor Portch entered his new office he had a good understanding of the Centers' budget and personnel deficiencies because of his five years as Dean of the Marathon County Center. Many of the budget problems were perennial ones—not enough money to keep laboratories up to date, a great decline in the rate of library acquisitions, and a far too small budget for Supplies and Expenses (S&E). In addition, Portch believed that the Central Office staff needed to be reorganized and expanded, to provide better service to students and the campuses. He found the annual backlog in handling applications in the Registrar's and Financial Aids Offices especially alarming. The lack of adequate personnel in Financial Aids meant that some students did not receive their aid checks until nearly the end of the Fall semester. And the Registrar's Office typically could not promptly fill requests for transcripts, which sometimes caused delays in the admission of Center students to a four-year campus.

To address these problems, Portch proposed adding at least one FTE staff person to the Registrar's operation and, at a minimum, 2.0 FTE staff and additional part-time student assistants to the Financial Aids Office. Portch also believed the time had arrived to request that the System Administration return the data processing staff, which Chancellor Polk had transferred to UW System's Office of Information Systems, to the Centers' central office. As enrollment continued to increase this arrangement had gradually became more cumbersome and had occasionally caused delays in receiving vital data. Portch also insisted that a computer resources manager was needed to take charge of the evolving computerization of the student and business office records, the establishment of student computer labs on the thirteen campuses and to assure the compatibility of both hardware and software. Then, he wanted to create a position for a student services coordinator, whose responsibilities would be to monitor the new Associate Degree Transfer Policy, the articulation agreements and joint admissions and to trouble-shoot any transfer problems. Portch also proposed adding at least a part-time grants officer to his staff, who would assist both individuals and the institution to apply for grants and to identify new grant opportunities. [74]

Because the Centers had reached the state and UW System mandated position limit, before any new Central Office appointment could be made the Chancellor had to convince President Shaw to increase that limit. Portch successfully presented his case during budget-building and goal-setting sessions with the President. [75] Actually, the more delicate part of this process was for Portch to persuade his own faculty and staff that the time had arrived to reverse the Central Office reductions made in the early 1980s and that this could be accomplished without getting the institution into fiscal hot water. Portch began this campaign by streamlining the chain-of-command, reducing redundance in paperwork, and assigning new responsibilities. Then, after all this had been accomplished, he noted where gaps still existed. [76]

Nineteen eighty-eight brought significant changes to the Central Office. In mid-year, it moved from cramped quarters in the Madison Board of Education building to more spacious surroundings in the Verex Building. The move immediately improved morale. A Grants Officer and a Director of Academic Services were appointed. The latter had responsibility for transfer liaison and for negotiating articulation and joint admission agreements with the baccalaureate campuses. [77]

Low salaries continued to plague the Centers. The Chancellor stressed that because of low starting salaries, the Centers were unable to attract and employ a larger number of minority and female faculty members, as urged by Board of Regents policy. Portch described a position in the Philosophy Department which had been vacant for three years. In that time, eleven women had declined the position or had refused to even come for an interview because of the Centers' miserly $20,000 starting salary. The position had finally been filled by a white male. In a separate incident, a black woman, who had applied for a tenure-track position in the English Department, instead took a similar position at UW-Milwaukee for almost $9,000 more than the Centers could offer. [78]

Meanwhile, the minuscule 2% raises in each year of the 1987-89 biennium had swiftly eroded the boost provided by the 1985-87 faculty "catch-up" salary increases. Once again, University of Wisconsin salaries had plummeted to near the bottom of its peer groups and some distinguished UW teachers and researchers had been lured away by higher salaries. Consequently, when Governor Thompson included another catch-up proposal in his 1989-91 budget, the legislature readily approved it. As in 1985, the new peer group salary comparisons demonstrated that Madison's and the Centers' faculty deserved the largest catch-up percentage (7.2%).[79]

The Board of Regents, because of its recent experience, quickly developed the guidelines for the individual UW institutions to follow in developing allocation plans. As with the first catch-up package, market factors and merit ratings drove the formula. The Centers' plan awarded the top market discipline weight (4.0) to the four academic disciplines—business, computer science, economics, engineering—whose members were most likely to be lured away by better salaries. Thirty percent of the catch-up dollars was awarded on the basis of these market discipline weights, while ten percent was distributed according to rank weightings (professor 4.0, associate professor 3.0, assistant professor 2.5, instructor 1.0). The remaining sixty percent was distributed by squaring the average of an individual's 1987 and 1988 merit ratings and adding the product to the other two formula factors. Squaring the average merit rating boosted the increase awarded to the most meritorious faculty members, hopefully preventing them from being hired away.[80] In due course, both the Board and the legislature's Joint Committee on Employment Relations approved the Centers' plan.

One significant difference in the 1989-91 salary catch-up process, compared to the first one, was the inclusion of the academic staff. The academic staff had undergone an exhaustive study which resulted in a regularization in their position titles and responsibilities. Consequently, staff salaries now could be compared to appropriate peer groups. The Centers' Academic Staff Catch-Up Plan was developed under the same guidelines as the faculty plan. Indeed, the plan for lecturers (instructional academic staff) paralleled the faculty plan, except for small changes in the weights given to the market and merit factors. In the case of the non-instructional academic staff, however, everyone was in uncharted territory. Fifty percent of the total catch-up dollars was allocated according to a market recruitment formula. This formula assigned extra weight to those titles/positions that were recruited nationally or regionally, while those advertised and recruited locally received no weight. The market merit factor, derived from an individual's 1987 and 1988 average merit rating, accounted for 35% of the distribution. The Board of Regents had directed that all UWs needed to bring their academic staff salaries closer to a peer median. The Centers used the UW System salary ranges as its peer and calculated an adjustment factor based on how far each person was from the median, thus providing the largest increments to persons in the lower pay ranges. However, just 10% of the total package was parcelled out on this basis. The final 5% was allocated on market degree, which was weighted in favor of a holder of a doctorate or master's degree.[81]

In terms of the budget, 1990 was a very good year for the Centers. As the year began, everyone was still celebrating the announcement, in December 1989, that AT&T Computer Systems would donate $2.7 million in equipment to the Centers. This gift enabled creation of CENTERSnet, which linked the Central Office and the thirteen campuses to each other and to the entire world.[82] The good news continued when Chancellor Portch announced that the Centers had received the largest percentage increase in its S&E allocation in the entire System, plus $150,000 to increase student access to computers and $66,000 to bolster library acquisitions.[83] During 1990, the Chancellor also called President Shaw's attention to vast improvements in the Centers' CSI and faculty productivity. Portch noted that internal reallocations and enrollment increases had enabled both Barron County and Richland to move out of the danger zone, by reducing their CSIs to 101.04% and 100.05%, respectively, of the Centers' average cost per student.[84] Indeed, the Fall 1990 enrollment put the entire institution in its best position within the UW System since merger. The Centers' CSI had declined to 99.6% of the University Cluster average, compared to 131% as recently as 1986. Now, six UW Cluster campuses (Green Bay, Oshkosh, Parkside, Platteville, River Falls, Superior) had a higher CSI than the Centers. The Centers' faculty productivity now reached 290 SCH per faculty member, which exceeded the undergraduate level of UW-Superior, UW-River Falls, UW-Parkside, and UW-Milwaukee.[85]

Unfortunately, 1990 ended on a sour note when Governor Thompson mandated a budget freeze for the remainder of fiscal 1991 (January through June 1991). UW System's giveback equalled $16 million over the period, to which the Centers contributed $416,000.[86] Naturally, the unwelcome budget freeze chilled the hope for approval of the UW's 1991-1993 biennial budget request.

In November 1990 President Shaw had presented a new budget strategy to the Board of Regents, for drafting the UW's 1991-1993 biennial funding request. Shaw proposed that the Regents should request the entire amount needed by the UW System to maintain the quality of its instructional program. Then, if the state did not provide the entire amount, he recommended that the University should reallocate resources to support its most essential programs. At some point, Shaw cautioned, the UW might be compelled to deny admission to qualified students because it did not have adequate finances.[87]

The Board had laid the groundwork for carrying out Shaw's proposal the previous month, when it adopted the Enrollment Management II plan, which would be in force from Fall 1990 to Fall 1994. EMII envisioned a further reduction in the University's enrollment of 5,685 FTE students. Unlike

195

EMI, when admissions standards for all but the Centers were raised to discourage under-qualified high school graduates from enrolling, the EMII reduction should occur naturally as the number of high school graduates decreased. This meant the UW would not need to fill some vacant positions and could reallocate the dollars to other uses, without increasing the student/faculty ratio, a key component in quality. EMII anticipated that all UW institutions, except Green Bay, would experience enrollment reductions. EMII expected that the Centers would achieve its reduction (448 FTE students) simply by receiving fewer applications for admission.[88]

Governor Thompson's budget proposal for the UW System for the 91-93 biennium contained $40 million less than the Board of Regents had requested. The next month President Shaw unveiled a reallocation proposal for the Board, which he labelled a Quality Reinvestment Program (QRP). Shaw's calculations predicted that the entire $40 million could be garnered by not filling vacant positions, most of which would occur through retirements, and by increasing tuition.[89] Because the vacancies would not occur in proportion to need in each institution, the president proposed that UW System should levy a "reallocation tax" on each UW institution and redistribute the proceeds to address the most pressing needs. Shaw recommended that the largest amount ($23.7 million) be dedicated to faculty compensation, in order to maintain the gains achieved through the 1990-91 catch-up plan. The next largest sum ($7.2 million) would be used to improve S&E budgets, while lesser amounts would be shifted to the UW-Madison School of Engineering, a Systemwide course assessment program, library acquisitions, improved computer access, and laboratory modernization. Fortunately, the final 1991-1993 state budget contained sufficient dollars for library acquisitions, computer access and laboratory modernization, which allowed these items to be removed from QRP. Ultimately, over three years, 1992-1995, the UW System reallocated $26.5 million.[90]

In late October 1989, Chancellor Portch appointed a thirteen member Planning Council and gave it a broad mandate to review all aspects of the UW Centers and to recommend necessary alterations in how the institution operated.[91] In its first meeting Portch observed that, because the Six Year Plan had elapsed in late 1988, the time was ripe for the Centers to evaluate how well the goals of the Six Year Plan had been achieved and to establish another long-range plan to carry the institution toward the 21st Century. Over the ensuing sixteen months, the Council invited individuals to identify problems and to suggest solutions; consulted with various constituent groups including department chairs, Deans Council, Faculty Senate, and Academic Staff Advisory Committee; and circulated numerous drafts of its report for comment.

In February 1991, the Council's report, Moving Toward the 21st

Century, was completed. When Portch transmitted the report to the faculty, academic staff, and classified staff, he urged everyone to keep an open mind about its sometimes bold suggestions. He also promised that the report would not gather dust and that action would be taken on each one of the recommendations. Portch asserted that he would personally implement some items, working groups would be created to tackle others, and some recommendations, because they involved policy changes, would be considered by the Senate. Portch closed his memo with,

> Some may ask if we can risk moving forward at a time of one of the tightest budgets in a long time and at a time when we are in transition to a new chancellor. I would respond that we cannot afford not to, that we cannot stand still if we are to become stronger, especially at a time when we need to assure North Central [Accrediting Association] that we are not just planning but also moving ahead. This report gives us that opportunity. Let's not miss it. [92]

The reference to a transition to a new chancellor reflected Portch's announcement, in mid-January 1991, that he had accepted an appointment as the UW System Vice President for Academic Affairs, an office he would assume on the first of May. On Portch's last day in the Chancellor's Office, he issued a "one-minute-to-midnight" memo which described the status of each one of the Planning Council's 35 recommendations. Most notably, great progress had been made by a working group toward a "zero-base curriculum" protocol that would annually require each campus and department to review its courses' enrollment history and determine how each one meshed with the Centers' associate degree. Portch announced that the protocol procedures would be implemented during the 1991-1992 academic year. On the other hand, Portch said that the Senate Steering Committee would slow down its development of a new annual faculty merit evaluation procedure, because of the great diversity of opinion that had arisen. Still, he urged the Steering Committee to work toward presenting a set of options for the Senate's consideration in September. [93]

Chancellor Stephen Portch left the UW Centers in excellent condition. Through his straightforward leadership style, he had secured approval for several policies that assured a smooth student transfer process. The most important of these, of course, was the Associate Degree Transfer Policy that encouraged a student to remain at a Center for two years by guaranteeing that the Associate Degree would fulfill the general education requirements of any four-year UW institution. The articulation agreements, negotiated by the Director of Academic Services, had removed uncertainties about which courses were needed for various majors. In addition, when a four-year institution changed its requirements, the implementation had to be delayed for one year, to allow Centers' advisors and students time to adjust to the new standards. Finally, a negotiation procedure was in place to iron out the few transfer problems which inevitably would arise. All in all, Stephen Portch had helped create a higher profile for the UW Centers and a broader acceptance of the thirteen two-year campuses as a truly integral part of the University of Wisconsin.

President Shaw, in late April 1991, announced that he would be leaving UW System to become the President of New York's Syracuse University. After his departure, the Board of Regents named Senior Vice President Lyall as acting president. This was a familiar position for Lyall, as she had led the System for five months in the interim between O'Neil's leaving and Shaw's arrival. Indeed, some argued that the Board should immediately name Lyall president, in recognition of her leadership talents and of her service to the University of Wisconsin. However, the Regents decided to conduct a full-scale presidential search so that, should Lyall eventually be appointed, it would be clear she was the best candidate. Ultimately, in April 1992, Lyall was named the fifth president of the University of Wisconsin System. [94]

Ten

The UW Centers Weathers another Crisis: 1991-1997

When Stephen Portch left the Centers, Vice Chancellor for Academic Affairs Arthur Kaplan was named acting chancellor to serve until a search and screen committee completed its work. The search and screen committee worked throughout the summer to screen the numerous applications and to interview a half-dozen candidates. Then it sent a list of candidates to Acting President Lyall and the Regents for final action. In September 1991, the Board of Regents and Lyall announced that Lee Grugel, the Dean of the School of Arts and Sciences at UW-Eau Claire, would become the Centers' Chancellor on the first of November. A historian, Grugel had earned bachelor's and master's degrees from the Ohio State University and a Ph.D. from the University of Chicago. Grugel had practiced his craft at Moorhead State University (Minnesota) as a teacher and also served as chair of the history department prior to assuming a deanship at UW-Eau Claire in 1981. In his tenure at Eau Claire, Grugel had led a school with 22 academic departments and 350 faculty members. Acting President Lyall stressed that Grugel's experience at Eau Claire had "prepared him well for his new administrative duties."[1]

Lee Grugel continued work on the full agenda he inherited from Stephen Portch and the Planning Council. A good example is the Council's recommendation that the faculty merit evaluation procedure be revised, an issue which had been under consideration by the Senate Steering Committee for several months. The current procedure had been bitterly complained about for years by practically everyone. Under it, each faculty member was evaluated annually by both a department merit committee (a role often filled by the department executive committee) and a campus merit evaluation committee. The merit scale consisted of 2.0 points for each member of the faculty. Consequently, when a faculty person was awarded a merit rating above 2.0, someone else necessarily had to receive a "below average" rating. This aspect of the procedure damaged the morale of both those who received a "below average" rating and of those top-notch faculty who felt their work was not being adequately rewarded because of the constraints of the procedure. [2]

The Steering Committee received suggestions for a new merit procedure through the Fall Semester 1991 and eventually presented a proposal to the faculty senators during the Senate's March 1992 session. First, the proposal entirely eliminated the detested 2.0 point scale and recommended that every faculty member automatically be considered "meritorious." Then a merit evaluation committee could place from 25% to 40% of its faculty in either a "highly meritorious" or an "exceptional merit" category. The other major change recommended that the department and campus merit evaluation committees operate on an alternate year schedule, thus reducing the hours devoted to the annual merit procedure by about half. In terms of the weight given to the four areas of evaluation—instructional activities, professional activities, university service (governance) and discipline-related public service and outreach—Steering proposed that the greatest weight be given to the effectiveness of ones instructional activities. In May 1992 the faculty senators voted eleven to six to adopt the new merit procedure. [3]

A related issue—post tenure review—was under discussion by the faculty senators at the same time the merit policy was revised. Post tenure review raised many alarms because some perceived it as a direct attack on tenure. However, the UW System and the Board of Regents defended its implementation as an integral and appropriate component of "The Undergraduate Imperative: Building on Excellence" which aimed at ensuring effective undergraduate teaching in all UW institutions. Accordingly, the Board had mandated that each UW institution develop a post tenure review policy which required a performance review of all tenured faculty members on a seven year cycle. Acting President Lyall pointed out that the process was aimed primarily at "reinforcing and rewarding high quality [teaching] performance" and that if a deficiency in teaching was uncovered, the UW would assist the faculty member to overcome the problem. [4] While these words somewhat reduced the anxiety level among tenured faculty, the Centers Professional Standards

Committee tried to dampen the concerns even more by including reassurances in the preamble to the guidelines for Tenured Faculty Review and Development: "Post tenure review and development is not a retenuring process but rather a review of performance and provides the opportunity to plan for developmental activities and identify strategies by which these activities may be implemented. This process will fully respect the concept of tenure."[5]

After spending all of 1992 writing and rewriting a post tenure review policy, the Professional Standards Committee finally asked the Faculty Session (the seventeen faculty senators of the Senate) to initiate the approval process in January 1993. The faculty senators agreed but also decided to delay the second and final vote until May, to allow sufficient time for discussion of the proposal at the campuses and during the spring department meetings. In March 1993 the Faculty Session initiated a slightly altered draft of the policy and directed Jerry Bower (Richland—History), Chair of the Senate Steering Committee, to conduct a referendum among the faculty on the proposal. In May Bower reported the results: only 178 faculty members (49%) had cast ballots, with 89 supporting the proposed policy and 58 voting no. The remaining 31 voted that the proposal needed further revisions. In view of this terribly split outcome, the faculty senators decided to delay the adoption vote until the October meeting. Finally, on October 2, 1993, the Faculty Session approved, 14-3, the Tenured Faculty Review and Development Policy.[6]

In the summer of 1992, Chancellor Grugel wrote a long letter to Vice President Stephen Portch detailing the Centers ongoing struggles with transfer issues. The major problem cited by Grugel concerned the nine baccalaureate institutions which insisted that transfer students earn a higher GPA than their own students to be regarded as "in good academic standing."[7] Grugel repeated the argument that a Centers' student who was transferring should be held only to the same academic standards as a student who began at a four-year campus. Grugel also again complained about the lack of timely notice to the Centers when a four-year campus changed its transfer policy. He related a horror story involving a recent incident with UW-La Crosse. In the 1991 Fall semester La Crosse had requested that Center transferees not submit their applications until after January 1, 1992. Then, on January 17, 1992, La Crosse suddenly announced that it would cease accepting transfer applications in one week! This notice came before the Centers' students had returned for second semester classes, thus making it nearly impossible to alert the transferees to La Crosse to mail their applications immediately. Although this incident was unusual, Grugel explained that many four-year UWs implemented changes in course equivalencies and/or majors requirements without sufficient notice. In the worst instances, the Centers only learned of such new policies when a student complained about transfer difficulties. Grugel suggested that the Board of Regents tighten up the nebulous language in the System Transfer Policy to absolutely require sufficient notice of changes in standards for transferees.[8]

Early in October 1992 Department of Administration Secretary James Klauser ordered each state agency to set aside 1.5% of its annual budget in an escrow account to be used to balance the state's budget. Once again, a decline in revenue had compelled this drastic action. A few days later President Lyall explained this latest budget blow's impact to the Board of Regents. She added this unexpected $10.2 million giveback to an earlier required $8.1 million S/E lapse and noted that the total was about 2.5% of the UW System annual budget. Indeed, Lyall stressed that the effect upon the 1993 Spring Semester operations would be 5%, for the announcement came too late to extract a significant sum from 1992 Fall Semester expenditures. Lyall sought assurances from Governor Thompson that these truly would be one-time givebacks rather than permanent reductions in the System's base budget.[9] After each UW institution had specified how its share of the giveback would be raised, President Lyall reported that approximately 200 fewer course sections would be offered in Spring 1993, 100 positions would not be filled, and efforts to streamline administrative procedures and to expand the Transfer Information System to include Technical College courses would be delayed. Moreover, the installation of computers and creation of networks would be slowed.[10]

The Centers' share of this mandated giveback was $340,700. This amount was in addition to an earlier directive to pare $109,500 from the S/E budget. Commenting on the latter, Assistant Chancellor Antone Kucera noted that the Centers, over the last four years, had been allocated an additional $300,000 for S/E but the repeated lapses had ultimately meant almost no increase in actual revenues.[11] The Centers pared its 1993 spring course offerings and held vacant several positions to pay off its debt. Grugel, in reporting this, observed that many Center students would be disadvantaged by the cancellation of courses, especially basic offerings in English composition and mathematics.[12]

In addition to the funds returned to the state in 1993, the Centers reallocated nearly $130,000 into salary increases as its share of the ongoing Quality Reinvestment Program. In view of the miserly 1% raises the state proposed to provide in the 93-95 biennium, the impact of the QRP dollars upon salaries was practically inconsequential and the UW once again sank below the median compensation of its peer groups. The Centers had extracted a sizable portion of its QRP contributions from summer session salaries which reduced summer sessions at several campuses to just a few courses. Finally, the

Centers began, in 1993, to commit $100,000 annually to maintenance agreements for its new Student Information system (SIS). SIS was used by the campus student services offices and the central office in Madison to store permanent student records. Naturally SIS was vital to providing good service to each student, but the cost of maintaining the network and files had to be pried from other areas of the budget. In the end, despite everyone's concerted efforts to reduce costs, the Centers had a $100,000 deficit at the end of the 1993-1994 academic year.[13]

During 1993 Chancellor Grugel and Assistant Chancellor Kucera worked with UW System Administration to find suitable space to relocate the Centers' Central Office. The impetus for this effort was the pending expiration of the Centers' lease in the Verex Building (in August 1994) where the Central Office had been housed since mid-1988. The owners of the Verex Building had warned that the rent would be substantially increased. The looming rent increase by itself might have been enough to compel a move but the Central Office staff had also become increasingly cramped due to the addition of more personnel and computers. Since the System Administration, itself, also was in the process of reorganizing, it appeared that the Centers might be able to obtain space in a UW System building. Eventually, Grugel and Kucera negotiated a fifteen year lease for 20% of the space in a new UW System Administration building erected at 780 Regent Street.[14]

In September 1992 an eleven-member North Central Association of Colleges and Schools evaluation team visited the Centers to decide whether the Centers' accreditation should be renewed. The team members visited ten of the two-year campuses and conferred with Central Office staff and UW System officials to gather data. In March 1993, the Centers received preliminary word that the NCA would renew the institution's full accreditation for another ten years. This was confirmed on June 4, 1993, when the Board of Regents officially received the NCA recommendation.[15]

Among the 25 strengths listed by the visitation team in its "Report of a Visit," a few deserve special note. The visitation team stressed how well Centers' personnel had learned to operate effectively with meager resources and to place the emphasis on the "success of students rather than the comforts of the work environment." But the team cautioned that the staff may have become too accustomed to "doing more with less" so that neither UW System nor the state government really understood the extent of the Centers' need for more money.[16] The Report commented favorably upon the dedicated, energetic and talented central administration which worked to promote the welfare of the Centers' students, faculty, and staff. It also described the faculty as highly qualified and well prepared to teach freshman and sophomore undergraduates. The updated associate of arts and sciences degree earned special commendation, especially the requirement that a student complete both a writing/speaking emphasis and a multicultural emphasis course.[17]

The North Central visitation team also cited numerous areas where the Centers needed to improve. Out of a list of twenty-six "Concerns" the team highlighted the three most important deficiencies and required the Centers to submit a progress report on overcoming them to the NCA by December 1995.[18] The first concern called upon the Centers to clarify and improve how the resources it received from UW System were allocated among the Centers' central office and the thirteen campuses. Second, the team noted the absence of an ongoing integrated planning process as a serious problem. Although each campus and department annually planned its budget and curriculum, the Centers lacked a master plan. Finally, the visitors chastised the Centers for its delay in implementing and using an assessment of student academic achievement to improve instruction.[19]

During the Centers' annual "budget exercise," as it was popularly labeled, each campus, in consultation with the academic departments, prepared a budget request. This budget also often contained requests for additional or replacement staff. In the 1990s the number of faculty retirements accelerated each year, leaving many tenure-track vacancies. The campuses' annual budget proposals routinely included pleas to have the faculty vacancies filled with tenure-track persons instead of by lecturers. When the thirteen campus budgets were totalled in the Central Office the sum was an astronomical figure that no reasonable person could ever expect to be totally funded. Consequently, faculty, staff, deans and indeed everyone had become increasingly disenchanted with the utter futility of preparing a comprehensive budget request that would never be funded. The state's almost routine budget freezes and givebacks also added uncertainty and anguish to the budget planning process. Early in 1996 the Centers new Assistant Chancellor for Administrative Services Christopher (Chris) Forrest initiated a revised and improved budget planning process which had been worked out in consultation with Senate Budget Committee and the deans.

The UW Centers 1996-97 Budget Guidelines carefully laid out the major areas for budget preparation—personnel, local campus considerations, institution-wide programs including plans for future givebacks and details for special budget initiatives such as the student technology fee and the upgrading of faculty computers. Although the new guidelines did not make more money available to the campuses, they did provide a clearer picture of the priority items for the entire institution and how the Centers' budget would be doled out. In succeeding years the budget guidelines were refined and tied into the long-range plans of the Centers and UW System.[20]

The NCA's special concern over the lack of an ongoing and integrated long-range planning procedure had been anticipated and noted in the Centers' Self-Study Report.[21] Therein the Centers planning procedure was described as reactive rather than proactive; when a problem arose the Centers created a committee, commission, or task force to investigate and to recommend remedial measures. After the group's report was submitted it dissolved.[22] The Self-Study also related that Chancellor Grugel, recognizing the limitations of this approach to long-range planning, had ". . . recently proposed the creation of an ongoing planning group. This group will monitor the educational environment, develop and maintain strategic plans on a continuing basis, and provide the chancellor with recommendations for the future direction of the UW Centers."[23] This reference described Chancellor Grugel's ill-fated Planning Commission proposal which he presented to the Centers' Senate in January 1993. From the beginning there was much resistance to Grugel's proposal emanating from a fear that this chancellor-appointed group would operate outside the governance process.[24] Even though the Planning Commission was staffed in May 1993, the group never succeeded in carving out an agenda or a role for itself. And, once again, urgent problems arising from successive fall enrollment declines and their negative impact upon the Centers' budget compelled the Centers to shunt aside long-range planning to concentrate upon immediate problems. Ultimately, with Chancellor Grugel's reluctant concurrence, the Planning Commission was dissolved in early 1996.[25] Nevertheless, the NCA approved the "progress report" the Centers submitted in December 1995 regarding efforts to address the agency's concerns for budget allocation and long-range planning.

Making sufficient progress toward drafting and implementing a plan for assessing student learning outcomes to satisfy the NCA visitation team's third major concern proved most difficult. The effort began in May 1993 when the Senate authorized its Steering Committee to draft a constitutional amendment to create an Assessment Committee. The amendment was duly drafted, initiated, and ratified; however, the Assessment Committee was not immediately launched because the Senate also decided to set up a ten-person General Education Task Force to undertake a broad review of the Centers' general education program, the associate degree, and the assessment of learning outcomes. In view of the obvious overlap between the agenda of the Task Force and the Assessment Committee, the Senate wisely opted to wait to activate the latter group.[26]

The General Education Task Force began its work in Fall 1994 coincident with an unanticipated dramatic decline in enrollment. [The Centers' Fall 1994 FTE enrollment plunged from 7,468 the previous fall to 6,728, putting the Centers 10.7% below its enrollment management FTE target.] [27] This development required that everyone focus on this emergency, which delayed the work of the Task Force. Consequently, in September 1995, only two months before the assessment progress report was due to the NCA, the Task Force reported to the Senate that it was just then organizing itself into three subcommittees to address particular issues. This report also indicated that each academic department had been directed to identify the specific educational proficiencies that would be stressed in one of its courses and be prepared to assess the achievement of these proficiencies in the Fall 1996 semester. [28] Although these steps addressed several of the NCA's worries about assessment of student learning, the agency pronounced the Centers' December 1995 progress report inadequate. In particular, NCA was disappointed that the Centers were still "planning for" assessment when the agency had expected that the process would be underway during the 1995-1996 academic year. Consequently, the NCA scheduled a "focused visit" to the Centers for December 1997 to determine whether sanctions would be necessary. [29]

In the fall of 1996 the General Education Task Force's work on assessment was taken over by the Assessment Initiation Working Group (AIWG) which would implement the Centers' assessment program. [30] The AIWG, using the NCA focused visit as a prod, relentlessly pushed the academic departments to begin their assessment programs. Consequently, the small NCA team that conducted a focused visit on assessment December 8-9, 1997, decided not to impose sanctions upon the Centers. [31]

A tangential outcome of the North Central review was the Centers' decision to withdraw from a long-standing Financial Aid Consortium which the Center System had formed with UW-Madison and UW-Green Bay in 1968 to process student financial aid applications more efficiently. As data was gathered for the Self-Study Report it became quite apparent that the Centers' students were not receiving a fair share of the financial aid generated by the Consortium. [32] The figures revealed that while Centers' students generated about 27% of the federal dollars dispensed through the Consortium, they received just 2% to 8% of the proceeds. In May 1992 Chancellor Grugel warned both partners that the Centers would withdraw from the arrangement unless the allocation formula was dramatically revised. Neither institution responded. But, after a 1993 U.S. Department of Education audit concluded that Centers' students should be awarded over one million additional dollars annually, both suddenly paid attention. Now thoroughly alarmed, Madison and Green Bay requested President Lyall's office to arrange a meeting to consider the Centers' concerns. Chancellor Grugel readily agreed to meet with his fellow chancellors on December 15. However, neither Chancellor Ward (Madison) nor Chancellor Outcault (Green Bay) attended; instead they sent representatives to argue that the consortium formula ought not be revised. Steamed by this affront, Grugel wrote to President Lyall to reiterate the Centers' position and to request her support for his decision to withdraw from the Consortium. His key argument was that the Centers' students, who were clearly more needy, ought not continue to subsidize their more well-to-do Madison and Green Bay colleagues' financial aid.[33] President Lyall reviewed the correspondence and supported Grugel's decision. Three years later the Financial Aid Consortium ceased to exist.[34]

Early in 1993 the Board of Regents began to work on a UW System plan for Enrollment Management III. EM III would encompass three biennia, 1995-2001. Unlike the two earlier enrollment management plans (1987-1995) when a gradual 20% decline in the number of high school graduates had permitted the UW System gracefully to orchestrate a small decline in enrollment, EM III would be carried out during years when the number of high school graduates would gradually return to the high levels of the mid 1980s. In addition to this increased demand for admission by high school graduates, UW System planners also anticipated that a larger number of adult learners, who needed to update their knowledge and skills, would call upon the University. Along with these changed demographics EM III would operate during years of tight fiscal constraints which would force the UW System to educate more students without a proportionate increase in its budget. Because of increased competition for state dollars to meet rapidly rising health care costs, to provide more prison cells, and to implement Governor Thompson's pledge to provide additional state aid to the local public schools, the University could not realistically anticipate any significant increase in its state support.[35]

In order to compile accurate estimates of how many additional students the UW System could accept, the Board of Regents directed each UW institution to predict how many more students it could accommodate within each of three budget parameters: 1) no additional state funding, 2) a slight increase in state dollars coupled with internal budget reallocations, and 3) full state support for each additional student. Chancellor Grugel enlisted the Senate Steering and Budget Committees to help prepare the Centers' estimates.

The Committees decided that the Centers could not accept any additional students under budget condition #1 because all of the campuses budgets were stretched very thin. In addition, the greatest number of new students would be expected to enroll at the Marathon, Fox Valley, and Marinette Centers because the nearby four-year UW campuses (Stevens Point, Oshkosh, Green Bay, respectively) had already achieved their enrollment limits. In the second budget scenario the Centers predicted it could accommodate 492 more students and with full state funding it could accept another 497, for a total of 989 FTE students. When all the estimates had been tallied, the UW

System predicted it would grow by 6.8% (8,510 FTE) during the six years of EM III. The Centers anticipated a 13.1% (989 FTE) growth rate.[36]

The UW System's emphasis in EM III upon increased development of distance education capabilities presented both opportunities and potential pitfalls to the Centers. Since the Centers had thirteen campuses scattered across the state and a central office in Madison, it stood to gain a great deal by linking them together via a personal computer network. But the start-up costs would be huge because each of fourteen sites would need the same basic equipment. Then, the ongoing costs of maintaining the network, the computer laboratories, and technology staff salaries would require a significant amount of money. Despite these daunting fiscal prospects the Centers could not ignore this trend in the delivery of college courses. Somehow it had to find the resources to expand and maintain a telecommunications network that permitted instantaneous communication among its scattered parts.

In the quest for funds to increase the capability of CentersNet (established in 1990-91) the Centers sought private grant monies and also campaigned for special state budget items dedicated to technology acquisition. For example, in August 1992, Chancellor Grugel announced that the Centers had won a $508,806 U.S. Department of Education grant which, over three years, would be used to develop a new Student Information System (SIS) to store student records.[37] The Centers fully supported the Regents' campaign to gain the legislature's permission to levy a special 1% student technology fee throughout the UW System. This special assessment proposal had even won the support of the student governments because the expenditures would be strictly devoted to increasing student access to computers and because students would have the majority vote on the committees which expended the funds. This campaign ended successfully when the state legislature included the technology fee in the 1995-97 biennial budget.[38] In the fall of 1994 the Centers received a grant specifically for designing a distance education (DE) network for the thirteen campuses and the Centers' central office. The money ($50,000) came from the Public Communications Facilities Program in the U.S. Department of Commerce. The Centers enhanced the value of this grant by collaborating closely with the Wisconsin Educational Communications Board to assure that its distance education network would be compatible across the state.[39]

Early in 1994, in response to all of this activity, the Centers set up a Distance Education Task Force to study technology issues and to recommend how the institution should respond. The DE Task Force met several times during the summer of 1994 and submitted its report in November 1994. At the very beginning of its Report the group tried to quiet a major faculty misgiving about DE courses when it stated that distance education ". . . is intended to complement and enhance, not supplant, regular classroom instruction."[40] Elsewhere the Report listed three primary criteria for determining whether a particular course should be offered via distance education—the course should increase sophomore retention, have a low enrollment at several Centers, and utilize special faculty expertise.

A Task Force survey had revealed that the human and physical space resources available for distance education were severely limited at almost all Centers. The data highlighted the fact that the current technology staff person on several campuses was an individual who had taken on the additional duties of trying to keep the network operating smoothly. But the workload had significantly increased and several now indicated that they could not continue much longer to juggle their regular duties and their technology work. On many campuses the audiographics equipment (then the only DE delivery system available in the Centers) was crammed into little more than a closet, while the goal was a computer, a document scanner, and an electronic notepad for each three students. If the Centers could ever acquire sufficient equipment to meet this standard, a larger space naturally would be required to house the equipment and the classes. The Report noted that only four Centers' faculty were then involved in the creation and delivery of DE courses; the Task Force proposed to entice more faculty to become engaged in DE by providing them with training and release time to prepare DE courses. The Task Force also suggested summer stipends for DE course development as a potential incentive. The Task Force's most important recommendation was that the Centers should immediately employ an external consultant to assist in the design of an improved CentersNet and the selection of the appropriate equipment to support the network.[41]

Shortly after the DE Task Force issued its Report, the Distance Education Strategic Planning Committee assumed the responsibility for carrying out the Task Force's recommendations. The DE Strategic Planning Committee, like its predecessor, issued a set of principles which sought to calm faculty members who feared that an increase in the number of distance education courses might jeopardize their jobs. The principles statement said,

> It is appropriate that the UW Centers engage in distance education when such engagement enhances its curricular array and/or enriches the curriculum. Such engagement must, however, seek to maintain the quality of education that has become the hallmark of the UW Centers and allow for the continuing personal contact and interaction that is consistent with the experiences our students have in face-to-face instruction. Rather than substituting for such instruction, distance education should become one of the tools of a technologically empowered

faculty and staff while at the same time helping to prepare their students to utilize technology after transfer.[42]

During January and February 1996 the DE Strategic Planning Committee reviewed the recommendations of Evans Associates, the external consultant employed to assist the Centers with technology issues. In brief form, Evans Associates proposed that the UW Centers create an interactive video system called "Centersview," that Centersview be compatible with other existing networks, that Centersview be integrated as soon as practical with CentersNet, and that the Centers seek compatible partners to share the carrying capacity of Centersview. To support both Centersview and CentersNet the Committee recommended that each Center be allotted one FTE network administrator and one FTE instructional support administrator. Finally, the Strategic Planning Committee and Evans Associates urged that personnel be trained in the use and advantages of Centersview so that each Center would eventually have a properly designed and utilized electronic classroom.[43]

The DE Strategic Planning Committee attached a half-dozen conditions to its endorsement of these proposals. The most important of these conditions stipulated "That sufficient funding additional to the current base budget be found [for the DE installation and operation] to guarantee that the quality and character of a UW Centers education will be maintained. . . ."[44] Chancellor Grugel accepted all six recommendations and the conditions attached to them. He pledged that additional resources would be sought through traditional UW System fiscal procedures and through vigorous pursuit of all appropriate grant opportunities.[45]

During the summer of 1994 political rhetoric intensified as both incumbents and their challengers geared up for the fall gubernatorial and legislative elections. Wisconsin's governor's race promised to be especially interesting because incumbent Republican Governor Tommy Thompson had decided to seek an unprecedented third four-year term. The Democrats launched state Senate Minority Leader Charles "Chuck" Chvala against Thompson. Chvala, a Madison-area political veteran, had served one term in the Assembly before being elected to the Senate in 1984. Once again the key election issues were taxes and the state budget. Thompson had been relentlessly pushing his proposal to increase the state's share of public school costs from the current 45% to 67%. This would require an estimated additional $1.5 billion. But Thompson still insisted that his plan could be funded without increasing either the income or sales tax. Thompson was counting upon continued economic growth, along with increased efficiencies in all state agencies, to generate the revenue needed for this huge cost shift. Chvala attempted to trump Thompson's plan with a pledge to have the state assume

100% of the public school operating costs, at an estimated cost of $2.5 billion. To finance his proposal Chvala conceded that some taxes would have to be modestly increased but he argued that most of the money could be garnered by closing sales tax loopholes. Thompson quickly labelled Chvala a "tax and spend liberal Democrat," a charge that proved very effective in the campaign.[46]

Long before the 1994 political campaign began in earnest, University of Wisconsin System officials had been grappling with budget issues arising from the pending increase in state aid to public school districts. They knew that the UW could not expect an increase in its state support because the K-12 schools would be the top priority for any additional state expenditure. In fact, a major concern was that the UW's share of the state budget would continue to decline, necessitating unpopular tuition increases and/or reductions in the quality of a UW education. In May 1994 the Department of Administration seemed to confirm these fears when it imposed a hiring freeze and ordered all state agencies to prepare budgets based upon both a 5% and a 10% decrease. Each agency also was directed to submit a narrative describing any adverse impacts of these reductions.

In the Centers Chancellor Grugel mobilized the Senate Budget Committee, department chairs, deans, and key academic staff to prepare the reduced budgets and a commentary about their negative impacts. Meanwhile President Lyall waged a well-conceived public relations campaign on the theme that Wisconsin must not allow its excellent system of higher education to deteriorate in order to shunt more resources to the public schools. Lyall asserted that the University, through former President Shaw's Quality Reinvestment Program, had made all of the position cuts and budget shifts it could afford. Perhaps in response to this campaign, in mid-September DOA Secretary James Klauser unexpectedly excused the UW from having to complete the 5% and 10% budget reduction exercise. Governor Thompson immediately used this announcement as evidence of his pledge to maintain the quality of the UW System while also improving Wisconsin's public schools. Challenger Chvala soon also promised to spare the University from huge budget cuts but admitted that some "discreet cuts" might be necessary to implement his plan to help the public schools.[47]

The November 8, 1994, election gave Wisconsin Republicans an astounding victory. Thompson crushed Chvala [1,019,599 (67%) to 465,772 (33%)] to win a third term. Adding to Thompson's elation was the fact that his party retained its narrow, 17 to 16, edge in the state Senate while it captured control of the Assembly by a 51 to 48 margin.[48]

Throughout the political campaigns the process for building the UW's 1995-1997 biennial budget had moved relentlessly forward. The work was done under a DOA mandate to all state agencies to submit a no-increase budget. However, the Regents proposed a very modest increase and warned that much larger future increases would be needed to maintain the quality of a University of Wisconsin degree. The Regents also requested that the special state allocations for laboratory and classroom modernization be continued.

Governor Thompson's budget proposal to the legislature, in February 1995, contained two pieces of bad news for the UW. First, he proposed a base budget reduction of 5.1% ($43 million), the first GPR cut for the UW System since merger. Thompson also, in the interest of increased efficiency, recommended that the UW System information technology and capital building project planning staffs be eliminated. DOA would assume their duties. This proposal especially alarmed UW officers because the University would lose control over its telecommunications network and direct access to the special planning skills required for academic buildings. Indeed, some disgruntled UW System officers predicted that DOA would soon realize that its personnel lacked the expertise to provide these services and would have to contract with consultants at greater expense to get the work done. On the positive side, the Governor proposed that the lab and classroom modernization programs be continued ($9 million annually) and that new special initiatives be funded for Distance Education ($5.3 million) and for the Improvement of Undergraduate Education ($17 million). He also concurred in the recommendation that the 1% student technology fee should be collected at all UW institutions to assure students' access to computers, the internet, and e-mail.[49]

President Lyall led the campaign to politely but firmly point out the negative repercussions of the Governor's budget upon the University. She noted, for instance, that the $43 million GPR reduction would slash all state aid for 7,000 FTE students—equivalent to wiping out entirely the budget of UW-La Crosse or UW-Stevens Point or the Centers, all of which had a full-time equivalent enrollment of about 7,000.[50] This campaign, while necessary, was fraught with political danger because Wisconsin's taxpayers were looking forward to local property tax relief and were not in a receptive mood to hear complaints from a group of allegedly pampered professors. Chancellor Grugel discovered this first-hand when he was quoted as saying, while addressing a "Budget Cut Awareness Day Rally" at UWC-Fond du Lac, "This budget is good for the governor but bad for the people of Wisconsin." Grugel had also noted that while the Governor's budget did not increase taxes, it contained $460 million in new fees—"Whether you call it a tax or a fee, you still pay for it!"[51] An angry Governor Thompson quickly protested to President Lyall about Grugel's remarks and she relayed the governor's complaint to the Chancellor. A few days later Grugel sent to Thompson a very carefully worded letter of apology in which he suggested that his remarks were quoted out of context and thus they appeared to be more personal than intended. In transmitting a copy of this "apology" to President Lyall, however, Grugel explained that he felt his remarks were appropriate for a political rally and that if Thompson's budget was adopted real damage would be done both to the Centers and the UW System.[52]

Early in June 1995 the powerful Joint Finance Committee (JFC) convened to review the Governor's 95-97 biennial budget proposal. The JFC accepted Thompson's $43 million GPR reduction for the University but offset it somewhat with $10.7 million in tuition and fee increases. The Committee members, however, deleted the Governor's proposal to transfer planning for technology and major building projects to DOA, thus saving the UW System staff from elimination. Chancellor Grugel, in relaying news of the JFC's action to the deans, noted that the Centers' share of the GPR reduction would be $948,999 for the biennium.[53] At the end of June 1995 the state legislature enacted a 1995-1997 University of Wisconsin System budget as crafted by the Joint Finance Committee.[54]

Beginning in the Fall Semester of 1994 the UW Centers experienced three successive years of enrollment decline. This unexpected development created a fiscal crisis reminiscent of the one faced by the old Center System from the mid 1970s into the early 1980s. The numbers were indeed grim: the Fall 1994 enrollment was 810 FTE (10.7%) below the target which meant a loss to the Centers budget of $1 million dollars; Fall 1995 brought a further decline of 300 FTE (now 14.7% below target) and an increase in the budget deficit to $1,590,000; and finally the Fall 1996 numbers represented a decline of another 366 FTE, which pushed the Centers fully 20% beneath its Enrollment Management III target enrollment of 7,505 FTE and created a huge, total liability of $2.2 million.[55]

After the disastrous Fall 1994 numbers were tallied, Chancellor Grugel polled the deans and student services directors for explanations of why the Centers' enrollment had unexpectedly plunged. Subsequently, Grugel cited three major reasons for the decline in a letter to President Lyall. First, the spring 1994 high school graduating class had been the smallest in two decades and a fierce competition ensued among all UW institutions to enroll the college-bound graduates. Second, Grugel contended that some baccalaureate institutions had reduced admission requirements to achieve freshmen enrollment goals. In the past, the Chancellor observed, many of the underprepared freshmen would have been advised to enroll in a Center. The baccalaureates had also heavily recruited students who had completed only one year's study in the Centers. This tactic, which reduced the Centers' sophomore retention rate, had contributed to the overall enrollment decline. Finally, Grugel maintained that the strong economy and job market had lured some high school graduates into delaying their college education. The strong economy had also convinced some Centers' students to postpone their enrollment to save for an eventual return to the classroom. He stressed that this phenomenon had especially harmed enrollment in eastern Wisconsin at Fox Valley, Washington County, and Waukesha County.[56]

When the Fall Semester 1995 numbers proved even more dismal, Chancellor Grugel reiterated all three of these explanations. But now he added data which revealed that the four-year UWs, excluding Madison and Milwaukee, had increased the number of new freshmen by about 1,000 FTE and transfer students by approximately 600 FTE. Grugel used these figures to strongly intimate that the four-year institutions had met their goals at the expense of the two-year campuses. Consequently, he requested President Lyall to regard the Centers' predicament ". . . as a systemic rather than [solely] an institutional issue."[57] In his third annual letter of explanation to President Lyall, in October 1996, Chancellor Grugel hopefully noted two reasons why the Centers' enrollment might begin to rebound in 1997. He wryly suggested that some baccalaureate campuses, thanks to vigorous recruitment of new freshmen and transfer students the past two years, would be at their enrollment limits and thus would again recommend that excess applicants should enroll at a Center. He also anticipated that the number of Wisconsin high school graduates would begin to rise in 1997.[58]

Although the record indicates that Lee Grugel worked tirelessly to convince System administrators that a major share of the Centers' enrollment and fiscal difficulties were the result of damaging decisions made by the four-year campuses under EM III guidelines, some Centers' faculty, staff and administrators felt that the Chancellor had become perplexed and discouraged. Consequently during the last two years of Chancellor Grugel's tenure institutional morale sank very low. The situation appeared to some faculty and staff to be entirely beyond their control and they though it terribly unfair to require the Centers to make huge budget adjustments which resulted from the "theft" of students who normally would have enrolled at a Center. The entire episode also reinforced the impression that the Centers was the UW institution of last resort for students who just were not well-prepared enough to be admitted elsewhere in the University of Wisconsin. There can be no doubt that this negative image of the Centers compounded the difficulty of attracting students to enroll.

Once again in September 1996 Chancellor Grugel plunged into negotiations with President Lyall and key members of her staff to convince them that a portion of the Centers' debt ought to be forgiven because the four-year UWs had "mined" the Centers for students. Consequently those institutions should, in fairness, be required to bear part of Centers' burden.

In the midst of these negotiations, on October 31, 1996, Lee Grugel died unexpectedly in his sleep of an apparent heart attack.[59] Because he was only 56, the Chancellor's death hit everyone in the Centers especially hard. Some people naturally wondered whether the stress of dealing with the enrollment and budget crises had contributed to his death. Lee Grugel's memorial service, held in Madison, was attended by numerous Centers' personnel, by colleagues from UW-Eau Claire, and by President Lyall and other UW System officials. Six weeks later, in mid-December 1996, President Lyall appointed Howard Thoyre, who had recently retired after a 34 year career at UW-Stevens Point as a professor of mathematics and an administrator, to serve as the Acting Chancellor.[60]

After Lee Grugel's untimely death, other Centers' personnel stepped forward to try to convince UW System officials that the Centers' debt should be reduced. Previously, in 1994 and 1995, President Lyall had generously slashed the Centers' uncollected tuition debt by half, to $500,000 and $795,000, respectively. Naturally it would also help tremendously to have the 1996 $2.2 million obligation sliced in half. But, because of shifting priorities in the state budget (as described earlier) the UW System now had less fiscal flexibility to assist the Centers. This was the clear message that Vice President David Ward delivered to Senate Steering Committee Chair Bellamy Hamilton. Ward stressed that the Centers' "only issue was enrollment" and that the institution needed to quit blaming external factors for its dilemma and get busy to recruit more students. Ward recommended, in view of the continued fierce competition to recruit traditional-aged students, that the Centers should target new pools of students through distance education courses and through partnerships with area high schools to bring the best junior and senior students into UW Centers' classes. Hamilton's report to the Senate of her visit with Vice President Ward triggered a wide-ranging discussion of the sources of the Centers' problems. During this exchange Fond du Lac Dean Judy Goldsmith described a recent meeting of the thirteen deans with President Lyall. The deans had stressed that ". . . the Centers' enrollments won't turn around until the four-year schools stop treating us like a colony to be exploited" and that UW System must forgive some of the mounting debt, ". . . otherwise the Centers will be in a death spiral."[61]

In yet another meeting, this time between Vice President Keith Sanders and the academic staff representatives of all fifteen UW institutions, information surfaced which supported the Centers' contention that the four-year campuses had adjusted admission requirements to assure achievement of their enrollment targets. Sanders, a former UW-Stevens Point Chancellor, related that Stevens Point, indeed, had acquired forty or fifty more last-minute students by making telephone calls and personal contacts with students previously refused admission. Sanders added that he knew this tactic had harmed enrollment at both UWC-Marathon County and UWC-Marshfield/Wood County. Sanders concluded with the observation that the Centers provided a valuable service to the UW System and that a way had to be found ". . . to subsidize and help the Centers or the rest of the UW institutions will suffer." [62]

During the ongoing enrollment/fiscal crisis more and more Centers personnel expressed the opinion that part of the enrollment problem was that prospective students and the general public did not clearly understand what the Centers were and how they meshed with the UW System. Older citizens in the host communities still held fast to the "Extension Center" label. [63] A second perception that dogged the Centers was that students lost credits when they transferred. This impression persisted despite the great strides that had been taken to create a "seamless transfer process" within the UW System. The best explanation for this misunderstanding is that students who had no problem transferring seldom advertised their experience while those who encountered difficulty complained loudly. Another image problem was the idea that the two-year campuses were not as good as the four-year UWs. Consequently, the impression was afoot that only students who could not gain admission at a baccalaureate institution enrolled in a Center. The Centers' lower tuition sometimes even hurt the image because of the commonly-held notion that "you get what you pay for." Evidently, when some prospective students read that the Centers were the "best educational value" in the UW System, they translated that to mean that the educational quality was not as high as at the four-year schools. [64]

Chancellor Grugel's response to these image issues had been brilliant—he requested that President Lyall reduce the Centers' giveback to UW System by $45,000 so that the Wisconsin Survey Research Laboratory (WSRL) could be employed to do a statewide image study. In less than a month the President gave her go-ahead. [65] The WSRL conducted a fifteen-minute telephone interview with at least 100 respondents in each of the thirteen Center communities. These interviews revealed that 89% of the respondents were aware of the local Center compared to a slightly lower (86%) awareness of the area technical college. However, when the queries focused on how much each interviewee knew about these institutions, 67% replied that they knew "some" or a "great deal" about the technical college while just 47% said the same about the Center. Conversely this meant that 53% of those who knew that their community had a Center answered that they either knew "little" or "almost nothing" about its actual operation! [66] The responses to the question about how well the local Center informed the public about itself and its activities disclosed that just 55% responded "excellent or good." [67] Obviously the

UW Centers needed to devise ways to better inform the public about its programs and about its status as fully accredited University of Wisconsin campuses.

Two months after receiving the Image Survey Chancellor Grugel, in June 1996, created a nine-member Marketing Task Force (MTF) to conduct a broad-range review of current marketing efforts and to make recommendations for "a comprehensive institutional marketing effort." [68] The MTF included in its study a Student Satisfaction Survey sent to just over 1,100 randomly selected Centers' students. This survey produced some heartening news—94% of the respondents expressed overall satisfaction with their UW Centers' experience, 95% were satisfied with the quality of instruction, and 67% had selected a Center as their first-choice college. On the debit side of the ledger, however, was a UW Centers Transfer Study which indicated that almost half of the students who transferred encountered some difficulty—either they lost credits or a course which they expected would fulfill a specific general education requirement transferred instead as an elective. [69]

The Marketing Task Force made nine recommendations in its final report. The MTF boldly urged that the name of the institution and each campus be changed by dropping "Center" and that this be accomplished before the end of 1997. The MTF recommended that an external consultant be employed to assist in the creation of an institution-wide marketing plan and that adequate resources be devoted to marketing efforts. [70] These suggestions were quickly implemented. One result was a unified across-the-state advertising campaign via television and radio spots and even a few billboards.

Back in 1992, just a few months after he had become Chancellor, Lee Grugel had written Acting President Lyall to suggest that the institution's title should be changed to the University of Wisconsin Colleges. [71] After the Marketing Task Force also recommended a name change, Acting Chancellor Thoyre pushed the idea by circulating various options and requesting reactions to them. In May 1997 the Senate chose University of Wisconsin Colleges, 19 to 7, as its preference; UW Regional Campuses came in second. [72] Thoyre promptly forwarded the recommendation to President Lyall who sent it to the Board of Regents with her endorsement. On July 25, 1997, the Board of Regents overwhelmingly approved the new title, to become effective with the 1997 Fall Semester. [73] In late August 1997 the UW Centers truly became HISTORY! but the two-year campuses are still hard at work in thirteen communities implementing the Wisconsin Idea by providing access to a high-quality University of Wisconsin education. [74]

2001 Locations

List of Campuses with Starting Dates

ANTIGO 1933-1942, 1946-1948 (FIRST OUT-STATE EXTENSION CENTER)
BARABOO/SAUK COUNTY 1946-1949, 1968-
BARRON COUNTY 1946-1949, 1966-
FOND DU LAC 1933-1941, 1946-1952, 1967-
FOX VALLEY 1938-1942, 1946-
GREEN BAY 1933-1969 (BECAME UW-GREEN BAY 1969)
KENOSHA 1933-1969 (ABSORBED BY UW-PARKSIDE 1969)
MANITOWOC COUNTY 1934-
MARATHON COUNTY 1934-
MARINETTE 1935-1937, 1946-
MARSHFIELD/WOOD COUNTY 1946-1949, 1964-
MEDFORD 1969-1982 (CLOSED BY REGENTS AND LEGISLATURE 1982)
MILWAUKEE 1919-1956 (MERGED WITH MILWAUKEE STATE TEACHERS COLLEGE TO FORM UW-MILWAUKEE 1956)
RACINE 1933-1969 (ABSORBED BY UW-PARKSIDE 1969)
RICHLAND 1967-
ROCK COUNTY 1937-1942, 1946-1947, 1966-
SHEBOYGAN 1935-
WASHINGTON COUNTY 1946-1947, 1969-
WAUKESHA COUNTY 1966-

The UW Colleges

photo by Tom Schmidt

UW Colleges Deans and Central Administration, 2002

Standing Left to Right: **Phil Zweifel, Assoc. Dean, UW-Waukesha, Brad Stewart, Dean, UW-Waukesha, Janet Philipp, Dean, UW-Rock County, Tom Pleger, Assoc. Dean, UW-Fox Valley, Jim Perry, Dean, UW-Fox Valley, Ray Hernandez, Dean, UW-Sheboygan, Jim Veninga, Dean, UW-Marathon County, Roland Baldwin, Dean, UW-Manitowoc, Steve Wildeck, Assistant Chancellor for Administrative Services, Sid Bremer, Dean, UW-Marinette, Carol McCart, Dean, UW-Marshfield/Wood County, Teri Venker, Assistant to the Chancellor for Marketing and University Relations**
Seated Left to Right: **Deborah Cureton, Dean, UW-Richland, Paul Chase, Dean, UW-Barron County, Judy Goldsmith, Dean, UW-Fond du Lac, Bill Messner, Chancellor, Margaret Cleek, Vice Chancellor, Joel Rodney, Dean, UW-Washington County, Patricia Roby, Assoc. Dean, UW-Washington County, Aural Umhoefer, Dean, UW-Baraboo/Sauk County**

Left: UW Center System Deans and Central Administration, 1967

Standing Left to Right: Murray Deutsch, Dean, Waukesha Center, Charles E. Miller, Dean, Rock County Center, Allen Dussell, Dean, Fox Valley Center, Paul Zehner, Dean, Marathon County Center, Earl Beard, Dean, Sheboygan County Center, Elmer Meyer, Central Administration, Ray Grosnick, Dean, Manitowoc County Center, Henry Duwe/Business Manager, Central Administration, Lon Weber, Dean, Marinette County Center, Norbert Koopman, Dean, Marshfield Wood County Center, Jim Batt, Director of Communications, Central Administration

Seated Left to Right: Gladys Meier, Registrar Central Administration, Trudi Stone, Secretary to Faculty, Central Administration, Steve Mitchell, Dean, Kenosha Center, Lorentz Adolfson, Chancellor, Central Administration, Marion Smith, Vice Chancellor, Central Administration, Al May, Dean, Racine Center, Ted Savides, Dean, Green Bay Center

Lorentz H. Adolfson

Durward Long

Edward B. Fort

Stephen R. Portch

Lee E. Grugel

William F. Messner

Administrators of the
University of Wisconsin Two-year Campus System

Robert R. Polk   Lorman A. Ratner

DEANS OF THE EXTENSION DIVISION
Louis E. Reber 1907-1926
Chester D. Snell 1926-1935
Frank O. Holt 1935-1944
Lorentz H. Adolfson 1944-1964

CHANCELLORS OF THE UW CENTER SYSTEM
Lorentz H. Adolfson 1964-1972
Durward Long 1972-1973
John F. Meggers 1973-1974 (Interim Chancellor)
Edward B. Fort 1974-1981
Robert R. Polk 1981-1983
Daniel K. Van Eyck 1983 (Interim Chancellor)

CHANCELLORS OF THE UW CENTERS
Daniel K. Van Eyck 1983 (Interim Executive Dean)
Lorman "Larry" A. Ratner 1983-1986 (Executive Dean)
Arthur M. Kaplan 1986 (Interim Chancellor)
Stephen R. Portch 1986-1991
Lee E. Grugel 1991-1996
Howard H. Thoyre 1996-1997 (Interim Chancellor)

CHANCELLORS OF THE UW COLLEGES
William F. Messner 1997-present

UW-Baraboo/Sauk County logo designed in the mid 1980's by Public Information staff member Catherine Trapani. The design emphasizes the natural beauty of the campus location near Devil's Lake and the Baraboo Range. It was used until 1998 when a uniform logo was adopted for the 13 UW Colleges campuses.

BARABOO/SAUK COUNTY

Left: The John and Murrel Lange Center. Built entirely from bequest funds of $4.5 million dollars, the largest bequest received in the Colleges, the 46,000 square foot facility includes a gymnasium, racquetball courts, studio, weight and workout rooms, food service, dining and conference areas, student services and activities offices, student recreation and lounge areas and the James A. Schwalbach Art Gallery.

Left: John and Murrel Lange Center Groundbreaking, June 12, 1996. Circus World Museum's Hanneford Elephants assist (from left) Aural Umhoefer, Campus Dean; Charles Montooth, Taliesin Architects; Joseph Wankerl, Chair Campus Commission; Lee Grugel, Chancellor; Mark Paschen, VP, Friends of the Campus; David Etzwiler, Chair Steering Committee and Steve Rundio, Athletic Director

Masthead of the original student newspaper *The Gauntlet*.

Student checking out materials from the T. N. Savides Library, named for founding dean Theodore Nelson Savides. This building along with the rest of the original campus was remodeled in a major campus-wide new construction and renovation project from 1997 to 2000.

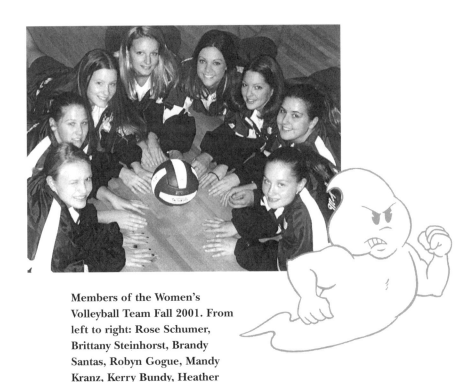

Members of the Women's Volleyball Team Fall 2001. From left to right: Rose Schumer, Brittany Steinhorst, Brandy Santas, Robyn Gogue, Mandy Kranz, Kerry Bundy, Heather Bohling and Jennifer Matyskela celebrating the fourth season of women's volleyball.

Above Right: Meet the *Spirit*, the logo and mascot of the *Fighting Spirits* campus athletic teams.

Right: Anne Forbes, one of three generations in her family to attend UW-Baraboo/ Sauk County, participates in a painting class. Exemplifying the epitome of life-long learning, Anne, a retired music educator who already holds a BA degree plus 83 graduate credits, has completed 54 credit hours and audited 275 credits on campus. Her son earned his Associate Degree here and her granddaughter, who has climbed the ranks through the College for Kids program, will return as a freshman for the fall 2002 semester.

UW-BC student Sarah Bowen walks in front of the Student Services Center building, which features a 20-ton relief sculpture. The facade, which was created by art professor Donald H. Ruedy, is a three-dimensional artwork that portrays student activities. *Below:* This logo was designed in 1984 by artist Janet Hartmann, daughter-in-law of the campus Student Services Director Dr. Eugene Hartmann. It incorporated symbols of northern Wisconsin, the pine trees and lakes, to form a "W" representing Wisconsin. The "Transferring Excellence" motto reflected the mission of the campus.

BARRON COUNTY

Students at UW-BC spend their after-class hours in the library, which houses the reference library, a computer lab along with quieter space in the new North Carrels Study Area that is equipped with individual PCs.

Right: Jennifer Lawton and Jason Randall are but two of the hundreds of students whom Dr. James M. Pannier has had the privilege of teaching over a 35 year career at the campus. He is the sole remaining charter faculty member, having joined the campus in 1966.

Right: Beyond the traditional classroom, students can now take classes online, receive courses through the audio-graphic system or via compressed video. UW-BC provides area high school students with ITV (interactive television network) courses.

The original logo of The Barron County Campus, Stout State University, 1966. It incorporates the symbol of UW-Stout – the clock tower on Bowman Hall and the historic Red Cedar River which runs along the edge of Barron County Campus.

Above: UW-BC students can participate in two unique programs. The Internship and Service Learning programs give students the opportunity to earn university credit, work with community professionals and add valuable work experience to their personal resumes.

Below: Eric Laidlaw and Heather Fankhauser take a moment to relax outdoors at the UW Colleges northwoods campus.

UW-BC is located on 110 acres of wooded land that is situated on the Red Cedar River along which winds the Cedar Side Trail, a hiking/biking path that winds through the City of Rice Lake.

The University of Wisconsin-Fond du Lac completed a $13 million renovation project in 2001. The University Center (above) was added to the campus and houses a new theater, library, music suite, cafeteria, art gallery, campus store and dramatic two-story student commons. *Below:* One of the earliest University of Wisconsin Center Fond du Lac logos included images which represented the shape of the campus buildings and the ponds on the campus grounds.

FOND DU LAC

The UW-Fond du Lac campus opened in 1968. Construction, land and equipment costs totaled just over $5 million. Planning for the campus began in 1963 when the Wisconsin Coordinating Council for Higher Education (CCHE) designated Fond du Lac as a potential site as part of its "outreach" plan.

Below: Musicals, dramas, comedies and more have been staged at UW-Fond du Lac. *Steel Magnolias* was performed by (left to right) Renee Hinn, Mary Halfman, Karla Larson and Ellen Ewaskowitz in the new 340-seat Prairie Theater in the fall of 2001. The theater features state-of-the art technical and production equipment.

The Quiz Bowl has been an annual event at UW-Fond du Lac since 1989. Each year area high schools are invited to send a three-person team to compete for scholarship money. One of the past winning teams from Goodrich High School in Fond du Lac is shown receiving their trophy.

UW-Fond du Lac basketball teams have produced several Wisconsin Collegiate Conference (WCC) All-Conference Players over the years. Student athletes are also able to participate in soccer, golf and volleyball teams at the campus.

Fox Valley

The world-class Barlow Planetarium and the Weis Earth Science Museum - Wisconsin's Official Mineralogical Museum – are now prominent parts of UW-Fox's campus. Leonard W. Weis, Ph.D., Associate Professor of Geology and Geography, Emeritus, and his wife, Donna, are the major financial contributors to the museum. During his tenure at UW-Fox and the UW System (1965-1989), his students knew him as "Doc Rock". *Below:* This award winning graphic design of the Barlow Planetarium logo was created by Directions, Inc., Neenah, in 1994 as part of their in-kind sponsorship of the state-of-the-art facility. Construction on the Barlow began in 1997, with the grand opening held March 20, 1998. To date, over 165,000 people have seen the variety of shows it has to offer.

Above: Students in Lecturer Joy Perry's biology #103 class study water and aquatic insect samples while wading in Kaukauna's Konkapot Creek in April 2001.

Lecturer Susan Benedict facilitates a small group mathematics tutoring session in her office in December 2000.

For many years prior to 1998, UW-Fox used this logo as the "Official Campus Visual Mark." It reveals the face of a fox (the dot being the nose). If viewed another way, it shows the Fox River Valley with the campus located south of the Fox River. The logo is also a stylized "UW."

Above: Dave Jordahl, Associate Professor of Music, leads student musicians and vocalists during a rousing mid-day concert celebrating the upcoming winter holiday season in December 2001.

In April 2001, students from Associate Professor Judith Baker's "Life Drawing" Art 201/202 class leave their solo easels in order to create a 40ft. long x 7 ft. high group drawing. The students were encouraged to approach this creation process in the manner of ensemble musicians, who must work together in order to realize a strong composition.

UW-Manitowoc opened its doors at its present location in 1962 on 40 acres of Lake Michigan shoreline donated by Manitowoc County. Shown in this photo is the original building, Founders Hall and the first logo of the campus. The fall of 2001 saw the dedication of UW-Manitowoc's third building, Lakeside Hall. *Below:* Math students, Mike Maes and Jimmy Dao, work out a problem during class in the 2001 fall semester.

Manitowoc County

One of the advantages of UW-Manitowoc is a caring faculty willing to spend individual time with students. Here, Geography/Geology Professor Cathy Helgeland answers questions from the 2001 fall semester students, Joan Sonnies and Jody Bruechert.

Below: Raymond Grosnick, center, was the first dean of UW-Manitowoc. Here, he is seen (circa 1960) with students in front of the entrance to the old Vocational Building on Clark Street, where classes were held for 29 years.

Above: An arsonist's fire destroyed the library and cafeteria in the fall of 1965. Almost all of the students volunteered their time to help with the clean up. Pictured are several students who sorted through the damaged books in the library.

Extra-curricular activities at UW-Manitowoc include intramural and collegiate sports. During the fall semester of 2001, Roberta LeCaptain took advantage of the volleyball opportunities.

In 1933 UW-Madison began holding classes in Wausau as part of its extension services. Classes were originally held in the old Central School, and in 1947 the University of Wisconsin Wausau Center, as it was called then, found a home in the County Normal School Building, above. Today the main campus building is located on the same site. The logo below, used in the 1980s and early 1990s, reflected UW-MC's location right next to Wausau's largest park, Marathon Park.

MARATHON COUNTY

Members of the Marathon County Board were so committed to having a UW campus in Wausau that in 1957 they persuaded the legislature to permit counties to finance the construction of a university building. Pictured above is the first such building in the state, built in Wausau at a cost of $530,000 and opened to students in 1959.

The 2001 Women's Varsity basketball players Jessica Beyer and Mindy Hartwig pose with the UW-MC athletic mascot, the Husky. Besides athletics, UW-MC students can participate in student government, the student newspaper and literary journal, drama, music, and over 20 different clubs and campus organizations.

Top: Student ambassadors Peter Xiong, David Cohn and Allyson McKensey staff a table during the summer 2001 student registration. Ambassadors represent the UW-MC at special functions, lead campus tours, serve on faculty selection committees and do general campus service.

Above: UW-MC's official logo from 1993 until 1998 when the current UW Colleges logo was adopted.

Josh King tests his skills on the climbing wall during the Student Activity Board's April 2001 picnic. To offset the rigors of academic life and to expand student experiences, several campus organizations plan special events. Musicians, theatre and dance troupes, speakers, mentalists, comedians, artists and poets all perform on campus.

UW-Marinette remains nestled among the pine trees along the bay. A granite entrance sign was installed in 1994 and redesigned in 1997 with the new campus logo. The Fine Arts Building addition completed in 2000 is seen in the background. *Below:* UW-Marinette's original logo was designed by Dwaine Naragon, a student (1969-71) of art professor James LaMalfa, and used until 1997 when the UW Colleges adopted a uniform look for all 13 campuses. *Bottom:* The Marinette Normal School for teacher preparation served the area from 1905 until the UW-Center opened in 1965.

Theatre on the Bay, which began in 1966, was directed for 30 years by Herbert L. Williams. The Theatre on the Bay Logo designed by Joe Paradis in 1976 was updated in 2001 with the addition of the seagull by TOB's new director Dr. Doug Larche.

Joe Gerend, Director of the UW Extension Center Marinette Campus from 1951 to 1963, is shown below teaching English classes in Goodman Hall at the old Marinette High School on Main Street.

Joe Gerend (left) helped recruit students for the Extension Center in the 50s.

Above: UW-Marinette continues to lead the UW Colleges in the creation and promotion on Learning Communities courses as a significant pedagogical movement. Here Dr. Jane Oitzinger (left) leads a discussion in the new seminar room overlooking the bay.

Before Campus Renewal 2000, chemistry lab students contended with summer heat and outdated equipment in a classroom that hadn't been renovated since 1965.

Today's chemistry lab is equipped with state-of-the-art instruments used in the separation and identification of chemical compounds and computers to assist in the acquisition and analysis of experimental data.

The original Marshfield campus includes the Aldo Leopold Science Building, front left. The Helen Connor Laird Fine Arts Building, right, and Physical Education Building, rear left, both added in 1971, were connected in 1998 with an addition that provided more space for the arts, distance education and student recreation. *Below:* One of many logos used by UW Marshfield/Wood County since 1964 until the adoption of a uniform logo in 1998 to create a strong and consistent visual institutional identity for the UW Colleges.

Marshfield/ Wood County

A full house gathers in Room 127 at UW-Marshfield/Wood, a photo probably taken during the campus's first decade. The lecture hall, which seats 72, was renovated in 1998's expansion project.

Intercollegiate athletic teams for basketball, volleyball, golf and tennis have flourished since the founding of UW-Marshfield/Wood County. The *Marauders* wear blue and gold on the court.

Through concerts performed by the Marshfield/Wood County Symphony Orchestra, theatre productions staged by Campus-Community Players, and guest artists hosted by the Performing Arts Series, UW-Marshfield/Wood County has built a strong tradition of providing quality arts programming to the community.

The original campus sign in 1967. *Below:* The historic logos of UW-Richland, which appeared in various incarnations over the years, were designed to reflect the shape of an important architecture element of the Richland Center campus - the copper roofs.

RICHLAND COUNTY

A student works on an "antique" computer from the 1980s.

This UWC-Richland campus promotional photo from 1980 brought together faculty, staff and students.

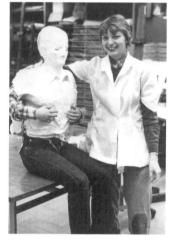

Above: A scene from the 1978 Campus-Community Theater production of "Where's Charley?" features two community actors – left, Paul Fowell and right, John Bart.

Above Right: In the art room in the late 1970s or early 1980s, Robin Chamberlain Transo works on an art project.

Rear View: every year since the first 1967, UW-Richland hold Burlap Olympics, a freshman-versus-sophomore competition which usually includes a human pyramid building contest, like this one from the mid-to-late 1970s.

ROCK COUNTY

"Winter fest Fun" on the UW-Rock County Campus.

Right: The Wells Cultural Center was the third building added to the UW-Rock County Campus. It was built in 1981, 15 years after the university opened its doors.

Previous Page: Front entrance to Williams Hall which houses the Science and Mathematics laboratories, lecture hall, seminar room, student gathering space, technical support and audio visual offices, computer labs and greenhouse. In 1971, it was named after Dr. Daniel Hale Williams (1856-1931) a Rock County resident who founded the first private African-American Hospital in Chicago where he performed the first recorded operation on the human heart. *Inset:* The "bubble" greenhouse attached to the south side of Williams Hall was used primarily for experiments by botany students. The greenhouse was taken down in 1999 during the renovation of Williams Hall.

University of Wisconsin Center—Rock County

One of the early campus logos.

Top: Ribbon cutting ceremony for the Williams Hall Renovation Project-Open House and Dedication, April 12, 1999. From left: Terry Maybee, Chair, Rock County Board of Supervisors; Betty Jo Bussie, Chair, General Services Committee, Rock County Board of Supervisors; Jane Crisler, Campus Executive Officer and Dean; Phil Boutwel, Assistant County Administrator, Steve Wildeck, Director of Business Services and Williams Hall Project Manager. Background: Bill Messner, Chancellor, UW Colleges.

Professor Dave Murray, Physics, Astronomy, ascending the stairway in Hyatt Smith Hall. Student banner illustrates the political culture of the day before the change in the legal drinking age.

The entrance to Main building which houses the administrative, student service, business and Continuing Education Offices, TV studio, classrooms, lecture hall and Wombat room in fall 2001. *Below:* In the fall 2001, almost 800 students enrolled at UW-Sheboygan. Thirty seven percent are nontraditional students, age 22 and older.

SHEBOYGAN

Spanish professor Alice Homstad works with student Miriam Flores in the language lab.

Below: William Hughes, choral director, conducts rehearsal in the campus music room shortly after the building was constructed in 1964.

A student worker operates the UNIVAC 9200, an early computer which was used on campus from 1969-1974.

Hannah Benton, Joe Feustel, and Brenda Sinnen starred in the University Theatre's March 2001 production of Cabaret.

Students studying in the library circa late 60's early 70's. *Below:* Students learning art from bare bones in the fall 2001.

WASHINGTON COUNTY

Above: Students in the "Writing across the Curriculum Program" word processing in the Writing Lab located in the library.

Professor Mohamed Ayoub instructing chemistry students.

Students Sara Uebele, Lisa Finkey and Angela Behnke plumb the secrets of the universe in the physics lab.

The 2001 Dance team – an athletic event in itself – brightens all the UW-WC home games. Pictured Row 1: Mary Spangola, Leah Nienow. Row 2: Jenny Jarvey, Karla Podewils, Erica Opitz,. Row 3: Tricia Fischer, Carly Schaefer, Stephanie Vetter, Brooke Nugent. Row 4: Connie Laudusdorf, Rose Marquardt, Theresa Schultzz

The University of Wisconsin-Waukesha Commons building has been serving the students of the Waukesha community since 1966. Photo taken after the Commons remodeling project was completed in 1966. The project added 20,000 square feet to the Commons and remodeled an existing 29,000 square feet. *Below:* Gertrude Sherman and Wisconsin Governor Warren Knowles at the 1967 ceremony honoring the 93 year-old's gift of 98 acres of farmland to UW-Waukesha. She stipulated that the area be used for educational purposes and the land restored to a natural condition. The land is now called the UW-Waukesha Field Station and includes the Gertrude Sherman classroom building built in 2001.

WAUKESHA COUNTY

Chemistry Professor Gary Udovich, left, and Mathematics Professor Ghulam Shah, right, prior to a UW-Waukesha Honors and Degree Ceremony. The ceremony is held each May and recognizes students receiving the associate degree or receiving special departmental honors.

Aerial view of the UW-Waukesha.

Members of the UW-Waukesha women's basketball team. The *Cougars* play and practice in the Field House remodeled in 2000. The facility was renovated and expanded to include 3 classrooms and a fitness center. This added close to 10,000 square feet to the original 1966 building.

Tonic Sol-Fa performs on the UW-Waukesha dining area stage at a *Nightclub at Noon* event on February 9, 1998. Because the campus does not have dorms, the student-run Activities Coordination Team (ACT) organizes the entertainment for the lunch crowd.

Bottom: Dr. Jane Burgess, UW-Waukesha Professor of Sociology, in a 1972 classroom photo. Robert Jozwiak of the campus University Relations office took the photo and labeled it: "Professor encourages adult students and younger students to share ideas in the classroom." Professor Burgess retired from teaching in 1990 and died in 1999 at the age of 81.

This logo was designed in 1981 by McGraphics of Milwaukee and marked the 15th Anniversary of the campus. It was used until 1998 when the UW Colleges mandated a uniform logo for all campuses.

Interim Dean Robert Larson distributing the new campus bumper sticker to students in 1978.

MEDFORD

Endnotes for Chapter One, Pages 7-20

[1]. Frederick M. Rosentreter, *The Boundaries of the Campus. A History of the University of Wisconsin Extension Division, 1885-1945.* (Madison: The University of Wisconsin Press, 1957), pp. 16-17.
[2]. Rosentreter, pp. 15-17.
[3]. Rosentreter, pp. 17-26.
[4]. Rosentreter, pp. 28-29.
[5]. Rosentreter, pp. 29-30.
[6]. Rosentreter, pp. 30-39.
[7]. Rosentreter, pp. 39-42.
[8]. Rosentreter, pp. 43-55, 65-77; George Clarke Sellery, *Some Ferments At Wisconsin. 1901-1947, Memories and Reflections* (Madison: The University of Wisconsin Press, 1960), p. 5; Clay Schoenfeld, editor, *History Digest: The University of Wisconsin, 1848-49 to 1948-49*, reprinted from the *Wisconsin Alumnus*, October 1948, pp. 13-14; "Six Men of Vision Started U. Extension," The Capital Times, January 31, 1956.
[9]. Extension Division, Annual Report, 1948-49.
[10]. Rosentreter, pp. 43-55; Maurice M. Vance. Charles Richard Van Hise, *Scientist Progressive* (Madison: State Historical Society of Wisconsin, 1960), pp. 108-112. Vance states that, "The Extension program would not have developed without Van Hise's support, nor could it have achieved acceptance without his active mediation." p. 110.
[11]. The College of Agriculture of course provided a home for the Farmers' Institutes and short courses. Lorentz H. Adolfson, "University Extension at Wisconsin: Policies, Practices, and Problems," an address delivered to the New England Rural Sociology Committee, April 23, 1964, University of Wisconsin Archives, Series 42/1/1, Box 16, asserts that the Extension Division deliberately was not rooted in the residence departments because Van Hise and McCarthy feared that the residence faculty would kill it.
[12]. Rosentreter, pp. 50-52, 65-66; Sellery, p. 5; *The Capital Times*, "Six Men of Vision Started U. Extension," January 31, 1956.
[13]. Rosentreter, pp. 54-55, and endnote 32 on p. 188; Adolfson, "University Extension at Wisconsin: Policies, Practices, and Problems." Merle Eugene Curti and Vernon Carstenson, *The University of Wisconsin, A History, 1848-1925*, two volumes (Madison: The University of Wisconsin Press, 1949), II: Chapter 17, "The Wider Campus: Extension," discusses in some detail the revival of General Extension during the Van Hise presidency.
[14]. Rosentreter, pp. 96-112.
[15]. Rosentreter, pp. 56-64, Sellery, p. 5.
[16]. Elisabeth Holmes, *The Urban Mission Anticipated: A Biography of the UW Extension Center in Milwaukee* (Milwaukee: Moebius Print Co., 1976), p. 4; Rosentreter, pp. 93-95.
[17]. Holmes, p. 4; Rosentreter, pp. 93-94; "The Development of the Milwaukee Extension Program of the University of Wisconsin," UW Archives, Series 18/1/1, Box 307, Enlarging College Opportunity; Extension Centers file.
[18]. Holmes, pp. 4-5; Chester Allen, *University Extension in Wisconsin*, 3 volumes, unpublished manuscript, 1955?, I: 122-125; Extension Dean Chester D. Snell to President Glenn Frank, April 2, 1931, Extension Deans' Papers, UW Archives, Series 18/1/1, Box 37, discusses briefly the initiation of freshman and sophomore courses in Milwaukee in 1920; University Extension Division, *University Extension in Wisconsin, 1906-1956. The 50-Year Story of the Wisconsin Idea in Education* (Madison: The University of Wisconsin, 1956), pp. 17-18.
[19]. Holmes, p. 5; Allen, I: 130-32.
[20]. Allen, I: 132.
[21]. Birge had been named Acting President shortly after Van Hise's unexpected death in November 1918. His tenure ultimately stretched out several years, until Glenn Frank was appointed President in 1925. Lawrence H. Larson, *The President Wore Spats: A Biography of Glenn Frank* (Madison: State Historical Society of Wisconsin, 1965), pp. 49-50.
[22]. Regents of the University of Wisconsin, Record K, 1921-23, pp. 433-34, UW Archives.
[23]. Dean Louis E. Reber, "MEMORANDUM. Re. A Building for the University Extension Division in Milwaukee," September 21, 1925, Glenn Frank Papers, Series 4/13/1. Box 14. RE file, UW Archives; Allen, I: 10-13; "The Milwaukee Extension Center—A Bit of History," Extension Deans' Papers, Series 18/1/1, Box 307, Enlarging College Opportunity file, UW Archives.
[24]. Larson, pp. 46-52.
[25]. Edward A. Fitzpatrick to Senator Teasdale, February 18, 1925, Glenn Frank Papers, Series 4/13/1, Box 14, RE file, UW Archives.
[26]. "MEMORANDUM. Day Credit Courses in Milwaukee Offering First and Second Year College Work," Glenn Frank Papers, Series 4/13/1. Box 86, Snell file, UW Archives. There is no date on this document but internal evidence suggests 1927. The unknown author (Snell?) is retracing the battle over the credit classes.
[27]. Allen, I: 134.
[28]. Allen, I: 134.
[29]. *The Capital Times*, July 11, 1928.
[30]. Chester D. Snell, "The University and the Adult," *Wisconsin Alumni Magazine*, July 1929.
[31]. W. H. Lighty, Director, Department of Extension Teaching, to Dean Snell, June 28, 1927, Glenn Frank Papers, Series 4/13/1, Box 86, Snell file, UW Archives.
[32]. Holmes, pp. 3-4; "Extension Classes Conducted by Members of the Faculty of the School of Education, September 1920-February 1925," Glenn Frank Papers, Series 4/13/1, Box 14, RE file, UW Archives.
[33]. Dr. George Parkinson, Director of the Milwaukee Extension Center, "An Analysis of the Administration of the Milwaukee Extension Division of the University of Wisconsin, August 1951, E. B. Fred Papers, Series 4/16/1, Box 147, Extension Division file, UW Archives.
[34]. Rosentreter, 78-95 passim.

[35]. See page 11 for the founding of the vocational high schools.
[36]. Rosentreter, pp. 78-95 passim.

Endnotes for Chapter Two, Pages 21-40

[1]. John E. Miller, *Governor Philip F. La Follette, The Wisconsin Progressives, and the New Deal* (Columbia & London: University of Missouri Press, 1982), pp. 8-9; Robert C. Nesbit, *Wisconsin, A History* (Madison: The University of Wisconsin Press, 1973), pp. 476-77, 488-89.
[2]. Nesbit, *Wisconsin, A History*, p. 480.
[3]. *Milwaukee Sentinel*, January 11, 1930; Capital Times, March 18, 1931.
[4]. *Capital Times,* March 18, 1931.
[5]. *Capital Times,* January 29, 1931 & November 25, 1932; Allen, II: 43-48.
[6]. EDUCATIONAL PLANS for HIGH SCHOOL GRADUATES, p. 1. This bulletin was written by Callahan, Hambrecht, Doudna, and Snell and distributed throughout the state to high school and vocational school administrators. There is a copy of the bulletin in the Glenn Frank Papers, Series 4/13/1, Box 122, Snell file, UW Archives. Reference to this committee and its work is also found in Allen, II: 74-76 and Rosentreter, Boundaries of the Campus, pp. 150-52.
[7]. EDUCATIONAL PLANS for HIGH SCHOOL GRADUATES, p. 1.
[8]. Ibid., pp. 8-10. Chester Allen to Dean Chester Snell, January 19, 1932, Extension Division Papers, Series 18/1/1, Box 34, Director of Field Organization file, UW Archives. In this letter Allen, who was Director of Field Organization for Extension, suggested that Snell send a letter to every high school principal urging them to consider freshman correspondence courses as a way their graduates could continue their educations. Apparently Snell enthusiastically accepted the recommendation and later worked the idea into his section of the bulletin.
[9]. Allen, II: 41-42. The twenty cities were Antigo, Appleton, Beloit, Edgerton, Fond du Lac, Green Bay, Hartland, Janesville, Kenosha, Manitowoc, Marinette, Mayville, Oconto, Racine, Shawano, Sheboygan, Sheboygan Falls, Waukesha, Wausau, and Wisconsin Rapids.
[10]. Allen, II: 77-78; Rosentreter, *Boundaries of the Campus,* p. 152; L.H. Adolfson, "The Early Days of University Centers in Wisconsin," *Wisconsin Academy Review,* Vol. 19, Number 2 (March 1973), pp. 14-15; University Extension Division, *University Extension in Wisconsin, 1906-1956. The 50-Year Story of the Wisconsin Idea in Education* (Madison: The University of Wisconsin, 1956), pp. 24-25.
[11]. Adolfson, "The Early Days of University Centers in Wisconsin," p. 15.
[12]. Ibid.; Chester Allen to (Extension) Dean Frank O. Holt, June 11, 1935, Extension Division Papers, Series 18/1/1, Box 62, Director of Field Organization file, UW Archives.
[13]. The Necessity of Educational Extension Work for the Unemployed, Extension Division Papers, Series 18/1/1, Box 61, Free Courses file, UW Archives.
[14]. Wisconsin Statutes, Chapter 363, Laws of 1933, Section 7(4b); Extension Division Papers, Series 18/1/1, Box 61, Free Courses file, UW Archives, contains much information about this program; Chester D. Snell to Voyta Wrabetz, Industrial Commission, no date, Glenn Frank Papers, Series 4/13/1, Box 171, Snell file, UW Archives, reports the use made of the money; Allen, II: 38.
[15]. Allen, II: 79-83, describes the episode in detail. Chester Allen to Glenn Frank, May 23 and July 6, 1934; Frank to Allen, August 14, 1934, Extension Division Papers, Series 18/1/1, Box 76, County Normals file, UW Archives.
[16]. Chester Allen to Dean Frank O. Holt, June 11, 1935, Extension Division Papers, Series 18/1/1, Box 62, Director of Field Organization file, UW Archives. Six vocational schools—Antigo Manitowoc, Marinette, Merrill, Rhinelander, Sheboygan—charged their students $25.00 per semester. The three county normal schools offered an even better deal, charging students just $12.50 per term. In Fond du Lac, Racine, Madison, and Richland Center the students paid the entire fee, $75.00. Chester Allen to M. G. Little, Assistant Dean, January 6, 1936, in Ibid.
[17]. Chester Allen to Dean Frank O. Holt, June 11, 1935, Extension Division Papers, Series 18/1/1, Box 62, Director of Field Organization file, UW Archives.
[18]. Chester Allen to Dean Chester D. Snell, February 1 and April 18, 1933 and January 31, 1934, Extension Division Papers, Series 18/1/1, Box 47, Director of Field Organization file, UW Archives; Chester Snell to Glenn Frank, July 27, 1933, Glenn Frank Papers, Series 4/13/1, Box 138, Snell file, UW Archives.
[19]. *Urban Mission Anticipated,* Extension Division, Annual Report 1948-49, pp. 11-12.
[20]. Chester Snell to Dr. C.M. Purin, Director of Milwaukee Center, January 18, 1932 and Snell to J.D. Phillips, UW Business Manager, June 29, 1932, Glenn Frank Papers, Series 4/13/1, Box 122, Snell file, UW Archives; Holmes, pp. 12-13. Allen indicates that the waivers in Extension totaled $140,339 over the three years. Allen, II: Appendix A: Budget Figures, notes 25, 26, 27.
[21]. W.H. Lighty, Memorandum Concerning Extension Appropriation 2A as a Dedicated Fund, February 3, 1932, Glenn Frank Papers, Series 4/13/1, Box 122, Snell file, UW Archives.
[22]. Chester D. Snell to President Glenn Frank, March 25, 1932, Glenn Frank Papers, Series 4/13/1, Box 122, Snell file, UW Archives.
[23]. Robert A. Carlson, "Merger in Extension: A History and Analysis of Merger at the University of Wisconsin," Master of Arts Thesis, 1968, University of Wisconsin-Madison, pp. 39-43.
[24]. Holmes, *Urban Mission Anticipated,* pp. 16-19; Larsen, *The President Wore Spats,* pp. 112-13; Rosentreter, pp. 141-44; Milwaukee Journal, April 23, 1935; E. Kurath, Chairman, Committee Investigating Extension Division Administration, Milwaukee County Federation of Teachers, to "Whom It May Concern," May 2, 1935, Glenn Frank Papers, Series 4/13/1, Box 171, Snell file, UW Archives. Chester Allen devoted three chapters to this important episode, see II: Chapters Seven, Eight, and Nine.

[25]. Investigating Committee on Communistic and Other Subversive Activities [in the University], Special Committee Reports, Wisconsin Senate Journal, 1935, pp. 2336-40; *Milwaukee Wisconsin News,* September 21, 1935; *Capital Times,* September 21, 1935.
[26]. Allen, II: 96-100.
[27]. M.E. McCaffrey, Secretary to President Frank, to Dean Chester D. Snell, April 25, 1935, Glenn Frank Papers, 4/13/1, Box 171, Snell file, UW Archives.
[28]. *Milwaukee Journal,* April 23, 1935. This article listed a half dozen reasons for the firing, all drawn from the Union's Fact Finding Committee's report.
[29]. *Wisconsin Senate Journal,* 1935, pp. 2334-35; Allen, II: Chapter Eight; *Capital Times,* September 21, 1935; Miller, Governor Philip LaFollette, pp. 72-3.
[30]. Meta Berger was the widow of renowned Milwaukee Socialist Victor Berger. Snell's allegation of immorality implicated her son-in-law Colin Welles, her daughter Doris (Mrs. Welles), and Professor Frank Hursley of the English Department. *Milwaukee Journal,* April 18, 1935; *Wisconsin State Journal,* April 26, 1935. In her testimony before the committee, Mrs. Berger essentially agreed with Snell's account—*Milwaukee Sentinel,* September 22, 1935. Snell's testimony received nation-wide news coverage, in the Presidents' Papers, Miscellaneous Files, Series 4/0/1, Box 29, UW Archives, there is an envelope bulging with clippings.
[31]. President Frank's statement, "The Snell Episode," is found in Presidents' Papers, Miscellaneous Files, Series 4/0/1, Box 30, Dismissal of Snell file, UW Archives.
[32]. *Milwaukee Journal,* September 21, 1935.
[33]. *Capital Times,* September 21, 1935.
[34]. *Wisconsin Senate Journal,* 1935, pp. 2336-40; *Capital Times,* September 21, 1935; *Milwaukee Journal,* September 21, 1935.
[35]. *Milwaukee Sentinel,* November 9, 1935. Holmes, *Urban Mission Anticipated,* pp.19-25, recounts the episode from the viewpoint of the Milwaukee Center faculty and states that several members of that faculty did not talk to one another for several years because of the rancor created over Snell's dismissal.
[36]. Allen, II: 123, 129; III: 1-2.
[37]. Larsen, *The President Wore Spats,* Chapters VIII-IX. Steven D. Zink, "Glenn Frank of the University of Wisconsin: A Reinterpretation," *Wisconsin Magazine of History,* 62 (Winter 1978-79): 91-127, see especially pp. 116-27. Zink concludes that while Snell's ouster was not primarily Frank's doing, his lack of attention to administrative detail had allowed the situation to fester until drastic action was required (p. 114). Miller, *Governor Philip LaFollette,* pp. 102-105. Miller observes that the *Capital Times* especially decried the affair as a heavy-handed bit of politics.
[38]. "Clarence Addison Dykstra" in *Wisconsin: Stability—Progress—Beauty* (Chicago: The Lewis Publishing Company, 1948), III: 32-33.
[39]. Rosentreter, pp. 161-65.
[40]. Ibid.
[41]. *Wausau Record Herald,* November 11, 1936.
[42]. T. Harry Williams, Lincoln Address Case, Extension Division Papers, Series 18/1/1, Box 90, UW Archives. Rosentreter, p. 167, notes that during the investigation by the History Department the *Record Herald* reporter admitted that he had not been present during Williams' speech and that he had written his story from an outline supplied by Williams.
[43]. T. Harry Williams, Lincoln Address Case, Extension Division Papers, Series 18/1/1, Box 90, UW Archives; Rosentreter, pp. 166-168.
[44]. Marshall C. Graff to Dean Holt, May 27, 1937; Chester Allen to Holt, May 27, 1937; F. O. Holt to S. I. Hayakawa, June 3 and 25, 1937, Extension Division Papers, Series 18/1/1, Box 79, S. I. Hayakawa file, UW Archives. Rosentreter, pp. 164-65.
[45]. Tape recorded interview with Chancellor L.H. Adolfson, March 21, 1968, "Transcriptions of Tapes on Early [Extension Center]History," Series 42/0/1, UW Archives.
[46]. Rosentreter, p. 157.
[47]. Extension Division Papers, Series 18/1/1, Box 65, Class Approval Blanks, 1st Semester, 1934-35 file, UW Archives.
[48]. *Milwaukee Journal,* September 20, 1936.
[49]. Tape recorded interview with Mrs. Frank Rentz, April 1968, "Transcriptions of Tapes on Early [Extension Center]History," Series 42/0/1, UW Archives. During her career Mrs Rentz taught in Beloit, Green Bay, Janesville, Kenosha, Manitowoc, Marinette, Racine, Sheboygan, Sturgeon Bay, Waupaca, Williams Bay and Wisconsin Rapids. Normally she had a four city circuit but one year she taught just in Manitowoc and Sheboygan.
[50]. John L. Bergstresser, "Classes Go to the Student," *Wisconsin Journal of Education,* September 1938, p. 50.
[51]. L. H. Adolfson, "The Early Days of the University Centers in Wisconsin," p. 15.
[52]. Mark H. Ingraham to Dean F. O. Holt, December 22, 1936, Extension Division Papers, Series 18/1/1, Box 78, Visits by Residence Staff to Freshman Classes file, UW Archives.
[53]. W. B. Hesseltine and R. L. Reynolds to Professor Paul Knaplund, Chairman, Department of History, April 27, 1937, in Ibid.
[54]. Holt to Evans, April 6, 1937, Extension Division Papers, Series 18/1/1, Box 81, Legislature (1937) file, UW Archives; John L. Bergstresser, "Classes Go To The Student," pp. 49-50.
[55]. Rosentreter, p. 157; Allen, III: 55.
[56]. Rosentreter, p. 157; Interview with Norbert E. Koopman, April 1968, Transcriptions of Tapes on Early [Extension Center]History, Series 42/0/1, UW Archives. Koopman attended the Sheboygan Center during 1938-39. He and his friends commuted fifteen miles from their homes in Plymouth to the old (1870 vintage) Sheboygan Central High School, where the college classes were held under the auspices of the Vocational School. Fees were $30 to $40 per semester; books were extra. Koopman mentioned that the students did not get to know their instructors very well because they had to leave soon after class to get to their next teaching assignment. In 1966 Koopman became the dean of the Marshfield/Wood County Center; he served until he retired in 1986.

[57]. Allen, III: Preface, 6-7, 18-22. Another factor in Holt's change of heart toward the Centers may have been President Glenn Frank's dismissal. Frank had rather adamantly opposed expanding the college credit classes beyond the Milwaukee Center and no doubt he would have had a great deal of influence upon Holt.
[58]. University Extension in Wisconsin, p. 30; Allen, III: 19-20; F. O. Holt to President Glenn Frank, July 9, 1936, Glenn Frank Papers, Series 4/13/1, Box 182, F. O. Holt file, UW Archives.
[59]. Allen, III: 35-38; *Capital Times*, March 11, 1937; Extension Division Papers, Series 18/1/1, Box 81, Legislature (1937) file, UW Archives. Leverich was a former member of the State Board of Vocational and Adult Education.
[60]. *Wisconsin State Journal*, February 25, 1937. The *Antigo Daily Journal*, March 13, 1937, and *Rhinelander News*, March 12, 1937, also rapped the bill, primarily because they feared that if Kannenberg succeeded their college credit programs would be shut down and their students would have to travel to Wausau.
[61]. *Capital Times*, March 5, 1937.
[62]. *Wisconsin State Journal*, February 25, 1937; Allen, III: 37-8. Late in the session, on June 17, Kannenberg introduced another budget amendment. This one paralleled Leverich's bill, but increased to $175,000 annually the amount available for the creation of one and two year university credit programs by local school board contracts with Extension. It also would have reduced the Extension fees to the same level as those paid by students in Madison; the reduction would have amounted to $3.00 per credit. The Senate passed this measure, too, but the Assembly refused to suspend its rules to discharge it from committee and it expired when the legislators went home on July 2. Allen, III: 37-8.
[63]. Allen, III: 48-53.
[64]. Allen, III: 63-4.
[65]. Allen, III: 64-5. Allen made a last minute appeal to George Hambrecht, asking him to try once more to persuade the State Vocational Board to continue the aid to the Centers. In sharp contrast to the $100,000 maximum requested from the legislature, Allen estimated that total aid for 1938-39 would probably not exceed $3,000. Of course, Allen wrote, the absence of even that small amount would spell disaster for the students and the local communities which were counting on it to keep the Centers going. Chester Allen to George Hambrecht, State Board of Vocational Education, June 26, 1939, Extension Division Papers, Series 18/1/1, Box 91, Chester Allen file, UW Archives.
[66]. Allen, III: 58-62.
[67]. F. O. Holt to Chester Allen, June 6, 1939, and Chester Allen to Dean Holt, July 8, 1939, Extension Division Papers, Series 18/1/1, Box 91, Chester Allen file, UW Archives; Allen, III: 70-1, 72, 78-9.
[68]. Allen, III: 66-9; Rosentreter, pp. 157-58; *Capital Times*, March 3, 1938, and August 16, 1939.

Endnotes for Chapter Three, Pages 41-56

[1]. William E. Leuchtenberg and the Editors of Life, *New Deal and Global War, 1933-1945*, Volume 11 in the Life History of the United States, 12 volumes (New York: Time Incorporated, 1964), pp. 99, 115; William F. Thompson, *The History of Wisconsin, Volume VI, Continuity and Change, 1940-1965* (Madison: State Historical Society of Wisconsin, 1988), pp. 66-67.
[2]. Thompson, *Continuity and Change*, pp. 66-67, 70-71, 83-93.
[3]. Holmes, *Urban Mission Anticipated*, pp. 115-16.
[4]. Holmes, Ibid.; Allen, III:88-9.
[5]. Allen, III:39-90, 127-28. Allen states that the surplus totalled just over $200,000 by the end of 1942-43 and reached $360,000 at the close of the following academic year.
[6]. The University of Wisconsin Press Bulletin, September 11, 1940; F.O. Holt to C.A. Dykstra, February 20, 1940, Dykstra Papers, Series 4/15/1, Box 48, F.O. Holt file, UW Archives.
[7]. University of Wisconsin Press Bulletin, July 16, 1941; Allen, III:86-7.
[8]. Allen, III:83-6. Allen provides a list of the Normal Schools and the number of education courses each sponsored: Eau Claire-4, LaCrosse-3, Oshkosh-4, Platteville-2, River Falls-1, Stevens Point-12, Superior-2 and Whitewater-1. A University of Wisconsin Faculty Employment Form, dated 1/25/41, in the Clarence Dykstra Papers, Series 4/15/1, Box 66, F.O. Holt file, UW Archives, indicates that W.W. Price taught two of these courses, at Mayville and Manitowoc, for a salary not to exceed $525.00. The professor's compensation depended upon how many students enrolled.
[9]. Allen, III:74-7.
[10]. Allen, III:81-2.
[11]. Holmes, *Urban Mission Anticipated*, pp. 33-36, 115; Milwaukee Center Day School Enrollments, 1939-1949, E.B. Fred Papers, Series 4/16/1, Box 126, Extension Division file, UW Archives. [12]. A. W. Peterson to President C. A. Dykstra, September 1, 1942, Dykstra Papers, Series 4/15/1, Box 105, F. O. Holt file, UW Archives.
[13]. Memorandum to Dean Holt, November 16, 1942, in Ibid.
[14]. Allen, III:112-13.
[15]. Allen, III:82-84, 98-120.
[16]. Allen, III:134-39.
[17]. *Capital Times* and *Wisconsin State Journal*, February 13, 1944; The Record of the Regents of the University of Wisconsin, Volume V, 1943-44, meeting of February 12, 1944, pp. 7-8.
[18]. Allen, III:134-39.
[19]. Record of the Regents of the University of Wisconsin, Volume VI, 1944-45, special meeting of January 25, 1945, pp. 21-4, and "Edwin Broun Fred," Donna S. Taylor, interviewer, 1976, University of Wisconsin Archives Oral History Project, pp. 1-3 of transcript.
[20]. L.H. Adolfson, "The University and State Policy Regarding the Freshman-Sophomore Program of the University Extension Division," Center System Papers, Series 42/1/1, Box 16, Addresses file, UW Archives.
[21]. *Milwaukee Journal*, June 13, 1943.
[22]. Allen, III:96; Chapter 225, Laws of 1943.

[23]. Record of the University of Wisconsin Regents, Vol. IV, 1942- 1943, meeting of February 27, 1943, p. 7. The Regents' Finance Committee discussed the issue and recommended no action be taken.
[24]. *Milwaukee Journal,* June 9 & 13, 1943.
[25]. *Capital Times,* February 15 & September 16, 1945; *Milwaukee Journal,* July 20 & September 16, 1945; *Milwaukee Sentinel,* September 17, 1945; and Record of the University of Wisconsin Regents, Vol. VII, 1945-1946, meeting of September 15, 1945, p. 4.
[26]. Nesbit & Thompson, *Wisconsin, A History,* pp. 529-30.
[27]. *Portage Register-Democrat,* March 22, 1946.
[28]. "Enrollment in the University of Wisconsin and Provisions for Veterans," E.B. Fred Papers, Series 4/16/1, Box 32, Enrollment file, UW Archives. There is no date on this document, but it must have been written in the late summer of 1946 because it includes enrollment figures for the 1946 summer session. Rosentreter, *Boundaries of the Campus,* pp. 160-61.
[29]. R.J. Colbert to L.H. Adolfson, April 24, 1946, Extension Division Papers, Series 18/1/8-2, Box 2, College Centers, 1945-46 file, UW Archives, describes a typical planning meeting in Rice Lake. *Milwaukee Journal,* May 6, 1946; *Sparta Democrat,* May 9, 1946; *Wisconsin Journal of Education,* May 1946; Wisconsin State Journal, July 12, 1946; and University of Wisconsin Press Bulletin, September 18, 1946.
[30]. "Edwin Broun Fred," Donna S. Taylor, interviewer. pp. 128-129 of transcript.
[31]. L.H. Adolfson, "The Plan for the Racine Extension Center," March 21, 1946; "The Extension Center Program," a radio address with President Fred, November 1, 1946; and "The Building of an Institution: The University Center System," April 20, 1967; Center System Papers, Series 42/1/1, Box 16, Addresses file, UW Archives. [Extension Centers] Annual Report, 1946-47, Extension Division Papers, Series 18/4/1, Box 1, Annual Reports, 1946-1954 file, UW Archives. Holmes, Urban Mission Anticipated, pp. 117-18.
[32]. Petition from Milwaukee students to Center Director Dr. George Parkinson, August 9, 1946, Fred Papers, Series 4/16/1, Box 32, Extension Division file, UW Archives; Holmes, *Urban Mission Anticipated,* pp. 36-37.
[33]. Adolfson to Fred, August 11 & 13, 1946, and Fred to Adolfson, August 21, 1946, Fred Papers, Series 4/16/1, Box 32, Extension Division file, UW Archives.
[34]. Alden White, Secretary of the Faculty, to Fred, May 12, 1947, Fred Papers, Series 4/16/1, Box 57, Extension Division file, UW Archives; Milwaukee Journal December 6, 1946, July 31 & August 12, 1947.
[35]. J. Martin Klotsche, *The University of Wisconsin-Milwaukee, An Urban University* (Milwaukee: University of Wisconsin-Milwaukee, 1972), pp. 3-6; hereafter cited as Klotsche, An Urban University. Proceedings of the Board of Regents of Normal Schools, 1948-1949, meeting of February 10, 1949, Resolution 411, p. 26.
[36]. Report of the Committee on Extension Centers, May 12, 1947, E. B. Fred Papers, 4/16/1, Box 57, Extension Division file, UW Archives.
[37]. Ibid. The ten out-state Centers were Fond du Lac, Green Bay, Kenosha, Manitowoc, Marinette, Menasha, Racine, Rhinelander, Sheboygan, and Wausau.
[38]. Adolfson to Fred, May 19 and John Guy Fowlkes, Chairman, Committee on Extension Centers, to Fred, June 16, 1947, E. B. Fred Papers, 4/16/1, Box 57, Extension Division file, UW Archives; Record of the University of Wisconsin Regents, Vol. VIII, 1946-1947, Meeting of June 25, 1947, p. 6.
[39]. Hanley to Roy Luberg, Assistant to the President, September 24, 1947, E. B. Fred Papers, 4/16/5, Box 4, Extension Division file, UW Archives.
[40]. John Guy Fowlkes and Henry C. Ahrnsbrak, Junior College Needs in Wisconsin, Bulletin of the University of Wisconsin, Serial 2907, General Series 1681, April 1947, see especially pp. 33-34, 55-57. The report received considerable press. As could be expected, the papers in the seven towns (Green Bay, Kenosha, Marinette, Menasha-Neenah, Racine, Sheboygan, Wausau) gave enthusiastic approval. See, for example, *The Sheboygan Press,* August 9, 1947. On the other hand, *The Wisconsin State Journal* (August 13, 1947) editorialized against the recommendation and urged, instead, that vocational courses be added at the nine state colleges if the state truly needed junior colleges.
[41]. L. H. Adolfson, A Memorandum Concerning the Proposed Extension Center Program for 1948-49, Extension Division Papers, Series 18/1/1, Box 183, Centers—General, 1948-50 file, UW Archives.
[42]. The E. B. Fred Papers, Series 4/16/1, Boxes 81 & 107, Extension Division file, UW Archives, contain many letters, notes and memoranda on this issue.
[43]. Progress Report of the Committee on Fond du Lac and Menasha Extension Centers in Relation to the Oshkosh State Teachers College, Extension Division Papers, Series 18/1/1, Box 183, Centers—Oshkosh Committee Report file, UW Archives.
[44]. Robert Doremus to Adolfson, March 17, 1949, in Ibid.
[45]. Fond du Lac Survey. Extension Center Students & High School Seniors, in Ibid.
[46]. Extension Division Annual Report, 1949-50, Extension Division Papers, Series 18/4/1, Box 1, UW Archives; Keith W. Olson, "World War II Veterans at the University of Wisconsin," *Wisconsin Magazine of History,* 53(Winter 1969-70):83-97; Lucille Bystrom, "U.W. Extension Centers Will Vie in Basketball League," *Milwaukee Sentinel,* December 3, 1946.

Endnotes for Chapter Four, Pages 57-70

[1]. Thompson, *The History of Wisconsin: Continuity and Change, 1940-1960,* pp. 616-17, 701.
[2]. Ibid. Highways and public welfare also claimed significant segments of the federal aid.
[3]. Hanley's memoranda are in the Extension Centers General Files, Series 18/4/1-2, Box 1, Budgets, 1948-1956 file, UW Archives.
[4]. Extension Division Annual Report, 1951-52 and 1952-53.
[5]. *Milwaukee Journal,* March 12, 1953; *Green Bay Press-Gazette,* March 25, 1953.
[6]. Statements before Senate Education Committee, Re; Resolution 41-A, March 24, 1953, Extension Division Papers,

Series 18/1/1-1, Box 229, Centers-General, 1952-54 file, UW Archives.
[7]. *Capital Times*, May 3, 1953.
[8]. I have used four major sources for my brief account of Kohler's 1955 attempt to achieve a merger of the state's two public higher education systems: Otto M. Carouthers, The Merger of the University of Wisconsin with the Wisconsin State Universities System (Ed. D. thesis, Indiana University, 1974), pp. 104-114; Gale Loudon Kelly, The Politics of Higher Educational Coordination in Wisconsin, 1956-1969 (Doctoral Thesis, UW-Madison, 1972), pp. 67-79; Klotsche, *an Urban University*, pp. 21-25; and Joseph C. Rost, The Merger of the University and the Wisconsin State University Systems: a Case Study in the Politics of Education (Doctoral Dissertation, UW-Madison, 1973), pp. 139-168.
[9]. Proceedings of the Board of Regents of State Colleges, 1953-1955, Resolution 1072, pp. 86-87.
[10]. *Milwaukee Journal*, February 18, 1995.
[11]. *Green Bay Press-Gazette*, August 22, 1950.
[12]. *Green Bay Press-Gazette*, May 20, 1953.
[13]. *Green Bay Press-Gazette*, May 2, 1957.
[14]. *Green Bay Press-Gazette*, October 11, 1957.
[15]. CCHE Background Study X. The Junior College. December 1957, pp. 1-2; *Wisconsin State Journal*, January 11, 1958.
[16]. CCHE Minutes, January 15, 1959; *Milwaukee Journal*, January 16, 1959.
[17]. Kelly, The Politics of Higher Educational Coordination in Wisconsin, pp. 101-106, 134-137.
[18]. Memorandum Concerning the Meeting of Extension Center Directors at Kenosha," November 13, 1951; "Green Bay Directorship," September, 1953; and "Memorandum for Files, R. J. Zorn," August 11, 1955, Extension Division Papers, Series 18/1/1-1/ Boxes 217, 229, 240, respectively,UW Archives. Chester Allen to Dr. L. H. Adolfson, February 5, 1952, Chester Allen papers, Series 18/1/8-1, Box 12, L. H. Adolfson file, UW Archives.
[19]. L. H. Adolfson to William H. Young, Assistant to the President, February 9, 1956, Extension Division Papers,Series 18/1/1-1, Box 240, Centers-Kenosha 1954-56 file, UW Archives.
[20]. L. H. Adolfson to W. M. Hanley, June 20 and November 20,1956, in Ibid., Box 253, Centers-General, 1956-58 file.
[21]. Profile of Center Students, 1953-54," Extension Division Papers, Series 18/1/1, Box 307, Enlarging College Opportunity file, UW Archives.
[22]. Extension Centers Annual Report, 1950-51, Student Personnel Services section; Green Bay Extension Center promotional brochure, 1956-57.
[23]. The *Kenosha News*, May 7, 1955.
[24]. Adolfson to Hanley, December 7, 1955, Extension Division Papers, Series 18/1/1-1, Box 240, Centers-General, 1954-56 file, UW Archives. Hanley's response was penciled on the bottom of the letter.
[25]. Record of the University of Wisconsin Regents, Volume XX, 1958-1959, meeting of April 11, 1959, p. 2.
[26]. "Attendance Patterns at University Centers," CCHE #7, Informational Item, January 1964, p. 3.
[27]. Chapter 619, Laws of 1955.
[28]. Section 67.04, Wisconsin Statutes.
[29].Board of Regents meeting, November 12, 1955. Clarke Smith,Secretary of the Board of Regents, to Mrs. Lucile Zielsdorf, County Clerk, November 14, 1955, E. B. Fred Papers, Series 4/16/1, Box 255, Extension Division file, UW Archives.
[30]. W. M. Hanley to President E. B. Fred, March 13, 1958, Extension Division Papers, Series 18/1/1-1, Box 253, Centers-General, 1956-58 file; W. M. Hanley, Memorandum: Status of Center Building Projects, no date but internal evidence suggests January or February 1960, Extension Division Papers, Box 263, Centers-General, 1958-60 file, UW Archives.
[31]. L. H. Adolfson, Honors Convocation Address, Fox Valley Campus, May 14, 1968, Center System Papers, Series 42/1/1, Box 16, Addresses file, UW Archives.
[32]. *Appleton Post-Crescent*, March 17, 1958; Milwaukee Sentinel, September 21, 1958.
[33]. Shirley E. Johnson, "University of Wisconsin System Outreach,"*Encyclopedia of Library and Information Services*, Volume 33 (New York: Marcel Dekker, Inc., 1982), pp. 232-33; Report on Extension Libraries, September 1956, Extension Division Papers, Series 18/1/1-1, Box 253, Centers-General, 1956-58 file, UW Archives; Henry C. Ahrnsbrak, Director [Wausau], to W. M. Hanley, November 3, 1960, in Ibid., Box 263, Centers-Wausau, 1958-60 file.
[34]. Record of the Regents of the University of Wisconsin and Executive Committee, Volume XX, 1958-59, meeting of June 9,1959, pp. 12-13.

Endnotes for Chapter Five, Pages 71-96

[1]. Nesbit & Thompson, *Wisconsin, A History*, p. 530; CCHE Working Paper #24, A Design For Future Development of Public Higher Education in Wisconsin, November 1960, pp. 12-14; Donovan Riley, Two Year Higher Education Institutions: Plans and Current Operation, A Report of the Committee on Legislative Organization and Procedure, December 1964, p. 13.
[2] . L.H. Adolfson, "University Extension Looks Ahead," Founders' Day speech, March 23, 1961, Green Bay, Center System Papers, Series 42/1/1, Box 16, Addresses file, UW Archives.
[3]. *Milwaukee Journal*, January 26, 1960; *Wisconsin State Journal*, June 8, 1961; CCHE Informational Item #48, Cooperation Between State Colleges or Extension Centers and Vocational Schools, January 1961.
[4]. CCHE Paper #43, Semi-Final Report of CCHE Subcommittee on County Teachers Colleges, July, 1962, and CCHE Working Paper #56, Final Report on County Teachers Colleges and Related Matters, October 1962. Kelly, The Politics of Higher Education Coordination in Wisconsin, pp. 137-143.
[5]. CCHE #32, Joint Staff Committee Concerned with the Development of New Criteria for the Establishment and Operation of New Extension Centers, Subcommittee Minutes, July 1962.

[6]. Kelly, Politics of Higher Education Coordination in Wisconsin, pp. 146-154.
[7]. Ibid.; *Wisconsin State Journal*, July 20, 1962.
[8]. These recommendations were included in the semi-final and final reports on the county teachers colleges. See note 4, above, for details. The committee had beefed up Adolfson's original proposal by increasing both the distance from another college and the required number of high school graduates within a given radius for a two year campus to be established. Thus, a Center located 15 to 29 miles from an existing college needed 1,250 high school graduates within 15 miles, while one 30 to 45 miles away needed at least 1,000 graduates in a 20 mile radius. A center more than 45 miles from a competitor required 750 graduates within a 30 miles radius. Smaller communities in rural areas, which could not meet these standards, had the right to appeal to the CCHE for special consideration. In addition, the CCHE requested that the legislature empower the state colleges to establish extension centers and authorize the CCHE to decide where new campuses would be located and who, the University or the State Colleges, would operate them.
[9]. Record of the University of Wisconsin Regents, Volume 24, meetings of January 5, 1962, pp. 6-7 and exhibits C, D, E, F; February 9, 1962, pp. 19-20; and June 5, 1962, pp. 16-17. *Wisconsin State Journal*, June 6, 1962.
[10]. Proceedings of the Board of Regents of State Colleges, 1960- 1966; Proceedings, 1961-62; Resolution 2004, adopted June 20, 1962; pp. 122-123. Capital Times, June 21, 1962; *Wisconsin State Journal*, June 21, July 20, and December 7, 1962. Kelly, The Politics of Higher Education Coordination in Wisconsin, pp. 146-154.
[11]. Gordon Haferbecker to President Harrington, August 8, 1962, Center System Papers, Series 42/1/1, Box 2, Suggested Central State College file, UW Archives.
[12]. Fred Harvey Harrington to Gordon Haferbecker, August 13, 1962; Harrington to Vice President Clodius and Dean Adolfson, August 13, 1962, F. H. Harrington Papers,, Series 4/18/1, Box 9, Extension Division file and L.H. Adolfson to Harrington, September 14, 1962, Center System Papers, Series 42/1/1, Box 2, Suggested Central State College file; W.H. Hanley, Memorandum on Proposed New Centers, October 23, 1962, Extension Division Papers, Series 18/4/1-2, Box 3, Proposed New Centers file; all in the UW Archives.
[13]. CCHE Working Paper #14, First Report of the Long-Range Planning Subcommittee: Distribution of Public Higher Education in Wisconsin, A Progress Report, March 1963; CCHE Working Paper #44, Proposal for the Distribution and Establishment of Two- Year University Centers and State College Branch Campuses, October 1963; Milwaukee Journal, October 26, 1963.
[14]. *Capital Times*, October 25, 1963; Kelly, Politics of Higher Education Coordination in Wisconsin, pp. 154-161.
[15]. Proceedings of the Board of Regents of State Colleges, 1963- 1964, pp. 106, 109-113; CCHE #33, State College Regents Report on Post-High School Education, April 1964; CCHE #55, Communication-Resolution from the Board of Regents of State Colleges, May 1964; Milwaukee Journal, April 12, 1964.
[16]. Kelly, The Politics of Higher Education Coordination in Wisconsin, pp. 160, 174-175; Fred Harvey Harrington to L.H. Adolfson, May 1, 1964, Harrington Papers, Series 4/18/1, Box 40, Center System—Provost file, UW Archives; Proceedings of the Board of Regents of State Colleges, 1960-1966, Proceedings, 1963-1964, pp. 117-18, Resolution 2234, May 22, 1964; *Milwaukee Journal*, May 23, 1964.
[17]. Grace Witter White, *Cooperative Extension in Wisconsin, 1962- 1982* (Dubuque, Iowa: Kendall/Hunt Publishing Company, 1985), pp. 6-9; Carlson, Merger in Extension, pp. 2-14, 66.
[18]. Recommendation Concerning Organization of University Center System, Record of the University of Wisconsin Regents, Volume 27, (July-December 1963), meeting of September 6, 1963, p. 17; *Capital Times* & *Milwaukee Journal*, September 7, 1963. Clara Penniman, "The University of Wisconsin System," in Allan G. Bogue and Robert Taylor, editors, *The University of Wisconsin, One Hundred and Twenty-Four Years* (Madison: The University of Wisconsin Press, 1973) observes that this important change in organization was made "with essentially no faculty input and little consultation with the Madison University administration." She asserts that little criticism ensued because everyone was in an expansive mood and because many felt that Harrington would protect Madison's interests.
[19]. R.L. Clodius, Vice President, to the Search Committee, September 16, 1963; W.M. Hanley to President Harrington, January 24, 1964; Harrington to Angus Rothwell, January 29, 1964; Emil Muuss, Mayor of Sheboygan, to Harrington, March 2, 1964; Sheboygan Center Faculty to Harrington, March 3, 1964; Resolution from Manitowoc County Board, February 12, 1964; Resolution from the Common Council of the City of Kenosha, February 4, 1964; *Kenosha News*, January 29, 1964; all in the Harrington Papers, Series 4/18/1, Box 40, Center System- Provost file, UW Archives.
[20]. Harrington to Dean Edwin Young, [Chairman of the Search Committee], March 24, 1964; Harrington to Adolfson, March 24, 1964; in Ibid. Record of the University of Wisconsin Regents, Volume 28, January-June 1964, meeting of April 10, 1964, p. 20. *Wisconsin State Journal*, April 11, 1964.
[21]. Working Paper on Separation of Center System from University Extension Division, February 13, 1964. A copy is located in the Center System Papers, Series 42/1/1, Box 1, Center System (Separate) file, UW Archives. Pages 21-24 dealt with the provost's office. L.H. Adolfson, "University of Wisconsin Centers, 1946-1972," *Wisconsin Academy Review*, Volume 19, Number 3 (June 1973), p. 28. Record of the University of Wisconsin Regents, Volume 30, January to June, 1965, meeting of January 8, 1965, p. 29.
[22]. Working Paper on Separation of Center System from University Extension Division, pp. 11-15.
[23]. Record of the University of Wisconsin Regents, Volume 31, July-December 1965, meeting of August 20, 1965, pp. 27-28.
[24]. Riley, Two Year Higher Education Institutions. . ., A Report of the Committee on Legislative Organization and Procedure, December 1964, pp. 17-18. This analysis was based upon the Center System October 1964 payroll. L.H. Adolfson, Remarks on the University Center System [to the Regents], October 16, 1964, Center System Papers, Series 42/1/1, Box 16, Addresses file, UW Archives.
[25]. Report of the Interim Committee on Organization of the University Center System Faculty, February 4, 1965, and L.H. Adolfson to Center Directors, March 9, 1965, Center System Papers, Series 42/1/1, Box 19, Center System Faculty Senate file, UW Archives; Record of the University of Wisconsin Regents, Volume 30, January-June 1965, meeting of May 7, 1965, p. 19 and Exhibit G.
[26]. Center System Document 14, November 12, 1966; Center System Document 17: The University Faculty Assembly,

February 24, 1967; and Center System Document 67, November 16, 1968, Center System Papers, Series 42/1/8, Box 7, UW Archives. In the inaugural Faculty Assembly Madison had 36 seats, Milwaukee had 10, Extension had 5, and the Center System had 2.

[27]. Bureau of Government, University Extension Division, University Extension Division Departments and Center Instruction: A Working Paper, January 1963, Center System Papers, Series 42/1/1, Box 8, Center Faculty Organization file, UW Archives; Working Paper on Separation of Center System from University Extension Division, pp. 5-10; Center System Faculty Senate Minutes, July 17, 1965, p. 2; L.H. Adolfson, "University of Wisconsin Centers, 1946-1972," p. 28; Center System Faculty Document 9: Divisional Structure of the University of Wisconsin Center System and Center System Faculty Document 10, Departmental Structure of the University of Wisconsin Center System, both September 24, 1966, Center System Papers, Series 42/1/8, Box 7, UW Archives.

[28]. Memorandum on the "60 Credit" Rule, November 1, 1965, Center System Papers, Series 42/1/1. Box 19, Center System Faculty Senate file, UW Archives.

[29]. Policy on Transferring of Courses and Credits within the University System, September 9, 1966; Pre-transfer Counseling and Advising Program for Center System Students, Summary of Planning Meeting Discussion, November 2, 1966; Martha Peterson, Dean for Student Affairs, to Fred H. Harrington, December 1, 1966, Harrington Papers, Series 40/1/1, Box 38, Center System, Chancellor file, UW Archives.

[30]. Riley, Two Year Higher Education Institutions: Plans and Current Operation, pp. 22-27; Roger E. Schwenn, "Center System Libraries," *Wisconsin Library Bulletin*, 63: 85-86, March 1967; Roger E. Schwenn, "Libraries," University Center System Progress Report, 1964-1967, pp. 60-66.

[31]. Warren P. Knowles to CCHE, December 23, 1964, Records of the Coordinating Council for Higher Education, Series 1841, Box 8, folder 2, the State Historical Society of Wisconsin.

[32]. CCHE Working Paper #4, Planned Two-Year Educational Opportunities, February 1965; David R. Obey to CCHE, February 13, 1965, in CCHE #11, Communication. *The Milwaukee Journal*, February 7, 1965, wondered whether pressure from Governor Knowles had led to this recommendation.

[33]. *Milwaukee Sentinel*, March 9, 1965.

[34]. *Wisconsin State Journal*, July 25, 1965; CCHE #42, Working Paper, Dual Track Institutions, May 1966; CCHE # 72, Communication (Frank Nikolay, Assembly Majority Leader, to CCHE Director Angus Rothwell, July 13, 1966); Milwaukee Journal, July 16, 1966; Kelly, Politics of Higher Education Coordination in Wisconsin, pp. 255-264.

[35]. Capital Times & Milwaukee Journal, March 24, 1965; Wisconsin State Journal, March 25, 1965; Kelly, Politics of Higher Education Coordination in Wisconsin, pp. 232-239.

[36]. *Racine Journal-Times*, October 15, 1965, a special issue in honor of the dedication of the new Racine Center; CCHE #53, Working Paper, First Report on Planning for the New Third and Fourth Year Campuses, November 1965.

[37]. Fred Harvey Harrington to L.H. Adolfson, January 18, 1967, and Adolfson to Harrington, January 23, 1967, Harrington Papers, Series 40/1/1, Box 38, Center System, Chancellor file, UW Archives.

[38]. John P. Nash [a Manitowoc lawyer] to President Fred H. Harrington, May 23, 1967, protesting the transfer of the Manitowoc Center to Green Bay's control. The points Nash makes about faculty concerns indicate that he was well informed or, perhaps, well coached. Harrington to Chancellor L.H. Adolfson and Chancellor Edward Weidner, no date but attached to Nash's letter in the file; Harrington still prefers the four-campus arrangement but does not want "another major conflict," he asked the two Chancellors to work to defuse the situation. Carolyn Pearson, Secretary of the Manitowoc Center Faculty, to Harrington, June 1, 1967, informs the President of the faculty's desire to remain with the Center System. Harrington's terse reply (June 6, 1967) simply said the issue would again be discussed. All these in the Harrington Papers, Series 40/1/1, Box 38, Center System- Chancellor file, UW Archives. Chancellors L.H. Adolfson & E.W. Weidner to Faculty of Fox Valley, Green Bay, Manitowoc & Marinette Centers, November 3, 1967, indicated the deadline for making a choice between Green Bay and the Center System; Nancy Janssen, Secretary of the Manitowoc Center Faculty to Adolfson and Weidner, November 10, 1967, reported that about one-third of the Manitowoc faculty had not supported the spring protest and had applied to Green Bay; in Ibid, Box 74.

[39]. Report of the Committee on the Future Role and Organization of the University of Wisconsin Center System, June 20, 1968, Center System Papers/UWC-Marathon County, uncatalogued collection, accession #86/112, Box 3, Wausau Plan file; and UW Center System Faculty Documents 70 (January 11, 1969), 72 (March 22, 1969), and 75 (May 10, 1969), Center System Papers, Series 42/1/8, Box 7, UW Archives.

[40]. Geographic Distribution of Students Registered at Centers, According to Post Office and County, lst Semester 1962-63, Harrington Papers, Series 4/18/1, Box 9, Extension Division file, UW Archives; Riley, Two Year Higher Education Institutions . . ., A Report of the Committee on Legislative Organization and Procedure, December 1964, pp. 28-30; the University of Wisconsin Center System Report, November 1966; *Milwaukee Sentinel*, January 9, 1968; the University of Wisconsin Center System Report, January 1970.

[41]. L.J. Lins and Allan P. Abell, Comparison of Madison Campus Achievement of University Center Transfer Students with Students Who Entered as New Freshmen at Madison, June 1963; L.J. Lins to Vice President Robert Clodius. December 7, 1964 Center System Papers, Series 42/1/1, Box 12, Institutional Studies file, UW Archives.

[42]. Record of the University of Wisconsin Regents, Volume 32, January-June 1966, meeting of May 6, 1966, p. 14; *Milwaukee Sentinel*, May 7, 1966.

[43]. Martha Peterson, Impressions of Center Students, manuscript of a speech delivered July 13, 1967, Center System Papers, Series 42/1/8, Box 4, Center System file, UW Archives.

[44]. Adolfson to Harrington, November 4, 1966; Harrington to Adolfson, November 10, 1966; Elmer Meyer, Jr., to Adolfson, December 15, 1966; R.L. Clodius to Adolfson, January 4, 1967, Harrington Papers, Series 40/1/1, Box 38, Center System, Chancellor file, UW Archives.

[45]. UW News press release, July 7, 1968. The northern division consisted of the basketball teams from Barron County, Fond du Lac, Fox Valley, Green Bay, Manitowoc, Marathon County, Marinette, and Marshfield/Wood County; the southern division members were Baraboo/Sauk County, Parkside, Richland Center, Rock County, Sheboygan, Washington

County, and Waukesha County.
[46]. Various issues of the University of Wisconsin Center System Report, 1966-1969.
[47]. University of Wisconsin Center System Report, February 1967; Faculty Document 51, Resolution of the Committee on Human Rights on Obstruction of University Activities, May 25, 1968; Faculty Document 55, Resolution on Student Participation in Center System Decisions, May 25, 1968.
[48]. Proceedings of the Board of Regents of the State Colleges, 1960-1966, Proceedings 1965-1966, p. 118; Board of Regents of the State Universities, press releases, April 17 & September 26, 1968; Office of the Governor, press release, April 26, 1968.
[49]. W.M. Hanley, Comments on Possible Sites for Future Centers, March 1963, Center System Papers, Series 42/1/1, Box 2, Possible Sites file, UW Archives; CCHE #18, Subcommittee Report: Joint Staff Comment on Medford, May 1965.
[50]. Proceedings of the Board of Regents of State Colleges; Proceedings, 1966-1967, meeting of January 27, 1967, p. 5; Proceedings, 1967-1968, meeting of January 18, 1968, Resolution 3055, p. 147; meeting of March 22, 1968, Resolution 3092, p. 172; meeting of April 26, 1968, Resolution 3117, p. 182; and Proceedings 1970, meeting of November 13, 1970, Resolution 3884, p. 154. CCHE #8, Informational Item: Wisconsin State University Branch Campus at Medford Enrollment Potential, March 1968. *Wausau Record-Herald*, March 22 & 25, 1968; *Milwaukee Sentinel*, April 27, 1968. Kelly, Politics of Higher Education Coordination, pp. 178-180, concludes that the decision to proceed with the Medford project was not a "straight political deal." Instead, Kelly believes an exception was made by the CCHE members because they felt the northern part of the state deserved more educational opportunities, even if Medford did not entirely meet the minimum criteria.
[51]. Jerry Bower, Personal Recollection.
[52]. Ad Hoc Committee on the Center System, A Mission Statement for the University of Wisconsin Center System, November 8, 1969, Center System Papers, Series 42/2/2, Box 4, Kellett Task Force file; Capital Times, December 11, 1969; *Wisconsin State Journal*, commentary by John Wyngaard, February 13, 1970.

Endnotes for Chapter Six, Pages 97-126

[1]. *Wisconsin State Journal*, January 17, 18, 22, February 13, 18, August 24, 25, 1970; February 28, 1993.
[2]. *The Capital Times*, September 9, 1970.
[3]. Patrick J. Lucey, "Statement on Campus Unrest," September 3, 1970; Jack Olson campaign, News Release, October 7, 1970. Olson blamed much of the unrest on out-of-state students and he supported proposals to limit their enrollment—*The Capital Times*, October 8, 1970.
[4]. Speech on Higher Education, Patrick J. Lucey, Democratic Candidate for Governor, September 23, 1970. Joseph Peter Heim, "Decision-Making in the Wisconsin Legislature: A Case Study of the Merger of the University of Wisconsin and the Wisconsin State University Systems," Ph.D. Dissertation, UW- Milwaukee, 1976, p. 20. Hereafter cited as Heim, "A Case Study of Merger."
[5]. *The Capital Times*, November 4, 1970.
[6]. See for example, "Lucey Election Adds Spice to Higher Education Stew," *Milwaukee Sentinel*, November 5, 1970.
[7]. "A Forward Look," final report of the Governor's Commission on Education, November 1970. Hereafter cited as "A Forward Look."
[8]. *Wisconsin State Journal*, January 24 & February 27, 1970.
[9]. Tony Baez, "The Community College Movement in Wisconsin: A Historical Perspective," October 1986, pp. 12-14, unpublished mss., copy obtained from author. *Milwaukee Sentinel*, December 8, 1969. "Summary of Major Policy Directions in Most Recent Kellett Policy Group Working Papers," Center System Papers, Series 42/2/2, Box 4, Kellett Task Force file, UW Archives. Wisconsin State Journal, February 13 & April 8, 1970.
[10]. "New Kellett Proposal Eyes College Mergers," *Wisconsin State Journal*, January 24, 1970, describes the Green Bay/Parkside plan. The faculty of the Barron County (Rice Lake) branch campus objected to the comprehensive college proposal in a "Position Paper on the Preliminary Report of the Governor's Commission on Education," May 5, 1970, Center System Papers, Series 42/2/2, Box 4, Kellett Task Force file, UW Archives.
[11]. L. H. Adolfson to President Harrington, February 3, 1970, Center System Papers, Series 42/2/2, Box 4, Kellett Task Force file, UW Archives.
[12]. *Green Bay Press-Gazette*, February 22, 1970; News of the University of Wisconsin Press Release, May 8, 1970; and "Summary Statement Concerning Recommendations Contained in the Kellett Commission Report as Related to the University of Wisconsin," November 1970, all in the Kellett Task Force file in Ibid.
[13]. *Wisconsin State Journal* and *Milwaukee Sentinel*, November 12, 1969. *The Wisconsin State Journal* article observed that this was perhaps the first time a board chairman had spoken against an opportunity to gain more power.
[14]. *Sheboygan Press*, April 15, 1970, and *The Capital Times*, December 28, 1970.
[15]. *Sheboygan Press, Milwaukee Sentinel*, and *Milwaukee Journal*, February 5, 1970.
[16]. "A Forward Look," p. vi.
[17]. Ibid., p. 12.
[18]. *Milwaukee Sentinel*, November 5, 1970. Joseph Rost, "The Merger of the University and Wisconsin State University Sys- tems: A Case Study in the Politics of Education," Ph.D. Dissertation, UW-Madison, 1973, p. 40, notes that the state faced a projected $510 million gap between state agency bud- get requests and projected revenues for the upcoming 1971-1973 biennium. Rost (pp. 73-79) also relates in detail the failure of the CCHE to pare down the UW and WSU requests for the 1971-1973 biennium. The result was that a proposal for an almost 55% budget increase was forwarded to the governor's office.
[19]. Rost, "The Merger of the University and the Wisconsin State University System," pp. 41-45. Rost observed that many

people believed that Lucey had asked Dreyfus to send up this merger trial balloon to gauge public and political reaction. Heim, "A Case Study of the Merger," pp. 20-23, agrees with Rost's assessment of Dreyfus's testimony and adds that Dreyfus also stressed the disparity in faculty salaries between Stevens Point and Green Bay as another measure of unjustified fiscal inequalities between the two similar institutions.

[20]. Governor Patrick Lucey, Budget Message, February 1971, cited in Rost, "The Merger of the University and the Wisconsin State University Systems," p. 98.

[21]. *Wisconsin State Journal*, January 21, 1971; *Milwaukee Sentinel*, February 5, 1971; and *Milwaukee Journal*, February 25, 1971. As the merger battle unfolded, additional reasons were advanced for Lucey's decision. For example, some believed that President Harrington's resignation in September 1970 and the pending retirement of Eugene McPhee, Executive Director of the WSU System, gave the Governor an opportunity to act while both systems had new, inexperienced leaders. And many noted that the political environment seemed conducive to pushing for merger: the Democrats had a huge margin in the Assembly, the Senate Republicans were in a state of disarray from Lucey's huge victory, and, finally, the Kellett Commission, a thoroughly Republican body, had urged a merger. *Green Bay Press-Gazette*, September 26, 1971, and *The Capital Times*, April 9, 1973 (a retrospective article).

[22]. *The Capital Times*, March 8, 1971; *Milwaukee Sentinel*, March 13, 1971; and *Wisconsin State Journal*, March 18 & 30 and April 30, 1971.

[23]. *Green Bay Press-Gazette*, March 6, 1971; March 6 & April 23, 1971; and *The Capital Times*, March 8, 1971.

[24]. Heim, "A Case Study of Merger," pp. 25-33, traces carefully the politics of the merger bill's passage. In Chapter III of his dissertation, where Heim analyzes the role of "influence" in the bill's enactment, he concludes that although lobbyists from both systems made numerous contacts with legislators, those contacts had little influence on legislators' votes because the general public expressed little interest in the merger debate. Put bluntly, Heim discovered through his survey that legislators felt they could vote on merger as they saw fit without incurring their constituents' wrath in the next election. The state press carried extensive coverage of the merger debate, see for example: *Milwaukee Journal*, July 29, September 15 & 18, 1971; *The Capital Times*, August 3, 5, & 18, and October 5, 1971; and *Milwaukee Sentinel*, August 4 and September 16, 1971.

[25]. *Milwaukee Journal*, February 16, 1971; *Milwaukee Sentinel*, September 16, 1971; and *Wisconsin State Journal*, October 9, 1971.

[26]. *The Capital Times*, February 16, 1971; *Milwaukee Sentinel*, February 17, 1971; and *Wisconsin State Journal*, February 17, 1971.

[27]. UW News press release, February 19, 1971, and Center System Office of Public Information press release, February 22, 1971, Center System Papers, Series 42/1/8, Box 7, Proposed Merger of CS with Tech Schools file, UW Archives.

[28]. *Green Bay Press-Gazette*, July 27, 1971. Noll expected very soon to be replaced as president of the SBVTAE by a Lucey appointee.

[29]. Although I was unable to find direct proof, my conclusion is that the furor over the take-over attempt caused an amendment protecting the Centers and branch campuses to be added to the merger budget. Certainly, the timing is right. The protective amendment is briefly described on page 12.

[30]. Vice Chancellor Durward Long to Center System Faculty and Staff, no date, Center System Papers, Series 42/1/8, Box 7, Merger—UW and State Universities file, UW Archives. Lucey did not elaborate his third option to explain whether he had in mind institutions with separate programs, administrations, and facilities that cooperated extensively or whether he envisioned moving toward the Kellett Commission proposal for comprehensive community colleges.

[31]. 31. Reorganization of Two-Year Institutions of Higher Education in Wisconsin, CCHE #71-32, June 1971, in Ibid. It is very important to note that, while the state aid to the technical schools' college transfer programs was less than that provided to the Centers, the revenue the VTAEs received from local property taxes pushed the total cost of their college parallel courses above the Centers' costs.

[32]. Clarke Smith, Secretary, Board of Regents of the UW System, to Attorney General Robert W. Warren, November 18, 1971, and Warren to Smith, December 9, 1971, in Ibid. Record of the Meetings of the Board of Regents of the University of Wisconsin System, Volume 1, October 1971—June 1972, meeting of 12/17/71, p. 4. Hereafter cited as Record of the Regents. *Milwaukee Journal*, December 10, 14, & 17, 1971, and *Wisconsin State Journal*, December 11, 16, & 17, 1971.

[33]. Record of the Regents, Volume 1, October 1971—June 1972, meeting of 6/9/72, p.7. The University of Wisconsin Center System Report, Volume Eight, Number One, May 1972, contains "A Tribute to Chancellor L.H. Adolfson" which thoroughly describes his career.

[34]. *Milwaukee Journal*, June 10, 1972; The University of Wisconsin Center System Report, Volume 5, Number One, September 1968; and Record of the Regents, Volume 1, October 1971-June 1972, meeting of 6/9/72, p. 37. In December 1972, the Board of Regents at Long's request, also appointed him a professor of history in the Center System.

[35]. *The Capital Times*, May 31, 1972, printed a long article by Bruce Swain which reviewed the controversy to that point. Swain wrote that the anti-Condon faculty at Rock had been especially upset recently when the Board of Regents had approved a $1,250.00 salary increase for Condon, an increase recommended by Adolfson. The faculty told Swain Adolfson had described Condon's position as "untenable" but Adolfson denied he had used that word, rather he had said Condon's position was "difficult."

[36]. *Wisconsin State Journal*, July 28 and August 1, 1972.

[37]. *Janesville Gazette* and *Beloit Daily News*, September 14, 1972, announced that Condon would become the Dean of Academic Administration at California State University in Northridge; *Wisconsin State Journal*, October 21, 1973, related that Dr. Thomas Walterman had been appointed dean at the Rock County Center and also gave a capsule account of the Condon affair.

[38]. Final Report to the President of the University of Wisconsin System Consolidation Task Force, May 1972, p. ii. Hereafter referred to as Final Report of the CTF.

[39]. Ibid. and Harold Hutchison to John C. Weaver, May 22, 1972, John C. Weaver Papers, Series 40/1/1/2-2, Box 45, Center System Consolidation Task Force file, UW Archives.

[40]. The Final Report of the CTF, Appendix D, pp. 25-28, lists 47 communications that it received regarding "Systemwide Instructional Organization." Copies of these items are located in Center System Papers, Series 42/0/2, Box 1, Consolidation Task Force files, UW Archives, and have been used for this summary.
[41]. Steve Bennion to Dallas Peterson, April 3, 1972, in Ibid.
[42]. Edward F. McClain, Chairman Philosophy Department, to All Department Chairmen, Center System, April 18, 1972, and Chairmen of Center System Departments to Consolidation Task Force, April 20, 1972, in Ibid.
[43]. Harold Hutchinson, Dean, College of Education, WSU Platteville, to John C. Weaver, May 22, 1972, John C. Weaver Papers, Series 40/1/1/2-2, Box 45, Center System Consolidation Task Force file, UW Archives.
[44]. Final Report of the CTF, pp. 7-10.
[45]. The CTF also proposed a system-wide Instructional Organization. Each academic department would elect a three-member Discipline Resource Committee to provide advice to the Center Executive Committees on personnel and curriculum issues. Each Discipline Resource Committee would elect one of its members to a Division Resource Committee. The five chairmen of the Division Resource Committees automatically became the System Executive Committee, whose duties included advising the chancellor on systemwide personnel policies and on the budget. Ibid, pp. 10-16.
[46]. John C. Weaver to Regent David Carley, May 1, 1972. In this letter, which predates the Final Report by three weeks, Weaver urged Carley to ignore the rumors he had heard about the CTF's recommendations and to suspend judgement until central administration could analyze the report and provide a full briefing to the Regents
[47]. Letter in Center System Papers, Series 42/2/2-3, Box 2, Merger Implementation Bill & Governance file, UW Archives.
[48]. Durward Long to Center System Deans, October 7, 1972, in Ibid.
[49]. Charter Governing the University of Wisconsin Center System, especially sections 1.03 Faculty and 2.01 System Collegium Membership. The inclusion of students in university governance was a hot issue for Governor Lucey's Merger Implementation Committee, which finally drafted legislation that made students "active participants" in governance and gave them primary responsibility for the formulation and review of policies concerning student life, services, and interests. The merger implementation law also specified that students must constitute a majority of the committees which established and allocated students fees. On the student participation issue, see for example: *Wisconsin State Journal*, June 16, 1972; *The Capital Times*, December 1, 1972; and *Milwaukee Sentinel*, December 2, 1972.
[50]. Durward Long to Center Deans, Faculty, Academic Support Staff, Center Student Government Presidents, October 26, 1972, Center System Papers, Series 42/2/2-3, Box 2, Merger Implementation Bill & Governance file, UW Archives.
[51]. Record of the Regents, Volume 2, July-December 1972, meeting of December 8, 1972, pp. 15-16; *Wisconsin State Journal*, December 8, 1972, and *The Capital Times*, December 9, 1972. The newspapers noted that Professor Clara Penniman of UW-Madison's powerful Liaison University Committee had spoken in opposition to Long's Charter because it diluted faculty governance by including non-faculty persons in both the local and system collegiums.
[52]. Willard J. Henken, Dean (Fond du Lac Center), to Bernard C. Ziegler, Vice President, Board of Regents, March 6, 1972, John C. Weaver Papers, Series 40/1/1/2-2, Box 45, Center System Consolidation Task Force file, UW Archives, *Wisconsin State Journal*, May 17, 1972; and Summary Review of the Joint Committee of UW Regents and VTAE Board Members Meeting at Fond du Lac on May 19, 1972, Center System Papers, Chancellor's Office, Accession #81/14, Box 6, UW/VTAE Joint Committee, 1972-74 file, UW Archives.
[53]. Summary Review of the Joint Committee of UW Regents and VTAE Members Meeting. . ., in Ibid.
[54]. Steve Bennion to Leonard Haas, Dallas Peterson, Bob Polk, September 20, 1972, RE: Immediate VTAE-UW Concerns, Center System Papers, Chancellor's Office, Accession #81/14, Box 6, UW/VTAE Joint Committee, 1972-74 file, UW Archives. In this memo Bennion describes Zien's proposal, which had not yet been leaked to the press.
[55]. Steve Bennion, Alternate Positions the UW System Can Take Visa Vis [sic] the VTAE System, September 1972, and Bennion to Regents Bertram McNamara and Bernard Ziegler, October 2, 1972, An Initial Proposal which you might want to offer to the Joint UW/VTAE Committee, in Ibid. In the introduction to the Initial Proposal Bennion notes that the matter has become urgent because "rumors of Zien's proposal have leaked" and already articles and editorials are casting "doom and gloom" on the Fond du Lac Center's future.
[56]. Minutes of Joint VTAE-UW Committee Meeting (Regents & VTAE Board Members), Milwaukee Club, October 23, 1972, and Bernard C. Ziegler to Chancellor Durward Long, November 7, 1972, in Ibid. In his letter Ziegler expresses his frustration that the UW/VTAE issue is being tried in the press. He said that at first he had been inclined to consider helping the VTAE in Fond du Lac solve its problem, but now ". . .to hell with lending a helping hand."
[57]. UWS-VTAE Information Report, December 19, 1972, in Ibid.; *The Capital Times*, December 19, 1972; *Green Bay Press Gazette*, December 30, 1972; and *Wisconsin State Journal*, January 31, 1973.
[58]. President John C. Weaver to Each Regent, Fee Experiment at Fond du Lac and Rice Lake, January 30, 1974, Robert R. Polk Papers, Accession #85/86, Box 3, UW Ctrs-Misc., 1971-78 file, and W. Lee Hansen, An Evaluation of the University of Wisconsin Low Tuition Experiment, November 1975, Donald K. Smith Papers, Series 40/1/2/4-2, Box 19, Center System 1974-75 file, both in UW Archives.
[59]. Legislative Audit Bureau, Analysis of Governor's Policy Paper #15: 1973-75 Budget. University of Wisconsin System. Other Policy changes—UW Center System, April 4, 1973, Center System Papers, Accession #81/14, Box 5, Governor's Policy Paper #15 file, UW Archives.
[60]. Durward Long to President John C. Weaver, May 18, 1973, and UW Press Release, May 18, 1973, Don Percy Papers, Series 40/1/2/3-2, Box 48, CS Chancellor file, UW Archives.
[61]. John C. Weaver to Durward Long, June 18, 1973, in Ibid. John C. Weaver to John N. Durrie, Secretary, Presidential Search and Screening Committee, The University of New Mexico, February 20, 1975, Weaver Papers, Series 40/1/1/2-2, Box 19, Durward Long file, UW Archives.
[62]. *Milwaukee Journal*, June 24, 1973.
[63]. *The Capital Times*, July 31, 1973; Record of the Regents, Volume 4, August 1973-June 1974, Meeting of August 8, 1973, Exhibit E, particularly pp. 8-10; and Response to Legislative Fiscal Bureau Paper Regarding the Center System,

April 3, 1973, Center System Papers, Accession #81/14, Box 5, Governor's Policy Paper #15 file, UW Archives.
[64]. *The Capital Times*, July 31, 1973.
[65]. Record of the Regents, Volume 4, August 1973-June 1974, meeting of August 3, 1973, p. 20, and Exhibit E, pp. 8-10; *The Capital Times* and *Wisconsin State Journal*, August 3, 1973.
[66]. "Merger Within Merger," a report to the President and Regents by Chancellor Durward Long, August 3, 1973, Center System Papers, unprocessed collection to be added to Series 42/1, Box 7, Annual Report, 1972-73, file, UW Archives; *The Capital Times*, August 4, 1973; *The Milwaukee Journal*, August 5, 1973.
[67]. The University of Wisconsin System, Student Statistics—Term I, 1977-78, Table I, Total Enrollment [of Center System] with 10-Year Profile reveals the following data by comparing fall 1970 enrollment with fall 1972—Barron, up 8 students; Fond du Lac, down 65; Manitowoc, down 89; Medford, down 99; and Richland, down 69.
[68]. *The Capital Times* and *The Milwaukee Journal*, November 15, 1973, reported on the mission hearings at Baraboo and Richland Center.
[69]. *The Capital Times*, November 15, 1973.
[70]. "Center System Annual Report, 1972-73," John C. Weaver Papers, Series 40/1/1/2-2, Box 18, UW Centers file, UW Archives; *Wisconsin State Journal*, December 2, 1973.
[71]. "Center System Annual Report, 1972-73, Budget Retrenchment," in Ibid.
[72]. Donald Percy to John C. Weaver, August 23, 1973, Don Percy Papers, Series 40/1/2/3-2, Box 48, Center System Chancellor file, UW Archives.
[73]. Record of the Regents, Volume 4, August 1973-June 1974, meeting of December 7, 1973, pp. 20-22; *The Milwaukee Journal*, December 2, 1973; *Wisconsin State Journal*, December 11, 1973.
[74]. Enrollment figures from University of Wisconsin System Student Statistics, Fall 1977, p. 2.
[75]. John C. Weaver to Acting Chancellor John Meggers, August 15, 1974, Donald Percy Papers, Box 48, Center System Chancellor file, UW Archives.
[76]. John C. Weaver to Regent President Frank J. Pelisek, August 8, 1974, marked "Confidential," in Ibid.
[77]. Record of the Regents, Volume 5, July 1974-June 1975, meeting of September 6, 1974, p. 5; *The Capital Times*, August 13, 1974; *Wisconsin State Journal*, August 14, 1974. It is interesting to note that Marjorie Wallace had been appointed dean of the Richland Campus in June 1974, thus becoming the first woman to lead a campus in the UW System, albeit a very small campus. *Wisconsin State Journal*, June 8, 1974.
[78]. The State of Wisconsin, 1975 Blue Book, pp. 795 & 816; *Wisconsin State Journal*, November 8, 1974; Mary Beth Norton et. al., *A People and A Nation, A History of the United States*, Houghton Mifflin Company, 1994/4th edition, pp. 975, 1024-25.
[79]. *Wisconsin State Journal*, October 17, 1974. Although he said nothing overt, reporters noted that Lucey appeared irritated that the Board had made this proposal.

Endnotes for Chapter Seven, Pages 125-152

[1]. Governor Patrick J. Lucey to All State Agency Heads, November 29, 1974; Joe E. Nusbaum, Secretary, Department of Administration, to All Department Heads, December 3, 1974; Donald E. Percy to Secretary Joe E. Nusbaum, Wisconsin Department of Administration, December 11, 1974; *Wisconsin State Journal*, December 19, 1974; and Chancellor Edward Fort to All Center System Deans, December 23, 1974, in Center System Papers, Accession #81/14, Box 5, Governor's Austerity Program 74-75 file, UW Archives.
[2]. Lucey to Pelisek, January 8, 1975, President's Report in Response to the Governor's Request On Reducing the Scope of the University of Wisconsin System, April 18, 1975, Appendix—Exhibit #1. Hereafter cited as: Scope Reduction Report.
[3]. *Milwaukee Journal*, January 19, 1975, front page; Joe E. Nusbaum, Secretary, DOA, to Governor Patrick J. Lucey, November 16, 1974, in the Donald Percy Papers, Series 40/1/2/3-2, Box 48, CS: Cost and Curriculum Controls file, UW Archives. The latter is the DOA study.
[4]. *Wisconsin State Journal*, January 20, 1975.
[5]. *Milwaukee Journal*, January 22 & 27, 1975; *The Capital Times*, January 20, 24, & 25, 1975; *Wisconsin State Journal*, January 20, 22, 26, & 30 and February 3, 1975.
[6]. *Wisconsin State Journal*, January 20 & 22, 1975.
[7]. Cammack, Arnn, and Kolka, "Alternatives for Dealing With the Problem of Underutilized Center System and University Campuses," no date, Don Percy Papers, Series 40/1/2/3-2, Box 48, CS: Cost and Curriculum Controls file, UW Archives; Book I, Report of the System Advisory Planning Task Force, March 1975, p. i. Hereafter cited as Book I.
[8]. Statement of Regent President Pelisek, January 10, 1975, in Scope Reduction Report, Appendix, Exhibit #2.
[9]. Book I, p. I-1; *Milwaukee Journal*, January 28, 1975; *Wisconsin State Journal*, January 30, 1975.
[10]. President John C. Weaver to Chancellors, "System Advisory Task Force," January 14, 1975, Center System Papers, Accession #81/14, Box 5, Governor's Austerity Program 74-75 file, UW Archives.
[11]. Book I, p. V-19.
[12]. Ibid.
[13]. Dean Darwin Slocum to Dr. Carol Marion, President's Task Force on Retrenchment, February 13, 1975, and Chancellor Edward Fort to [UW-Madison] Vice Chancellor Irving Shain, Chairperson, Committee #4, Institutional Feedback re: Carol Marion Paper on Stevens Point/Center System Nucleation, March 4, 1975, Center System Papers, unprocessed collection to be added to 42/1, Box 15, UWC-Medford, 1974-75 file and Nucleation file, respectively, UW Archives.
[14]. Donald K. Smith to Chancellors, Report concerning simulations requested by the Study Committee of the System Advisory Task Force, February 3, 1975, Center System Papers, unprocessed collection to be added to 42/1, Box 15, System Advisory Task Force file, UW Archives.

[15]. Book I, pp. IV: 58-114.
[16] 16. Ibid.
[17]. Steve Bennion to Don Percy, "My Initial Reactions to the Draft Portions of the President's Report Dealing with the Center System," March 17, 1975, Donald Smith Papers, Box 19, Center System 1974-5 file, UW Archives.
[18]. Statement by President John C. Weaver, In Presenting His Report to the Board of Regents in Response to the Governor's Request on Reducing the Scope of the University of Wisconsin System, April 18, 1975, in Scope Reduction Report, pp. ii-vii.
[19]. Scope Reduction Report, pp. vii-xiii and Appendix—Exhibit #4.
[20]. Ibid., pp. xiv-xvii, and *The Milwaukee Sentinel*, April 19, 1975.
[21]. Scope Reduction Report, pp. 21-24
[22]. Record of the Regents, Volume 5, July 1974-June 1975, Special Board Meeting, April 18, 1975, pp. 18-22.
[23]. Ibid., *The Capital Times*, April 18, 1975, and *The Milwaukee Journal*, April 22, 1975.
[24]. Frank J. Pelisek, President, Board of Regents, to Governor Patrick J. Lucey, Senate President Pro Tem Fred Risser, and Assembly Speaker Norman Anderson, April 18, 1975, in Scope Reduction Report, page not numbered. Every member of the legislature received a copy.
[25]. *The Capital Times* & *Wisconsin State Journal*, April 23, 1975.
[26]. *The Milwaukee Sentinel*, April 29, 1975.
[27]. "May 2nd Action of Legislative Joint Finance Committee," Center System Papers, Unprocessed collection to be added to 42/1, Box 15, Scope file, UW archives.
[28]. *Wisconsin State Journal*, May 24, 1975.
[29]. Regent John M. Lavine to William L. Mossman, President, Friends of the Campus, UWC-Baraboo/Sauk County, June 9, 1975, Center System Papers, Unprocessed collection to be added to 42/1, Box 17, Scope file, UW Archives.
[30]. "The Center System: A Progress Report," Elwin Cammack, Associate Vice President, to Phil Arnold, Legislative Fiscal Bureau, November 25, 1975, Center System Papers, Unprocessed collection to be added to 42/1, Box 17, Scope file, UW Archives. The six two-year institutions were the University Branches of Edinboro (Penn.) State, Penn State, Ohio State, Wright (Ohio) State, Kent (Ohio) State, and the University of South Carolina.
[31]. Ibid.
[32]. Chancellor Edward Fort to Provost Wilson Thiede, July 1, 1975, and Fort to Senior Vice President Donald Smith, July 3, 1975, Center System Papers, Unprocessed collection to be added to 42/1, Box 17, Scope file, UW Archives.
[33]. However, there were concerns that the facilities would be unsuitable for the types of programs that NCTI could offer; the validity of these concerns was confirmed a few months later when a study of joint UW-VTAE use of the Baraboo campus concluded that many of the most popular vocational programs, such as automobile mechanics, could not be housed at Baraboo, due to a lack of appropriate shop space and equipment. Possible Joint UW-VTAE Utilization of the UW Center-Baraboo/Sauk County—A Feasibility Study, October 14, 1975 (Central Office Files) The authors of the study were Albert J. Beaver, UW-System, Daniel K. Van Eyck, Vice Chancellor, Center System, George R. Kinsler, Wisconsin VTAE Board, and Dean H. Wessels, Madison Area Technical College. (The Central Office Files will eventually be sent to the UW Archives, where they will be added to the Center System Papers.)
[34]. The options are found in Chancellor Edward Fort, Chancellor's Recapitulation of Scope Reduction meeting held on 7-16-75, July 21, 1975, Donald Smith Papers, Box 19, Center System Miscellaneous, 1975-76 file, UW Archives. This document is marked, "Confidential. Do Not Reproduce."
[35]. Provost Wilson Thiede to President John C. Weaver and Board of Regents, December 2, 1975, Center System Papers, Unprocessed collection to be added to 42/1, Box 17, Scope file, UW Archives.
[36]. Statement of Joseph Koelsch, UWC-Richland's representative to the Center System Board of Visitors, Record of the Regents, volume 6, July 1975-June 1976, meeting of January 9, 1976, pp. 6-7.
[37]. Provost Wilson Thiede, Progress Report on Cost Reductions at Certain Centers, and Chancellor Edward Fort, Institutional Reaction to Continuing Pressures of Cost Effectiveness RE the Scope Reduction Scenario: The Center System in the Eye of the Hurricane, both found in Ibid.
[38]. Ibid., *Milwaukee Sentinel* & *Wisconsin State Journal*, January 10, 1976, *Marshfield News Herald*, January 12 & 14, 1976.
[39]. Chancellor Edward B. Fort, Report on the Liberal Arts Core Curriculum, Prepared for the University of Wisconsin System Board of Regents, February 1977.
[40]. UW Center System Senate Minutes, December 10, 1976, & January 21, 1977.
[41]. Record of the Regents, volume 7, July 1976-June 1977, meeting of February 11, 1977.
[42]. Record of the Regents, volume 7, July 1976-June 1977, meeting of March 11, 1977, Exhibit B; North Central Association of Colleges and Schools, Report of a Visit to the University of Wisconsin Center System, October 25-29, 1976, pp. 110-112.
[43]. UW Center System Collegium Minutes, October 11, 1974. Because the new constitution was considered to be an "amendment" to the Charter, this elaborate procedure was spelled out in University of Wisconsin Center System Charter, 6.01 Amendments. However, this procedure was also written into the new constitution, to take into account the Center System's unique structure, with faculty and staff dispersed at 14 separate campuses.
[44]. Chapter 36: University of Wisconsin System, 36.05(8) "Faculty"; University of Wisconsin System Faculty Personnel Rules, 1.04 Faculty; Donald K. Smith to Education Committee, Board of Regents, October 23, 1974, Donald Smith Papers, 40/1/2/4-2, Box 19, Center System 1974-5 file, UW Archives. Hereafter cited as Smith papers.
[45]. University of Wisconsin Center System Collegium Minutes, Special Meeting, November 14, 1974.
[46]. Ibid.
[47]. William R. Schmitz, President, AAUP UW-Marathon County Chapter, to President John C. Weaver, July 18, 1973, and Durward Long to Weaver, August 30, 1973, Weaver Papers, Box 19, Marathon County file, UW Archives.
[48]. Fred Moss, Chairman, Internal Charter Review Committee, to Center System Collegium, March 14, 1975. Moss's report is attached to that day's Collegium Minutes, as Appendix 6.

[49]. UW Center System Collegium Minutes, Special Meeting, November 22, 1975. Chancellor Edward Fort to Senior Vice President Donald Smith and Provost Wilson Thiede, October 1, 1975; UW Center-Waukesha Collegium to Fort, October 23, 1975; Smith to Thiede, Fort, and John Tallman, October 23, 1975; Fort to Smith, November 10, 1975; Fort to all Deans, Local Campus Collegia, and Central Office Staff, November 22, 1975; President John C. Weaver to Fort, December 16, 1975; Smith Papers, Box 19, Center System 1975-76 and Chancellor's Correspondence files, UW Archives. The vote breakdown on each side: Yes—12 faculty senators, 3 student senators and 1 academic staff senator; No—3 faculty, 2 students and 1 academic staff.

[50]. The University of Wisconsin Center System Constitution, 2.02 Senate Membership. A Center with 36 to 70 ranked faculty earned a second senator and one with more than 70 elected three.

[51]. Ibid.

[52]. Ibid, 2.03 D. and 2.04.

[53]. Ibid, Chapters 4 and 5.

[54]. Provost Wilson Thiede to Senior Vice President Donald Smith, June 1, 1976, Smith Papers, Box 19, Center System 1975-76 Miscellaneous file, UW Archives.

[55]. University of Wisconsin Faculty Personnel rules, 1.05 Faculty Status and the UW Center System Constitution, 1.04 Faculty Status.

[56]. Record of the Regents, volume 16, July 1985-June 1986, Meeting of September 6, 1985.

[57]. The UW Center System Constitution, 1.05 Students & 3.01 Membership [of the Collegium]; Chancellor Edward Fort to UW System Academic Planner Steve Karges, December 9, 1975, Center System Papers, Unprocessed collection to be added to 42/1, Box 17, Chancellor Fort 1974-75 correspondence file, UW Archives.

[58]. Herman Kroll, A Survey of Student Opinion, 1975-76, pp. 6-8.

[59]. Ibid, pp. 47-52.

[60]. Ibid, pp. 10-25.

[61]. "Abstract of Results"; *Racine Journal*, March 13, 1977; and the *Milwaukee Journal*, May 1, 1977.

[62]. Central Administration Analysis Paper #15, Completion of Facilities in the UW Center System, November 1976, Smith Papers, Box 30, Campuses: Center System-Waukesha County file, UW Archives.

[63]. Ibid.; the *Milwaukee Journal*, November 4, 1977; the *Milwaukee Sentinel*, September 9, 1978: The latter article reports that the Waukesha County Board had approved an expansion project to increase campus capacity to 1,500. Waukesha's Fall 1978 enrollment was 1,688.

[64]. *Appleton Post-Crescent*, July 31, September 24 & 27, 1978. In the September articles, the *Post-Crescent* editor noted that the Winnebago County supervisors had defeated a one-third/two-thirds cost sharing formula because they did not want to lose control over the Center campus! Chancellor Edward Fort to Regent Mary Walter, May 3, 1979, Smith Papers, Box 29, Campuses: Center System-Fox Valley file, UW Archives. Fort's letter reviews the now-four- year-old squabble and explains to Regent Walter that neither he nor anyone in System Administration can bring any "pressure" to bear on the two county boards to resolve their differences.

[65]. Reuben J. Schmahl, Washington County Board Chairman, to Governor Martin J. Schreiber, August 23, 1977; Dean Robert Thompson, Washington County Center, to Chancellor Edward Fort, October 7, 1977; [Center System Assistant Chancellor] Antone Kucera to Lon Sprecher, Department of Administration, September 19, 1977; and Governor Martin J. Schreiber to Reuben J. Schmahl, October 13, 1977, Smith Papers, Box 30, Campuses: Center System—Washington County file, UW Archives. *The Milwaukee Journal*, September 12, 1978. This lengthy article reviews the ongoing city/county contest, noting that the county board had, so far in 1978, three times voted down a 20%/80% cost-sharing formula. Center Dean Robert Thompson lamented that the ownership split meant neither party felt responsible for the campus. Schmahl said Thompson's observation had merit; West Bend's mayor declined to comment.

[66]. Chapter 36.09(1)(h), Wisconsin Statutes; Section 726m, Assembly Substitute Amendment 1 to 1975 AB222.

[67]. UW Center System Senate Minutes, December 10, 1976, Steering Committee Report; Annual Report, 1977, of the Faculty Salary Equity Committee, UW Center System Senate Minutes, May 13-14, 1977, Appendix 7.

[68]. Annual Report, 1977, of the Faculty Salary Equity Committee, UW Center System Senate Minutes, May 13-14, 1977, Appendix 7, pp. 4-12.

[69]. Ibid.; UW Center System Senate Minutes, January 10, 1978, report the election of an Academic Staff Salary Equity Committee and those of May 17, 1979, indicate that the Senate approved the appropriation of $20,000 to make the internal academic staff salary adjustments recommended by the Committee.

[70]. John C. Weaver and H. Edwin Young, Biographical File, UW Archives. The "Biofiles" are a collection of UW press releases and newspaper articles about prominent persons connected with either UW System or UW-Madison. Their content is pretty hit and miss.

[71]. *Wisconsin State Journal*, November 2, 1978, carried a pre-election profile of gubernatorial candidate Schreiber.

[72]. *The Capitol Times*, June 22 & July 12, 1978; *Wisconsin State Journal*, June 12 & November 5, 1978; *Green Bay Press Gazette*, July 28, 1978. The primary tallies were: Dreyfus 197,279; Kasten 143,361 and Schreiber 217,572; Carley 132,901, The State of Wisconsin 1979-80 Blue Book, p. 893.

[73]. *The Wisconsin State Journal*, November 1-8, 1978; The State of Wisconsin 1979-80 Blue Book, p. 770. The political composition of the 1979-81 Senate was 21 Democrats and 10 Republicans (2 seats vacant), and in the Assembly 60 Democrats and 39 Republicans.

[74]. *The Milwaukee Journal*, September 21, November 30, December 2, 1978; *Manitowoc Herald-Times*, December 1, 1978; *Appleton Post-Crescent*, December 2, 1978.

Endnotes for Chapter Eight, Pages 153-172

[1]. Fall Headcount Enrollments Historical Table 1862-1992, 1993 UW System Fact Book, pp. 31-32; Milwaukee Journal, December 8, 1978.

[2]. Preparing for a Decade of Enrollment Decline, A Report from the Board of Regents of the University of Wisconsin System to State Government and the People of Wisconsin, November 30, 1979, pp. 8-13. These three Centers, all former WSU branch campuses, had experienced a considerable enrollment decline, from their post-merger peaks. The figures were as follows: Barron County, -185 headcount, -34%; Medford, -59 headcount, -32%; And Richland, -84 headcount, -26%. Barron County's difficulty was compounded by the ending of the low fee experiment in Fall 1976, when her headcount dropped by 25.5%. Chancellor Fort pled in vain with System to have the low fees restored and expanded to all Center campuses. System administrators explained that the loss of income ($600,000) had been offset by revenue from the other UWs, an unpopular policy that they could no longer support. President John C. Weaver to Each Regent, Fee Experiment at Fond du Lac and Rice Lake, January 30, 1974; W. Lee Hansen, UW-Madison Department of Economics, An Analysis of the University of Wisconsin Low Tuition Experiment, December 1975; Donald E. Percy to Chancellor Edward Fort, Deans Wilbur Henken and John Meggers, Senator Walter Hollander, April 12, 1976; Chancellor Edward Fort to Associate Vice President Elwin Cammack, December 9, 1976; Donald Smith Papers, Box 19, Center System, 1974-5 and 1975-6 files, UW Archives.

[3]. Chancellor Edward Fort to Vice President Donald Smith, November 8, 1979, Smith Papers, Box 29, Campuses: Center System 1979 file, UW Archives.

[4]. Donald K. Smith to Chancellor Edward Fort, November 13, 1979, in Ibid.

[5]. President Edwin Young to Special Task Force Members, January 4, 1980, Chancellor Fort 1980 correspondence file, Central Office Files; Wisconsin State Journal, January 10 and 23, 1980.

[6]. Robert M. O'Neil, Biographical File, UW Archives.

[7]. The Madison press, especially, traced the Task Force's proceedings: *Wisconsin State Journal*, January 23, April 28, May 2, 14, 15, 1980.

[8]. Report to the President by the Special Task Force to Review the Programs of Three UW Centers Within the Mission of the UW Center System, June 4, 1980, pp. 2-3. Hereafter cited as Report to the President.

[9]. Report to the President, pp. 3-5.

[10]. Ibid., p. 12.

[11]. Ibid., pp. 6-12, Appendices 1-5; *Capital Times*, June 4, 1980; *Wisconsin State Journal*, June 5, 1980, *Appleton Post-Crescent*, June 8, 1980.

[12]. Report to the President, pp. 13-14, Appendix 7.

[13]. Ibid., pp. 15-17.

[14]. Provost Wilson Thiede to Senior Vice President Donald Smith, October 2, 1975, Smith Papers, Box 19, Center System Miscellaneous 1975-76 file, UW-Archives. In this letter Thiede relates that he and Fort had agreed that no one would be recommended for tenure until action was required under the law. Thiede also observed, "We specifically checked the Medford and Richland promotions to tenure to be certain they were not in departments where they had 100% tenure density and would cause difficulty." Edward Fort to Don Smith, October 10, 1979, RE: Instructional Tenure Density in the Center System, in Ibid., Box 29, Campuses: Center System 1979 file. With this letter Fort transmitted to Smith tables listing the tenure density by campus and by academic department. In the memo's key sentence, Fort said, "Tenure decisions for the next academic year will be made on a case-by-case basis, taking under strong advisement the impact of any high density figures upon campuses and/or departments. . . ."

[15]. Statements by Ronald V. Mershart, President of the Association of the University of Wisconsin Faculties, and Judy Clark [one of the persons denied tenure], to the Education Committee, Board of Regents, Record of the Regents, volume 11, July 1980-June 1981, meeting of September 4, 1980; Resolution on Tenure Denial, UWC-Washington County Collegium, October 6, 1980, in University of Wisconsin Center System Senate Minutes, November 22, 1980, Appendix 5; University of Wisconsin Center System Senate Minutes, January 17, 1981; Kerry Trask, Chairman, Center System Appeals and Grievances Committee to Chancellor Edward B. Fort, February 4 and 24, 1981, Senate Committees 1980-81 file, Central Office Files. In his February 4 letter Trask indicated that the Committee had reached its decision because ". . . the Chancellor, acting alone without the required consultation with the faculty, evoked and applied 'tenure density and fiscal and enrollment uncertainty' as standards for his not awarding tenure. . . ."

[16]. Statement of Committee A of the American Association of University Professors, approved by the AAUP Council, October 20, 1973. This statement was adopted by the Center System Senate as part of its official reaction to Chancellor Fort's tenure denial decisions. Senate Minutes, January 17, 1981.

[17]. John Tallman, UWS Office of Legal Counsel, to Executive Vice President Joseph Kauffman, February 17, 1981; Joseph F. Kauffman to Chancellors, Vice Chancellors, and Faculty Representatives, February 24, 1981, Chancellor's Correspondence 1980-81 file, Central Office Files. An attachment to Kauffman's letter, "UW Institutions Having Formal Policies and Practices Relating to Tenure Density, Tenure Management or Tenure Ratio," indicated that eight UWs (Eau Claire, La Crosse, Oshkosh, Platteville, Stevens Point, Stout, River Falls, Superior) had established tenure density ratios.

[18]. University of Wisconsin Center System Senate Minutes, January 17, March 20, May 15-16, September 19, 1981.

[19]. Chancellor Edward Fort to Coordinating Committee for Response to the Task Force Report, May 30 and June 24, 1980.

[20]. Meeting the Challenge of the 1980s: Response of the Coordinating Committee to the Task Force Report, September 2, 1980.

[21]. Antone Kucera to Coordinating Committee, RE: Administrative Responsibilities in the Center System, July 24, 1980, and Steven Bendrick to Herman Nibbelink, Chair, Coordinating Committee, July 9, 1980, Kucera's Grandson of Scope file, Central Office Files.

[22]. Stephen R. Portch, "An Educational Impact Study of the Report to the President by the Special Task Force to Review

the Programs of Three UW Centers Within the Mission of the UW Center System," 35 pp., July 25, 1980, Kucera's Grandson of Scope file, Central Office Files. Portch was on a sabbatical at Penn State to complete his doctoral work when he wrote this analysis. These were the primary disadvantages the 1975 Scope Reduction Report had also cited in its examination of possibly nucleating Marathon, Marshfield, and Medford to UW-Stevens Point.

[23]. Chancellor Edward Fort, "The Issue Before The House: The UW Center System and Access For the 1980s, A Report to the President of the University of Wisconsin System," October 1, 1980. Fort followed up with a letter to President O'Neil and Vice President Kauffman, October 10, 1980, which greatly elaborated his request for a basic financial module. This letter is in Kucera's Great Grandson of Scope file, Central Office Files.

[24]. William Lenehan to Richard Rossmiller, October 16, 1980, and Dick Rossmiller to Joe Kauffman, October 21, 1980, Robert O'Neil Papers, series 40/1/1/4-2, Box 4, Special Task Force file, UW Archives. Hereafter cited as O'Neil Papers.

[25]. Record of the Regents, volume 11, July 1980-June 1981, Meeting of December 5, 1980, Exhibit C.

[26]. Robert Mergendahl, Chairman of the UW Center-Marathon Steering Committee to President Robert O'Neil, November 20, 1980, O'Neil Papers, Box 3, Marathon file, is an invitation to O'Neil to come to Wausau to discuss affiliation with Madison. O'Neil replied that he would schedule a visit as soon as possible. Chancellor Fort to President O'Neil, RE: UW Center System Resolution reaffirming institutional integrity, November 26, 1980, O'Neil Papers, Box 2, UW Center System 1980-82 file, UW Archives. Fort's memo outlines his objections to permitting these affiliation discussions to continue.

[27]. The letters that set up the President's meeting with the Steering Committee are, O'Neil to Fort, April 8, 1981, and Fort to O'Neil, April 21, 1981. The conditions O'Neil announced were communicated via Herman Nibbelink, Chair, Senate Steering Committee, to Senators, April 28, 1981, all in O'Neil Papers, Box 3, Chancellor Edward Fort and Medford files, UW Archives.

[28]. Chancellor Edward Fort to Long Range Planning Committee, December 31, 1980, Assistant Chancellor Kucera's Great Great Grandson of Scope file, Central Office Files.

[29]. *Wisconsin State Journal*, May 15, 1981.

[30]. *Chippewa [Falls] Herald-Telegram*, July 1, 1981. UW Regent John Lavine, the owner-editor of the *Herald Telegram*, used this interview with O'Neil to argue eloquently that UW could not sustain Dreyfus's decrease without seriously damaging the quality of its academic programs.

[31]. Daniel Putman, Chairman, Senate Budget Committee, to Chancellor Edward Fort, RE: Advisory Process for Dealing with Current State-Imposed Cuts, May 29, 1981, and Long Range Planning Committee to Chancellor Fort, RE: Response to Senate Budget Committee Recommendations Regarding 1981-82 Budget, June 29, 1981, Assistant Chancellor Kucera's Great Great Grandson of Scope file, Central Office Files. The Long Range Planning Committee completely endorsed the Budget Committee's proposals.

[32]. *Milwaukee Sentinel*, June 13, 1981, and *Wisconsin State Journal*, June 14, 1981.

[33]. Chancellor Edward Fort to Senior Vice President Donald Smith, November 8, 1979, Smith Papers, Box 29, Campuses: Center System 1979 file, UW Archives, is an example of Fort's pleading. See also p. 154, above.

[34]. Deans to Chancellor Fort, RE: Deallocation of positions for 1981-82, May 20, 1981, Assistant Chancellor Kucera's Great Great Grandson of Scope file, Central Office Files. In their memo, the Deans said, "Before any additional position cuts are levied on the Centers, the Chancellor's staff, classified and unclassified, should be reduced to a total of no more than 15 to 17 positions."

[35]. *Wisconsin State Journal*, June 14, 1981.

[36]. *Milwaukee Journal*, June 28, 1981.

[37]. *Appleton Post-Crescent*, April 14, 1982.

[38]. Byron Barrington, Earl Nelson, Herman Nibbelink, Laraine O'Brien, Bill Schmidtke to Deans, Department Chairmen, Senate, Academic Staff Advisory Committee and Long Range Planning Committee, July 15, 1981, O'Neil Papers, Box 4, Chancellor Robert Polk file, UW Archives.

[39]. Center System Senate Minutes, September 19, 1981, Chancellor's Report to the Senate, p. 5.

[40]. Ibid., pp. 3-5. The SPC membership included the five faculty members of the Senate Steering Committee, a dean, a department chair, an academic staff person, and a student representative.

[41]. UW Center System Long Range Planning Committee, Adjusting the UW Center System to the Demands of the 1980s. A Six Year Plan, November 1981, 20 pp., 7 appendices.

[42]. Ibid., pp. 3-16, Appendices 2 through 4.

[43]. Ibid., pp. 16-18.

[44]. Special Planning Committee Report, February 15, 1982, pp. 1-6. The SPC requested that Polk be permitted to continue as the Acting Chancellor, at least until January 1983, at which time it recommended a search committee be appointed to select a new chancellor.

[45]. Ibid., p. 4.

[46]. Ibid., pp. 6-10.

[47]. Bob Polk to President O'Neil, Executive Vice President Kauffman, Academic Vice President [Katharine] Lyall, February 25, 1982, and Polk to Members of the Special Planning Committee, March 1, 1982, O'Neil Papers, Box 2, UW Center 1980-82 file, UW Archives. Polk also expressed to O'Neil his desire to have the transitions completed before the Central Office moved from its cramped quarters at 602 State Street to offices in the Madison Board of Education Building on Dayton Street on July 1.

[48]. UW Center System Senate Minutes, April 6, 1982.

[49]. *Wisconsin State Journal*, April 12, 1982.

[50]. Chancellor Polk to President O'Neil, April 30, 1982, O'Neil Papers, Box 2, UW Center 1980-82 file, UW Archives.

[51]. Chancellor Robert R. Polk to Ms. Therese Rozga, Chair, Senate Steering Committee, April 23, 1982, Chancellor Polk's 1982-83 correspondence file, Central Office Files.

[52]. Transcript of the Remarks of President O'Neil at the Meeting of the UW Center System Senate, May 14, 1982, con-

cerning the Special Planning Committee Report and the Issue of Affiliation.
[53]. Robert M. O'Neil to Robert R. Polk, May 24, 1982, O'Neil Papers, Box 4, Chancellor Robert Polk file, UW Archives.
[54]. Bob Polk to Deans, "Confidential," RE: Outcome of Meeting with President O'Neil on 9-24-82, September 28, 1982, Chancellor Polk's 1982-83 correspondence file, Central Office Files. A great deal of the external pressure on O'Neil had arisen from Assembly Representative Virgil Roberts' suggestion, via a public letter, that the inefficient Center System be completely closed down. Indeed, Roberts had suggested that all tenured Center System faculty be given immediately the required one-year notice that their positions would be terminated. Roberts to O'Neil, May 21, 1982, O'Neil Papers, Box 35, Wisconsin Legislature, State Representative V. D. Roberts file, UW Archives.
[55]. Polk to O'Neil, "Confidential," October 20, 1982, Chancellor Polk's 1982-83 correspondence file, Central Office Files.
[56]. Ibid.
[57]. UW Center System Steering Committee to President Robert M. O'Neil, October 29, 1982, Chancellor Polk's 1982-83 correspondence file, Central Office Files.
[58]. Polk to O'Neil, November 4, 1982, Chancellor Polk's 1982-83 Correspondence file, Central Office Files.
[59]. Record of the Regents, volume 13, July 1982-June 1983, Meeting of November 5, 1982, Report of the President of the System. Both the *Capital Times* (November 5) and the *Wisconsin State Journal* (November 6) called O'Neil's recommendations a "surprise move."

Endnotes for Chapter Nine, Pages 173-198

[1]. Daniel Van Eyck, The Centers' Vice Chancellor from September 1973 through June 1984, in his interview, April 5, 1993, stressed the pivotal role the BOV had played in the late 1970s and early 1980s in preventing greater damage from being done to the Centers.
[2]. Larry Ratner to President O'Neil, May 3, 1984, Executive Dean Ratner 1984 correspondence file, Central Office Files, recaps the grand success of the inaugural luncheon. Chancellor Lee Grugel to Participants, UW Centers Board of Visitors Breakfast, February 22, 1995, Chancellor Grugel 1995 correspondence file, Central Office Files, indicates that mayors and county board chairs have been added as participants in these gatherings.
[3]. Record of the Regents, Volume 15, July 1984-June 1985, Meeting of October 5, 1984, "The Current Status of the UW Centers," pp. 3-9; *Wisconsin State Journal*, October 14, 1984.
[4]. Republican Dreyfus decided not to seek reelection in 1982. Earl, with 57% of the votes, handily defeated Republican Terry Kohler. *Wisconsin State Journal*, November 4, 1982.
[5]. Ibid., October 26, 1982.
[6]. Larry Ratner to President O'Neil, 1984-85 Annual Budget Presentation, January 19, 1984, Appendix IV-Percentage Change in the Composite Support Index 1972-73 through 1982-83, Executive Dean Ratner 1984 correspondence file, Central Office Files. The data reveals that the Centers' CSI had declined 41.4% during the decade following merger and its CSI in 1983-84 ($29.15) was beneath that of UW-Superior ($36.64), UW-Parkside ($30.57), UW-Green Bay ($30.30), UW-Stevens Point ($30.10), and UW-River Falls ($29.28).
[7]. Ibid.; Ratner to O'Neil, 1985-86 annual Budget Presentation, January 11, 1985; Ratner to Executive Vice President Katharine Lyall, March 4, 1985; Ratner to Elwin Cammack, November 21, 1985, Executive Dean Ratner 1985 correspondence file.
[8]. UW Centers Senate Minutes, January 9 and May 10-11, 1985.
[9]. See especially Ratner to Elwin Cammack, October 11, 1985, which transmits to Cammack a report, UWC Library Automation, Microcon Project, and asks for fiscal assistance to continue the catalog conversion project, Executive Dean Ratner 1985 correspondence file. The OCLC was a major project to link libraries via computers and the internet. OCLC began strictly within Ohio higher education but soon recognized the advantage of inviting out of state university libraries to join. Today its initials stand for Online Computer Library Center.
[10]. UW System Faculty Representatives to Governor Anthony Earl, October 16, 1983. A draft of this letter is in UW Centers Senate Minutes, September 17, 1983, Appendix 5.
[11]. UW Centers Senate Minutes, January 11, 1984.
[12]. This is the data that Kerry Trask used for his presentation to the Board of Regents in October 1984. See note 3, above.
[13]. UW Centers Senate Budget Committee, Faculty and Staff Salary Study: a preliminary report, May 1997, pp. 1-2.
[14]. Speech of Lorman A. Ratner to UW-Stevens Point meeting of legislators and Board of Regents, August 20, 1984, Executive Dean Ratner 1984 correspondence file, Central Office Files. Ratner also noted that 67 faculty members (26%) would earn less than $20,000 in 1984.
[15]. Executive Dean Ratner's report, UW Centers Senate Minutes, November 10, 1984. In his report, Ratner also described the status of the academic staff catch-up proposal. Because of the vast variety of titles and functions of the academic staff, the Board of Regents had decided to focus on those academic staff whose duties most advanced the "instructional, research, and service missions of the UW." Thus, the instructional academic staff, librarians, and research academic staff would receive the following average increases: Centers - 17.6%, Madison - 13.9%, Milwaukee - 10.2%, University Cluster - 6.0%. The academic staff catch-up plan ultimately approved by the Regents totaled $19.4 million, *Wisconsin State Journal*, October 5, 1984
[16]. Ratner to Dr. Ben Lawton, President, Board of Regents, February 11, 1985, Executive Dean Ratner 1985 correspondence file; both the *Milwaukee Journal*, August 19, 1984, and the *Wisconsin State Journal*, August 21, 1984, carried articles in which various state legislators warned the UW faculties not to fight among themselves over the division of the catch-up salary increases, lest the struggle give the anti-university faction an opportunity to defeat the entire proposal.
[17]. UW Centers Senate Minutes, January 9, 1985.
[18]. UW Centers Senate Minutes, October 12, 1985, Appendix 6: Report of the Joint Senate Budget and Steering

Committee; Ratner to Acting President Katharine C. Lyall, September 20, 1985, transmitted the Centers distribution plan to System for approval. The two committees also developed an allocation plan for the librarians and instructional academic staff (lecturers). For the librarians, 40% of their catch-up was based on their merit ratings, 50% on salary market considerations, and 10% was distributed at Executive Dean Ratner's discretion. For the instructional academic staff, 25% was parceled out by the deans, according to their assessment of the lecturer's performance, 50% was used to address salary compression, 20% was awarded by the department chairs to their most valuable lecturers, and 5% was reserved for the executive dean's discretionary use.

[19]. *Chippewa Herald-Telegram,* December 16, 1985.

[20]. Ratner to Acting President Katharine Lyall, January 2, 1986, Executive Dean Ratner 1986 correspondence file.

[21]. Ibid., Ratner to President Kenneth Shaw, February 13, 1986, Ratner to Campus Steering Committee Chairs, February 26, 1986, Executive Dean Ratner 1986 correspondence file; UW Centers Senate Minutes, January 18 and March 15, 1986.

[22]. Report of the Special Regent Study Committee on Extension, Record of the Regents, volume 12, July 1981-June 1982, meeting of April 9, 1982, Exhibit A, especially p. 3. Hereafter cited as Special Regent Report on Extension.

[23]. Executive Dean Larry Ratner to Extension Chancellor Patrick Boyle, April 16, 1984, UWC Continuing Education Long Range Plan, P. 1, Executive Dean Ratner 1984 correspondence file. Hereafter cited as Continuing Education Long Range Plan.

[24]. Ibid., pp. 1-3.

[25]. Larry Ratner to Harold Montross, Dean, General Extension, March 21, 1984, in Executive Dean Ratner's 1984 correspondence file discusses the mechanics of this transfer. Although the continuing education coordinators were on the Centers' payroll, they remained employees of UW Extension, which continued to provide administrative services to them.

[26]. Continuing Education Long Range Plan, pp. 1, 3-4.

[27]. In January 1988, Centers Chancellor Stephen Portch informed the Regents that the UW Extension Integration Plan was proceeding on schedule. At that time, each Center had at least a half-time coordinator. In 1986-1987, the thirteen coordinators had, collectively, offered 830 courses to over 18,000 individuals and had generated in excess of $500,000 in revenue.

[28]. Record of the Regents, Volume 14, July 1983-June 1984, meeting of September 9, 1983. Katharine Lyall had begun her duties as Vice President for Academic Affairs in January 1982.

[29]. Policy on the Use of Teaching Academic Staff in the UW Center System, Center System Senate Minutes, February 2, 1980 (adopted) and May 16-17, 1980 (ratified).

[30]. *Milwaukee Journal,* January 24, 1985, and Katharine C. Lyall Biographical File, UW Archives.

[31]. *The Capital Times,* September 14, 1985, *Milwaukee Sentinel,* September 20, 1985; *Wisconsin State Journal,* September 20 & 24, 1985.

[32]. Larry Ratner to Acting President Katharine Lyall, December 30, 1985, Executive Dean Ratner's 1985 correspondence file informs Lyall of his intention to leave the Centers. Ratner to Lyall, September 16, 1985, in ibid., requests consideration of restoring the chancellor title. Record of the Regents, volume 16, July 1985-June 1986, meeting of February 7, 1986, records the Regents' approval.

[33]. *Appleton Post Crescent,* November 14, 1986, reporting Portch's remarks at UWC-Fox Valley.

[34]. *Eau Claire Leader Telegram,* August 11, 1986.

[35]. *The Capital Times,* October 10, 1986.

[36]. *Wisconsin State Journal,* November 5, 1986.

[37]. Ibid., November 6, 1986.

[38]. State of Wisconsin, Legislative Fiscal Bureau, University of Wisconsin Enrollment and Admission Policies, Informational Paper #37, January 1995, pp. 1-2; *Wisconsin State Journal,* June 7, 1986.

[39]. *Wisconsin State Journal,* February 16, June 7 & October 26, 1986; *Milwaukee Sentinel,* April 4, 1986; *Stevens Point Journal,* October 26, 1986.

[40]. *Wisconsin State Journal,* June 6, 1986. The article reported that tuition at UW-Madison and UW-Milwaukee would be $1,431 for a resident undergraduate, $1,202 at the seven Cluster campuses, and $1,153 at the thirteen Centers.

[41]. *Wisconsin State Journal,* February 16, 1986; *Marinette Eagle Star,* May 30, 1986.

[42]. Record of the Regents, Volume 16, July 1985-June 1986, Meeting of February 7, 1986, and Executive Dean Ratner's Speeches file, 1983-1986.

[43]. *Glenwood City Tribune Press,* February 27, 1986, reporting on the legislative luncheon held on February 12th.

[44]. James J. Lorence, Chair, UW Centers Senate Steering Committee, to Regent Ody Fish, February 26, 1986, transmitting Working Together: The Centers in the University of Wisconsin System, 8 pp., quote on p. 3, UW Centers Senate Minutes, March 15, 1986, Appendix 4.

[45]. Ibid.

[46]. Ibid., p. 5.

[47]. Ibid., p. 4.

[48]. Ibid., pp. 5-6.

[49]. Ibid., pp. 3-8 passim, but especially p. 7. The fifth issue stressed keeping Centers' tuition the lowest in the System, to make enrollment economically attractive, p. 6.

[50]. Report of the Regents Study Group on the Future of the University of Wisconsin System, in Record of the Regents, Volume 17, July 1986-June 1987, Meeting of December 5, 1986, Exhibit A, p. 9. The Study Group explained that it anticipated requiring all UW undergraduate credit courses to be recorded on a transcript would eliminate the perception that a transferee "lost" credits in transferring.

[51]. Ibid., p. 11; the Regents' planning thresholds were reaffirmed on p. A5.

[52]. Chancellor Stephen Portch to President Kenneth Shaw, January 6, 1987, Chancellor Portch's 1987 Correspondence file; the *Oshkosh Northwestern,* March 9, 1987, reported the proposed tuition differentials.

[53]. Record of the Regents, Volume 18, July 1987-June 1988, Meeting of July 10, 1987, Resolution 3850 and Exhibit A.
[54]. Chancellor Stephen Porch to President Kenneth Shaw, October 2, 1987, Chancellor Portch's 1987 Correspondence file.
[55]. Chancellor Stephen Porch to President Kenneth Shaw, October 19, 1987, in Ibid. There is also a copy in the Kenneth Shaw Papers, accession #90/84, Box 10, UW Centers Miscellaneous file, UW Archives.
[56]. Chancellor Stephen R. Portch to UW Chancellors, November 4, 1987, Chancellor Portch's 1987 Correspondence file.
[57]. Ibid., a sample articulation agreement was attached to the letter.
[58]. Chancellor Portch to Deans, Department Chairs, Chancellor's Council, January 5, 1988, Chancellor Portch's 1988 Correspondence file.
[59]. Kenneth A. Shaw to Chancellors, RE: Progress on Facilitating UW Center Transfers, January 12, 1988, Shaw Papers, Accession #90/84, Box 10, UW Centers Miscellaneous file, UW Archives.
[60]. Chancellor Portch to Deans, February 17, 1988, Chancellor Portch's 1988 Correspondence file.
[61]. Chancellor Stephen Portch to Board of Regents, UW Center Legislators, January 13, 1989, Chancellor Portch's 1989 Correspondence file.
[62]. *Wisconsin State Journal,* February 4 and November 2, 1986, and *Milwaukee Sentinel,* December 9 and 25, 1986. The maximum levy was 1.5 mills per $1,000 valuation.
[63]. *Milwaukee Sentinel,* August 16, 1986; *Superior Evening Telegram,* January 12, 1987; and *Stevens Point Journal,* January 15, 1987.
[64]. *Racine Journal-Times,* March 17, 1987, carried an article which quoted Gateway Technical Institute Director John Birkholtz as favoring "collapsing" the Centers into the VTAE System; *Green Bay Press-Gazette,* May 15, 1987, cited Robert Sorenson's support of a merger. Sorenson, state director of the VTAE System, said "They should be put together in a community college system."
[65]. Chancellor Stephen Portch to President Kenneth Shaw and Vice Presidents Lyall, Trani, Bornstein, May 21, 1987. After some refinements Portch sent the same memo to the Campus Deans, June 25, 1987, for them to use to argue against a merger. Chancellor Portch's 1987 Correspondence file.
[66]. Chancellor Stephen Portch to President Kenneth Shaw, Katharine Lyall, Ron Bornstein, and Gene Trani, July 22, 1987, reporting testimony received at a recent Study Commission hearing, Chancellor Portch's 1987 Correspondence file.
[67]. Chancellor Stephen Portch to Governor Tommy Thompson, July 1, 1987, thanks Thompson for comments that Portch had read in a *Milwaukee Journal* article, Chancellor Portch's 1987 Correspondence file.
[68]. Dean Nancy Aumann [Marshfield/Wood County Center], to District Director Mel Schneeberg, March 23, 1988; M. H. Schneeberg to Nancy Aumann, March 31, 1988; and Stephen Portch to Buzz Shaw, Katharine Lyall, Gene Trani and Ron Bornstein, April 13, 1988, Chancellor Portch's 1988 Correspondence file. Portch's letter indicates that he believed Schneeberg was pushing the college parallel agenda with backing from other VTAE directors. Portch worried that Schneeberg would attempt to convince one of the Wisconsin Rapids area legislators—Marlin Schneider, Dave Helbach, or Stan Gruszynski—to introduce legislation to permit at least Midstate to establish a college parallel program.
[69]. State of Wisconsin Legislative Audit Bureau Informational Memorandum, University of Wisconsin System and Vocational, Technical and Adult Education Credit Transfer Policies and Practices, January 1988.
[70]. Chancellor Stephen Portch to President Kenneth Shaw, December 19, 1988, citing the summary page of the LAB report, Chancellor Portch's 1988 Correspondence file.
[71]. *Wisconsin State Journal,* July 30, 1987.
[72]. Record of the Regents, volume 19, July 1988-June 1989, Meeting of June 9, 1989, Exhibit A.
[73]. Ibid.
[74]. Chancellor Stephen Portch to Kathleen Sell [UW System Budget Analyst], November 24, 1986 and January 8, 1987; Portch to Buzz Shaw, March 12, 1987 and October 15, 1987; Chancellor Portch's 1986 and 1987 Correspondence files.
[75]. Chancellor Stephen Portch to President Kenneth Shaw, March 12, 1987 (Talking Points for the UW Centers Budget Conference), and November 1989 (1988-89 in Review), Chancellor Portch's 1987 and 1989 Correspondence files, respectively.
[76]. Chancellor Portch to Campus Deans, Department Chairs, Senators, Board of Visitors, July 10, 1987, Chancellor Portch's 1987 Correspondence file. This memo announced the Central Office reorganization and listed these major gaps: "Computer Resources Manager, Student Services Coordinator, Grants Officer, Personnel Administrator, and support staff."
[77]. Chancellor Stephen R. Portch to UW Chancellors, July 13, 1988, announced the appointment of a Director of Academic Services, and Steve Portch to Buzz Shaw, November 1989, 1988-89 in Review, Chancellor Portch's 1988 and 1989 Correspondence files.
[78]. Chancellor Stephen Portch to President Kenneth Shaw, Talking Points for UW Centers Budget Conference, March 12, 1987, Chancellor Portch's 1987 Correspondence file.
[79]. UW System, Unclassified Compensation Planning and Implementation for 1989-91 Salary Catch-Up, revised March 17, 1989, p. 1.
[80]. Ibid., pp. 3-5; the UW Centers Faculty Catch-Up Plan, April 14, 1989.
[81]. UW Centers Academic Staff Catch-Up Plan, March 13, 1989.
[82]. Centron, of the UWC Sheboygan County, December 12, 1989, and Minutes, UW Centers Board of Visitors, March 7, 1990, Chancellor Portch's 1989 and 1990 Correspondence files. CENTERSnet was developed with the invaluable assistance of UW-Stevens Point, where the hub of the network was located. Its development greatly sped up completion of the ongoing library automation project.
[83]. Chancellor Portch to Deans, July 28, 1989; Minutes, UW Centers Board of Visitors, March 7, 1990; Chancellor Portch's 1989 and 1990 Correspondence files. The memo to the deans contained these figures: the S&E budget would be boosted by $100,414 in the first year of the biennium and by another $94,919 in the second, for a total increase of $295,333.

[84]. Chancellor Stephen Porch to President Kenneth Shaw, January 22, 1990, Chancellor Porch's 1990 Correspondence file.
[85]. Chancellor Stephen Porch to President Kenneth Shaw, October 10, 1990, Chancellor Porch's 1990 Correspondence file.
[86]. Chancellor Porch to Deans, Department Chairs, Chancellor's Council, Senate Budget Committee, Dave Gratz [Chair, Senate Steering Committee], Rhonda Uschan [Chair, Academic Staff Advisory Council], December 26, 1990, and Chancellor Stephen Porch to President Kenneth Shaw, January 14, 1991, Chancellor Porch's 1990 and 1991 Correspondence files. The December memo outlined the parameters of the budget freeze and described the Department of Administration's directive that most of the required "savings" were to be garnered from the instructional budget. The January letter reports that the Centers will pay their 1990 share by drawing $198,000 from salaries and wages, plus $10,000 from S&E.
[87]. State of Wisconsin, Legislative Fiscal Bureau, University of Wisconsin Enrollment and Admissions Policies, Informational Paper #37, January 1995, p. 4, hereafter cited as LFB #37; Chancellor Porch to Deans, Department Chairs, Senators, Chancellor's Council, Academic Staff Advisory Committee, Planning Council, November 13, 1990, Chancellor Porch's 1990 Correspondence file.
[88]. LFB #37, pp. 2 and 4. The LFB reported that EMI had decreased the number of students by 5,709 FTE (4.1%), while the Centers' enrollment had grown by 868 FTE.
[89]. Record of the Regents, Volume 21, July 1990-June 1991, Meeting of March 8, 1991, pp. 15-16.
[90]. LFB #37, pp. 4-6. The $26.5 million was allocated as follows: $19.4 million—faculty salary increases, $3.3 million—S&E, $3.0 million—UW-Madison School of Engineering, and $0.8 million—assessment program. Altogether 270 FTE faculty and staff positions were held vacant to generate these funds; the Centers, UW-Superior, and UW-Green Bay did not contribute any positions to QRP.
[91]. Chancellor Porch to UW Centers Planning Council, October 26, 1989, Chancellor Porch's 1989 Correspondence file.
[92]. Chancellor Porch to All UW Centers Faculty, Academic Staff, and Classified Staff, RE: Planning Council Report, February 12, 1991, Chancellor Porch's 1991 Correspondence file.
[93]. Chancellor Porch to All UW Center Employees, RE: Status of Planning Council Report Recommendations, April 30, 1991, One-Minute-to-Midnight, Chancellor Porch's 1991 Correspondence file.
[94]. *The Capital Times, Milwaukee Sentinel*, and *Milwaukee Journal*, April 27, 1991, all carried the news of Shaw's resignation and the discussion of Lyall's status.

Endnotes for Chapter Ten, Pages 199-217

[1]. *Eau Claire Leader-Telegram*, September 6, 1991.
[2]. Dave Gratz, (English—Manitowoc), Chair, Senate Steering Committee, to Campus Steering Committee Chairs and Department Chairs, February 28, 1991, requested a critique of the existing merit procedure and suggestions for changes. The preliminary results were reported to the Senate by Gratz in May, UW Centers Senate Minutes, May 3-4, 1991, when he said the Senate Steering Committee had found "widespread support for some changes in merit."
[3]. Dave Gratz to Senate Steering Committee, Draft Proposal on Merit, January 23, 1992; Lee Grugel to Steering Committee, Draft Merit Proposal, January 27, 1992, both in Chancellor Grugel's 1992 Correspondence file; UW Centers Senate Minutes, January 17, March 20, and May 9, 1992. The Senate Minutes for May 7-8, 1993, noted that the department chairs had reported the new merit procedure was a great improvement.
[4]. The Undergraduate Imperative: Building on Excellence, Executive Summary, December 3, 1991.
[5]. UW Centers Senate Policy #35, Tenured Faculty Review and Development, p. 1.
[6]. UW Centers Senate, Faculty Session Minutes, January 15, March 13, May 7-8, and October 2, 1993.
[7]. Chancellor Lee Grugel to Vice President Stephen R. Porch, June 18, 1992, Chancellor Grugel's 1992 Correspondence file. Grugel explained that Green Bay, Oshkosh, Stevens Point, Superior, and Whitewater demanded a GPA between 2.25 and 2.75 for admission while Eau Claire, Madison, and River Falls specified a GPA greater than 2.0 but reserved the right to adjust it "as necessary!" La Crosse required a 2.5 GPA of transfer students.
[8]. Ibid. Vice President Porch raised these concerns with the Education Committee of the Board of Regents which reiterated support for the Transfer Policy and its enforcement by Porch's office.
[9]. Record of the Regents, volume 23, July 1992-June 1993, meeting of October 9, 1992, pp. 6-7.
[10]. Ibid., meeting of December 11, 1992, pp. 4-5.
[11]. Chancellor Lee Grugel to UWC Deans, October 22 and 28, 1992, Chancellor Grugel's 1992 Correspondence file; Tony Kucera to Lee Grugel, November 1, 1992, in Ibid.
[12]. Chancellor Lee Grugel to UW System Vice President Ray Marnocha, November 3, 1992 and to President Katharine Lyall, November 19, 1992, Chancellor Grugel's 1992 Correspondence file.
[13]. Assistant Chancellor Antone F. Kucera to UW Centers Deans, March 22, 1993; Chancellor Lee E. Grugel to President Katharine Lyall, March 26, 1993; Lee Grugel to Campus Deans, RE: Financial Outlook, August 2, 1993; Lee Grugel to Members, Senate Budget Committee, September 22, 1993, all in Chancellor Grugel's 1993 Correspondence file.
[14]. Chancellor Lee Grugel to President Katharine Lyall, February 25 and June 1, 1993; Grugel to Senior Vice President Ron Bornstein, December 23, 1993, Chancellor Grugel's 1993 Correspondence file.
[15]. Record of the Regents, volume 23, July 1992-June 1993, meeting of June 4, 1993, p. 24; Report of a Visit to the University of Wisconsin Centers (September 21-23, 1992) for the Commission on Institutions of Higher Education of the North Central Association of Colleges and Schools, February 1993, pp. 38-39, hereafter cited as Report of a Visit.
[16]. Report of a Visit, p. 27.
[17]. Ibid, pp. 34-35, especially Strengths #2, 3, 4, 10, and 20.
[18]. Report of a Visit, pp. 35-36, 38-39.

[19]. Ibid., pp. 38-39.
[20]. UW Centers 1996-97 Budget Guidelines and succeeding versions.
[21]. University of Wisconsin Centers Self-Study Report, July 1992, pp. 107-09.
[22]. Ibid, p. 108.
[23]. Ibid.
[24]. Senate Minutes, January 15, 1993, Attachment 5: Strategic Planning in the UW Centers, A Proposal to the Senate Steering Committee.
[25]. Senate Minutes, January 11, 1996. The Planning Commission's struggles can be traced in the Senate Minutes for May 7-8, 1993; May 6-7, 1994; May 5-6, 1995; and September 23, 1995.
[26]. Senate Minutes, May 7-8, 1993; November 13, 1993; January 13, 1994; and May 6-7, 1994.
[27]. The University of Wisconsin System Office of Policy Analysis and Research, Informational Memorandum, Trends and Enrollment: Fall 1998 Update, issued April 1999, Tables 3 and 7.
[28]. Senate Minutes, September 23, 1995, Report of the General Education Task Force.
[29]. Senate Minutes, September 20-21, 1996, Attachment 4a-Assessment.
[30]. Senate Minutes, September 20-21, 1996.
[31]. Assessment Lite, A Newsletter of Assessment Activities at the University of Wisconsin Centers, Winter 1997, Volume 1, Number 1, p. 4; Fall 1997 (sic), Volume 2, Number 1, printed the Plan for and Initial Implementation of the Assessment of Student Academic Achievement and Institutional Effectiveness authored by the AIWG; and Spring 1998, Volume 2, Number 2, p. 4.
[32]. University of Wisconsin Centers, Self-Study Report for the North Central Association of Colleges and Schools, July 1992, pp. 60-62.
[33]. Chancellor Lee E. Grugel to President Katharine Lyall, December 23, 1993, Chancellor Grugel's 1993 Correspondence file.
[34]. Chancellor Grugel to President Lyall, February 9, 1994, explains a three-year phase-out of the consortium, Chancellor Grugel's 1994 Correspondence file. UW Centers Senate Minutes, March 12, 1994, record Grugel's announcement that the first year of the phase-out would increase financial aid for Centers' students by $400,000.
[35]. David Suchman, Informational paper #37, University of Wisconsin Enrollment and Admissions Policies, Wisconsin Legislative Fiscal Bureau, January 1995, pp. 1-3. Hereafter cited as Suchman, Informational paper #37.
[36]. Suchman, Informational Paper #37, pp. 8-9 and Table 3: FTE Students Under Enrollment Management III. Record of the Regents, Volume 24, July 1993-June 1994, meetings of February, April, and May, 1994, record the Board's actions in developing EM III.
[37]. Chancellor Lee E. Grugel, "News and Views," sent to UW Centers Board of Visitors, August 17, 1992; Chancellor Lee E. Grugel, UW Centers Annual Report to the UW System President, January 6, 1993, in Chancellor Grugel's 1992 and 1993 Correspondence files, respectively.
[38]. Chancellor Lee E. Grugel to Deans, March 30, 1994, Chancellor Grugel's 1994 Correspondence file. Grugel requested that each dean indicate how the special technology funds would be spent on his campus—Grugel intended to use this information in the ongoing political drive to get the fee included in the budget. It was estimated that the Centers would have about $225,000 to expend from the levy in 1995-96.
[39]. On September 20, 1994, Chancellor Grugel wrote thank-you notes to three persons who had assisted in the acquisition of this grant: Glenn A. Davidson, Executive Director, Wisconsin Educational Communications Board, and United States Senators Herbert Kohl and Russ Feingold, Chancellor Grugel's 1994 Correspondence file.
[40]. Draft Report of the UW Centers Distance Education Task Force, November 1994, p. 7. Hereafter cited as DE Report.
[41]. DE Report.
[42]. Distance Education Strategic Planning Committee to Chancellor Lee E. Grugel, March 1, 1996, p. 1, Chancellor Grugel's 1996 Correspondence file.
[43]. Ibid., pp. 1-2.
[44]. Ibid., p. 2.
[45]. Chancellor Grugel to Distance Education Strategic Planning Committee, May 13, 1996, Chancellor Grugel's 1996 Correspondence file.
[46]. *Wisconsin State Journal*, September 4, October 18, & November 6, 1994.
[47]. *Wisconsin State Journal*, November 6, 1994.
[48]. *Wisconsin State Journal*, November 9, 1994.
[49]. Record of the Regents, Volume 25, July 1994-June 1995, meeting of August 19, 1994, President Lyall's report, pp. 3-6; "UW System's Major Budget Concerns," March 20, 1995; and Chancellor Lee Grugel to Deans, June 6, 1995, describes the Joint Finance Committee's action to date on the Governor's budget, Chancellor Grugel's 1995 Correspondence file. The UW Centers especially relied upon the UW System capital planning staff for assistance with its building projects. Chancellor Grugel worried that Centers' projects would constantly be pushed to the bottom of DOA's list.
[50]. "UW System's Major Budget Concerns," March 20, 1995, and Record of the Regents; Volume 25, July 1994-June 1995, meeting of June 9, 1995, pp. 5-6.
[51]. *Fond du Lac Reporter*, March 22, 1995.
[52]. Chancellor Lee E. Grugel to Governor Tommy Thompson, Grugel to President Katharine Lyall, both March 30, 1995, Chancellor Grugel's 1995 Correspondence file.
[53]. Chancellor Lee Grugel to Deans, "Summary of UW System's 1995-97 Budget Following Action of Joint Finance Committee," June 6, 1995, Chancellor Grugel's 1995 Correspondence file.
[54]. Chancellor Grugel to UW Centers Board of Visitors, transmitting statement by UW President Katharine C. Lyall Regarding Legislative Approval of the 1995-97 state budget, June 30, 1995, Chancellor Grugel's 1995 Correspondence file.
[55]. The University of Wisconsin System Office of Policy Analysis, Informational Memorandum, Trends in Enrollment: Fall 1998 Update, Tables 1 (Historical Profile of Undergraduate FTE enrollment) and 7 (Historical Profile of Percent

Deviation from FTE Targets). Hereafter cited as Trends in Enrollment. The amount of indebtedness was gleaned from various of Chancellor Grugel's memos and from Senate Minutes for each of the Fall Semesters.

[56]. Chancellor Lee E. Grugel to President Katharine C. Lyall, October 11, 1994, Chancellor Grugel's 1994 Correspondence file.

[57]. Chancellor Lee E. Grugel to President Katharine C. Lyall, October 18, 1995, Chancellor Grugel's 1995 Correspondence file.

[58]. Chancellor Lee E. Grugel to President Katharine C. Lyall, October 1, 1996, Chancellor Grugel's 1996 Correspondence file.

[59]. *Wisconsin State Journal*, November 1, 1996.

[60]. *Stevens Point Journal*, December 13, 1996.

[61]. Senate Minutes, November 16, 1996.

[62]. Senate Minutes, May 2-3, 1997, p. 6.

[63]. Chancellor Lee Grugel to Acting President Katharine Lyall, February 1992, relates that a Center dean had recently received a check made out to the "Extension Center," Chancellor Grugel's 1992 Correspondence file.

[64]. Wisconsin Survey Research Laboratory, University of Wisconsin Centers Image Survey: Consolidated Report, April 1996, included (Appendix B, p.3) comments from interviewees about their perception of their local Center such as, "Good place for higher ed for people who can't afford other schools; a two-year college, many kids that can't afford 4-year college go there." and "I think of it just as a prep school—just as a school you go to before you go to a regular school." UW Centers Marketing Task Force Final Report, February 1997, relates that one Center had ". . . lessened emphasis on affordability because students told us we were thought of as the K-Mart of education, an image we didn't like.", p. 8.

[65]. Chancellor Lee E. Grugel to President Katharine Lyall, February 21, 1995, proposes the project, and March 17, 1995, thanks Lyall for approving his "bold proposal," Chancellor Grugel's 1995 Correspondence file.

[66]. Wisconsin Survey Research Laboratory, University of Wisconsin Centers Image Survey: Consolidated Report, Table 2, p. 3, and Comparative Report, Table 1, p. 2, April 1996. The Comparative Report reveals that the Fox Valley Center had the greatest awareness (65%) while Rock County scored only 32%.

[67]. WSRL, Image Survey: Comparative Report, Table 7, p. 8. For this question Richland rated best (72%) and Rock County worst (44%).

[68]. UW Centers Marketing Task Force Final Report, February 1997, p. 1.

[69]. Ibid., pp. 3-4, 5-6.

[70]. Ibid., VI. Recommendations, pp. 15-16.

[71]. Chancellor Lee E. Grugel to Acting President Katharine C. Lyall, February 27, 1992, Chancellor Grugel's 1992 Correspondence file.

[72]. Senate Minutes, May 2-3, 1997.

[73]. Record of the Regents, volume 28, July 1997-June 1998, meeting of July 25, 1997, p. 17. Only one regent voted against the resolution.

[74]. It is unfortunate that Lee Grugel did not live to see the enrollment increase, which he had been steadfastly predicting, begin in the Spring 1997 Semester. This small gain caused the Centers' debt to be reduced by $200,000. Since then the two-year campuses have experienced four successive Fall enrollment increases to slightly exceed their FTE target. Simultaneously the budget crunch also eased. The Fall enrollments were as follows: 1997 6,108 FTE (+2%), 1998 6,901 FTE (+13%), 1999 7,672 FTE (+11%) and 2000 7,917 FTE (+3.2%). The Fall 2000 Enrollment Management III target for the two-year campuses was 7,835 FTE, which was exceeded by 81 FTE (+1.0%).

Campus Directors, Deans and CEOs

Titles under UW Extension were Director
Titles under UW Center System, and UW Centers were Campus Deans
Titles under UW Colleges are CEO and Campus Dean

UW-Baraboo/Sauk County
Theodore N. Savides 1967-1980
Aural Umhoefer, Acting 1980-1981
Aural Umhoefer 1981-2002

UW-Barron County
John Meggers 1966-1973
Eugene Hartmann, Interim 1973-1974 (while Meggers was Interim Chancellor)
John Meggers 1974-1988
Mary Somers 1988-1997
Paul Chase 1997-present

UW-Fond du Lac
Willard Henken 1966-1987
Bradley Gottfried 1987-1993
Judy Goldsmith, Acting 1993-1994
Judy Goldsmith 1994-2002

UW-Fox Valley
Vern Imhoff 1957-1965
Robert Najem 1965-1966
Allan Bussell, Acting 1966-67
Henry Hutson 1967-1969
Leander Schwartz 1969-1972
Franklin Doverspike, Acting 1972-1973
Rue Johnson 1973-1986
Jack Silha, Acting 1986-1987
Robert E. Young 1987-1992
Janice Green, Acting 1992-1993

Rhonda Uschan, Interim 1993
James Perry 1993-present

UW-Manitowoc
Raymond Grosnick, 1962-1972
Leroy Purchatzke, Interim 1972
Michael Karnis 1972-1976
Chester Natunewicz 1976-1984
Herman Nibbelink, Interim 1984
Roland A. Baldwin 1984-present

UW-Marathon County
Henry Ahrnsbrak 1947-1965
Paul A. Zehner 1965-1969
Byron Barrington, Acting 1969-1971
William Peters 1971-1981
Jordan Nash, Interim 1981
Stephen Portch 1981-1986
Harlan Grinde, Acting 1986-1987
George Newtown 1987-1990
Bryant Kearl, Interim 1990-1991
G. Dennis Massey 1991-1999
Howard Thoyre, Interim 1999-2000
James Veninga 2000-present

UW-Marinette
Lyman Funkey 1946-1947
R. D. Wagner 1947-1951
Joseph J. Gerend 1951-1963
Lon W. Weber 1963-1967
William A. Schmidtke, Interim 1967-1968
James Olson 1968-1969
William A. Schmidtke, Interim 1969
William A. Schmidtke 1969-1995
Nancee I Bailey, Interim 1995-1995
Sidney H. Bremer 1995-present

UW-Marshfield/Wood County
Norbert Koopman 1964-1986
Nancy Aumann 1986-1990
Thomas Bitner, Acting 1990-1991
Carol McCart 1991-2002

UW-Medford
Russell L. Oliver 1969-1974
Darwin Slocum 1974-1981
Bob Larson, Interim 1978
Campus Closed 1982

UW-Richland
Ross Papke 1967-1973
Marjorie Wallace, Interim 1973
Marjorie Wallace 1974-1979
Donald Gray 1979-1984
Jerry Bower, Acting 1984-1985
Thomas Oates 1985-1989
Jean Birkett & Patricia Fellows,
 Co-Acting 1989-1990
Dion Q. Kempthorne 1990-2001
Deborah B. Cureton 2001-present

UW-Rock County
Charles E. Miller 1965-1968
Allan A. Spitz 1968-1969
George A. Condon 1969-1972
Martin Stabb, Interim 1972-1973
Gerald Henry, Interim 1973
Thomas W. Walterman 1973-1990
Elizabeth Schoenfeld, Interim
 1990-1991
Jane E. Crisler, 1991-2000
Janet Philipp 2000-present

UW-Sheboygan
Myron Lowe
Earl S. Beard 1963-1967
R. Gordon Goodrum, Interim
 1967-1968
James Smith 1968-1972
Alex Nagy, Interim 1972
Kenneth Bailey 1972-1985
Barbara Losty 1985-1991
G. Kathleen O'Connor 1992-1996
Kerry A. Trask, Acting 1996-1997
Mark J. Tierno 1996-2000
Tom Brigham, Interim 2000
Raymond Hernandez 2000-present

UW-Washington County
Harry Maxwell 1968-1972
R. Gordon Goodrum, Acting
 1972-1973
Robert O. Thompson 1973-1989
Dion Kempthorne, Acting 1989-1990
Joel Rodney 1990-present

UW-Waukesha
Murray Deutsch 1966-1972
Delbert Meyer, Interim 1972-1973
Kenneth Oliver 1973-1981
Mary Knudten 1981-1999
Brad Stewart 1999-present

Index

A

Abell, Allan P., 90–91
absenteeism, 66
accreditation, 203–6
Adolfson, Lorentz H., 35, 46–54, 59–60, 64, 66, 72–84, 88–89, 92–93, 99–100, 104–7, 136, 220–23
affiliation issue, 161–62
Affiliation Protocol, 167–68
agriculture courses/programs, 8–9, 11–12, 46
Ahrnsbrak, Henry, 52–53, 62
Allen, Chester, 24–26, 28, 37, 39–40, 42–43, 46
American Federation of Teachers Union, Local 253, 27–28, 30
Anderson, Norman, 136
anti-Extension/Center sentiments, 8–12, 14, 18, 27, 48, 66, 69, 91, 102, 108
Antigo Extension Center, 23, 33–34, 38, 40, 44, 52–53, 75, 218
Appleton Center, 39–40
Arnn, Gene, 129
Articulation Agreements, 187–89, 193
Assembly Bill 922, 24
Assembly Bill 194A, 44
Associate Degree, 138, 183, 185–89, 192, 197, 203–4. See also Liberal Arts Core Curriculum
Associate in Arts certificate, 66, 203
Associate in Science certificate, 66, 203

B

Bablitch, William, 135
Baldwin, I. L., 74
Baldwin, Roland, 220–21
Baraboo/Sauk County Center
 evolution of, 89, 103–4, 116, 120–21
 scope reduction years, 126, 131, 133–38, 148, 156–57
 as UW Campus, 218, 224–26

Barron County Center
 evolution of, 77, 94, 113–16, 120–22
 scope reduction years, 126, 131, 133, 142–43, 148, 154, 156–57, 161, 166
 as UW Campus, 218, 227–29
Barrows, Thomas, 39–40
Batt, Jim, 220–21
Beard, Earl, 220–21
Beaver Dam Center, 77
Bendrick, Steven, 160
Bennion, Steve, 109, 132–33
Berger, Meta, 29
Bergstresser, John, 35–36
Berquist, Henry J., 43–44
Birge, Edward A., 14–15
Blackenburg, Howard, 34
Board of Regents. See individual subjects
Board of Visitors, 47, 169, 174–75
Bower, Jerry, 144, 201
Boyle, Patrick, 180–81
Bremer, Sid, 220–21
Brunette, E. F., 29
Brunette Committee, 29–31, 37

C

Callahan, John, 23, 25, 38–39
Cammack, Elwin, 129
Carley, David, 149
Carter, Jimmy, 149
Catlin, Mark, 61
Center System, launching of, 79–96
Center System constitution, 140, 142–44. See also Long's Charter
Center System Task Force (1980), 154–61
Chamberlain, Thomas C., 9
chancellor, 7, 80–81, 170–71, 182
Chase, Paul, 220–21
Chvala, Charles (Chuck), 210–11
circuit riders/riding, 9–10, 17, 32–35,

39, 64, 81, 160
Clausen, Fred, 28, 30
Cleek, Margaret, 220–21
Clodius, Robert, 76, 79
Colbert, R. J., 34
communistic activities. See Brunette Committee
community colleges. See junior colleges
Community Institutes, 12
commuting (instructors). See circuit riders/riding
compensation/salaries. See salaries/compensation
Composite Support Index (CSI), 112–22, 128, 136–38, 140, 151, 154, 157, 165–66, 173, 176, 195
compulsory attendance law, 11–12
computerization, 195–96, 203, 208, 210
Condon, George, 107
Consolidation Task Force (CTF) (1972), 106–12
constitutional challenges, 16, 22, 25. See also Tallman, John
Coordinating Committee for Higher Education (CCHE), 61–64, 69, 72–79, 85–88, 90, 94–96, 101–5, 159–61
correspondence study courses/programs, 10–13, 18, 23–25, 40, 42–44, 50
County Normal Schools, 25, 27, 67–68
County Teachers Colleges, 71–73, 75, 77, 94
credit courses/lectures, 9, 11, 13–19, 22–23, 39, 42–47, 50, 53, 62, 78. See also Associate Degree; 60 credit rule; 72 credit rule; Liberal Arts Core Curriculum
60 credit rule, 22, 50–51, 83–84
72 credit rule, 83–84, 120–21, 186
credit transfer. See transfer of credits
Crofts, Albert E., 32

Cureton, Deborah, 220–21

D
Deutsch, Murray, 220–21
directors. See governance
distance education, 208–10
Doremus, Robert, 55
Doudna, E. G., 23
Drake, Louis E., 28, 36
Drexler, Carl, 38–39
Dreyfus, Lee S., 95, 101, 118, 149–50, 163, 175
Drier, Beverly, 146
Dunn, Robert, 127
Duren, Joanne, 128, 136
Duwe, Henry, 220–21
Dyke, William, 123–24
Dykstra, Clarence A., 31, 44–46

E
Earl, Anthony, 135, 175, 177–79, 182–84
Edsall, Bessie, 33
Ekern, Herman, 16, 22
Elvehjem, n.s., 73, 75
Ely, Richard T., 9–11
Enrollment Management I, 184–87
Enrollment Management II, 195–96
Enrollment Management III, 207–8, 214
enrollments, 40–45, 48–51, 53, 58–60, 64–65, 72–74, 79, 115. See also Enrollment Management I; Enrollment Management II; Enrollment Management III
charts, 45, 65, 141
post-war baby boom, 56–57, 67–68, 71
Erdman, Joyce, 138
Ermene, John, 22
Evans, Jean, 164

292

Evans, L. R., 36
Executive Dean. See chancellor
extracurricular activities, 19, 37, 51,
  55–56, 65–66, 91–93. See also student
  government

F

facilities, 16, 35–36, 50, 54, 56, 212. See
  also libraries; science facilities
faculty/instructors. See circuit riders/
  riding
Faculty Senate, 81–84, 90, 94–95
Farmers' Institutes, 8–9
Farrell, Michael, 136
Federal Educational Facilities Act of
  1963, 76
fee parity, 22, 47–48, 53–54, 56
fees/tuition, 8–9, 16, 25, 37–38, 43, 49,
  92, 115, 187
field representatives, 26, 42–43, 45, 49,
  64
Fish, Ody, 138, 182–84
Fitzpatrick, Edward A., 15–16
Fond du Lac Center
  evolution of, 77, 94, 104, 106, 113–16,
    120–21
  as extension, 32, 34–36, 52–55, 59
  scope reduction years, 126, 142–43,
    148, 156–57
  as UW Campus, 218, 230–32
foreigners, 33
Forrest, Christopher (Chris), 204
Fort, Edward B., 122–25, 128–31,
  134–35, 137–38, 140–41, 143–45,
  148–50, 153–54, 157–62, 164, 167,
  171, 174, 181, 222–23
Fowlkes, John Guy, 52–53, 62
Fox Valley Center
  evolution of, 82, 86, 88–89, 108
  as extension, 65, 68
  scope reduction years, 142, 147,
    156–57
  as UW Campus, 218, 233–35
Frank, Glenn, 15, 22, 24–25, 27–31, 37
Fred, Edwin Broun, 46, 49–52, 60–61
free union high schools, 22
Freshman Extension Centers, 11,
  23–27, 31, 33–34, 38–40, 48–49,
  67–68, 84
Freshman-Sophomore Centers, 13–14,
  16–17, 37, 44, 46–47, 69, 72, 74
funding, federal, 8, 13, 42, 49, 58, 76,
  85, 95
funding, local, 9, 11, 25, 74, 76, 195
funding, state
  for extension centers, 8–9, 11–16,
    24–26, 37–39, 44, 47–49, 54, 58–60,
    67, 69
  1980's and 1990's, 175, 179, 183–84,
    195–96, 211–13
  during scope reduction years, 76, 85,
    125–27, 133–35, 149–50, 163

G

Gale, Zona, 15, 31
Gelatt, Charles, 61
Gelatt/McIntyre compromise, 61
Gilley, Clarence, 62–63
Goldsmith, Judy, 215, 220–21
Goodland, Walter, 47–48
governance, 74–81, 88–90, 106–12,
  144–45, 205
Graff, Marshall, 32–33, 39
Green Bay Center, 218
  evolution of, 77, 82, 88–89
  as extension, 32, 35, 45, 49–50,
    52–54, 56, 64, 69
Greiber, Clarence L., 63, 100
Gribble, Roger, 128
Grosnick, Ray, 220–21, 237
Grugal, Lee E., 199, 201–3, 205–8,
  210–17, 222–25

H

Haferbecker, Gordon, 75–76
Hambrecht, George P., 23, 38
Hamilton, Bellamy, 215
Haney, Jim, 191
Hanley, Wilbur (Bill), 50, 52, 58, 64, 66, 79, 94–95
Hansen, W. Lee, 115
Harrington, Fred Harvey, 75–76, 78–79, 84, 88–89, 92, 96–97, 99
Hayakawa, S. I., 33
Heil, Joseph P., 39
Hernandez, Ray, 220–21
Hershfield, Allan, 112
Hesseltine, William Best, 35–36
Hoard, William Dempster, 8, 12
Holm, E. A., 32
Holt, Frank O., 24, 30–33, 36–40, 42–45, 223
housing, 14, 19, 50–51
Hutchins, Frank, 10
Hutchison, Harold, 107, 110
Hutnik, Willis J., 62–63
Hutson, Henry, 220–21

I

image/image survey, 216–17
industrial courses, 10–12
Ingraham, Mark, 35
itinerants. See circuit riders/riding

J

Janesville Center. See Rock County Center
junior college debate, 52–53, 62–64, 72–73, 85–87, 99–100, 128

K

Kannenberg, Roland E., 38
Kaplan, Arthur M., 199, 223
Kasten, Robert, 149
Kauffman, Joseph, 158, 161, 164
Kellet Commission/Report, 96, 98–104
Kellett, William, 96. See also Kellett Commission/Report
Kenosha Center, 218
  evolution of, 77, 82, 86, 88–89
  as extension, 52–53, 59, 64–69
Kinnaman, Ted, 177
Klauser, James, 202, 211
Knowles, Warren, 85–88, 96, 98, 100–101, 260
Kohler, Terry, 175
Kohler, Walter J. Jr., 58–62
Kolka, Jim, 129
Koopman, Norbert, 220–21
Kopitzke, Veldor, 129
Kroll, Herman, 146
Kucera, Antone, 160, 202–3

L

Ladysmith Center, 49, 53, 62
LaFollette, Philip, 28–29, 31
LaFollette, Robert M. (Fighting Bob), 10, 15, 28
Lake Geneva Center, 77
Land Grant Act of 1862, 8
Lawrence College, 39
lecture series, early, 8–10, 12, 18
legal issues, 16, 22, 25. See also Tallman, John
Legislative Audit Bureau, 115–17
Legislative Luncheon, 174, 178, 185
Lehrmann, Gene, 113–15
Lenehan, William, 161
Leverich, Earl, 37–38
Levine, John, 138
Liberal Arts Core Curriculum, 138-40, 159, 187
library facilities, 24, 35–36, 51, 68–69, 84–85, 160, 176, 192, 195–96
Liechty, Thornton, 155

Lighty, William H., 11, 27
Lins, L. J., 90–91
Local 253, 27–28, 30
Long, Durward, 104, 106–7, 111–12, 117–20, 122, 136, 145, 222–23
Long Range Planning Committee. See Six Year Plan
Long's Charter, 111–12, 140, 142–45
Lorence, Jim, 185
Lucey, Patrick A., 98, 101–3, 105, 112–13, 115, 119, 123–29, 133, 149
Lyall, Katharine, 181–82, 198–200, 202, 206–7, 211–17

M

Manitowoc County Center
  evolution of, 82, 85, 88–89, 103–5, 108, 120–21
  as extension, 32, 35, 42, 45, 52–53, 55, 59, 65
  scope reduction years, 126, 156–57
  as UW Campus, 218, 236–38
Marathon County Center
  evolution of, 75, 82, 89, 94, 103–4
  as extension, 25, 32–36, 38, 45, 52–56, 64–65, 67, 69
  scope reduction years, 126, 130, 142, 156–57
  as UW Campus, 218, 239–41
Marinette Center
  evolution of, 82, 88–89, 103, 105, 108
  as extension, 49, 52–53, 55, 59, 64–65
  scope reduction years, 126, 131, 133, 156–57
  as UW Campus, 218, 242–44
Marquette University, 15–16, 22, 50
Marshfield/Wood County Center
  evolution of, 74–75, 77, 79, 82, 85, 89, 94, 103–4
  as extension, 53
  scope reductions years, 126, 130,

  156–57
  as UW Campus, 218, 245–47
May, Al, 220–21
Mayville Center, 25, 34
  3M campuses, 88–89, 105, 108–9, 113. See also Fox Valley Center; Manitowoc Center; Marinette Center
McCart, Carol, 220–21
McCarthy, Charles, 10–12, 27
McClain, Edward, 109
McIntyre, William, 61–62
McNamara, Bertram, 113–14, 128
McPhee, Eugene, 95, 102
Medford Center, 218, 263
  evolution of, 75, 77, 94–95, 104–5, 113, 116, 120–22
  scope reduction years, 126–28, 130–38, 142–43, 148, 150, 154, 156–57, 159, 161–62
Meggers, John F., 122–23, 140, 223
Meier, Gladys, 220–21
Menasha Center. See Fox Valley Center
merger law, 142–44
mergers
  1960's, 74, 77–78, 80, 96
  1940's and 1950's, 45–46, 51, 60–62
  1970's and 1980's, 127–28, 130, 132, 190–91
merit evaluations, faculty, 194, 200
Merrill Center, 33, 35, 49, 50, 75
Messner, William F. (Bill), 220–23, 253
Meyer, Elmer, 220–21
military, effect of, 13, 41–42, 44–46, 48, 53–54, 58, 93. See also veterans
Miller, Charles E., 220–21
Miller, Jess, 94
Milwaukee Center, 13–19, 22, 26–29, 44–47, 49–53, 60, 62, 218
Mitchell, Steve, 220–21
Monroe Center, 77
Morrill, Justin, 8

Morrill Act, 8
Morrison, Kathryn, 128
Moss, Fred, 143

N
National Youth Administration, 36, 43
Nelson, Gaylord, 74
New Richmond Center, 52
Nicolet Community College, 87, 191
Nikolay, Frank, 87
Nixon, Richard, 97
Noll, Joseph, 100, 103–4
non-credit courses/lectures, 8–9, 14, 18–19, 23, 39, 42, 62, 78, 118
non-tenure instructors, 180–82

O
Okray, Peter, 155
Olson, F. I., 73
Olson, Jack, 98
O'Neil, Robert M., 155, 161–65, 167–71, 174, 176, 178, 182, 198
Outcault, n.s., 206
out-state classes/centers, 23–27, 32–34, 37, 45–46, 49, 51–52, 58–59, 69, 149

P
Parkinson, George A., 42
Patch, Foster, 128
Pelisek, Frank J., 125–27, 135
Percy, Donald, 132
Perry, Jim, 220–21
Peterson, A.W., 44
Peterson, Dallas, 109
Peterson, Martha, 91–92
Philipp, Janet, 220–21
Phillips Center, 62
Pleger, Tom, 220–21
politics, 7, 12, 15, 28–29. See also funding, state; state legislature
Polk, Forrest, 54–55

Polk, Robert R., 164–74, 192, 223
Portch, Stephen R., 160, 175, 183, 187–90, 192–93, 195–97, 199, 201, 222–23
post tenure review, 200–201
Pound, Roscoe, 15
prestige issue, 8–11, 14, 18, 48, 102, 108
Provost for University Outreach, 78–80, 118–20, 129
Public Law 88-204, 76, 95
Purin, Frank C., 30

R
Racine Center, 218
 evolution of, 77, 82, 88–89, 99
 as extension, 45, 49, 53–54, 56, 64–65, 67–69
racism, 33
railroads, 8, 17
Ratner, Lorman A. (Larry), 173–74, 176–78, 180, 182, 185, 223
Reagan, Ronald, 163
Reber, Louis E., 11–16, 223
recruiting, 40, 43
regents. See individual subjects
regionalization, 156, 160–61
Rennebohm, Oscar, 62
Rentz, Mrs. Frank, 34–35
Resolution 41-A, 59–60
retention rates, 66, 183
Reynolds, R. L., 35–36
Rhinelander Center, 33–34, 44, 49, 52–53, 62, 75, 77, 86
Rice Lake Center, 49, 52–53, 86, 94, 103, 105, 109, 113–16
Richland Center
 evolution of, 77, 86, 94, 105, 116, 120–22
 scope reduction years, 126–28, 131, 133–38, 142–43, 148, 150, 154,

156–57, 159, 161, 166
   as UW Campus, 218, 248–50
Roby, Patricia, 220–21
Rock County Center
   evolution of, 77, 85–86, 89, 104, 107
   as extension, 49, 52–53
   scope reduction years, 126, 156–57
   as UW Campus, 218, 251–53
Rodems, Leo, 120
Rodney, Joel, 220–21
Roosevelt, Franklin D., 26, 42
Rossmiller, Richard, 155, 161
Rozga, Therese, 169

S
salaries/compensation, 17, 25–26, 28, 34, 46, 64–65, 98, 147–48, 176–79, 193–94
Sanders, Keith, 215
Sauk County. See Baraboo/Sauk County Center
Savides, Theodore N. (Ted), 220–21, 225
Schmahl, Reuben, 147
Schneeberg, Mel H., 191
Schreiber, Martin J, 147, 149–50
Schwartz, Richard, 146
Schwenn, Roger E., 68–69, 84–85
science facilities, 50–51, 67–68, 72, 76, 174, 176, 180, 192, 196, 212
scope reduction study/report, 126, 133–34, 138, 174
Senate Bill 279S, 61
Shaw, Kenneth (Buzz), 182–83, 185, 187–89, 193, 195–96, 198, 211
Sheboygan Center
   evolution of, 82, 85, 89, 103–4, 106
   as extension, 23, 34–36, 42, 45, 52–53, 55, 59, 65
   scope reduction years, 126, 156–57
   as UW Campus, 218, 254–56

Shen, Teresa, 146
Shorewood Center, 49
Six Year Plan (1980's), 162–63, 165–68, 173, 196
Slocum, Darwin, 130–31
Smith, Donald, 119, 128–29, 131, 137, 143–44, 154
Smith, Kenneth, 13
Smith, Marion, 220–21
Smoller, Jeff, 128
Snell, Chester D., 16, 22–31, 37, 223
social activities. See extracurricular activities
Social Gospel of the Progressive Era, 12
South Milwaukee Center, 49
Special Planning Committee (SPC) (1982), 166–69
Spooner Center, 49, 52–53
sports. See extracurricular activities
State Board of Adult and Vocational Education, 38–40, 72, 86–87, 103–104, 113–16
State Colleges, 72–78
state legislature, 7–9, 11–12, 14–16, 22, 24, 37–39, 43–44, 47–48, 53 54, 58–59, 61, 63, 67, 69, 78, 175
State Normal Schools, 9, 10, 16, 23, 43
State Teachers Colleges, 51, 53–55, 60–61, 75, 95
Stewart, Brad, 220–21
Stone, Trudi, 220–21
student body, compositions of, 8–10, 12–13, 18, 36–37, 55, 65, 90–92, 132, 146
student government, 55, 93–94
student learning assessment, 205–6
student services, 36, 51, 73, 84, 130–31, 160, 167, 192–93
subsidies. See funding
subversive activity. See Brunette Committee

System Advisory Planning Task Force (1975), 129–30, 132, 134–35

T
Tallman, John, 142–43, 158
Taylor County. See Medford Center
teachers courses/institutes, 8–9, 16, 18, 43, 73
Teasdale, Howard, 15
telecommunications, 208, 212
tenure, 26, 30, 83, 200–201. See also post tenure review
tenure density, 157–59
Thiede, Wilson, 129, 137–38
Thompson, Carl, 58
Thompson, Tommy, 182–84, 190–91, 193–96, 202, 207, 210–13
Thomson, John, 77–78
Thomson Plan, 78
Thoyre, Howard H., 215, 217, 223
Tomah Center, 77
trains. See railroads
transferees, performance of, 14, 17, 36, 90–91, 146
transfer of credits
  from centers, 83–84, 87, 89–90, 99–100, 103–4, 108
  from extensions, 17, 39, 43, 50, 53
  1980's and 1990's, 183, 185–89, 191–93, 197, 198, 201–2, 216–17
  during scope reduction, 130–31, 167, 183
Trask, Kerry, 175
Truman Doctrine, 57
tuition/fees. See fee parity; fees/tuition
Turner, Frederick Jackson, 9–11

U
Umhoefer, Aurel, 220–21, 224–25
unions, 12, 27–30, 100, 102, 191
UW Centers, 171, 173
UW Green Bay, 7, 82, 88, 99, 101, 105, 108–9

UW Parkside, 82, 88, 218. See also Kenosha Center; Racine Center

V
Valitchka, Roy, 175
Van Eyck, Daniel K., 223
Van Hise, Charles R., 10–11
Veninga, Jim, 220–21
Venker, Terri, 220–21
veterans, 13–14, 18, 48–55
vocational courses/schools
  1960's, 71–72, 78, 86–87, 95–96
  1940's and 1950's, 43, 50, 52–54, 62–64, 68–69
  through the 1930's, 11–12, 14, 18, 22–25, 37–39
vocational high schools, 11–12, 18, 22–25, 38–39, 87
Vocational Technical and Adult Education, 100, 126–28, 150, 190–92

W
Wallace, Marjorie, 94, 120–21, 128
Ward, David, 215
Ward, n.s., 206
Warren, Robert W., 105
Washington County Center
  evolution of, 77
  scope reduction years, 125, 142, 147, 156–57
  as UW Center, 218, 257–59
Watertown Center, 42
Watson, George, 62
Waukesha County Center
  evolution of, 85–86, 104
  scope reduction years, 126, 142–43, 147, 156–57
  as UW Center, 218, 260–62
Wausau Center. See Marathon County Center
Wauwautosa Center, 49
Weaver, John, 105–112, 114, 117–20, 122–23, 129–30, 132–34, 137, 149
Weber, Lon, 220–21

Weidner, Edward, 89
Weinstein, Laurence, 184
Welles, Colin, 29
West Allis Center, 49
West Bend Center. See Washington
 County Center
Wildeck, Steve, 220–21, 253
Wilkie, Harold, 28, 30–31
Williams, T. Harry, 32–33
Wisconsin Idea, 7, 11, 19, 47, 53, 60,
 72, 96, 117–18, 133, 135, 174, 181,
 217
Wisconsin Rapids Center, 25, 74–75,
 77, 86, 191
Wisconsin's constitution, 7, 16, 22
Withey, Morton, 51
Wood County Center. See
 Marshfield/Wood County Center;
Wisconsin Rapids Center
Wrigley, Victor, 144

Y
Young, H. Edwin, 73, 149–51, 154–55

Z
Zehner, Paul, 220–21
Ziegler, Bernard, 114
Zien, Burt, 114
Zweifel, Phil, 220–21

Author

Jerry Bower began his college education at the Marathon County Extension Center in 1956. He completed a Bachelor of Science degree with a major in history in 1960 at the Wisconsin State College in Stevens Point. Over the following seven years Bower earned a Master of Arts degree and completed the coursework for a Ph.D. in history at Michigan State University and taught for three years at Port Huron Junior College. He received his Ph.D. from MSU in 1971.

In the fall of 1967 Bower began teaching history at the Richland Campus, a branch campus of the Wisconsin State University at Platteville. He continues to teach at UW-Richland. He has participated in many of the events of the past thirty-five years that are described in this book. He has served as Richland's senator for twenty years and twice chaired the UW Centers' Senate, 1982-83 and 1992-94. In 1992 Bower received an Underkoefler Excellence in Teaching Award from the UW System.

Jerry and his wife, Donna, are the parents of four grown sons, all graduates of the University of Wisconsin, and the doting grandparents for six grandchildren.